INTERNATIONAL LAW AS WE KNOW IT

International legal scholars tend to think of their work as the interpretation of rules: the application of a law 'out there' to concrete situations. This book takes a different approach to that scholarship: it views doctrine as a sociolinguistic practice. In other words, this book views legal scholars not as law-appliers, but as constructing knowledge within a particular academic discipline. By means of three close-ups of the discourse on cyberwar and international law, this book shows how international legal knowledge is constructed in ways usually overlooked: by means of footnotes, for example, or conference presentations. In so doing, this book aims to present a new way of seeing international legal scholarship: one that pays attention to the mundane parts of international legal texts and provides a different understanding of how international law as we know it comes about.

Lianne J. M. Boer is Assistant Professor in the Department of Transnational Legal Studies, Faculty of Law, VU Amsterdam. She previously coedited *Backstage Practices of Transnational Law* (2019, with Sofia Stolk) and she was a Kathleen Fitzpatrick Visiting Postdoctoral Fellow at Melbourne Law School. Her research deals with the (socio)linguistics of knowledge construction in the field of international peace and security law.

International Law As We Know It

CYBERWAR DISCOURSE AND THE CONSTRUCTION OF KNOWLEDGE IN INTERNATIONAL LEGAL SCHOLARSHIP

LIANNE J. M. BOER
VU Amsterdam

CAMBRIDGE
UNIVERSITY PRESS

CAMBRIDGE
UNIVERSITY PRESS

University Printing House, Cambridge CB2 8BS, United Kingdom

One Liberty Plaza, 20th Floor, New York, NY 10006, USA

477 Williamstown Road, Port Melbourne, VIC 3207, Australia

314–321, 3rd Floor, Plot 3, Splendor Forum, Jasola District Centre, New Delhi – 110025, India

103 Penang Road, #05–06/07, Visioncrest Commercial, Singapore 238467

Cambridge University Press is part of the University of Cambridge.

It furthers the University's mission by disseminating knowledge in the pursuit of education, learning, and research at the highest international levels of excellence.

www.cambridge.org
Information on this title: www.cambridge.org/9781108484831
DOI: 10.1017/9781108676564

First published 2021

A catalogue record for this publication is available from the British Library.

Library of Congress Cataloging-in-Publication Data
NAMES: Boer, Lianne J. M., author.
TITLE: International law as we know it: cyberwar discourse and the construction of knowledge in international legal scholarship / Lianne J. M. Boer, Vrije Universiteit Amsterdam.
DESCRIPTION: Cambridge, United Kingdom; New York, NY: Cambridge University Press, 2021. | Based on author's thesis (doctoral – Vrije Universiteit Amsterdam, 2017). | Includes bibliographical references and index.
IDENTIFIERS: LCCN 2021009552 (print) | LCCN 2021009553 (ebook) | ISBN 9781108484831 (hardback) | ISBN 9781108676564 (ebook)
SUBJECTS: LCSH: Cyberspace operations (International law)
CLASSIFICATION: LCC KZ6718 .B64 2021 (print) | LCC KZ6718 (ebook) | DDC 341.6/3 – dc23
LC record available at https://lccn.loc.gov/2021009552
LC ebook record available at https://lccn.loc.gov/2021009553

ISBN 978-1-108-48483-1 Hardback

Contents

Acknowledgments

This book has benefited from the generosity of many people.

Thanks to Tanja Aalberts, Matilda Arvidsson, Leila Brännström, Alan Cienki, Galina Cornelisse, Jillian Dobson, Merel Ekelhof, Geoff Gordon, Markus Gunneflo, Lisette ten Haaf, Laura Henderson, Ester Herlin-Karnell, Marieke de Hoon, Sara Kendall, Martti Koskenniemi, Dion Kramer, Jessica Lawrence, Prosper Maguchu, Kenneth Manusama, Anne van Mulligen, Gregor Noll, Anne Orford, Amin Parsa, Hadi Purnama, Tom Randall, Lisa Schweiger, Sofia Stolk, Renske Vos and Tijmen Wisman, for being so generous with your time, and for your thoughtful engagement with this book.

Thanks are also due to Ratna Parsan for her help in compiling the index.

The final stages of the writing of this book were greatly assisted by a grant from the Gezina van der Molenfonds, and I am grateful to the Faculty of Law at VU Amsterdam for awarding it.

I am particularly indebted to Arno Lodder and Wouter Werner for their supervision of the PhD thesis on which this book is based. Arno, thank you for continuing to remind me that there is nothing self-evident about international legal reasoning – quite the contrary. Wouter, thank you for your ongoing encouragement and support, and for always letting curiosity prevail over every other reason for pursuing research.

Thanks to Eline, Barbara, Judit, Markus, Erik, Froukje, Reint, Janny, Christa, Annette, Maarten, Mirjam, Mardi and Willem Jan, for solid ground.

To my parents: you have been and continue to be unwavering and inexhaustible in your love and support. Thank you.

Pieter-Jan, you have brought so much light, and love, and happiness. Thank you. I love you.

In this book I further develop and/or draw on parts of previously published work: 'Backstage Practices of Transnational Law,' in: *Backstage Practices of Transnational Law* (ed., with Sofia Stolk), Routledge 2019; 'Narratives of Force: Plot and the Presence of the Writer in International Legal Scholarship' (2019) 66 *Netherlands International Law Review* 1; '"It Could Probably Just as Well be Otherwise": Imageries of Cyberwar,' (with Wouter Werner) in: *Risk and the Regulation of Uncertainty in International Law*, Mónika Ambrus, Rosemary Rayfuse and Wouter Werner (eds.), Oxford University Press 2017, 39–55; '"Echoes of Times Past': On the Paradoxical Nature of Article 2(4)' (2015) 20 *Journal of Conflict and Security Law* 5; '"Restating the Law "As it Is"': On the Tallinn Manual and the Use of Force in Cyberspace' (2013) 5 *Amsterdam Law Forum* 4; 'Cyberwar? What War? Meer in het bijzonder: welk recht?' (with Arno Lodder) (2012) 38 *Justitiële Verkenningen* 52; 'Cyberwar,' (with Arno Lodder) in: *Cyber Safety: An Introduction*, Rutger Leukfeldt and Wouter Stol (eds.), eleven international publishing 2012, 157–166. References to the relevant parts of these works are given where appropriate in the text.

Chapter 4 of this book was previously published as Lianne J. M. Boer (2016) '"The Greater Part of Jurisconsults": On Consensus Claims and Their Footnotes in Legal Scholarship,' *Leiden Journal of International Law*, 29(4), 1021–1042 © Foundation of the Leiden Journal of International Law 2016, published by Cambridge University Press. Reproduced with permission. Section 5.1.3 of Chapter 5 uses and expands on pp. 77–78 of Lianne J. M. Boer (2019) '*Lex Lata* comes with a Date; or, What Follows from Referring to the "Tallinn Rules,"' *AJIL Unbound*, 113, 76–80 © 2019 by The American Society of International Law and Lianne J. M. Boer, published by Cambridge University Press. Reproduced with permission.

Olivia Give us the place alone: we will hear this divinity.
[*Exeunt* MARIA and Attendants]
Now, sir, what is your text?

Viola Most sweet lady,–

Olivia A comfortable doctrine, and much may be said of it. Where lies your text?

Viola In Orsino's bosom.

Olivia In his bosom! In what chapter of his bosom?

Viola To answer by the method, in the first of his heart.

Olivia O, I have read it: it is heresy. Have you no more to say?

Viola Good madam, let me see your face.

Olivia Have you any commission from your lord to negotiate with my face? You are now out of your text: but we will draw the curtain and show you the picture.

Twelfth Night, *Act I Scene V*

1

Knowing International Law

In February 2017, Cambridge University Press published the *Tallinn Manual 2.0 on the International Law Applicable to Cyber Operations*.[1] Written by a group of international lawyers, it presents a series of rules on the application of the *jus ad bellum*, *jus in bello* as well as peacetime international law to operations conducted by states in cyberspace.[2] The *Tallinn Manual 2.0* is, in fact, a sequel: it revises and expands on the first *Tallinn Manual*, which focused solely "on the law governing cyber warfare."[3] Even though there is hardly any treaty or customary law speaking directly to the subject, in the words of the project's director "[t]his … does not mean … that cyber operations exist in a normative void. [The] International Groups of Experts were unanimous in their estimation that existing international law applies."[4] Thus, the issues addressed in the Manuals range from the right of self-defense against a non-state hacker group to "[c]yber operations in the exclusive economic zone"; from "the duty to protect cyber infrastructure on the premises of a mission or post" to what *levée en masse* would look like online.[5]

The *Tallinn Manuals* are part of a larger body of scholarly work detailing if, and if so how, international law applies to war in cyberspace. But the debate

[1] Michael N. Schmitt (ed.), *Tallinn Manual 2.0 on the International Law Applicable to Cyber Operations*, Cambridge University Press 2017 (hereafter: 'Tallinn Manual 2.0').

[2] The second *Tallinn Manual* briefly deals with non-state actors; see ibid., specifically rule 33.

[3] Meaning the *jus ad bellum* and *jus in bello*; Michael N. Schmitt (ed.), *Tallinn Manual on the International Law Applicable to Cyber Warfare*, Cambridge University Press 2013, 1, 4 (hereafter: 'Tallinn Manual'). For a comment on the revisions in the second Manual see Schmitt (ed.), 'Tallinn Manual 2.0,' 1–2.

[4] Schmitt (ed.), 'Tallinn Manual 2.0,' 3; Schmitt (ed.), 'Tallinn Manual,' 5; these pages display minor differences in the ways they describe this absence of law.

[5] Schmitt (ed.), 'Tallinn Manual 2.0,' rule 71 para. 18 et seq.; rule 47; rule 42 para. 4 and rule 40; rule 88. The word 'Manual' is capitalized throughout this book when referring to the *Tallinn Manual* (1 or 2) proper.

goes back to the mid-1990s, when scholars began interpreting existing rules and coming up with new ones when they thought the old did not suffice.[6] In 1996, one of the earliest contributors to the debate described the problem in doing so as follows:

> Today, public international law faces perhaps its greatest challenge as information technology transforms international society. Just as territorial boundaries and natural resources formed the theoretical foundation for an international legal paradigm in an age of geopolitical borders, so too must a conceptual framework based on information undergird the legal institutions of the twenty-first century.[7]

These phrases indicate that from very early on international legal scholars took note of the features of cyberspace that, in the words of one of them, makes it "nearly impervious to regulation."[8] What is more, roughly twenty-five years later scholars still have very little to go by. Even though *opinio juris* has started to emerge over the last few years and the use of cyberspace as part of conventional warfare is increasing – for example, during the armed conflict in Ukraine – a stand-alone cyberwar has rarely, if ever, taken place.[9] This doesn't mean states aren't *preparing* for war in cyberspace: by now, many have included "cyber units"[10] in their military apparatus. It is a given though, as noted by one of the critics of the first *Tallinn Manual*, that it was written in anticipation of a war that "has hardly occurred so far."[11]

[6] See also Lianne J. M. Boer, '"Restating the Law 'As It Is'": On the Tallinn Manual and the Use of Force in Cyberspace' (2013) 5 *Amsterdam Law Forum* 4, 4–6.

[7] Sean P. Kanuck, 'Information Warfare: New Challenges for Public International Law' (1996) 37 *Harvard International Law Journal* 272, 274. Kanuck's use of the word 'information' rather than 'cyber' has to do with the origins of this debate, which lie in the notion of an 'information revolution.' On these origins, see Myriam Dunn Cavelty, *Cyber-Security and Threat Politics: US Efforts to Secure the Information Age*, Routledge 2008, chapters 1 and 4.

[8] Kanuck, 'Information Warfare,' 272.

[9] Depending on one's definition. On these issues, and the importance of the Stuxnet worm in this respect, see Chapter 2. For a legal analysis of the use of cyberattacks in Ukraine see Jan Stinissen, 'A Legal Framework for Cyber Operations in Ukraine,' in: *Cyber War in Perspective: Russian Aggression against Ukraine*, Kenneth Geers (ed.), NATO CCD COE Publications 2015, 123–134.

[10] Marco Roscini, *Cyber Operations and the Use of Force in International Law*, Oxford University Press 2014, 10; Johann-Christoph Woltag, *Cyber Warfare: Military Cross-Border Computer Network Operations Under International Law*, Intersentia 2014, 147. For the argument that the creation of these units constitutes state practice see ibid.; see, however, Sergei Boeke and Dennis Broeders, 'The Demilitarisation of Cyber Conflict' (2018) 60 *Survival* 73.

[11] Dieter Fleck, 'Searching for International Rules Applicable to Cyber Warfare – A Critical First Assessment of the New *Tallinn Manual*' (2013) 18 *Journal of Conflict and Security Law* 331, 332.

What this means for the international legal debate is that, in the words of one scholar, "it is the work of academia which currently importantly influences the development of a common understanding within the international community."[12] This being the case, scholarly work has taken center stage with regard to giving the legal answers to the questions arising in this debate. The shared concern of those involved is that the possibilities provided by cyberspace for engaging in hostile action necessitate regulation by means of international law.[13] For example, scholars write that

> [t]he most important task confronting international lawyers is to clarify various criteria by which the legitimacy of a state's use of forcible measures in information operations situations can be appraised, with the ultimate goal of bringing the international system closer to a more orderly, predictable environment for interstate intercourse.[14]

What emerges from these and similar proclamations is a mission statement for the public international lawyer: that the uncertainties created by the possibility of cyberwar require an answer from international law, in order to guide state behavior in a way that will increase international peace and security.[15]

This book takes this mission statement – solving the problem of cyber – as the common denominator of the group of scholars involved, and looks at the ways in which they construct legal knowledge on cyberwar.[16] By means of three close-ups it shows how doctrine in this debate is made out of "mundane" words that are not usually included in analyses of international legal knowledge construction, and how "people and ideas" can get entangled in the making; how scholars can assign themselves, and others, the authority to speak or be heard.[17] In other words, this book looks at doctrine as a (socio)linguistic

12 Katharina C. Ziolkowski, '*Ius ad bellum* in Cyberspace – Some Thoughts on the "Schmitt-Criteria" for Use of Force,' in: *Proceedings of the 4th International Conference on Cyber Conflict*, Christian Czosseck, Rain Ottis and Katharina Ziolkowski (eds.), NATO CCD COE Publications 2012, 295–309, 297 (she states this with regard to the *jus ad bellum* specifically). For a similar statement see Marie Aronsson-Storrier, *Publicity in International Law-Making: Covert Operations and the Use of Force*, Cambridge University Press 2021, 10. See also Chapter 2 of this book.

13 Martti Koskenniemi refers to this resort to law as "legal problem-solution"; see Martti Koskenniemi, *From Apology to Utopia: The Structure of International Legal Argument*, Cambridge University Press 2005, 28; 24 et seq. See also Chapter 2 of this book.

14 Christopher C. Joyner and Catherine Lotrionte, 'Information Warfare as International Coercion: Elements of a Legal Framework' (2001) 12 *European Journal of International Law* 825, 863. On the origins of the phrase 'information operations' see note 7 above.

15 See note 13 above.

16 Below, I will elaborate on the use of the phrase 'knowledge construction' in this book.

17 For "mundane" see Fleur Johns, *Non-Legality in International Law: Unruly Law*, Cambridge University Press 2013, 18. Ken Hyland refers to the "relationships between people, and between

practice: it asks what exactly is said in the cyberwar debate, and who is doing the saying.[18] Through these close-ups, it becomes possible to see how international legal knowledge is formed on the level of its "patterned activities and often mundane modes of work":[19] those parts of legal academic work that are not normally considered relevant to the construction of doctrine.

In so doing this book proposes a new "way of seeing"[20] international legal scholarship. It seeks to 'read between the lines' of what we normally consider to be part of and relevant to scholarly legal reasoning, in order to uncover there "that which is so close, which is so immediate, which is so intimately linked to us, that because of that we do not perceive it."[21] One of the principal claims of this book is that a focus on the 'microlevel' of international legal scholarship changes our understanding of what it means to make law.[22] This has significant implications for what we scrutinize and how; for what we think matters to the way international legal knowledge comes about and what it is we do as legal scholars. What it entails is an "attentiveness" to the particular, individually spoken and written word, as well as to the part played by the individual scholar who utters it.[23] In this way my aim is to show how international law, as we know it, comes about.

1.1 SCHOLARSHIP AND INTERNATIONAL LAW

To write about international legal scholars and the knowledge they construct is first and foremost associated with questions about the part they play in

people and ideas"; Ken Hyland, *Disciplinary Discourses: Social Interactions in Academic Writing*, The University of Michigan Press 2004, 1; see also the illustration in ibid., 34–37.

18 Cf. Hyland, 'Disciplinary Discourses,' xi. This book is heavily influenced by the way Hyland writes about academic discourses, though it approaches this particular one differently. I will elaborate on this further on in this introduction.

19 Johns, 'Unruly Law,' 23.

20 Ibid., 21.

21 Anne Orford, 'In Praise of Description' (2012) 25 *Leiden Journal of International Law* 609, 617, quoting and translating M. Foucault, 'La philosophie analytique de la politique,' in D. Defert and F. Ewald (eds.), with J. Lagrange, *Dits et écrits*, 1954–1988, 4 vols., Vol. 3 (1994), 534, at 540–1. Where I didn't have access to the quoted publication I adopted the citation style of the citing author. Annelise Riles similarly refers to our failure to see what's too obvious; see Annelise Riles, 'A New Agenda for the Cultural Study of Law: Taking on the Technicalities' (2005) 53 *Buffalo Law Review* 973, 981. On 'reading between the lines' see Michel Foucault, *The Archeology of Knowledge*, transl. A. M. Sheridan Smith, Pantheon Books 1972, 27.

22 Aalberts and Werner use the word "micropractices," see Tanja E. Aalberts and Wouter G. Werner, 'International Law,' in: *Routledge Handbook of International Political Sociology*, Xavier Guillaume and Pınar Bilgin (eds.), Routledge 2017, 36–45, 41. See also Anthony Carty, 'Sociological Theories of International Law,' *Max Planck Encyclopedia of Public International Law* (hereafter: MPEPIL) 2008, Rüdiger Wolfrum (ed.), 22.

23 Anne Orford refers to the "attentiveness to the material with which we work"; see Orford, 'Description,' 625. I will return to this in the conclusion.

international lawmaking; about the impact they have on the development and creation of international law by states. "Scholarship about scholarship"[24] is on the rise, focusing for instance on the use of doctrine by the International Court of Justice and international criminal courts, or asking how we know a 'most highly qualified publicist' when we see one.[25] Central to these inquiries are questions about the impact of the work of scholars; how it can be measured and how these (empirical) findings relate to questions such as whether scholars make law.[26] The same happens in the cyberwar debate: for example, one article asks how the 2017 *Tallinn Manual*'s chapter on human rights may in fact be "used by States … to *limit* human rights"; another analyzes the Manuals "as a case study of how legal scholarship may affect the making of international law."[27]

These kinds of questions are asked against the background of Article 38(1) of the Statute of the International Court of Justice, (arguably) listing the sources of international law – or at least, those sources the Court "shall apply" in its

[24] Jörg Kammerhofer, 'Lawmaking by Scholars,' in: *Research Handbook on the Theory and Practice of International Lawmaking*, Catherine Brölmann and Yannick Radi (eds.), Elgar 2016, 305–326, 305.

[25] For examples see Michael Peil, 'Scholarly Writings as a Source of Law: A Survey of the Use of Doctrine by the International Court of Justice' (2012) 1 *Cambridge Journal of International and Comparative Law* 136; Avidan Kent and Jamie Trinidad, 'International Law Scholars as *Amici Curiae*: An Emerging Dialogue (of the Deaf)?' (2016) 29 *Leiden Journal of International Law* 1081; Sandesh Sivakumaran, 'The Influence of Teachings of Publicists on the Development of International Law' (2017) 66 *International and Comparative Law Quarterly* 1; Sondre Torp Helmersen, 'Finding "The Most Highly Qualified Publicists": Lessons from the International Court of Justice' (2019) 30 *European Journal of International Law* 509; Nora Stappert, 'A New Influence of Legal Scholars? The Use of Academic Writings at International Criminal Courts and Tribunals' (2018) 31 *Leiden Journal of International Law* 963; Luíza Leão Soares Pereira, 'International Lawyers as Lawmakers' (PhD, Cambridge University 2021, forthcoming). For more general reflections see, for example, Jochen von Bernstorff, 'International Legal Scholarship as a Cooling Medium in International Law and Politics' (2014) 25 *European Journal of International Law* 977; Anne Peters, 'International Legal Scholarship Under Challenge,' in: *International Law as a Profession*, André Nollkaemper et al. (eds.), Cambridge University Press 2017, 117–15 9; Gleider Hernández, 'The Responsibility of the International Legal Academic,' in: ibid., 160–188; Jan Klabbers, 'On Epistemic Universalism and the Melancholy of International Law' (2019) 29 *European Journal of International Law* 1057.

[26] Kammerhofer, 'Lawmaking by Scholars,' 305, who distinguishes this question from the normative one whether "scholars [are] empowered by the law" to actually do that (he vehemently denies this; see for example 320).

[27] Robert E. Barnsby and Shane R. Reeves, 'Give Them an Inch, They'll Take a Terabyte: How States May Interpret Tallinn Manual 2.0's International Human Rights Law Chapter' (2017) 95 *Texas Law Review* 1515, 1516, emphasis added; Papawadee Tanodomdej, 'The Tallinn Manuals and the Making of the International Law on Cyber Operations' (2019) 13 *Masaryk University Journal of Law and Technology* 67, abstract.

legal reasoning.[28] Next to treaties, custom and general principles, Article 38(1)(d) states that in its application of international law the Court can draw on "judicial decisions and the teachings of the most highly qualified publicists of the various nations, as subsidiary means for the determination of rules of law."[29] In other words, the Court can use doctrine: a somewhat confusing word, as in international law it is used to denote an idea about where its rules derive their "legitimacy" from ("positivist doctrine");[30] a declaration by a state on "a particular subject-matter … intended … to have legal consequences for other States" (the "Monroe doctrine")[31] or, as in this book, the work of legal scholars that deal with substantive questions of international law, "interpreting and systematizing the normative materials"[32] before them. The common denominator of these understandings of doctrine is that they all refer to "[t]hat which is taught or laid down as true concerning a particular subject or department of knowledge … a belief, theoretical opinion; a dogma."[33] In other words, rather than – remaining with the logic of Article 38 – a source of law, doctrine expresses that which is (already) known.[34]

The distinction between the making of law and its interpretation has a specific function in legal argumentation: it means that whoever makes a legal argument will have to base their claims on the primary sources of law – or at least make it seem as if they do.[35] But at the same time this distinction tells us very little about "the 'how' … of international legal work."[36] As pointed out by Martti Koskenniemi, "[t]he metaphor of sources

[28] Statute of the International Court of Justice, June 26, 1945, 1 UNTS XVI, Article 38(1). For differences of opinion on the status of Article 38(1) compare Kammerhofer, 'Lawmaking by Scholars,' 306–307; Sir Michael Wood, 'Teachings of the Most Highly Qualified Publicists (Art. 38 (1) ICJ Statute),' MPEPIL 2010, A.1. For a historical view on this question see Ole Spiermann, '"Who Attempts Too Much Does Nothing Well": The 1920 Advisory Committee of Jurists and the Statute of the Permanent Court of International Justice' (2003) 73 *British Yearbook of International Law* 187, section V.

[29] ICJ Statute, Article 38(1)(d). For the ICJ's references to itself see Wolfgang Alschner and Damien Charlotin, 'The Growing Complexity of the International Court of Justice's Self-Citation Network' (2016) 29 *European Journal of International Law* 83.

[30] Alexander Orakhelashvili, 'Natural Law and Justice,' MPEPIL 2007, B.29.

[31] Thomas D. Grant, 'Doctrines (Monroe, Hallstein, Brezhnev, Stimson),' MPEPIL 2014, A.1; B. This is a crude synopsis of the way Grant defines these doctrines; see A.1.

[32] Martti Koskenniemi, 'International Legal Theory and Doctrine,' MPEPIL 2007, A.1.; see also Peil, 'Scholarly Writings,' 137.

[33] "doctrine, n.," Oxford English Dictionary Online, June 2020, Oxford University Press, 2.b.

[34] See also Gregor Noll, 'International Law as Discipline and Doctrine,' in: *Routledge Handbook of International Law and the Humanities*, Shane Chalmers and Sundhya Pahuja (eds.), Routledge 2021 ("doctrine deals with that which has been revealed in the law already," at 37).

[35] Martti Koskenniemi (ed.), *Sources of International Law*, Ashgate 2000, xviii; Peil, 'Scholarly Writings,' section 2.2, 144.

[36] Johns, 'Unruly Law,' 218; see also 23.

aiding in 'finding' the law is premised upon a (positivist) understanding of the law existing 'out there' to be 'found'."[37] What we miss when adhering to it is a sense of "the law's constructive side, the aspect of law as a *result* of the legal argument and not a condition of it."[38] This does not mean we can do without the texts (of treaties, or customary law, if we know where to find it), but it does mean that to say that rules may be located in these texts, is different from saying their meaning is enclosed ("contained and conserved")[39] in them. In this view, the law is 'made' by those working with it, and there are very many different people doing so, in many different capacities.[40] To resort once more to Koskenniemi, "[i]t may be too much to say that international law is *only* what international lawyers do or think. But at least it is that."[41]

Whereas a doctrinal reading of the cyberwar debate would focus on the kind of legal reasoning we are familiar with, in this book the analysis shifts to the seemingly trivial and usually "overlooked"[42] parts of scholarly writing and speech. This means that this book doesn't offer, for example, an interpretation of the UN Charter in light of cyberattacks, nor does it assess the correctness of other scholars' attempts in doing so. Instead, it asks after the minuscule steps writers take to come to those conclusions in the first place, and how they linguistically reinforce the idea that this is, indeed, what we 'know' to be law – for example, through their footnotes or conference presentations. With this focus on legal scholars' actual

37 Koskenniemi (ed.), 'Sources,' xvi. Similarly, Ingo Venzke, *How Interpretation Makes International Law: On Semantic Change and Normative Twists*, Oxford University Press 2012, 53–54 and Ingo Venzke, 'Understanding the Authority of International Courts and Tribunals' (2013) 14 *Theoretical Inquiries in Law* 381, 393–394. On the metaphors used to sustain this idea, see Steven L. Winter, 'Transcendental Nonsense, Metaphoric Reasoning, and the Cognitive Stakes for Law' (1988) 137 *University of Pennsylvania Law Review* 1105, 1207–1224 and somewhat differently, Pierre Schlag, 'The Problem of the Subject' (1991) 69 *Texas Law Review* 1627.

38 Koskenniemi (ed.), 'Sources,' xvi, emphasis added. On the identification of customary law see Wouter G. Werner, 'Godot Was Always There: Customary Law as Restatement Practice,' in: *Repetition and International Law*, Cambridge University Press 2021, forthcoming (on file with the author).

39 Venzke, 'Interpretation,' 17, and chapter 2 of his book.

40 See, in a general sense, Hyland, 'Disciplinary Discourses,' chapter 1, particularly 1, 5–8. On different roles in international law see Martti Koskenniemi, 'Between Commitment and Cynicism: Outline for a Theory of International Law as Practice,' in: *Collection of Essays by Legal Advisers of States, Legal Advisers of International Organizations and Practitioners in the Field of International Law*, United Nations 1999, 495–523, 512–523 and Jean d'Aspremont et al. (eds.), *International Law as a Profession*, Cambridge University Press 2017. For a strong critique, see Kammerhofer, 'Lawmaking by Scholars,' 320–324.

41 Martti Koskenniemi, *The Gentle Civilizer of Nations*, Cambridge University Press 2001, 7.

42 Jens Meierhenrich, 'The Practice of International Law: A Theoretical Analysis' (2014) 76 *Law and Contemporary Problems* 1, 8, quoting Vincent Pouliot, 'The Logic of Practicality: A Theory of Practice of Security Communities' (2008) 62 *International Organization* 257, 258.

practice this book draws, among others, on the "turn to practice" as has already taken place in other disciplines and which is finding its way to international law.[43] Up to date, international legal scholars have taken up the practice turn in the form of Bourdieusian analyses (of which more later) of international commercial arbitration and the 'field' of international humanitarian law, and studied different practices of legality.[44] However, what is missing is an account of international legal *scholarship* on the level of the "everyday"[45] doings of scholars; the seemingly trivial parts of the making of international legal doctrine.[46] Without aiming to provide a comprehensive definition of the practice turn, what matters for the purposes of this book is the sensitivity practice theory presents toward the

[43] Johns, 'Unruly Law,' 23; Jeffrey L. Dunoff and Mark A. Pollack, 'International Judicial Practices: Opening the Black Box of International Courts' (2018) 40 *Michigan Journal of International Law* 47, 49, 57; see also Gavin Sullivan, '"Taking on the Technicalities" of International Law – Practice, Description, Critique: A Response to Fleur Johns' (2017) 111 *AJIL Unbound* 181, 181–182. All these authors state how international law is only slowly catching up to the practice turn. Some of the works they nonetheless identify in this vein are those by Tanja Aalberts and Ingo Venzke, 'Moving Beyond Interdisciplinary Turf Wars,' in: *International Law as a Profession*, André Nollkaemper et al. (eds.), Cambridge University Press 2017, 287–310; Tanja Aalberts and Thomas Gammeltoft-Hansen (eds.), *The Changing Practices of International Law*, Cambridge University Press 2018; Nikolas M. Rajkovic, Tanja E. Aalberts and Thomas Gammeltoft-Hansen (eds.), *The Power of Legality: Practices of International Law and Their Politics*, Cambridge University Press 2016; Annelise Riles, *The Network Inside Out*, University of Michigan Press 2000; Annelise Riles, *Collateral Knowledge: Legal Reasoning in the Global Financial Markets*, The University of Chicago Press 2011. For two examples in international criminal law see Meierhenrich, 'Practice' and Nora Stappert, 'Practice Theory and Change in International Law: Theorizing the Development of Legal Meaning through the Interpretive Practices of International Criminal Courts' (2020) 12 *International Theory* 33. On the practice turn more generally see Christian Bueger and Frank Gadinger, 'The Play of International Practice' (2015) 59 *International Studies Quarterly* 449.

[44] Yves Dezalay and Bryant G. Garth, *Dealing in Virtue: International Commercial Arbitration and the Construction of a Transnational Legal Order*, The University of Chicago Press 1996; Frédéric Mégret, 'Thinking about What International Humanitarian Lawyers "Do": An Examination of the Laws of War as a Field of Professional Practice,' in: *The Law of International Lawyers: Reading Martti Koskenniemi*, Wouter Werner, Marieke de Hoon and Alexis Galán (eds.), Cambridge University Press 2017, 265–296; Rajkovic, Aalberts and Gammeltoft-Hansen (eds.), 'The Power of Legality.'

[45] Dunoff and Pollack, 'International Judicial Practices,' 49, quoting Rebecca Adler-Nissen, *Why International Relations Theory Needs Bourdieu*, on 'e-International Relations,' October 23, 2012.

[46] Bueger and Gadinger, 'Play of Practice,' 457; see also Johns, 'Unruly Law,' 23; she in turn refers to Charles Camic, Neil Gross and Michèle Lamont (eds.), *Social Knowledge in the Making*, The University of Chicago Press 2011. For other work on scholarship and international law as a discipline see, for example, Fleur Johns, Thomas Skouteris and Wouter Werner, 'Editors' Introduction: Alejandro Álvarez and the Launch of the Periphery Series' (2006) 19 *Leiden Journal of International Law* 875, Kammerhofer, 'Lawmaking by Scholars'; d'Aspremont et al. (eds.), 'International Law as a Profession'; Lianne J. M. Boer and Sofia Stolk (eds.), *Backstage Practices of Transnational Law*, Routledge 2019; Leão Soares Pereira, 'International Lawyers as Lawmakers.'

importance of "concrete situations of life in which actors perform a common practice"; a view in which "the intentions and motivations of actors are less relevant. Their actual activities and practical enactments in concrete situations matter."[47] After all, what works as a practical, everyday account of the legal world 'out there' – international law's courts, or its financial institutions – also works as an approach to international law as an academic discipline.[48] It allows for "examining the practical activities involved in generating knowledge";[49] for scrutiny of how scholars construct legal knowledge in ways we do not see when focusing purely on arguments we identify as legal ones. As explained by Fleur Johns, it means to look at "international law as a form of social knowledge,"[50] similar to the knowledge constructed by "sociologists, anthropologists, historians, political philosophers, and so on."[51] So in this book the discipline of international law is considered as a place where, as in the disciplines of, say, linguistics or philosophy, knowledge is constructed: in all of these "academics work within communities in a particular time and place, and ... the intellectual climate in which they live and work determine [*sic*] the problems they investigate, the methods they employ, the results they see, and the ways they write them up."[52]

1.1.1 *Sociological Approaches to Legal Knowledge Construction*

Asked with regard to international legal scholarship specifically, the question is "how legal knowledge[...] [is] formed through practice."[53] This view of academic knowledge construction is very common in relation to the natural sciences, predominantly in Science and Technology Studies (STS).[54] With regard to *legal* knowledge, however, the same does not apply. There is a lack of scrutiny, not of doctrine as doctrine,[55] but of doctrine as a form of knowledge construction. For example, in the cyberwar debate doctrine is assessed in terms of its adoption

47 Bueger and Gadinger, 'Play of Practice,' 451.
48 As pointed out by ibid., 457.
49 Ibid., 457.
50 Johns, 'Unruly Law,' 23.
51 Camic, Gross and Lamont (eds.), 'Social Knowledge,' 4; see also 11, 13.
52 Hyland, 'Disciplinary Discourses,' 6; this is the way he defines "[t]he basic premise of constructionism" (ibid.).
53 Sullivan, 'Taking on the Technicalities,' 182, he refers here to the work of Annelise Riles and Mariana Valverde.
54 Riles, 'New Agenda,' 1032; Camic, Gross and Lamont (eds.), 'Social Knowledge,' 1, 11. STS is increasingly concerned with the social sciences; see ibid., 11–12 and the references on those pages.
55 For example Helmersen, 'Most Highly Qualified'; in the cyberwar debate see Michael N. Schmitt, 'International Law in Cyberspace: The Koh Speech and Tallinn Manual Juxtaposed' (2012) 54 *Harvard International Law Journal Online* 13.

by states: a 2019 article published in the *American Journal of International Law* asked whether states act in accordance with the rules on cyber operations listed in the second *Tallinn Manual*.[56] With one or two exceptions, there is a lack of scrutiny of how the legal scholars involved in the Manual came to their answers in the first place, and by means of which words and phrases we come to view the Manual as particularly relevant to the debate on cyber and international law.[57] By contrast, within "[Science and Technology Studies] scholars have long recognized the value of an ethnographic approach to the production of scientific and technical thought."[58] This includes, for instance, the work of Bruno Latour and Steve Woolgar in *Laboratory Life*, an anthropological inquiry into "the mundane daily routines of scientists in order to understand the social and material production of scientific truth."[59] Nor has the 'social and material production' of law remained out of focus: Latour himself later studied the French Conseil d'État, in a book that he described as "the *Laboratory Life* . . . for the construction of legal arguments."[60] Similarly, Annelise Riles has adopted an ethnographic approach to international law, including in her study of financial markets and the use of brackets in negotiations on international legal documents.[61] Though the current book shares the curiosity expressed by Riles when she writes how she is after a "far more nuanced and fine-grained"[62] image of what it is the people she studies do, this book differs from both hers and Latour's as it is not an ethnography of international legal scholarship on cyberwar. Instead, the intent here is different: the aim throughout this book is to remain situated 'in law,' all the while retaining the possibility of reflecting on the practices employed. The practices this book analyzes are not 'out there' but belong to a discipline I consider myself to be a part

56 Dan Efrony and Yuval Shany, 'A Rule Book on the Shelf? Tallinn Manual 2.0 on Cyberoperations and Subsequent State Practice' (2019) 112 *American Journal of International Law* 583. I participated in an online forum on this article; see Lianne J. M. Boer, '*Lex Lata* Comes with a Date; or, What Follows from Referring to the "Tallinn Rules"' (2019) 113 *AJIL Unbound* 76.

57 These exceptions include Oliver Kessler and Wouter Werner, 'Expertise, Uncertainty, and International Law: A Study of the Tallinn Manual on Cyberwarfare' (2013) 26 *Leiden Journal of International Law* 793; Boer, 'Restating'; Roos van Keulen, 'Introducing a Critical Stylistic Analysis: How Linguistic Features Contributed to the Tallinn Manual's Power Position' (LLM, Vrije Universiteit Amsterdam 2018).

58 Riles, 'New Agenda,' 985.

59 As referred to by ibid., 985; Bruno Latour and Steve Woolgar, *Laboratory Life: The Construction of Scientific Facts*, Princeton University Press 1986.

60 Bruno Latour, *The Making of Law: An Ethnography of the Conseil d'État*, transl. Marina Brilman and Alain Pottage (revised by the author), Polity Press 2010, ix.

61 Annelise Riles, 'Infinity within the Brackets' (1998) 25 *American Ethnologist* 378; Riles, 'Collateral Knowledge'; see also Riles, 'New Agenda.' For more work in this vein see the brief summary in Riles, 'Collateral Knowledge,' 18–19.

62 Riles, 'Collateral Knowledge,' 13; she describes her own method at 11 et seq.

of:[63] the (socio)linguistic approach taken here – about these linguistics more later – can never be fully detached from the practices it scrutinizes. The attempt is to take a (socio)linguistic approach to international law while allowing for and recognizing the particularities of that practice.[64] In short, the attempt here is to consider international legal scholarship as particular, but to simultaneously allow for the possibility that it is not:[65] "If the internal perspective would be completely denied, the argument would no longer be recognizable as legal argument; if the external perspective would be completely denied, the argument would cease to be sociological."[66]

There are two reasons for taking this perspective. First, a purely sociological approach may not only run counter to how legal practice is "experience[d]" by those engaging in it;[67] it may also, secondly, limit our ability to differentiate between legal and other practices.[68] Concluding his Bourdieusian analysis of international humanitarian lawyers, Frédéric Mégret argues that "[Bourdieu's] model of law . . . is powerfully explanatory but notoriously frustrating for lawyers themselves. It 'explains away' the law as it were as a product of social competition in ways that fail to match lawyers' own understanding of what it is they do."[69] Bourdieu's idea that a "field" is defined, inter alia, by "the specific power relations which give it its structure and which order the competitive struggles"[70] is in that sense problematic ('frustrating,' in Mégret's words) as it excludes other reasons scholars may (feel they) have for engaging with the question of cyber

63 Bueger and Gadinger, 'Play of Practice,' 457.

64 Wouter G. Werner, 'The Use of Law in International Political Sociology' (2010) 4 *International Political Sociology* 304, 305; see also Martti Koskenniemi, 'Letter to the Editors of the Symposium' (1999) 93 *American Journal of International Law* 351, 356, 360 (both refer to 'recognition'). For a reference to a similar distinction and a suggestion for a new approach see Jakob V. H. Holtermann and Mikael Rask Madsen, 'European New Legal Realism and International Law: How to Make International Law Intelligible' (2015) 28 *Leiden Journal of International Law* 211; see also Sally Engle Merry, 'New Legal Realism and the Ethnography of Transnational Law' (2006) 31 *Law & Social Inquiry* 975. For a critical reflection see Sara Kendall, 'On Academic Production and the Politics of Inclusion' (2016) 29 *Leiden Journal of International Law* 617, in particular 619–620. I will return to this point in the last chapter of this book.

65 Cf. Latour, 'The Making of Law,' ix.

66 Werner, 'Use of Law,' 305.

67 Koskenniemi, 'Apology to Utopia,' 25; Koskenniemi, 'Letter to the Editors,' 360; similarly, Mégret, 'Thinking About,' 286.

68 Aalberts and Werner, 'International Law,' 41, who refer to Ron Levi and Mariana Valverde, 'Studying Law by Association: Bruno Latour Goes to the Conseil d'État' (2008) 33 *Law & Social Inquiry* 805, 822–823.

69 Mégret, 'Thinking About,' 286.

70 Pierre Bourdieu, 'Force of Law: Toward a Sociology of the Juridical Field' (1987) 38 *Hastings Law Journal* 814, 816, see also 818, 821; Ken Hyland similarly refers to "fields"; see Hyland, 'Disciplinary Discourses,' 169–170.

and international law: they might instead consider themselves involved in a genuine attempt at assessing the law applicable to cyberwar, for the sake of increasing international peace and security. Borrowing from Anne Orford, this kind of approach "flatten[s] everything" to the point where "people . . . turned out to be describable in terms of an extremely limited set of characteristics."[71] More fundamentally, however, the questions asked in this book are of a different kind: it asks what scholars say and how they construct legal knowledge in the cyberwar debate; the "'why' of international legal work"[72] is left aside. There is no scrutiny, for instance, of why scholars should say that force includes armed force, but not economic coercion.[73] Similarly, even though Chapters 4 and 5 conclude on the prominence of a very limited number of scholars in establishing certain "knowledge claims,"[74] it does not attempt to explain *why* these scholars became so important in the first place. This does not mean that this book may not conclude on, for example, authority (relations), especially in its second half; it does mean, however, that I did not enter the analysis presupposing 'struggle' to take place.

Secondly, the question is not just what it means to those involved to engage in international legal scholarship, but also how we might recognize an argument as a legal one.[75] The basic assumption underlying this book is that in their academic writing and speaking international legal scholars will, to some extent, perform their discipline in a similar way as those engaged in other academic disciplines, but that allowance has to be made for "interdisciplinary diversity."[76] A view of legal scholars as simply academics means we can look at their writing and speech as *academic* writing and speech and use, for example, the analytical tools developed by linguists to scrutinize these kinds of texts (I will elaborate on this shortly). At the same time, "[e]ach discipline [has] its particular norms, nomenclature, bodies of knowledge, sets of conventions and

[71] Orford, 'Description,' 622, and 620, where she refers to Foucault's "attentiveness and responsiveness to the archives he assembled"; see also Anne Orford, 'On International Legal Method' (2013) 1 *London Review of International Law* 166, 178–180. But see Didier Bigo, 'Pierre Bourdieu and International Relations: Power of Practices, Practices of Power' (2011) 5 *International Political Sociology* 225, 232.

[72] Johns, 'Unruly Law,' 218, 23. See also Orford, 'Description,' 618.

[73] On this question see, for example, Matthew C. Waxman, 'Cyber-Attacks and the Use of Force: Back to the Future of Article 2(4)' (2011) 36 *Yale Journal of International Law* 421, section IV.

[74] Hyland, 'Disciplinary Discourses,' 12–16; defined at 8.

[75] See note 68 above.

[76] Hyland, 'Disciplinary Discourses,' 10; cf. Martti Koskenniemi, 'Law, Teleology and International Relations: An Essay in Counterdisciplinarity' (2012) 26 *International Relations* 3, 19. On similarities see Hanne Andersen and Brian Hepburn, 'Scientific Method,' *Stanford Encyclopedia of Philosophy* 2015, Edward N. Zalta (ed.), section 1.

modes of inquiry constituting a separate culture."[77] The fact that there are "discipline-specific knowledge-making practices"[78] is already contained in the word 'discipline' itself: it entails an "allegiance"[79] to particular doctrines, as well as restraints on what can and cannot be said and *how* it is to be said within a given discourse. With regard to international legal scholarship, the kind of allegiance it entails is toward a specific way of solving world problems, and a shared expectation and idea of what it is international law is for. I will elaborate on this in the next chapter, but a few notes are in order here.

To take part in a discipline is "both restrictive and authorizing":[80] it means some things are heard, and others are left aside. A particular statement needs to be made according to the 'rules of the game' in order to be heard and understood as "belonging to" that discourse.[81] In turn, these rules are imposed and maintained by (those participating in) discourses themselves through (to cite Foucault again) "permanent re-actuation."[82] This is another way of saying that if I want to contribute to the body of knowledge that is international law, I will have to do so by speaking of those topics ("objects")[83] which my audience recognizes as belonging to the field of international law proper; that I have to approach my questions in ways that are acknowledged by that field and uphold certain assumptions about what it means to do law.[84] Moreover, these standards are constantly reproduced ('re-actuated') by myself and my colleagues. Put differently, my words are aimed at an audience; they need to be recognized by others.[85] What this means for academic legal writing is that we "shap[e] [our] actions to the presumed understandings and needs of [our] readers."[86]

The knowledge claims about 'what the law is' as posited by scholars are therefore understood in this book as "the outcome of socially agreed-upon ways of discussing academic problems that are always subject to dialectical revision."[87] In other words, academia is as much a "cognitive project" as it is

77 Hyland, 'Disciplinary Discourses,' 8; see also xi.
78 Ibid., xii.
79 Noll, 'Discipline and Doctrine,' 36.
80 Hyland, 'Disciplinary Discourses,' 10, referring to Foucault.
81 Foucault refers to the "rules of . . . discourse"; Michel Foucault, 'The Order of Discourse,' in: *Untying the Text: A Post-Structuralist Reader*, Robert Young (ed.), Routledge & Kegan Paul 1981, 48–78, 61. For "belonging to" discourse see ibid., 60; more elaborately 59–61.
82 Ibid., 56 ("discourses themselves exercise their own control"); for "permanent re-actuation" see 61.
83 Ibid., 59–61.
84 Foucault refers to being "within the true"; see ibid., 61. Cf. Aalberts and Venzke, 'Moving Beyond,' 306.
85 Foucault, 'Order of Discourse,' 60; Hyland, 'Disciplinary Discourses,' 8.
86 Hyland, 'Disciplinary Discourses,' xi.
87 Ibid., 8.

an "interactive" one.[88] Such a "community"-based perspective on knowledge construction also means it doesn't take much to see that if it matters how something is said, it also matters who is doing the saying.[89] International legal doctrine on cyberwar is constructed through our articles, books and conference presentations, but it matters very much who the audience and who the speakers are in these linguistic exchanges.[90] In this context Ken Hyland refers to "the voices used by academics when addressing one another rather than outsiders, the voices that define disciplinary boundaries, exclude outsiders and authorise contributions as new knowledge."[91] The authority to speak or to be heard is controlled, among other things, by means of the language we use: through our own individual acts of speaking and writing we can similarly assign others the authority to speak, or "validat[e]"[92] their knowledge claims. Not everyone is listened to with the same level of attention, and not everyone has equal "access": "Not all the regions of discourse are equally open and penetrable," Foucault writes, "[t]here is a rarefaction ... of the speaking subjects."[93]

The above can be summarized as saying that how we write and speak about international law has a bearing on what we know that law to be.[94] What we say exactly and who is doing the speaking, matters. It is this importance of the exact words we use when constructing international legal knowledge this book is concerned with.

1.2 'MAKING VISIBLE WHAT WE ALREADY SEE'

The way this book treats spoken and written words emanates from its main question – how do we know what we know? In answering this question I follow Anne Orford's call to engage in "description as a method for writing

88 Ibid., xi, comma omitted.
89 Ibid., 168; Hyland also elaborately discusses the notion of "community" on this page. See also Chapter 5 of this book.
90 Ibid., x–xi.
91 Ibid., 168.
92 Ibid., xi.
93 Foucault, 'Order of Discourse,' 62, 61; see also Hyland, 'Disciplinary Discourses,' 157.
94 See also Gerald B. Wetlaufer, 'Rhetoric and its Denial in Legal Discourse' (1990) 76 *Virginia Law Review* 1545, 1548; more elaborately, Winter, 'Transcendental Nonsense' and Marianne Constable, *Our Word Is Our Bond: How Legal Speech Acts*, Stanford University Press 2014. This is precisely why Lisa Eichhorn criticizes the distinction law schools make between "skills" training and doctrinal law courses; see Lisa Eichhorn, 'Writing in the Legal Academy: A Dangerous Supplement?' (1998) 40 *Arizona Law Review* 105, section II.B.

about law," a turn which she primarily situates in the work of Michel Foucault.[95] What it entails is a kind of analysis which starts with what is right in front of us; "that which is so close, which is so immediate, which is so intimately linked to us, that because of that we do not perceive it."[96] Foucault refers to it as a "project of a pure description of discursive events" which "rediscover[s] the silent murmuring, the inexhaustible speech that animates from within the voice that one hears, re-establish[es] the tiny, invisible text that runs between and sometimes collides with them."[97] The aim of such a descriptive project is to move "beyond" the desire of much critical work to expose the workings of power and instead take a step closer toward the text.[98] With 'text' I mean to refer to both written and spoken words. The attempt is to describe what we read or hear, what is right in front of us: "to make visible" what is already there.[99] As Fleur Johns says, this is about "amplifying, annotating, and burrowing through work *already ongoing*": the "critical project" is description itself.[100] Johns uses the word "quasi-ethnography" to describe this method; 'quasi' as the specific research she refers to does not draw on any fieldwork or interviews, and only to a degree on participant observation.[101] Neither is this project, as explained above, an ethnography of the cyberwar discourse. 'Quasi-ethnography,' rather, entails taking a very close look at what it is scholars

95 Orford, 'Description,' 609; see also Orford, 'International Legal Method,' 177–182. For a theoretical outlook similar to the one outlined here see Boer and Stolk (eds.), 'Backstage Practices,' introduction.

96 Orford, 'Description,' 617, quoting and translating Foucault (see note 21 above); see in that same piece part III; similarly, Riles, 'New Agenda,' 981. See also Bueger and Gadinger, 'Play of Practice,' 457 and Sullivan, 'Taking on the Technicalities,' 184.

97 Foucault, 'Archeology of Knowledge,' 27, emphasis omitted.

98 For 'moving "beyond"' see Mariana Valverde, '"Non-Legality" and Society: Fleur Johns, *Non-Legality in International Law: Unruly Law*, Cambridge, Cambridge University Press, 2013, 259 pp., ISBN 9781107014015' (2014) 27 *Leiden Journal of International Law* 961, 964. For this focus on power see Orford, 'Description,' 622; Sullivan, 'Taking on the Technicalities,' 183–184; Valverde, 'Non-Legality,' 963; Sharon Marcus, Heather Love and Stephen Best, 'Building a Better Description' (2016) 135 *Representations* 1, 3.

99 "[T]he role of philosophy is not to discover what is hidden, but to make visible precisely what is visible"; Foucault in Orford, see note 21 above. The title of this section is derived from this quote.

100 Fleur Johns, 'Author's Response – Fleur Johns, *Non-Legality in International Law: Unruly Law*, Cambridge, Cambridge University Press, 2013, 259 pp., ISBN 9781107014015' (2014) 27 *Leiden Journal of International Law* 966, 967; for "critical project" see Orford, 'Description,' 618.

101 Johns, 'Unruly Law,' 21 et seq. (cf. Riles, 'Collateral Knowledge,' 14); see also Fleur Johns, 'Data, Detection, and the Redistribution of the Sensible in International Law' (2017) 111 *American Journal of International Law* 57, 66. For an alternative label ("post-sociological") of Johns' method see Valverde, 'Non-Legality,' 963.

"actually do"[102] in their academic writing and speech, and attempt to account for what results from their words – without wanting to lay claim to producing a full ethnography or being "naïve" about the correspondence of the description of these actual doings to "reality."[103]

In this book the "turn to description"[104] as advocated by Orford and Johns materializes into four basic questions asked of the cyberwar discourse: Which words are used; where in these texts are they used; who is using these words; and what does it do to use these, rather than others? The aim of asking these questions is to make knowledge construction at the microlevel at which it is studied as tangible and concrete as possible. In this book this happens, for example, by means of appendices which form the empirical backbone of both the fourth and fifth chapter.[105] These appendices present the material underlying the analysis and show how it was "arranged"[106] in order to come to these chapters' conclusions. Hereby the aim is to "describe what the people in some particular place or status ordinarily do and the *meanings* they ascribe to the doing . . . presenting that description in a manner that draws attention to regularities that implicate cultural process."[107] In other words, the aim of the appendices in particular and of description in general is to highlight which words are used exactly; by assembling them to uncover 'regularities,' and, essentially, to be able to point out in a text where they are: literally to be able to say, 'there, there they are.'

Importantly, the 'way of seeing' described here does not just pertain to how we look at text but also *where* we look. The word 'mundane' has been used several times already, and it appears in different guises in the research referred to as bearing close affinity to this study. Bruno Latour and Steve Woolgar, for example, refer to "the routinely occurring minutiae of scientific activity"; Annelise Riles to "the taken-for-granted agreed bases of social life"; Anne Orford to "prosaic and everyday practices" and Fleur Johns to "the patterned activities and often

102 Andersen and Hepburn, 'Scientific Method,' section 1; a similar phrase is used by Meierhenrich, 'Practice,' 9; see also Camic, Gross and Lamont (eds.), 'Social Knowledge,' 6–7 and Riles, 'New Agenda,' 1032.

103 Orford refers to the "complicated relationship" between "practice[s] of description" and "reality" (625); she uses the word "naïve" in this context as well, at 624. See Orford, 'Description'; Clifford Geertz, *The Interpretation of Cultures*, Basic Books 1973, 316–317; and Marcus, Love and Best, 'Better Description,' 5.

104 Orford, 'Description,' 609; see also Chapter 6 of this book.

105 The Appendix of Chapter 4 is published online as supplementary material to Lianne J. M. Boer, '"The Greater Part of Jurisconsults": On Consensus Claims and Their Footnotes in Legal Scholarship' (2016) 29 *Leiden Journal of International Law* 1021. The Appendix of Chapter 5 can be found at the back of this book.

106 Orford, 'Description,' 623, 618.

107 Johns, 'Unruly Law,' 21–22, quoting Harry F. Wolcott, *Ethnography: A Way of Seeing*, Second Edition, (Lanham: AltaMira Press, 2008), pp. 72–73. See also note 21 above on citation styles.

mundane modes of work in which social knowledge-makers engage."[108] It is precisely the mundane character of these 'modes of work' that risks their being overlooked and not considered relevant for legal analysis.[109] This point is already well understood in US scholarship operating at the cross-section of law and linguistics and in legal anthropology. For example, both Marianne Constable and Elizabeth Mertz study the effect of language on our understanding of law: one by analyzing the rendition of facts by a Court, the other by asking how law schools train students in specific ways of using and understanding language.[110] Specifically, Mertz shows that to be trained as a lawyer means to learn to focus on a distinct set of arguments and dissect a text in a particular way.[111] This primes us to dismiss a lot of text as not "legally relevant" – starting with that which we do not recognize as an 'argument' proper (pronouns, adverbs, etc.).[112] Similarly, outside of the discipline of international law linguists have started to focus on legal discourse, for example in the form of analyzing metadiscourse and hedging in legal writing.[113] However, these approaches seem to make it to international legal scholarship only hesitatingly, with linguistic research on occasion grouping it together with domestic legal writing[114] and work in and specifically on international legal scholarship being thin on the ground.[115]

108 Latour and Woolgar, 'Laboratory Life,' 27; Riles, 'Collateral Knowledge,' 13; Orford, 'Description,' 614; Johns, 'Unruly Law,' 23; similarly, Meierhenrich, 'Practice,' 8, quoting Pouliot ("self-evident" and "commonsensical"); Camic, Gross and Lamont (eds.), 'Social Knowledge,' 6–7 ("day-to-day actions and processes"); Valverde, 'Non-Legality,' 964 ("hidden in plain sight").

109 Orford, 'Description,' 617, referring to Foucault.

110 Specifically, Constable, 'Our Word,' chapter 2 and Elizabeth Mertz, *The Language of Law School: Learning to 'Think Like a Lawyer,'* Oxford University Press 2007, chapters 4 and 5; see also Nina Philadelphoff-Puren and Peter Rush, 'Fatal (F)laws: Law, Literature and Writing' (2003) 14 *Law and Critique* 191.

111 Mertz, 'The Language of Law School,' chapter 4. On differences in international law training see Anthea Roberts, *Is International Law International? A Study in the Globalization of Legal Education and Scholarship*, Oxford University Press 2017, preface.

112 Mertz, 'The Language of Law School,' 67; the conveyance of "legal (ir)relevance" plays a big part in her fourth chapter. On learning how to make "legal arguments" specifically see ibid., 79–82.

113 For example, Michele Sala, 'Interpersonal and Interactional Markers in Legal Research Articles,' in: *Interpersonality in Legal Genres*, Ruth Breeze, Maurizio Gotti and Carmen Sancho Guinda (eds.), Peter Lang 2014, 63–86; Holly Vass, 'Analysing Hedging in Legal Discourse Using Small-Scale and Large-Scale Corpora' (2015) 3 *Research in Corpus Linguistics* 27.

114 Michele Sala, 'Plain Language in Legal Studies: A Corpus-Based Study' (2014) 16 *European Journal of Law Reform* 651, 656.

115 For some exceptions see Maks Del Mar, 'Metaphor in International Law: Language, Imagination and Normative Inquiry' (2017) 86 *Nordic Journal of International Law* 170; Jennifer Smolka and Benedikt Pirker, 'International Law and Pragmatics: An Account of

Yet as Johns, Orford and others have pointed out, these overlooked parts of international legal knowledge construction are in fact "worthy of [our] legal scholarly attention," and will only come into view as a result of changing the way we read or listen.[116] The ambition of this book is precisely this: to point out those sites that are not usually the subject of close (critical) scrutiny, and to show how the practices employed there do matter to what we know.[117] Taking such a close look at the fabric of legal texts highlights the "slow, practical craftwork"[118] involved in academic knowledge construction. This, moreover, explains the preference in this book for the word 'construction' when referring to the way knowledge comes about, as it comes closest to indicating how a legal argument is 'crafted' in legal writing. I take my lead here from a chapter in *Laboratory Life* which details the "characterisation" of TRF, one of the substances established in the laboratory where Latour and Woolgar conducted their research.[119] What they object to is the idea that TRF is "discovered" by the scientists involved; instead, what they show in this particular chapter is how a scientific fact comes into existence "through microsocial phenomena."[120] Hence, they prefer verbs such as "constructed" and "constituted" rather than "discovered" or "found," for "[t]o employ [these latter] expressions would be to convey the misleading impression that the presence of certain objects was a pregiven and that such objects merely awaited the timely revelation of their existence."[121] Likewise in this book, the image that emerges is that of a law which, rather than pre-given, is constructed in legal scholars' acts of writing and speaking, 'making law a given.'[122]

Interpretation in International Law' (2016) 5 *International Journal of Language & Law* 1. In this (2016) piece Smolka and Pilker similarly conclude that "[l]inguistics . . . has not yet been fully integrated into the study of interpretation in international law" (at 2); they repeat this a few years later in Benedikt Pirker and Jennifer Smolka, 'The Future of International Law Is Cognitive – International Law, Cognitive Sociology and Cognitive Pragmatics' (2019) 20 *German Law Journal* 430, 439.

116 Johns, 'Unruly Law,' 152; Marianne Constable, Leti Volpp and Bryan Wagner (eds.), *Looking for Law in All the Wrong Places: Justice Beyond and Between*, Fordham University Press 2019; see also Riles, 'Infinity'; Camic, Gross and Lamont (eds.), 'Social Knowledge,' introduction.

117 Similarly, Constable, Volpp and Wagner (eds.), 'Looking for Law' and the contributions in Boer and Stolk (eds.), 'Backstage Practices.'

118 Latour and Woolgar, 'Laboratory Life,' 236.

119 Ibid., 106.

120 Ibid., 128, 253–254; 236.

121 Ibid., 128–129; emphasis omitted for "constructed." On the use of verbs see, for example, Sarah Thomas and Thomas P. Hawes, 'Reporting Verbs in Medical Journal Articles' (1994) 13 *English for Specific Purposes* 129.

122 Latour and Woolgar, 'Laboratory Life,' 236, 128. See also Venzke, 'Interpretation,' 29 and 29 note 60.

The question remains how this is done, exactly. The above has linked the questions asked in this book to, among others, the practice turn as well as STS scholarship, and it explained how I go about answering them. In terms of accounting for what I find, however, I draw primarily on (socio) linguistic analyses of academic writing and speech. The introductions of the different chapters will elaborate on their respective methods; here, however, the work of Ken Hyland merits separate mention. He was already quoted, above, as referring to the 'voices' scholars use 'when addressing one another rather than outsiders.' This is precisely the focus of his work, which primarily deals with the differences and similarities of language use across disciplines. For example, using corpus linguistics he analyzes how and why the use of first person pronouns in philosophy textbooks is much higher than in biology textbooks, or how the structure of abstracts written in physics journals differs from those written in sociology journals, and why.[123] His work takes place within the subdiscipline of English for Academic Purposes (EAP), a domain in which linguists are concerned with the textual particularities of different academic disciplines.[124] One of the aims of EAP is "to show how different academic contexts place demands on communicative behaviours which are likely to be unfamiliar to disciplinary novices."[125] In other words, there is a clear "pedagogic"[126] aim to EAP: to instruct 'disciplinary novices' into the most efficient ways of bringing their points across in whichever discipline they seek to engage in. This is not the point of this book. It does not seek to improve international legal scholarship or to point out where it might differ from academic writing in other disciplines. What I borrow from EAP – and the work of Ken Hyland in particular – is its way of scrutinizing academic texts: a very close, textual analysis of the minute elements of legal writing and speech, and an attempt at accounting for what all these different elements signify or 'do' in a text. Its analytical importance, moreover, lies in that it radically opens up the scope of inquiry to include those parts of a text that are from a *legal* perspective irrelevant to the conclusions drawn by the writer on the application of international law to cyberattacks: adjectives, adverbs,

[123] Both examples are taken from Hyland, 'Disciplinary Discourses,' chapters 6 (114) and 4 (70) respectively.

[124] Ibid., ix. The introductions of Chapters 4 and 5 of this book deal more elaborately with the (socio)linguistic theories they draw on.

[125] Ibid., x.

[126] Eija Ventola, Celia Shalom and Susan Thompson, 'Introduction,' in: *The Language of Conferencing*, Eija Ventola, Celia Shalom and Susan Thompson (eds.), Peter Lang 2002, 9–14, 10.

pronouns, etc. Applied linguistics shows how these words are relevant to the knowledge constructed in an article, book chapter or conference presentation. In other words, and in line with the turn to description this book takes, it makes those parts of the text visible which are otherwise overlooked, and shows how these words and phrases matter to the knowledge we construct in this discipline.

1.3 OUTLINE OF THE BOOK

The above already referred to three close-ups of the cyberwar discourse this book offers. These close-ups are presented in Chapters 3, 4 and 5 and form the heart of this book. First, however, the second chapter details which parts of the cyberwar discourse this book is concerned with.[127] It functions as the background to Chapters 3 to 5 and in so doing demarcates the analysis by, first, elaborating on the notion of 'war' in cyberspace, and second, on "legal problem-solution"[128] as the shared aim of the international legal scholars involved. It furthermore explains the focus of Chapters 3 and 4 on the debate on Article 2(4) of the UN Charter in particular, and discusses some of the problems scholars run into as they try to apply the prohibition on the use of force to cyberattacks. The last part of the chapter provides a broad sketch of these attempts, and as a contrast to legal problem-solution details the work of those scholars who claim that the characteristics of cyberattacks preclude their regulation under international law.

Chapters 3, 4 and 5 all carry quotes as their titles, representative for the discussion in that particular chapter. Chapter 3 is titled "*Not 'Armed Force' in the Literal Sense.*"[129] It is taken from one of the articles written on Article 2(4) and cyberattacks, and signifies how scholars reconstruct the meaning of the

[127] Two previously published pieces in particular served as the background for and run-up to what would become Chapters 1, 2 and 3 of this book: Lianne J. M. Boer, '"Restating the Law 'As It Is'": On the Tallinn Manual and the Use of Force in Cyberspace' (2013) 5 *Amsterdam Law Forum* 4 and Lianne J. M. Boer, '"Echoes of Times Past": On the Paradoxical Nature of Article 2(4)' (2015) 20 *Journal of Conflict and Security Law* 5. References to specific parts of these articles have been inserted in the body text of this book where appropriate; see also note 129 below.

[128] See note 13 above.

[129] Joyner and Lotrionte, 'Information Warfare,' 849. A piece I published in the *Journal of Conflict and Security Law* in 2014 provided the run-up to this chapter; see Boer, 'Echoes.' However, during the writing of the dissertation (2017) on which this book is based my ideas on the cyberwar discourse changed so fundamentally that, even though some elements of the cyber/Article 2(4) discussion may be found in both the JCSL piece and in the third chapter of this book, and the literature used in both pieces overlaps, in terms of the argument made the 2014 article only served as a stepping stone for this chapter.

prohibition in light of the "novel features" of cyberwar.[130] The chapter starts with a general introduction into how the prohibition is given meaning through legal reasoning, subsequently zooming in on how exactly its boundaries are constructed. As will be more elaborately dealt with in the next chapter, given the range of effects cyberattacks can have the question these scholars struggle with is where to draw the boundary of the prohibition on the use of force. Cyberattacks may not always resemble what we think force looks like: on those occasions, they are 'not "armed force" in the literal sense.' By creating a dialogue between a number of different pieces and juxtaposing the arguments scholars make in this "gray area"[131] of law, the first close-up shows what legal knowledge construction in relation to the boundaries of Article 2(4) looks like. Specifically, it identifies two argumentative turns scholars take in their writing, be it journal articles or book chapters. The first pertains explicitly to the boundaries of the norm, and the chapter shows the subsequent trajectory of an argument about the (in)sufficiency of Article 2(4) in regulating these kinds of cyberattacks.[132] The second turn pertains to the classification of the threat. Whereas to some scholars cyberattacks simply constitute a new means to wage war or exercise coercion, to others the change is much more fundamental. Whether a scholar opts for the first label or the second, matters to how the legal analysis proceeds toward, again, a diagnosis about the (in)sufficiency of the norm. By bringing these junctions to the surface and contrasting them with the other possible turns a scholar could have taken at this point, this chapter shows how exactly legal writing 'creates what it claims to find' in relation to Article 2(4).[133]

The second close-up, in Chapter 4, is titled *"The Greater Part of Jurisconsults."*[134] This phrase is taken from a speech given by Baron Descamps,

130 As explained in Chapter 3 of this book, the notion of legal interpretations as reconstructions is based on Koskenniemi, 'Apology to Utopia,' specifically chapter 8 and its Epilogue, and Venzke, 'Interpretation,' chapters 1 and 2. The phrase "novel features" is from Marco Benatar, 'The Use of Cyber Force: Need for Legal Justification?' (2009) 1 *Goettingen Journal of International Law* 375, 391.

131 Todd C. Huntley, 'Controlling the Use of Force in Cyber Space: The Application of the Law of Armed Conflict During a Time of Fundamental Change in the Nature of Warfare' (2010) 60 *Naval Law Review* 1, 26.

132 On (the room for) decisions and the over- and underinclusiveness of rules, including the prohibition on the use of force, see Chapter 3 note 25.

133 As paraphrased from Ingo Venzke, who writes that "interpretations contribute to creating what they find." See Venzke, 'Interpretation,' 54. I will return to this in the conclusion.

134 This chapter was previously published as Lianne J. M. Boer (2016) '"The Greater Part of Jurisconsults": On Consensus Claims and Their Footnotes in Legal Scholarship,' *Leiden Journal of International Law*, 29(4), 1021–1042 © Foundation of the Leiden Journal of International Law 2016, published by Cambridge University Press. Reproduced with permission. Though large parts of the text remain unchanged, the

who was in charge of the Committee of Jurists that designed the Statute of the Permanent Court of International Justice in 1920. At some point during the Committee's deliberations, Descamps addressed the Jurists on the sources of law the Court should use to come to its judgments. One of the sources its judges should be allowed to draw on, Descamps referred to as "the concurrent teaching of the authors whose opinions have authority." After all, he said, "when the greater part of jurisconsults agree upon a certain rule – the presumption in favour of that rule becomes so strong, that only a person who makes a mock of justice would gainsay it."[135]

This agreement among 'the greater part of jurisconsults' is the main theme of the second close-up of this book. Remaining with scholarly interpretations of Article 2(4) it focuses on the use of one particular argument: consensus claims. With 'consensus claim' I refer to appeals to majority opinion, generally accepted interpretations, unanimity, etc.: phrases such as "the *generally accepted* interpretation is that the term force within Article 2(4) is limited to armed force."[136] Examples of these kinds of claims abound in reference to a whole range of different issues; for example, scholars might conclude that there "is a *general consensus* that some cyber operations will constitute a use of force,"[137] meaning that apparently most scholars agree that the *jus ad bellum* lends itself to application in the cyber context. Others are more specific when they state that "[t]he *leading view* ... among legal experts ... calls for an effects-based analysis of a particular cyber incident to determine whether or not it equates to an 'armed attack'."[138] This chapter considers one specific set of consensus claims: that Article 2(4) includes (armed) force, but excludes economic coercion.

chapter presents a somewhat edited version of the article. This overview of Chapter 4 is largely based on ibid., 1023–1026.

135 Permanent Court of International Justice, 'Advisory Committee of Jurists, Procès-Verbaux of the Proceedings of the Committee, June 16th–July 24th 1920, The Hague,' 323. These "concurrent teachings" (323) were part of Descamps' suggestion that the Court's judges should have resort to "objective justice" (324), which would be made up of these teachings as well as "the legal conscience of civilised nations" (323). See, more elaborately, the introduction of Chapter 4 of this book.

136 Russell Buchan, 'Cyber Attacks: Unlawful Uses of Force or Prohibited Interventions?' (2012) 17 *Journal of Conflict and Security Law* 211, 216; emphasis added for "generally accepted," omitted for "armed."

137 Andrew C. Foltz, 'Stuxnet, Schmitt Analysis, and the Cyber "Use-of-Force" Debate' (2012) 67 *Joint Force Quarterly* 40, 40; emphasis added for "general consensus," omitted for "some."

138 Charles J. Dunlap Jr., 'Perspectives for Cyber Strategists on Law for Cyberwar' (2011) 5 *Strategic Studies Quarterly* 81, 85, emphasis added for "leading view," omitted for "effects-based."

The chapter starts by examining what these kinds of claims *do* in a scholar's argument about the meaning of 'force.' It asks what is invoked when these kinds of claims are made, and rather than question whether they are 'empirically' correct it seeks to account for what these appeals to consensus signify in a scholarly piece of writing. The chapter then proceeds by looking at the footnotes following these claims. For example, the phrase "the *prevailing and commonly accepted view* put forward by scholars is that the force referred to in Article 2(4) is limited to armed force,"[139] is followed by a footnote. The 'sources' listed in this footnote seemingly function to substantiate the claim that this is, indeed, 'the prevailing and commonly accepted view.' However, as shown in the online Appendix of this chapter the footnotes following these consensus claims most of the time consist of references to largely the same, limited set of scholars.[140] Simply put, in order to support their consensus claims scholars largely refer to the same publicists. Making use of the notion of "concept symbols" as coined by Henry Small in the sociology of science, the chapter seeks to account for the function of these references to the most-cited scholars; what these scholars represent and how they turn into the bearers of majority opinion.[141] The chapter concludes that even though in an individual piece one single reference can appear to be quite innocuous, when considered as a more widespread practice of "self-referentiality"[142] it seriously impacts who gets a say – and thus, ultimately, what we know – in international law.

In this manner, halfway through the book focus changes from the 'what' of legal knowledge construction to an inquiry into 'who is doing the saying' in the cyberwar discourse. Whereas the third chapter and the first half of the fourth focus on what it is scholars say exactly, halfway through Chapter 4 emphasis shifts to the 'who' of legal knowledge construction. In Chapter 4 this happens by considering footnotes as distributing the authority to speak to other

139 Heather Harrison Dinniss, *Cyber Warfare and the Laws of War*, Cambridge University Press 2014, 41, emphasis added.

140 The chapter looks not only at the footnotes immediately following the consensus claim: these 'primary' footnotes in turn are 'trackbacked' to see to which sources they themselves refer. This is then repeated once over to come to a list of 'tertiary' references. The Appendix of this chapter is published online as supplementary material to the article originally published in the *Leiden Journal*, see note 134 above.

141 Henry G. Small, 'Cited Documents as Concept Symbols' (1978) 8 *Social Studies of Science* 327.

142 This term is also used by Urška Šadl, 'Case – Case-Law – Law: *Ruiz Zambrano* as an Illustration of How the Court of Justice of the European Union Constructs Its Legal Arguments' (2013) 9 *European Constitutional Law Review* 205, 208; by Thomas Skouteris, 'The New Tribunalism: Strategies of (De)Legitimation in the Era of International Adjudication' (2006) 17 *Finnish Yearbook of International Law* 307, 334; and by Roberts, 'International Law,' 101–104 to refer to somewhat similar dynamics.

participants in this discourse.[143] In Chapter 5 this happens by focusing on the self-positioning of the most prominent figure in the cyberwar debate, Michael Schmitt.

Schmitt has been described as "one of the most prolific writers on [international humanitarian law] issues ... enjoy[ing] a dominant position in contemporary discourse."[144] In the cyberwar discourse, in fact, his position is the most dominant one; most importantly, he chaired both groups of experts that drafted the *Tallinn Manuals*, mentioned on the opening pages of this book. The Manuals constitute what Ingo Venzke calls "authoritative reference points": those parts of a discourse its participants cannot escape.[145] In other words, if a scholar writes a piece about cyberwar and international law it is almost impossible *not* to mention them. The title of Chapter 5, "*Call Me Again If You're Ever Ready to Begin Answering the Questions*," is a quote from one of Schmitt's conference presentations on the first *Tallinn Manual* in particular,[146] and is taken as emblematic of the way in which he positions himself at the heart of the cyberwar discourse. The chapter briefly addresses the ways in which authority is ascribed to Schmitt by others, before moving on to its main focus: how, in these presentations, he himself contributes to this construction. It does so by thinking of his presentations as entailing a kind of map-drawing. The first part of the chapter shows how Schmitt relates to 'time' and international legal thinking; the second, how he constructs a spatial map of the field within which he functions. With regard to 'time,' Schmitt positions himself as well as the *Tallinn Manual* squarely within the history of international legal thinking; secondly, he has a strong sense of certainty about the substance of existing law and lastly, he proclaims the possible futures of international law on cyber. The second part of the chapter shows how Schmitt discursively relates to several 'others': nonlawyers; other(s) (lawyers) who, in his view, misinterpret international law as well as those he refers to as "pure academics";[147] third, the group of experts involved in the composition of the Manual; and finally, himself in the third person. Following the construal

143 See, more elaborately, the discussion of and references to the work of Ken Hyland in this chapter as well as in Chapter 4.

144 Gregor Noll, 'Analogy at War: Proportionality, Equality and the Law of Targeting,' in: *Netherlands Yearbook of International Law 2012*, Janne E. Nijman and Wouter G. Werner (eds.), T.M.C. Asser Press 2013, 205–230, 209. I will elaborate on this in the introduction of Chapter 5.

145 Venzke, 'Interpretation,' 48, and chapter 2 of his book.

146 CyCon 2012 | Michael Schmitt: Tallinn Manual Part I (hereafter: CyCon 2012 (I)), 0.49. The Appendix of Chapter 5 explains why this chapter focuses on the first *Tallinn Manual* only.

147 This is taken from a presentation held in 2013: The Tallinn Manual on the International Law Applicable to Cyber Warfare (hereafter: Brown 2013), 1.04.38.

of all these links, what is left at the heart of the discursive map is Schmitt himself, holding the key to legal knowledge as well as functioning as gatekeeper for those he considers suitable to partake in this debate.[148]

Together, these three close-ups aim to show how international legal knowledge is constructed by means of minor twists and turns in a piece of writing, and of words placed either metaphorically – in the case of conference presentations – or literally – in the case of footnotes – at the margins of what we consider to be the "real work" of international law.[149] This not only raises questions as to what that 'real work' is and what other places might be worth looking at, but also about how we look at the way international legal knowledge comes about. The sixth, concluding chapter will reflect on these questions, and on the kind of engagement the new way of seeing this book proposes entails.

148 Ken Hyland similarly speaks of "gatekeepers"; see Hyland, 'Disciplinary Discourses,' 157, and Chapter 5 of this book. Thanks to Jessica Lawrence for suggesting 'map-drawing' as a metaphor.

149 Sarah-Jane Koulen, 'Blind Justice and the Portraits on the Wall,' in: *Backstage Practices of Transnational Law*, Lianne J. M. Boer and Sofia Stolk (eds.), Routledge 2019, 91–107, 97.

2

"Legal Problem-Solution" and the Cyberwar Discourse

The previous chapter provided a first sketch of the cyberwar discourse. It explained how the international legal scholars engaged in this debate are faced with a lack of treaty and customary law on the subject, and that even though *opinio juris* has been emerging over the last few years there is still a lot of uncertainty as to how exactly states will approach the legal problem of cyberwar. Furthermore, the actual examples of cyberattacks that would qualify for consideration under the *jus ad bellum* are thin on the ground. One of the ensuing questions, then, is how scholars face these conditions and how their problem-solving "posture"[1] manifests itself concretely in this discourse.

This chapter is the beginning of an answer to those questions, as it provides a more detailed image of those parts of the cyberwar discourse with which this book is concerned. Though subversion and disruption by means of cyberspace are becoming more frequent, the kind of destructive all-out cyberwar envisioned in numerous "doomsday scenarios"[2] has not (yet) happened – which makes some scholars wonder whether it will happen at all. Therefore, I first consider more closely those few 'real-life' examples of cyberattacks relevant to this discourse, and identified as such by its participants. Though this scarcity of '*jus ad bellum*-like incidents' means scholarly writing occupies prime position in this debate, states have not remained completely quiet on the subject: the chapter moves on to discuss what they have, in fact, already said, of their own accord as well as in institutional

[1] Jean d'Aspremont, 'Cyber Operations and International Law: An Interventionist Legal Thought' (2016) 21 *Journal of Conflict and Security Law* 575, 578; see the text below for an elaboration.

[2] Isabelle Duyvesteyn, 'Between Doomsday and Dismissal: Collective Defence, Cyber War and the Parameters of War' (2014) 38 *Atlantisch Perspectief* 20, 20.

settings. This part of the chapter furthermore addresses several non-state regulatory proposals,[3] with a particular focus on the two *Tallinn Manuals*.

I then take a step back and ask how, given these conditions, scholars approach the problems posed by cyberwar. I elaborate on what I mean exactly with "legal problem-solution"[4] as the common denominator of their efforts, and inquire into the disciplinary force it exerts. The chapter subsequently draws the contours of how this approach manifests itself in the discourse on the application of Article 2(4) to cyberattacks, which is the focus of Chapters 3 and 4 of this book. I first elaborate on the reasons underlying this choice: first, the fundamental importance of the prohibition on the use of force to the international legal system, and second, the specific attributes of cyberattacks that pose a particular challenge to applying this norm. Based on this I explain what legal problem-solution entails in this specific debate; this furthermore allows for a brief note on what legal scholars mean exactly when they talk about 'cyberattacks.' Finally, and as a contrast to legal problem-solution this chapter concludes with the arguments of those few scholars who argue that the very characteristics of cyberattacks precludes their regulation under international law.

2.1 THE PRACTICE OF CYBERWAR

Up until the mid-2000s, scholars' interpretations of the *jus ad bellum* and *jus in bello* in relation to cyberattacks were guided by the use of hypotheticals: the 'what-ifs' of war in cyberspace.[5] One of the earliest contributors to the debate wrote that

> [w]hile real-world conflicts are a superb way to demonstrate [the *jus ad bellum*] in practice ... there are no reported information operations in cyberspace that will exemplify these principles. Accordingly, somewhat simplified hypothetical scenarios will be used to demonstrate how [they] may restrict state activities in cyberspace.[6]

3 Kubo Mačák refers to "non-state initiatives"; see Kubo Mačák, 'On the Shelf, but Close at Hand: The Contribution of Non-state Initiatives to International Cyber Law' (2019) 113 *AJIL Unbound* 81.

4 Koskenniemi, 'Apology to Utopia,' 28, 60.

5 As also pointed out by Marco Benatar, 'Cyber Warfare,' Oxford Bibliographies 2014, *Case Studies*. On the use of hypotheticals in legal writing see Jane B. Baron and Julia Epstein, 'Is Law Narrative?' (1997) 45 *Buffalo Law Review* 141 and Lianne J. M. Boer, 'Narratives of Force: The Presence of the Writer in International Legal Scholarship' (2019) 66 *Netherlands International Law Review* 1, 2–3 and 2 note 8, drawing on the same examples.

6 Thomas C. Wingfield, *The Law of Information Conflict: National Security Law in Cyberspace*, Aegis Research Corporation 2000, 91 note 235; see also Michael N. Schmitt, 'Computer Network Attack and the Use of Force in International Law: Thoughts on a Normative Framework' (1999) 37 *Columbia Journal of Transnational Law* 885, 892–893. See however,

The 'hypothetical scenarios' scholars came up with ranged from "virtual blockade[s]" to "pandemonium and violence in the skies" to "deadly crashes deliberately engineered."[7] At some point, however, legal writing started to change: in 2014 Marco Benatar noted that "[w]hereas earlier pieces sought inspiration from hypothetical cases ... more recent scholarship invariably draws to lesser or greater extent upon actual events."[8] The 'actual events' Benatar refers to include the cyberattacks on Estonia in 2007, and the deployment of the Stuxnet worm to target Iran's nuclear program, widely published in 2010. These attacks are the ones that come closest to the 'use of force' boundary set by Article 2(4) – or according to some, they cross it – and therefore serve as standard reference points in this debate.[9]

The cyberattacks on Estonia followed the removal of the statue of a Soviet soldier from Estonia's capital, Tallinn, in 2007. What ensued were weeks of cyberattacks on online banking systems and government websites.[10] Though the cyberattacks did not physically destroy anything, in the words of one contributor they "captured the world's attention ... because by now, Estonia was a member of NATO."[11] This suggests that Estonia could invoke Article 5 of the

Richard W. Aldrich, 'How Do You Know You Are at War in the Information Age?' (2000) 22 *Houston Journal of International Law* 223, 227–228 (publishing in the same year as Wingfield).

7 Wingfield, 'Information Conflict,' 92; Joyner and Lotrionte, 'Information Warfare,' 836; Yoram Dinstein, 'Computer Network Attacks and Self-Defense,' in: *Computer Network Attack and International Law*, Michael N. Schmitt and Brian T. O'Donnell (eds.), Naval War College 2002, 99–119, 105.

8 Benatar, 'Cyber Warfare,' *Case Studies*. As an illustration, in that same year the introductory chapter of a book on cyberattacks and the laws of war included a section headed "A word about examples and hypotheticals." See Harrison Dinniss, 'Cyber Warfare,' section 5.3.

9 Benatar similarly states that these attacks (and the ones on Georgia; see below) "have been examined with some frequency"; see Benatar, 'Cyber Warfare,' *Case Studies*; see also Kriangsak Kittichaisaree, *Public International Law of Cyberspace*, Springer 2017, 154; Schmitt (ed.), 'Tallinn Manual,' 1–2; Kubo Mačák, 'From the Vanishing Point Back to the Core: The Impact of the Development of the Cyber Law of War on General International Law,' in: *Defending the Core*, Henry Rõigas et al. (eds.), NATO CCD COE Publications 2017, 1–14, 5 (describing the Estonian attacks as "a prime reference point"); Arno R. Lodder and Lianne J. M. Boer, 'Cyberwar? What War? Meer in het Bijzonder: Welk Recht?' (2012) 38 *Justitiële Verkenningen* 52, 53 et seq. On the attacks on Estonia see Rain Ottis, 'Analysis of the 2007 Cyber Attacks against Estonia from the Information Warfare Perspective,' in: *Proceedings of the 7th European Conference on Information Warfare and Security*, Dan Remenyi (ed.), Academic Publishing Limited 2008, 163–168; Samuli Haataja, *Cyber Attacks and International Law on the Use of Force: The Turn to Information Ethics*, Routledge 2019, chapter 5. For an explanation of Stuxnet see Ralph Langner, 'Cracking Stuxnet, a 21st-Century Cyber Weapon,' March 2011, at TEDx. For an 'inside' account of the development of the worm see David E. Sanger, *Confront and Conceal: Obama's Secret Wars and Surprising Use of American Power*, Crown Publishers 2012, chapter 8.

10 Ian Traynor, 'Russia Accused of Unleashing Cyberwar to Disable Estonia,' *The Guardian*, May 17, 2007; Ottis, 'Analysis,' 163–165.

11 Michael N. Schmitt: PILAC Lecture on Cyber Operations and IHL: Fault Lines and Vectors (hereafter: PILAC 2015), 10.53.

North Atlantic Treaty and appeal to collective self-defense against these cyberattacks – but according to another report, this "was never seriously considered."[12] In any case, Article 5 was not invoked, and even though there were suspicions the hackers who had perpetrated the attacks were connected to the Russian state, this was never proven.[13] NATO did, however, create the 'Cooperative Cyber Defence Centre of Excellence' (the CCDCOE) in Estonia's capital – the same Centre which later commissioned the *Tallinn Manuals*.[14]

The other example often referred to in scholarly discourse is the release of the Stuxnet worm in a nuclear enrichment facility in Iran, by the US and Israel.[15] Discovered in June 2010, as a result of the worm the centrifuges that enrich uranium were "spinning . . . to enormous speeds, or slamming on their brakes," ultimately leading to their destruction – without giving its operators any indication that something was wrong until they had actually broken down.[16] In the words of one scholar, "with the discovery of the Stuxnet worm . . . theory became reality."[17] Its relevance to the international legal discourse lies in its kinetic effect: the destruction of the centrifuges. Stuxnet was the first example of a state (or states) targeting another state, inflicting a level of harm usually associated with the *jus ad bellum*. In other words, this is arguably the first time a cyberattack violated Article 2(4) of the UN Charter.[18]

12 Eneken Tikk, Kadri Kaska and Liis Vihul, *International Cyber Incidents: Legal Considerations*, Cooperative Cyber Defence Centre of Excellence (CCD COE) 2010, 26; but see Kevin Poulson, '"Cyberwar" and Estonia's Panic Attack,' *wired.com*, August 22, 2007 and Schmitt, PILAC 2015, 11.10. Article 5 provides that "an armed attack against one or more of [the Parties] . . . shall be considered an attack against them all," triggering collective defense against the attacking state. North Atlantic Treaty, April 4, 1949, 34 UNTS 243, Article 5.

13 See also Tikk, Kaska and Vihul, 'International Cyber Incidents,' 23, 33.

14 Note that Estonia had been urging the creation of such a center since 2004; see the CCDCOE website, 'About Us,' *History*.

15 Sanger, 'Confront and Conceal,' 188; Haataja, 'Cyber Attacks,' chapter 6. According to a 2019 Dutch newspaper article Germany, France and The Netherlands were also involved. See Huib Modderkolk and Kim Zetter, 'AIVD Speelde Cruciale Rol bij Sabotage Kernprogramma Iran,' *De Volkskrant*, September 2, 2019.

16 Sanger, 'Confront and Conceal,' 199, 189; Langner, 'Cracking Stuxnet,' 4.48 et seq; BBC News, 'Stuxnet "Hit" Iran Nuclear Plans,' November 22, 2010.

17 Foltz, 'Stuxnet,' 41; see also Sanger, 'Confront and Conceal,' 200, quoting the former director of the CIA. For an overview of the attack and the responses to it see Peter W. Singer, 'Stuxnet and its Hidden Lessons on the Ethics of Cyberweapons' (2015) 47 *Case Western Reserve Journal of International Law* 79.

18 For a legal analysis of Stuxnet see Buchan, 'Cyber Attacks,' 219–221; David Weissbrodt, 'Cyber-Conflict, Cyber-Crime, and Cyber-Espionage' (2013) 22 *Minnesota Journal of International Law* 347, section V.B.; Foltz, 'Stuxnet.' Some of the experts involved in the drafting of the *Tallinn Manual* even argued it constituted an armed attack "unless justifiable on the basis of anticipatory self-defence"; see Schmitt (ed.), 'Tallinn Manual 2.0,' 342; see also Weissbrodt, 'Cyber-Conflict,' 378.

Contrary to the scarcity of examples relevant to the *jus ad bellum*, the use of cyberspace during armed conflicts seems to become more common.[19] Examples include the defacement of Georgian government websites prior to and during the war between Georgia and Russia in 2008,[20] and the use of cyberattacks during the armed conflict taking place in Crimea.[21] Similarly, the UK has stated it used cyberattacks in the conflict against ISIS, which in its own words "made a significant contribution to the coalition's efforts to suppress [ISIS] propaganda [and] hindered their ability to coordinate attacks."[22] However, a 2019 study on the cyberattacks conducted during the Ukrainian and Syrian conflicts concluded that most of the attacks analyzed took place "alongside physical fighting," rather than that they had a serious impact on kinetic operations.[23] Drawing on quantitative analyses of these cyberattacks, the researchers claimed that "[e]ach group of hackers seems to operate in its own bubble, disengaged from unfolding events in both cyberspace and the physical world."[24]

The above led one contributor back in 2019 to reflect that "[o]ver the course of the past decade ... it has become increasingly apparent that the vast majority of hostile cyber operations neither cross the threshold required to constitute a prohibited use of force nor occur in the context of existing armed conflicts."[25]

19 Lesley Swanson pointed this out as early as 2010; Lesley Swanson, 'The Era of Cyber Warfare: Applying International Humanitarian Law to the 2008 Russian-Georgian Cyber Conflict' (2010) 32 *Loyola of Los Angeles International and Comparative Law Review* 303, 305.

20 Roscini, 'Cyber Operations,' 7–8. According to Stephanie Handler "[this was] the first use of cyberattacks as part of a broader armed conflict"; see Stephanie Gosnell Handler, 'The New Cyber Face of Battle: Developing a Legal Approach to Accommodate Emerging Trends in Warfare' (2012) 48 *Stanford Journal of International Law* 209, 222; more elaborately 224–225. See also Emilio Iasiello, 'Are Cyber Weapons Effective Military Tools?' (2015) 7 *Military and Strategic Affairs* 23, 32–33; for a legal analysis see Swanson, 'Era of Cyber Warfare.' On possible Russian state involvement, see ibid., 319–322; Iasiello, 'Cyber Weapons,' 33; Tikk, Kaska and Vihul, 'International Cyber Incidents,' 83, 89. Handler is more firm; see Handler, 'New Cyber Face,' 225, 234–235.

21 See Stinissen, 'Legal Framework,' 126–128.

22 BBC News, 'UK Launched Cyber-Attack on Islamic State,' April 12, 2018, at 0.10.

23 Nadiya Kostyuk and Yuri M. Zhukov, 'Invisible Digital Front: Can Cyber Attacks Shape Battlefield Events?' (2019) 63 *Journal of Conflict Resolution* 317, 318; similarly in general terms Mačák, 'Vanishing Point,' 7; but see Handler, 'New Cyber Face,' 234–235. For the legal relevance of this point see Roscini, 'Cyber Operations,' 122–125.

24 Kostyuk and Zhukov, 'Invisible Digital Front,' 333. For a few more examples of cyberattacks in addition to those mentioned here, see Handler, 'New Cyber Face,' 222–223; Katharina C. Ziolkowski, 'Computer Network Operations and the Law of Armed Conflict' (2010) 49 *Military Law and the Law of War Review* 47, 57–61.

25 Barrie Sander, 'The Sound of Silence: International Law and the Governance of Peacetime Cyber Operations,' in: *Silent Battle*, Tomaš Minárik et al. (eds.), NATO CCD COE Publications 2019, 1–21, 2. This has also entailed a shift in the focus of the debate, away from the laws of war – and a recurrence of the term 'information operations' rather than 'cyberwar.'

One of the reasons this situation may be slow to change is that, depending on the specifics of the operation, states may have an interest in keeping quiet on what they are capable of:[26] they don't always want to let the attacking side know they are aware of what is going on. (The reverse may also apply: in June 2019 the *New York Times* published an article on how US Cyber Command had found its way into Russia's power grid. The article's authors stated that "the National Security Council … said they had no national security concerns about the details of [the article], perhaps an indication that some of the intrusions were intended to be noticed by the Russians.")[27] This means that even though hostile operations in cyberspace may occur with increasing frequency,[28] not many of them are known to the outside world and if they are, they don't necessarily qualify for regulation under the *jus ad bellum* or *jus in bello*.[29]

In the field of security studies, this absence has led to the question whether "cyberwar will [actually] take place."[30] On the one side of that debate we find those warning of impending doom, a "cyber-Pearl Harbor"[31] with devastating consequences; on the other, those who are far more skeptical about the actual threat emanating from the hostile use of cyberspace.[32] Underlying this question about the likelihood of cyberwar are different understandings of what is

See ibid., 2; Mačák, 'Vanishing Point,' 2, 7; Sean Lawson, 'Does 2016 Mark the End of Cyber Pearl Harbor Hysteria?' *Forbes*, December 7, 2016.

26 See also Benatar, 'Cyber Warfare,' *State Practice* and *Case Studies*; d'Aspremont, 'Cyber Operations,' 587; Kubo Mačák, 'From Cyber Norms to Cyber Rules: Re-engaging States as Law-Makers' (2017) 30 *Leiden Journal of International Law* 877, 881; Jack Goldsmith, 'Cybersecurity Treaties: A Skeptical View,' in: *Future Challenges in National Security and Law*, Peter Berkowitz (ed.), Hoover Institution 2011, 1–16, 11; Director of National Intelligence, 'Background to "Assessing Russian Activities and Intentions in Recent US Elections": The Analytic Process and Cyber Incident Attribution,' January 6, 2017, 1; Sander, 'Sound of Silence,' 8–9.

27 David E. Sanger and Nicole Perlroth, 'U.S. Escalates Online Attacks on Russia's Power Grid,' *New York Times*, June 15, 2019.

28 Benatar, 'Cyber Warfare,' *Case Studies*.

29 For a similar comment pertaining to the secrecy of these operations see ibid., 'State Practice'; see also Efrony and Shany, 'Rule Book,' 586.

30 Thomas Rid, 'Cyber War Will Not Take Place' (2011) 35 *Journal of Strategic Studies* 5. The comparison in this section between security studies and international law is based in large part on Wouter G. Werner and Lianne J. M. Boer, '"It Could Probably Just as Well Be Otherwise": Imageries of Cyberwar,' in: *Risk and the Regulation of Uncertainty in International Law*, Mónika Ambrus, Rosemary Rayfuse and Wouter Werner (eds.), Oxford University Press 2017, 39–55.

31 Elisabeth Bumiller and Thom Shanker, 'Panetta Warns of Dire Threat of Cyberattack on U.S.,' *New York Times*, October 11, 2012, quoting then-US Secretary of Defense Leon Panetta; see also Werner and Boer, 'Imageries of Cyberwar,' 42 et seq.

32 See also Duyvesteyn, 'Between Doomsday and Dismissal.'

meant, exactly, when scholars (and states) refer to 'cyber*war*.'[33] Thomas Rid, one of the better known opponents of the 'cyber-Pearl Harbor' idea, categorically rejects the notion because, he says, "[a]ny act of war has to have the potential to be lethal; it has to be instrumental; and it has to be political."[34] In his 2012 piece, Rid argued that when understood as such none of the cyber-incidents that had happened so far would qualify as 'war' – nor did he consider it very likely that future cyberattacks would.[35]

Contrary to the International Relations debate, international legal scholarship is far less concerned with the "real possibilities" of cyberwar or how many times it has already happened.[36] The pertinent issue for lawyers is not how *likely* it is that states will actually attack each other by means of cyberspace:

> [T]he question whether cyberwar has happened, is happening, or will happen, and what form or shape this will assume, is largely irrelevant. Instead, the legal experts are concerned only with those scenarios that can follow from existing legal categories; these categories limit the shape and form of the possible realities of cyberwar.[37]

In other words, cyberwar is approached "through the lens" of what "the legal framework allows" to happen: it is framed in terms of what, for example, a use of force or armed attack would look like in cyberspace.[38] I will return to this later on in this chapter.

However, the absence of actual examples *is* relevant to the legal debate to the extent that it creates uncertainty as to which laws apply and how: both customary as well as treaty law speaking specifically to cyberattacks or cyberwar more generally have, for a long time, been nonexistent.[39] Jean d'Aspremont refers to this absence as a lack of "any serious legislative initiative

33 Werner and Boer, 'Imageries of Cyberwar,' 44–45; compare Rid, 'Cyber War Will Not Take Place' and Richard A. Clarke and Robert K. Knake, *Cyberwar: The Next Threat to National Security and What to Do About It*, HarperCollins 2010. For a discussion of the definition of 'cyberwar' see Lianne Boer and Arno Lodder, 'Cyberwar,' in: *Cyber Safety: An Introduction*, Rutger Leukfeldt and Wouter Stol (eds.), eleven international publishing 2012, 157–166, section 11.2; see also Lodder and Boer, 'Cyberwar?,' 64 et seq.

34 Rid, 'Cyber War Will Not Take Place,' 6.

35 His thesis was confirmed by a legal scholar in 2017; see Mačák, 'Vanishing Point,' 2. The cyberwar debate may have taken a turn in this respect; see note 25 above.

36 Werner and Boer, 'Imageries of Cyberwar,' 41–42; the phrases "real possibility" and "possible reality" are used in that piece (at 39) and are taken from Robert Musil, *The Man Without Qualities* [Der Mann ohne Eigenschaften], transl. Sophie Wilkins and Burton Pike, Picador 2011, 12, 10–12.

37 Werner and Boer, 'Imageries of Cyberwar,' 41.

38 Ibid., specifically 45, 50.

39 See also Kubo Mačák, 'Is the International Law of Cyber Security in Crisis?' in: *Proceedings of the 8th International Conference on Cyber Conflict: Cyber Power*, Nikolaos Pissanidis, Henry

or express conferral of new technical and administrative responsibilities upon international lawyers in relation to cyber operations."[40] Yet the degree to which those involved in the cyberwar discourse signal or problematize this absence varies. For example, some of them discuss the applicability of existing treaties such as UNCLOS, the Outer Space Treaty as well as that of the International Telecommunications Union.[41] Similarly, in a 2014 book Marco Roscini refers to a piece by Anthony d'Amato who "more than ten years ago ... predicted that 'computer network attack will soon be the subject of an outright prohibition under customary international law'."[42] Roscini proceeds by opposing this view to that of "[o]ther commentators [who] have been more sceptical and have argued that no customary international law has yet developed because the phenomenon is still too recent and there is no state practice."[43] Though he doesn't assert there is such a thing as customary law on cyberwar specifically, Roscini does claim it is certain that "existing *jus ad bellum* and *jus in bello* customary rules extend to cyber operations," but that the question is "when and how" they do so.[44] Similarly, another scholar writes that "[t]oday, it is generally recognised that international law applies ... the better question now concerns exactly *how* to apply international law in the cyber domain, and this is not a debate that will be resolved in the near future."[45]

Rõigas and Matthijs Veenendaal (eds.), NATO CCD COE Publications 2016, 127–139; Mačák, 'From Cyber Norms to Cyber Rules'; Efrony and Shany, 'Rule Book,' 588; Kristen E. Eichensehr, 'Review of *Tallinn Manual on the International Law Applicable to Cyber Warfare*. Edited by Michael N. Schmitt. Cambridge, New York: Cambridge University Press, 2013. pp. xix, 282. Index. $120, cloth; $58.99, paper' (2014) 108 *American Journal of International Law* 585, 587; cf. David Wallace and Mark Visger, 'Responding to the Call for a Digital Geneva Convention: An Open Letter to Brad Smith and the Technology Community' (2017) 6 *Journal of Law & Cyber Warfare* 3, 19–20. For the debate in the 1990s on the governability of the internet in general see, for example, David R. Johnson and David Post, 'Law and Borders: The Rise of Law in Cyberspace' (1995) 48 *Stanford Law Review* 1367; John P. Barlow, 'A Declaration of the Independence of Cyberspace,' *Electronic Frontier Foundation*, February 8, 1996; Jack Goldsmith and Tim Wu, *Who Controls the Internet? Illusions of a Borderless World*, Oxford University Press 2006. For a reflection on this debate, see Julie E. Cohen, 'Cyberspace as/and Space' (2007) 107 *Columbia Law Review* 210.

40 d'Aspremont, 'Cyber Operations,' 576.

41 Woltag, 'Cyber Warfare,' 127–134; Haataja, 'Cyber Attacks,' 89. See also Tara Davenport, 'Submarine Cables, Cybersecurity and International Law: An Intersectional Analysis' (2015) 24 *Catholic University Journal of Law and Technology* 57, 66 et seq.

42 Roscini, 'Cyber Operations,' 25.

43 Ibid.

44 Ibid., 25, 40, emphasis omitted for "when and how"; similarly with regard to treaties, see 23–24.

45 Stinissen, 'Legal Framework,' 124; similarly Weissbrodt, 'Cyber-Conflict,' 356.

However, other scholars are, simply put, less firm. Writing about 'cyber-violations' of Article 2(4) of the UN Charter in particular Johann-Christoph Woltag stated in 2014 how

> no particular State practice can be observed that would shed light on the question when [computer network operations] qualify as armed force. While several statements denounce the use of this measure in international relations, States fail to classify both which norms of international law are violated by [computer network operations] and the threshold needed in the particular case.[46]

Two years earlier Katharina Ziolkowski had already stated that "[p]otential State practice is not perceivable in the public, declarations of *opinio iuris* by States are rare and general in nature, and respective national or international jurisdiction does not yet exist on the matter."[47] At the time, she concluded that "it is the work of academia which currently importantly influences the development of a common understanding within the international community."[48] Thus, exactly how much can be known about states' views on the subject, in the form of 'declarations of *opinio iuris* that are rare and general in nature,' is part of the scholarly discourse. Even though developments over the last few years seem to suggest that existing law applies, this does by no means imply certainty as to *how* it does.[49] What is more, "a policy of silence and ambiguity in relation to their legal positions" affords states greater leeway – or "operational flexibility" – when acting in cyberspace, possibly leaving them with little incentive to publicly state their views.[50] What is clear is that states have been, and to an extent remain, absent from this discourse.[51]

46 See Woltag, 'Cyber Warfare,' 150; Johann-Christoph Woltag, 'Cyber Warfare,' MPEPIL 2015, B.5.

47 Ziolkowski, 'Ius ad Bellum,' 297; see also Schmitt (ed.), 'Tallinn Manual 2.0,' 3 – though the Manual does not make a similar statement about the absence of "national or international jurisdiction" (but see Anders Henriksen, 'The End of the Road for the UN GGE Process: The Future Regulation of Cyberspace' (2019) 5 *Journal of Cybersecurity* 1, 7).

48 Ziolkowski, 'Ius ad Bellum,' 297 (as also quoted in Chapter 1).

49 François Delerue, 'International Cooperation on the International Law Applicable to Cyber Operations' (2019) 24 *European Foreign Affairs Review* 203, 205; d'Aspremont, 'Cyber Operations,' 577; Stinissen, 'Legal Framework,' 124.

50 Efrony and Shany, 'Rule Book,' 588; see also Wallace and Visger, 'Responding to the Call,' 22 and Henriksen, 'End of the Road,' 5. Barrie Sander argues that states' "offensive" and "defensive interests" might point in opposite directions in this regard; see Sander, 'Sound of Silence,' 10. On silence in the formation of customary law, see Elisabeth Schweiger, 'Listening to Silence: "Targeted Killing" and the Politics of Silence in Customary International Law' (PhD, University of Groningen 2018).

51 Aronsson similarly refers to the "absence of states," see Aronsson-Storrier, 'Publicity,' 10. See also Sander, 'Sound of Silence,' 3 note 4; Efrony and Shany, 'Rule Book,' 648; Attorney General Jeremy Wright QC MP, 'Cyber and International Law in the 21st Century,' May 23, 2018.

This doesn't mean they haven't said anything about cyber and international law.[52] For example, at their 2014 Wales Summit NATO Member States declared that the collective self-defense provision of the Washington Treaty applies to cyberattacks.[53] In addition, several states have publicly announced their views: in a 2012 speech the US State Department legal advisor stated that a cyberattack that caused death or "significant destruction" would qualify as a use of force; a similar position has been adopted by the Dutch and UK governments.[54]

Moreover, a number of states have submitted their views on information security in general, both by means of Governmental Groups of Experts (GGEs) established by the UN General Assembly, as well as through annual reports submitted to the Secretary General.[55] The number of states participating in the GGE's in particular is not very large: it increased from fifteen in 2004/2005 to twenty-five for the 2019/2021 one.[56] In its 2013 report the GGE reached consensus on the applicability of the UN Charter to what it referred to as the "Information and Communication Technologies ... environment."[57] Similarly, the 2015 GGE used the language of Article 2(4) to state that

> of central importance [are] the commitments of States to the following principles [inter alia] refraining in their international relations from the threat or use of force against the territorial integrity or political independence of any State, or in any other manner inconsistent with the purposes of the United Nations.[58]

52 See also Roscini, 'Cyber Operations,' 21–22. He also refers to the UN GGE talks, which I discuss in greater detail on the next couple of pages. For the sake of brevity I am leaving out quite some (non-)governmental work on these questions; for these see Mačák, 'On the Shelf,' and Delerue, 'International Cooperation.'

53 North Atlantic Council, 'Wales Summit Declaration,' September 5, 2014, para. 72.

54 Harold Hongju Koh, 'International Law in Cyberspace' (2012) 54 *Harvard International Law Journal Online* 1, 3–4; Kabinetsreactie op het AIV/CAVV-advies Digitale Oorlogvoering, DVB/VD-38/12, April 6, 2012, section 4; Wright, 'Cyber and International Law.' See also Benatar, 'Cyber Warfare,' *State Practice*. UNIDIR collects states' cyber policies on its "Cyber Policy Portal," but this is not particularly geared towards the *jus ad bellum*. See UNIDIR, 'Cyber Policy Portal.'

55 UNODA, 'Developments in the Field of Information and Telecommunications in the Context of International Security,' 2019. On the status of the GGE Reports under international law see Elaine Korzak, *The 2015 GGE Report: What Next for Norms in Cyberspace?*, on 'Lawfare,' September 23, 2015.

56 UNODA, 'Fact Sheet,' July 2019, 1.

57 Report of the Group of Governmental Experts on Developments in the Field of Information and Telecommunications in the Context of International Security, A/68/98*, June 24, 2013, 2.

58 Report of the Group of Governmental Experts on Developments in the Field of Information and Telecommunications in the Context of International Security, A/70/174, July 22, 2015, para. 26.

The 2015 GGE report was "welcome[d]" by the US and China, who in turn concluded an agreement in September 2015 in which they decided "to create a senior experts group for further discussions on this topic."[59] The agreement also provided for, inter alia, cooperation in tackling cybercrime and the cessation of "cyber-enabled theft of intellectual property."[60]

Notably, however, the 2017 GGE backtracked on its 2015 progress: it "failed to reach a consensus" and no final text was agreed upon by the participating states.[61] Specific contentious issues included the application of Article 51 of the UN Charter, as well as how countermeasures would work exactly in cyberspace.[62] In response to this "deadlock"[63] the United States proposed a General Assembly Resolution in which it called for the creation of a *new* GGE "to be established in 2019 … to continue to study … how international law applies" to or in cyberspace.[64] During the same Assembly session, however, Russia proposed an "open-ended working group" (OEWG), open to all GA states.[65] Both proposals were accepted, which means that there are now "two processes" taking place at the UN in parallel, both considering how cyberspace should be regulated.[66] One author framed this dual process as "reflect[ing] recurrent divergence regarding states' visions of what needs to be regulated in the global information space, and how"; another adds that what we will probably end up with is a "fragmented international normative structure."[67] The first meetings of the OEWG took

59 The White House, Office of the Press Secretary, 'Fact Sheet: President Xi Jinping's State Visit to the United States,' September 25, 2015; see also Scott Warren Harold, *The U.S.-China Cyber Agreement: A Good First Step*, on the RAND Blog, August 1, 2016; Jack Goldsmith, *Don't Get Too Excited About A US-China Arms Control Agreement for Cyber*, on 'Lawfare,' September 21, 2015; David E. Sanger, 'U.S. and China Seek Arms Deal for Cyberspace,' *New York Times*, September 19, 2015.

60 Office of the Press Secretary, 'President Xi Jinping's State Visit.'

61 Delerue, 'International Cooperation,' 207; Michael N. Schmitt and Liis Vihul, *International Cyber Law Politicized: The UN GGE's Failure to Advance Cyber Norms*, on 'Just Security,' June 30, 2017.

62 Schmitt and Vihul, 'International Cyber Law Politicized.'

63 Adam Segal, *The Development of Cyber Norms at the United Nations Ends in Deadlock. Now What?*, Council on Foreign Relations Blog, June 29, 2017.

64 United Nations General Assembly, First Committee, Seventy-third session, 'Advancing Responsible State Behaviour in Cyberspace in the Context of International Security,' October 18, 2018, A/C.1/73/L.37, para. 3.

65 Alex Grigsby, *The United Nations Doubles Its Workload on Cyber Norms, and Not Everyone Is Pleased*, Council on Foreign Relations Blog, November 15, 2018.

66 Delerue, 'International Cooperation,' 211, 209–211; Grigsby, 'The United Nations Doubles Its Workload.'

67 Samuele De Tomas Colatin, *A Surprising Turn of Events: UN Creates Two Working Groups on Cyberspace*, CCDCOE INCYDER Articles, March 11, 2019; Henriksen, 'End of the Road,'

place in June 2019; the newly established GGE gathered in December that same year.[68]

In sum, what the 2015 GGE report as well as the decision made at the Wales Summit render is basically similar to what the scholars cited above point out: to say that international law applies, does not explain *how* it does – something which became clear during the 2017 GGE.[69]

This is the gap the *Tallinn Manuals*, mentioned here several times already, sought to fill. Their origin story may be briefly outlined: Michael Schmitt, then chairman of the International Law Department of the US Naval War College, was asked by NATO's Cyber Defence Centre to assemble a group of lawyers and write a manual on international law and cyberwarfare. Following the publication of the first *Tallinn Manual* in 2013 the second, 2017 Manual dealt with a much larger body of law and included inter alia human rights and space law.[70] The starting point of the Manuals is that existing international law applies: its application to cyberspace is then presented in a number of "black-letter rules"[71] followed by a commentary which explains the rule in question, offers concrete examples and provides possible interpretations. The Manuals are sponsored by the CCDCOE, but are not NATO doctrine – Michael Schmitt once referred to the first Manual as "a product that represents the personal views of the participants that were involved in the process and

2; similarly Wallace and Visger, 'Responding to the Call,' 21–22 and on these different positions Delerue, 'International Cooperation,' 207–208.

68 UNODA, 'Group of Governmental Experts'; UNODA, 'Open-Ended Working Group.' For a preliminary analysis of the first OEWG see Maria Tolppa, *Overview of the UN OEWG Developments: Continuation of Discussions on How International Law Applies in Cyberspace*, CCDCOE INCYDER Articles, March 23, 2020.

69 As pointed out by Henriksen, 'End of the Road,' 2; already in 2015 by Korzak, 'The 2015 GGE Report'; more optimistically Henry Rõigas and Tomáš Minárik, *2015 UN GGE Report: Major Players Recommending Norms of Behaviour, Highlighting Aspects of International Law*, CCDCOE INCYDER Articles, June 26, 2016. As a contrast, consider the response to the 2013 GGE report; see Detlev Wolter, *The UN Takes a Big Step Forward on Cybersecurity*, on 'Arms Control Association,' September 4, 2013. Almost the exact same phraseology as the one used here is used by Duncan B. Hollis, 'Why States Need an International Law for Information Operations' (2007) 11 *Lewis and Clark Law Review* 1023, 1037.

70 Schmitt (ed.), 'Tallinn Manual 2.0,' chapters 6 and 10. Kubo Mačák claims that this expanded scope of the second *Tallinn Manual* might be related to the move away from cyber 'war'; see Mačák, 'Vanishing Point,' 7, and note 25 above.

71 The Manual uses the term "black-letter" to refer to those rules that "reflect consensus among the Experts as to the applicable *lex lata*, that is, the law currently governing cyber conflict." See Schmitt (ed.), 'Tallinn Manual,' 5. On the history of the term see Kasia Solon Cristobal, 'From Law in Blackletter to Blackletter Law' (2016) 108 *Law Library Journal* 181; on their use in the *Tallinn Manual* see Wouter G. Werner, 'Absence, Restatement and Imagination: The Tallinn Manual on International Law Applicable to Cyber Operations,' in: *Repetition and International Law*, Cambridge University Press 2021, forthcoming (on file with the author).

nothing more."[72] Both Manuals position themselves as the work of "a group of independent experts acting solely in their personal capacity"; they "must be understood only as an expression of the opinions of the two International Groups of Experts as to the state of the law."[73] For the second Manual, however, states were invited to participate in consultations with the expert group, during which they could "unofficially comment on the working drafts of the Manual."[74] More than fifty states took part in what was referred to as the "Hague Process," as these consultations were hosted by the Dutch Ministry of Foreign Affairs in The Hague.[75] The introduction to the second Manual explains that as part of this process "[s]ome States also provided unofficial written comments that in many cases resulted in additional refinement of the text of the Manual."[76] Though these contributions by states do not change the formal legal status of the book[77] the fact that they were providing input on the experts' drafts at the very least gives the second Manual a different standing compared to the first.[78] As Rebecca Inger notes, "[a]s states participating in The Hague Process no doubt concluded, it would be naïve to assume that the *Tallinn* processes would have no effect on development of the law."[79]

72 Schmitt, CyCon 2012 (I), 1.48.

73 Schmitt (ed.), 'Tallinn Manual,' 11; Schmitt (ed.), 'Tallinn Manual 2.0,' 2.

74 Schmitt (ed.), 'Tallinn Manual 2.0,' 6.

75 Ibid., 6; Bert Koenders, Minister of Foreign Affairs of the Kingdom of the Netherlands, 'Foreword,' in: *Tallinn Manual 2.0 on the International Law Applicable to Cyber Operations*, Michael N. Schmitt (ed.), Cambridge University Press 2017, xxv–xxvii, xxvi. This 'Hague Process' continues up to the present day and involves a significant amount of funding by the Dutch government for initiatives that seek to develop international law in cyberspace. It frames these efforts as "taking to heart its constitutional task of advancing the international legal order, also in cyberspace" (my translation); see Veilige Wereld – Veilig Nederland, 'The Hague Process: Courses on the International Law Applicable to Cyber Operations,' Facebook, May 16, 2017. It includes the sponsoring of workshops organized by Cyber Law International, a company set up by Michael Schmitt and Liis Vihul (who served as project manager and managing editor on the first and second *Tallinn Manual* respectively); see Cyber Law International, 'Another successful int'l cyber law capacity-building seminar for gov't officials' on Twitter, May 21, 2019 and Liisi Adamson and Zine Homburger, 'Let Them Roar: Small States as Cyber Norm Entrepreneurs' (2019) 24 *European Foreign Affairs Review* 217, 228. For a more extensive discussion of the Dutch approach, see ibid., section 5.1.

76 Schmitt (ed.), 'Tallinn Manual 2.0,' 6.

77 As also pointed out by ibid., 6.

78 See also Wallace and Visger, 'Responding to the Call,' 20.

79 Rebecca Ingber, 'Interpretation Catalysts in Cyberspace' (2016) 95 *Texas Law Review* 1531, 1533; see also Mačák, 'On the Shelf,' 85–86 and Anton O. Petrov, *Expert Laws of War: Restating and Making Law in Expert Processes*, Edward Elgar 2020, chapter 1; but see Efrony and Shany, 'Rule Book,' 588. For a comment on this point, as well as an example of where states influenced the substance of the Manual see Michael Schmitt, *Tallinn Manual 2.0 on the International Law of Cyber Operations: What It Is and Isn't*, on 'Just Security,'

What the above means for the academic discourse studied here, is that *opinio juris* may be said to be emerging.[80] Importantly, however, for a long time it took place in the absence of confirmation that existing law applies, let alone specifics about how it would do so. As stated on the first few pages of this book, it means that for a little under two decades the debate has been – and to a large extent still is – dominated by scholars.[81] This chapter next takes a step back and asks what it means for them to legally solve the problem of cyber. I specifically consider what 'legal problem-solution' entails, in terms of scholars' expectations of what can be achieved through legal reasoning and what international law can *do* with regard to 'solving problems.' As such, the aim is to give a better understanding of the common denominator of this group.

2.2 LEGAL PROBLEM-SOLUTION EXPLAINED

The phrase "legal problem-solution" is taken from Koskenniemi's *From Apology to Utopia*, and in its most succinct form it refers to an approach to international law which "is premised on the idea that it can produce determinate results."[82] This doesn't mean there are no uncertainties about how international law applies in concrete cases, but it *does* entail the promise of these questions being solved at some point in the future. As Koskenniemi explains, the presumption is that

> [w]hatever uncertainty there might be about some particular application or interpretation of the law, the legal system itself is coherent, or at least it is possible, by the use of consistent principles, to make it appear so. If only subjective backgrounds and interpretation would be excluded, then full determinacy would follow.[83]

The term 'legal problem-solution' thus refers to a particular "attitude"[84] towards international law, one which is shared by the group of scholars whose work is considered in this book. It is a view of international law and legal reasoning as, in Koskenniemi's words, 'coherent': the problem at hand – cyberwar – requires

February 9, 2017. An attempt at measuring the impact of the *Tallinn Manuals* may be found in Efrony and Shany, 'Rule Book.'

80 Leaving aside the question of the particular status of the *Tallinn Manuals* and the GGE Reports; on the latter see Korzak, 'The 2015 GGE Report.'

81 See notes 48 and 51 above.

82 Koskenniemi, 'Apology to Utopia,' 60.

83 Ibid., 62.

84 Judith N. Shklar, *Legalism: An Essay on Law, Morals and Politics*, Harvard University Press 1964, 1.

a response from the side of (the) international law(yer); and this response can be arrived at in a structured, "rational" fashion.[85] So this group of legal scholars can be identified by their "common pursuit"[86] – solving the problem of cyber by means of international law – and by the expectations they have of what this effort will result in.

Among this group a wide range of legal solutions is proffered. Most conclude that existing law applies; some argue its insufficiency and suggest a treaty on the subject; yet others argue that, for example, the boundaries of particular norms have to be stretched in order to facilitate the inclusion of particular kinds of cyberattacks.[87] What they have in common is the idea that cyberwar, as a new means of waging war, requires an international legal response. In this context Jean d'Aspremont refers to "the manifestation of a presupposition that disorder and injustice need to be addressed by international legal rules and that the absence of such rules brings about a risk of great harm."[88]

Something more happens here, however, which has to do with what one expects international law to be able to do. Generally speaking, the response to legal uncertainty given by these scholars is that (more, new, better) law is needed to mitigate that uncertainty. Gregor Noll describes something similar when he writes about the "application-oriented international humanitarian lawyers" involved in the question of what 'proportionality' means in the context of targeting under IHL.[89] The notion of proportionality "relat[es] expected civilian losses to anticipated military advantage."[90] Noll describes how, according to the 'application-oriented' lawyer, it is uncertain what the principle of proportionality requires when measuring these two against each other. Yet, as Noll states, the effort to understand the meaning of the norm "obviously does not seem altogether futile . . . Had it been, [this lawyer] would hardly have spent his and our time on further details of its application. This move first expresses agnosticism on the functioning of the norm to then perform continued allegiance to it."[91] With 'agnosticism,' Noll means to say

85 Koskenniemi, 'Apology to Utopia,' 25, 24.

86 Hyland, 'Disciplinary Discourses,' 1. For the use of the word 'construction' in this book, see Chapter 1.

87 See also d'Aspremont, 'Cyber Operations,' 582. For all of these different options, see Chapter 3 of this book.

88 Ibid., 581.

89 Noll, 'Analogy at War,' he uses the phrase "application-oriented lawyer" specifically at 210.

90 Ibid., 205 (abstract).

91 Ibid., 210. Noll refers to a piece by Michael Schmitt here: Michael N. Schmitt, 'The Law of Targeting,' in: *Perspectives on the ICRC Study on Customary International Humanitarian Law*, Elizabeth Wilmshurst and Susan Breau (eds.), Cambridge University Press 2007, 131–168.

that the scholars writing on the application of this principle "openly avow the impossibility to explain its precise content."[92] However, this does not bring them to question the principle of proportionality itself. On the contrary, what these writings show is a 'continued allegiance' to the norm:

> Where legal doctrine falls silent, it appears that legal discipline continues to operate, and, indeed, operates in a more proper sense of the word . . . We do not know what the law demands of us: this seems to escalate the importance that we practice it.[93]

So, for example, we find in the introductions of both *Tallinn Manuals*, first, an assessment that the (almost complete) absence of both treaty and customary law gives rise to "uncertainty," followed by, second, the claim that "[t]his . . . does not mean cyber operations exist in a normative void."[94] The discourse studied in this book continuously displays this 'move' from agnosticism to allegiance. For, despite the uncertainties identified in the application of existing law the scholars participating in the cyberwar discourse still anticipate that at some point in the future this uncertainty will be remedied by law itself.[95] In the words of Gregor Noll, "discipline prepares for revelation to come."[96]

This thinking thus entails the idea that any deficiencies in the legal fabric have to be remedied by means of the development of (more, new, better) law. Application-orientation, then, is a resort to law even if that law in this particular situation doesn't quite suffice in covering the phenomenon it seeks to regulate. Law operates here as its own safety net; and this is also where Koskenniemi's reference to the supposed coherence of the legal system comes from. d'Aspremont similarly describes the attitude of the scholars involved in the cyberwar debate as an "interventionist posture"; a "belief in international law's primacy as method of practical intervention to solve the problems of the world."[97] This demonstrates these scholars' continued faith in

92 Ibid., 209.
93 Noll, 'Discipline and Doctrine,' 36.
94 Schmitt (ed.), 'Tallinn Manual,' 5, as already cited in the previous chapter; similarly Schmitt (ed.), 'Tallinn Manual 2.0,' 3. As pointed out by Kessler and Werner the "logic of uncertainty" has an uneasy relationship with the "logic of legalism." What they mean is that defining "issues in terms of danger, threats, and insecurity," conflicts with the idea that these phenomena could be constrained by the rational application of rules. See Kessler and Werner, 'Expertise,' 801–802; they refer to Judith Shklar for the 'logic of legalism,' which is discussed in this section.
95 Koskenniemi, 'Apology to Utopia,' 60–62.
96 Noll, 'Discipline and Doctrine,' 37.
97 d'Aspremont, 'Cyber Operations,' 578.

the ability of international law to regulate cyberattacks, despite their shared acknowledgment of the difficulties involved in doing so by means of existing law.

The word 'faith' brings this discussion to the work of Judith Shklar. In *Legalism*, Shklar doesn't use this word specifically, but she does talk of "rule-oriented thinking" as a "belief system."[98] This "legalism," Shklar writes, is "the ethical attitude that holds moral conduct to be a matter of rule following, and moral relationships to consist of duties and rights determined by rules."[99] She claims that this "political preference" for rule following supersedes other considerations, including those on the rightness of the substance of these rules.[100] In one of her most polemic phrases, legalism means lawyers "fear tyranny ... because it tends to be arbitrary, not because it is repressive."[101] Here, she refers in turn to Max Weber[102] who "identified [the European legal system] with logically formal rationality"; "an extreme version of the basic idea that law is a consciously shaped autonomous technique that can be applied to resolve social conflict."[103] As a system it operates according to "five basic postulates," which bring us back to Koskenniemi's notion of legal problem-solution:

> (1) Every concrete legal decision is the application of an abstract legal proposition to a concrete fact situation; (2) it must be possible in every concrete case to derive the decision from abstract propositions by means of legal logic; (3) the law is, or must be treated as, a gapless system; (4) whatever cannot be "construed" rationally is legally irrelevant; and (5) all human action is *ordered* by law.[104]

What results from such a system, as David Trubek points out, is a "society [whose] normative ordering is a logically consistent set of rules ... created by the use of highly specialized forms of thought which allow the construction of an intellectual system which can be applied only by trained professionals."[105] So it's not just law that operates independently of other systems (such as

98 In the preface to the 1986 edition of her book, see Judith N. Shklar, *Legalism: Law, Morals, and Political Trials*, Harvard University Press 1986, viii.

99 Shklar, 'Legalism' (1964), 1.

100 Ibid., 4.

101 Ibid., 15, in reference to Alexis de Tocqueville.

102 Ibid., 15-17; she equates his notion of "rationality" with her own understanding of "legalism" at 21.

103 David M. Trubek, 'Max Weber on Law and the Rise of Capitalism' (1972) 1972 *Wisconsin Law Review* 720, 730 and 723–724; 739.

104 Ibid., 730–731.

105 Ibid., 736.

religion):[106] the same goes for the legal profession. Trubek explains that according to Weber "the emergence of a distinct legal profession ... was not only unique; it was absolutely essential for the emergence of logically formal rationality and underlies much of the contemporary dynamics of legalism."[107] In other words, this kind of legal system requires secluded and "[s]pecialized professional or 'status' groups of lawyers" for its continued existence.[108] This notion of 'access' will resonate throughout this book, especially in its second half.

'Application-orientation' is thus understood as faith in the regulatory capacity of international law. The above highlights, first, the belief these scholars have in the rationality and problem-solving capacity of the legal system; second, that there is nothing self-evident about the resort to law to solve the problems presented by cyberwar. This resort may best be described as a 'reflex,' as these scholars approach the world from the lens of international law.[109] That this is not self-evident will become clear in the last part of this chapter, which elaborates on the work of those scholars who fundamentally question the ability of international law to 'solve' the problem of cyberwar.

The remainder of this chapter provides the necessary background specifically for the close-ups presented in Chapters 3 and 4, which deal with the discourse on Article 2(4) and cyberattacks. To reiterate, the reasons for the focus on Article 2(4) in the bulk of this book are, first, the fundamental nature of the norm, and second, one of the very specific features of cyberattacks. The next couple of pages elaborate on both of these reasons, first discussing the prohibition itself, followed by a taxonomy of cyberattacks as found in scholarly discussions of Article 2(4). Finally, as a precursor to Chapter 3 the last part of this chapter gives a brief overview of scholars' suggestions for how the norm could be applied to cyberattacks.

2.3 ARTICLE 2(4) AND THE CYBERWAR DISCOURSE

The prohibition on the use of force is both a customary as well as a treaty-based rule.[110] The scholars involved in the cyberwar discourse, however, rarely distinguish between the prohibition as located in both bodies of law; and if they do, the distinction hardly matters for the way they 'translate' the norm to

106 Ibid., 730.
107 Ibid., 739, see also 737.
108 Ibid., 724.
109 See also Robin West, 'Reconsidering Legalism' (2003) 88 *Minnesota Law Review* 119, 120.
110 *Military and Paramilitary Activities in and against Nicaragua (Nicaragua* v. *United States of America), Merits, Judgment, ICJ Reports 1986, p.* 14 (1986), para. 174 et seq., specifically 181.

cyberattacks.[111] Specifically, Article 2(4) of the UN Charter states that "[a]ll Members shall refrain in their international relations from the threat or use of force against the territorial integrity or political independence of any state, or in any other manner inconsistent with the Purposes of the United Nations."[112] Most scholars involved in the cyberwar debate, as well as in the debate on the use of force in general, understand this text to prohibit *all* kinds of force, unless explicitly permitted under the UN Charter: either because it is authorized by the Security Council, or because a state defends itself against an armed attack.[113] This means that the second half of the text of Article 2(4) is not to be read as an 'escape clause,' in the sense that any use of force that does not violate another state's 'territorial integrity or political independence' would be a permissible use of force.[114]

Once described by the International Court of Justice as the "cornerstone"[115] of the Charter, the prohibition takes center stage in international law. It is the next step in the attempt started by the League of Nations: to restrict states' resort to military force.[116] Whereas the League system only outlawed war, the Charter goes much further in that it prohibits "*all* resorts to armed force."[117] This means that it is much broader in scope than the prohibition imposed by the League.[118] In charting the history of war as a legal notion, Stephen Neff shows the radical change prompted by the prohibition on the use of force: he

111 Nor do states, according to Marco Roscini; see Roscini, 'Cyber Operations,' 21. For an exception in legal scholarship see Schmitt, 'Normative Framework,' 920–922. Those scholars using or referring to that part of his work which deals with the treaty norm specifically, however, do not seem to maintain the distinction Schmitt himself originally made. The word "translation" in this context is also used by Hollis; see Hollis, 'Why States Need,' for example 1039.

112 Charter of the United Nations, June 26, 1945, 1 UNTS XVI, Article 2(4).

113 Ibid., Articles 42 and 51. For a discussion of consent given by a state to another state to use force on its territory, see Yoram Dinstein, *War, Aggression and Self-Defence*, Cambridge University Press 2017 (6), chapter 4 section VII; Christine Gray, *International Law and the Use of Force*, Oxford University Press 2008 (3), 168–171.

114 Tom Ruys, *'Armed Attack' and Article 51 of the UN Charter: Evolutions in Customary Law and Practice*, Cambridge University Press 2010, 56–57; more elaborately, Christine Gray, 'The Use of Force and the International Legal Order,' in: *International Law*, Malcolm D. Evans (ed.), Oxford University Press 2010, 615–647, 619–623; in the cyberwar debate see for example Aldrich, 'Information Age,' 246–247 and Jackson Maogoto, *Technology and the Law on the Use of Force: New Security Challenges in the Twenty-First Century*, Routledge 2015, 10.

115 *Armed Activities on the Territory of the Congo (Democratic Republic of the Congo v. Uganda), Judgment, ICJ Reports 2005, p.* 168 (2005), para. 148.

116 The account of Article 2(4) that follows is based on Stephen C. Neff, *War and the Law of Nations: A General History*, Cambridge University Press 2005, 314 et seq.

117 Ibid., 314.

118 For the League of Nations system, see Neff, 'Law of Nations,' 279–280. Neff specifies that the Charter outlaws a whole range of measures under Article 2(4); see ibid., 317–318.

explains how Article 2(4) completely reset the international legal system by "the establishment of a thoroughgoing general norm of pacifism in international relations."[119] As he explains, Article 2(4) assumes peace to be the normal state of affairs in international relations (that is, from the perspective of international law):

> Perhaps the most important point of all about the UN Charter's ban on the use of force ... is the widespread ... agreement that a resort to force in violation of the ban does *not* constitute a war, but rather ... an unlawful act of aggression committed in peacetime. If the country that was attacked responded by exercising its right of self-defence in the narrow sense (i.e., by fending off the attack but going no further than that), then the situation would be a case of aggression-and-self-defence – but still not a war. If the victim country responded by going further than the law of narrow self-defence allowed ... then there was room for debate as to whether the struggle would be a war.[120]

Considered in this light, any debate on the meaning of 'force' has to do with what a peacetime state of affairs looks like, and at which point interstate relations approach something not quite so peaceful. This is the background against which the debate on cyberwar and Article 2(4) is held. The key question for those involved in this debate is what force means when perpetrated by means of zeroes and ones, rather than with the kind of kinetic force envisioned when the Charter was drafted in 1945.[121] In the words of one of the contributors, there "is [a] need to reach consensus on how the international law can and should bring a potential technical 'beast,' made of '1s' an '0s,' to heel on this very human journey down the cyber roadway."[122] In other words, when does a cyberattack constitute a use of force?

The above reveals the first reason for the focus in this book on the prohibition on the use of force: the fundamental nature of the norm. If Article 2(4)

119 Ibid., 314. Neff adds, though, that for all the similarities between the UN Charter and "mediaeval just-war doctrine" ("the pacifistic vision of the early Christian era" (314)), "Article 2(4) of the UN Charter was a thin brew indeed. It was simply a rule prohibiting force, with no indication that that rule has deep roots in any comprehensive and widely shared view of human social relations in general, as was the case in the Middle Ages ... It was an urgent response to local and immediate demands and conditions rather than an expression of eternal verities." Ibid., 317.

120 Ibid., 318–319.

121 For a concise example see Buchan, 'Cyber Attacks,' 212–213. I similarly explored this question in Boer, 'Restating,' 9–10 and Boer, 'Echoes,' section 3; parts of this chapter are based on these articles. I will provide some more historical context to the 'use of force'-debate in Chapter 3.

122 Kenneth Watkin, 'The Cyber Road Ahead: Merging Lanes and Legal Challenges' (2013) 89 *International Law Studies* 472, 478.

does, indeed, constitute the 'cornerstone' of the international legal system, it matters a great deal how its violation is assessed: the question what 'peace' looks like in cyberspace then is similarly a fundamental one.[123] The second reason for this focus is one of the main characteristics of cyberattacks: their wide range of effects. A cyberattack can either destroy its target or merely disturb its proper functioning, and its effects can be physical as well as non-physical.[124] It is precisely this feature which makes it extraordinarily difficult to assess the boundary of force. The scholars involved in this discourse wrestle not only with the question as to the boundaries of the norm itself (as discussed on the previous pages) but also with what cyberattacks can *do*, as their effects range from minor disturbances to death and destruction on a massive scale.

The following pages elaborate on this specific feature of cyberattacks. They first provide a taxonomy: what exactly do scholars mean, when they talk about cyberattacks? In other words, what is it that should be subjected to Article 2(4)? Some of the general features of cyberattacks are discussed as they emerge in this discourse, ultimately focusing on the feature that is most prevalent in the discussion on the applicability of Article 2(4): the wide range of effects cyberattacks can have.

2.3.1 *Cyberattacks and Article 2(4)*

In general language use the word 'cyberattack' can refer to a whole range of things. News media report the theft of credit card data, the hacking of personal bank accounts, or even, in one notorious case, the hacking of the digital

[123] On the notion of 'new wars' more generally, see Errol A. Henderson and J. David Singer, '"New Wars" and Rumors of "New Wars"' (2002) 28 *International Interactions* 165; cf. Bradley Raboin, 'Corresponding Evolution: International Law and the Emergence of Cyber Warfare' (2011) 31 *Journal of the National Association of Administrative Law Judiciary* 602, 604–605.

[124] Herbert S. Lin, 'Offensive Cyber Operations and the Use of Force' (2010) 4 *Journal of National Security Law & Policy* 63, 68; Myriam Dunn Cavelty, 'Unraveling the Stuxnet Effect: Of Much Persistence and Little Change in the Cyber Threats Debate' (2011) 3 *Military and Strategic Affairs* 11, 14; Lawrence T. Greenberg, Seymour E. Goodman and Kevin J. Soo Hoo, *Information Warfare and International Law*, National Defense University Press 1998, 1, 2; Emily Haslam, 'Information Warfare: Technological Changes and International Law' (2000) 5 *Journal of Conflict and Security Law* 157, 162; Hollis, 'Why States Need,' 1031; Duncan B. Hollis, 'An e-SOS for Cyberspace' (2011) 52 *Harvard International Law Journal* 373, 375, 390; Joyner and Lotrionte, 'Information Warfare,' 829, 835–839; Walter G. Sharp Sr., *CyberSpace and the Use of Force*, Aegis Research Corporation 1999, 19; Daniel B. Silver, 'Computer Network Attack as a Use of Force under Article 2(4) of the United Nations Charter,' in: *Computer Network Attack and International Law*, Michael N. Schmitt and Brian T. O'Donnell (eds.), Naval War College 2002, 73–98, 76; Waxman, 'Cyber-Attacks,' 422.

control systems of sewage works.[125] Alternatively, the word 'cyberattack' can refer to espionage in cyberspace: for example, the extraction of the design of a new military weapon from a Department of Defense network, or the theft of commercial trade information.[126]

Yet, in the scholarly works considered in this book the word 'cyberattack' signifies something very specific, and something different from the examples just mentioned.[127] In the mind of the international legal scholar the first set of attacks would amount to cybercrime, which is primarily subject to domestic law enforcement.[128] The second would constitute espionage, which might be punishable under the victim state's domestic laws but not under international law (though there are calls for considering cyber espionage as a use of force in some cases).[129] However, in this debate scholarly focus chiefly lies on "[cyber] attacks [that] aim at altering or destroying the information contained in the targeted computer or computer network with the purpose of incapacitating the adversary's command, control and communication system and/or of causing damage extrinsic to the targeted computer/network."[130] This is somewhat cryptic, but what it means is that as far as this debate is concerned cyberattacks

125 Shelly Banjo, 'Home Depot Hackers Exposed 53 Million Email Addresses,' *The Wall Street Journal*, November 6, 2014; Spencer Kelly, 'Hackers Outwit Online Banking Identity Security Systems,' *BBC News*, March 8, 2012; Michael Crawford, 'Utility Hack Led to Security Overhaul,' *Computerworld*, February 16, 2006.

126 Ellen Nakashima, 'U.S. Developing Sanctions Against China over Cyberthefts,' *Washington Post*, August 30, 2015.

127 For an illustration see Anders Henriksen, 'Lawful State Responses to Low-Level Cyber-Attacks' (2015) 84 *Nordic Journal of International Law* 323, 330. He writes that "harmful cyber-activities are actually better classified according to three basic categories," which is followed by the three *legal* categories mentioned here. See also Boer and Lodder, 'Cyberwar,' para. 11.3.

128 For example, the 2004 Council of Europe's Convention on Cybercrime imposes on its signatories the obligation to adopt national legislation on a number of crimes listed in the Convention (chapter II); it furthermore seeks to improve international cooperation (chapter III). See Council of Europe, *Convention on Cybercrime*, November 23, 2001, ETS No. 185. For the EU's policies combating cybercrime, see European Commission, Migration and Home Affairs, 'Cybercrime'; for initiatives taken by the UN, see UNODC, Organized Crime, *Emerging Crimes*, 'Cybercrime.'

129 See Anna Wortham, 'Should Cyber Exploitation Ever Constitute a Demonstration of Hostile Intent That May Violate UN Charter Provisions Prohibiting the Threat or Use of Force?' (2012) 64 *Federal Communications Law Journal* 643, who deliberately refers to "cyber exploitation" rather than cyber espionage (at 658); see also Iñaki Navarrete, 'L'Espionnage en Temps de Paix en Droit International Public' (2016) 53 *Canadian Yearbook of International Law/Annuaire canadien de droit international* 1 for a discussion. This assumes these distinctions are still tenable; see BBC News, 'UK Launched Cyber-Attack.'

130 Marco Roscini, 'World Wide Warfare: *Jus ad Bellum* and the Use of Cyber Force,' in: *Max Planck Yearbook of United Nations Law*, Armin von Bogdandy and Rüdiger Wolfrum (eds.), Koninklijke Brill N.V. 2010, 85–130, 93. This is the definition broadly maintained for the

are understood as those hostile attacks that make use of a digital tool to either disrupt or destroy a target likewise connected to a "system," which here is understood as "a set of mutually dependent components or variables … [E]ach component in the system is interrelated with every other component in the set and also interacts with the system environment within the system's boundaries."[131] The kind of 'connectivity' referred to here may be understood in two ways: first, it signifies the connection between an individual computer and a digital infrastructure; it can also refer to a system which is 'air-gapped' (as was the case for the nuclear power plant which suffered the Stuxnet attack), meaning the digital infrastructure itself is not connected to the world wide web.[132]

Plainly put, a cyberattack destroys or alters digital information, leading to a malfunction in its target. This target can either be digital, for example, financial information on the New York Stock Exchange, or it can operate in the physical world, such as air traffic control systems. Crucially, however, two assumptions have to be made before Article 2(4) can be applied to a specific cyberattack: first, that the attack can be traced to its origin, and second, that given the scope of application of Article 2(4) it can be attributed to a state.[133]

To start with the last point: Article 2(4) holds that the use of force is prohibited between the 'members' of the United Nations: the prohibition only applies between states.[134] This is the first problem for its application to cyberattacks, as it has no relevance to those attacks perpetrated by individual, private hacker(s) (groups), unless they are in some way connected to the state

purpose of the application of Article 2(4); see, for example Vida M. Antolin-Jenkins, 'Defining the Parameters of Cyberwar Operations: Looking for Law in All the Wrong Places' (2005) 51 *Naval Law Review* 132, 138 et seq. There are some, however, who maintain a much broader definition, which impacts their legal analysis. For an example see Oona A. Hathaway et al., 'The Law of Cyber-Attack' (2012) 100 *California Law Review* 817, 826–827, and the discussion of Duncan Hollis's work in Chapter 3 of this book.

131 Dunn Cavelty, 'Cyber-Security,' 17, 21–23 (she includes the use of physical tools against cyber targets in her definition, at 22 – this is usually not the case in the cyberwar debate); see also Jason Barkham, 'Information Warfare and International Law on the Use of Force' (2001) 34 *New York University Journal of International Law and Politics* 57, 64. This is not intended as an exhaustive, comprehensive definition, but as an identification of the common denominator of the various definitions given in this discourse.

132 Sanger, 'Confront and Conceal,' 194.

133 See also d'Aspremont, 'Cyber Operations,' 592; on the latter point see Barkham, 'Information Warfare,' 58–59.

134 Nicholas Tsagourias argues that the customary norm also applies to non-state actors; see Nicholas Tsagourias, 'The Tallinn Manual on the International Law Applicable to Cyber Warfare: A Commentary on Chapter II – The Use of Force,' in: *Yearbook of International Humanitarian Law 2012*, Terry D. Gill et al. (eds.), T.M.C. Asser Press 2014, 19–43, 21.

(which would be the province of the laws of state responsibility).[135] Cyberspace, however, presents a wide range of possibilities for non-state actors to perpetrate harmful attacks. Specifically, cyberattacks differ from conventional attacks in that they allow a single hacker to create damage to an extent previously mainly the preserve of states – a point noted by many commentators.[136] One of them observes how "a little high technology may provide leverage to a numerically or technologically weak combatant against a much larger or more advanced adversary";[137] another speaks of the "deference traditionally reserved for the state."[138] In other words, conflict in cyberspace is potentially highly asymmetric.[139] Additionally, one of the more remarkable features of cyberattacks is that a high level of technological development also implies a high level of vulnerability.[140] The strongest states are often also the most 'wired' ones which, paradoxically, turns them into the ones most vulnerable to cyberattacks.[141]

This notion of asymmetry, however, sits uneasily with the application of Article 2(4). After all, and as stated above, scholars' interpretations of the

135 For a discussion of how these issues play out in cyberspace, see Scott J. Shackelford and Richard B. Andres, 'State Responsibility for Cyber Attacks: Competing Standards for a Growing Problem' (2011) 42 *Georgetown Journal of International Law* 971; for a concrete example see Michael Schmitt and Sean Fahey, *WannaCry and the International Law of Cyberspace*, on 'Just Security,' December 22, 2017. See also Boer and Lodder, 'Cyberwar,' para. 11.4.

136 Joyner and Lotrionte, 'Information Warfare,' 832; Seymour E. Goodman, 'War, Information Technologies, and International Asymmetries' (1996) 39 *Communications of the ACM* 11, specifically 12; see also Barkham, 'Information Warfare,' mainly 108–109; Kanuck, 'Information Warfare,' 285; Sharp, 'CyberSpace,' 19; Silver, 'Computer Network Attack,' 73; Waxman, 'Cyber-Attacks,' 422; Schmitt, 'Normative Framework,' 897–898; Greenberg, Goodman and Soo Hoo, 'Information Warfare,' 21; Hollis, 'Why States Need,' 1049. As also stated in Boer, 'Restating,' 8.

137 Goodman, 'International Asymmetries,' 13; see also Barkham, 'Information Warfare,' 66–67; Hollis, 'e-SOS,' 407.

138 Jon P. Jurich, 'Cyberwar and Customary International Law: The Potential of a "Bottom-up" Approach to an International Law of Information Operations' (2008) 9 *Chicago Journal of International Law* 275, 287, also on power distributions. On asymmetric conflicts generally, and a critique of and reflection on the concept see Emily Crawford, 'From Inter-state and Symmetric to Intra-state and Asymmetric: Changing Methods of Warfare and the Law of Armed Conflict in the 100 Years Since World War One,' in: *Yearbook of International Humanitarian Law 2014*, Terry D. Gill et al. (eds.), T.M.C. Asser Press 2016, 95–118.

139 See generally Goodman, 'International Asymmetries'; Dunn Cavelty, 'Cyber-Security,' chapter 4; see also Lodder and Boer, 'Cyberwar?,' 59 and Boer, 'Restating,' 8.

140 See Dimitrios Delibasis, 'The Right of States to Use Force in Cyberspace: Defining the Rules of Engagement' (2002) 11 *Information & Communications Technology Law* 255, 257–258.

141 This is a point raised by many, using basically the same phraseology. See for example Mačák, 'On the Shelf,' 82; Iasiello, 'Cyber Weapons,' 24; Waxman, 'Cyber-Attacks,' 424, 450–451; Joyner and Lotrionte, 'Information Warfare,' 834; Hathaway et al., 'Law of Cyber-Attack,' 842; Kanuck, 'Information Warfare,' 285.

prohibition are contingent on the assumption that the (actual, hypothetical or future) cyberattack they seek to subject to international law is perpetrated by a state.[142] If the cyberattack were to be perpetrated by a non-state actor it would be subjected to law enforcement. The fact that scholars work on the basis of this assumption can sometimes be found quite literally in these pieces, for example when Marco Roscini writes that his "analysis will be limited to the use of cyber force by a state against another state: cyber attacks conducted by non-state actors will be discussed only for the purpose of determining when they can be attributed to a state."[143] Thus, the supposition that the cyberattack originates from a state is a necessary one for the scholar writing an article on the applicability of the prohibition, or for the scholar giving a conference presentation on the subject. Without it, the exercise becomes moot.[144] What is more, to apply Article 2(4) to cyberattacks assumes that the attack can, in fact, be traced.[145] Presumably, it is known where the attack came from. A few remarks on this are in order.

According to some scholars, attribution is a major assumption to make, as the intent and origin of the cyberattack may be unknown.[146] Bradley Raboin, for example, says that non-attribution "is typically the case in cyber warfare operations."[147] To sketch the extremes, a cyberattack on a dam could come from a seventeen-year old hacker who is unaware of how close s/he is to digitally breaking it; alternatively, it could come from a state intent on targeting critical national infrastructure.[148] This uncertainty as to the origins of the attack in turn implies uncertainty as to the applicable legal framework.[149] Whereas the first

142 See also Boer, 'Restating,' 7–8. This assumption is particular to the scholarly discourse on cyberattacks and Article 2(4). It may be less of a necessity once the debate moves to the right to self-defense against an armed attack. Cf. *Armed Activities*, para. 146; Raphaël van Steenberghe, 'Self-Defence in Response to Attacks by Non-State Actors in the Light of Recent State Practice: A Step Forward?' (2010) 23 *Leiden Journal of International Law* 183.

143 Roscini, 'World Wide Warfare,' 91.

144 Similarly d'Aspremont, 'Cyber Operations,' section 5; see also note 97 above. d'Aspremont considers this assumption part of an argumentative strategy employed by those scholars who argue that existing law applies to cyberattacks: by evading the issue of attribution scholars can uphold the claim that, for example, Article 2(4) can be applied. The absence of evidence, after all, would preclude the application of existing law. See also Wortham, 'Cyber Exploitation,' 651; Michael Preciado, 'If You Wish Cyber Peace, Prepare for Cyber War: The Need for the Federal Government to Protect Critical Infrastructure from Cyber Warfare' (2012) 1 *Journal of Law & Cyber Warfare* 99, 136.

145 d'Aspremont, 'Cyber Operations,' 587 with alternatives, 592; see also Silver, 'Computer Network Attack,' 78–79; Ziolkowski, 'Ius ad Bellum,' 306.

146 Raboin, 'Corresponding Evolution,' 644; see also Lodder and Boer, 'Cyberwar?,' 58.

147 Ibid.

148 Erik Larson, Patricia Hurtado and Chris Strohm, 'Iranians Hacked from Wall Street to New York Dam, U.S. Says,' *Bloomberg.com*, March 24, 2016.

149 Neff, 'Law of Nations,' 18 et seq.; see also Lodder and Boer, 'Cyberwar?,' 57 and Boer, 'Restating,' 8.

would be subject to domestic law enforcement, the second potentially violates the prohibition on the use of force. As a result, in some imageries of cyberattacks "[t]he 'enemy' becomes a faceless and remote entity, a great unknown that is almost impossible to track"[150] – while it is precisely "the nature of the enemy [that serves] to distinguish war from domestic law enforcement."[151]

Secondly, anonymity in cyberspace leads to the question of what kind of evidence is needed for what Jack Goldsmith terms "good-enough attribution."[152] For these purposes, as Nicholas Tsagourias in turn explains, what is required is not just "technical investigation" of the attack, but also "intelligence and information analysis . . . in order to profile the authors of the attack, and to provide information about their capabilities and intentions or their links with States or other entities."[153] This has led, however, to doubts about the reliability of what is basically "circumstantial evidence"[154] relevant to, inter alia, assigning state responsibility.

Third, and finally, the capacities of states in this respect may differ. For example, in March 2016 the US accused Iranian hackers allegedly "linked to the Iranian government"[155] of hacking into US financial institutions and a dam near New York. The US Attorney General was subsequently quoted as saying that "the move against the Iranians reflects the increasing ability of U.S. investigators to identify hackers operating from abroad, sometimes with the help of foreign powers or on their behalf."[156] In sum, whereas one scholar downplays the difficulties of attribution, another asserts that "anonymity is a norm destroyer."[157] I will return to this last view at the end of this chapter.

As mentioned above, next to the necessity of state attribution and the problem of anonymity, a third issue in applying the prohibition to cyberattacks is their wide range of effects. As a first example, consider the hacks during the 2016 US elections. It is doubtful whether these constitute 'force,' though they might violate

150 Dunn Cavelty, 'Unraveling,' 13; see also Waxman, 'Cyber-Attacks,' 443–444; Wortham, 'Cyber Exploitation,' 651.

151 Neff, 'Law of Nations,' 18 et seq. See also Boer, 'Restating,' 8.

152 Goldsmith, 'Skeptical View,' 10; see also Raboin, 'Corresponding Evolution,' 640–646 and d'Aspremont, 'Cyber Operations,' section 5.

153 Nicholas Tsagourias, 'Cyber Attacks, Self-Defence and the Problem of Attribution' (2012) 17 *Journal of Conflict and Security Law* 229, 234.

154 Ibid., quoting the ICJ's *Corfu Channel* case.

155 Larson, Hurtado and Strohm, 'Iranians Hacked.'

156 Ibid. On publicizing these findings, see notes 26–29 above.

157 Jack Goldsmith, 'How Cyber Changes the Laws of War' (2013) 24 *European Journal of International Law* 129, 136. Contrast, for example, Roscini, 'World Wide Warfare,' 96–102, who does not regard this as a fundamental problem, with Preciado, who considers it to be one of the main obstacles in applying Article 2(4); see Preciado, 'Cyber Peace,' 136.

other norms of international law such as the principle of non-intervention.[158] Alternatively, a cyberattack may cause the New York Stock Exchange to shut down completely, bringing financial trade to a full stop. Though very severe, these are not the kinds of attacks usually associated with the kind of 'force' prohibited under Article 2(4) – though as will be shown in Chapter 3, this is not necessarily a reason not to include them. A third, frequently mentioned example is the disruption of an air traffic control system, causing airplanes to crash and leading to the deaths of hundreds of people.[159] This particular kind of cyberattack comes closest to what is usually associated with 'force': death and the destruction of property.

These three examples are exactly why Herbert Lin states that "because virtually anything can be connected to a computer system or network, the scope and nature of effects resulting from a cyber attack can span an enormous range."[160] In other words, they raise the question where to draw the line of 'force': when does a cyberattack pass the threshold from permissible to impermissible under Article 2(4)? Few scholars taking part in this debate would argue that all three scenarios mentioned here should be considered to constitute 'force.'[161] On the other hand, few would argue that *none* of them would. One of the contributors to this debate, Matthew Waxman, puts it quite plainly when he says, "I am not aware of any serious proposal that cyber-attacks categorically could *never* constitute 'force'."[162] Similarly, Jason Barkham states that "using computers to destroy targets *certainly* should be considered a use of force."[163] The last example mentioned above – where a cyberattack leads to airplane crashes and the deaths of civilians – would, according to most of the

158 See Haataja, 'Cyber Attacks,' 168. On this interference see Sabrina Siddiqui, 'What the Mueller Report Tells us About Trump, Russia and Obstruction,' *The Guardian*, April 18, 2019. For different views on the applicable international legal framework compare Patrick C. R. Terry, '"Don't Do as I Do" – The US Response to Russian and Chinese Cyber Espionage and Public International Law' (2018) 19 *German Law Journal* 613; Jens David Ohlin, 'Did Russian Cyber Interference in the 2016 Election Violate International Law?' (2016) 95 *Texas Law Review* 1579; Christina Lam, 'A Slap on the Wrist: Combatting Russia's Cyber Attack on the 2016 U.S. Presidential Election' (2018) 59 *Boston College Law Review* 2167.

159 For this specific example see Joyner and Lotrionte, 'Information Warfare,' 836.

160 Lin, 'Cyber Operations,' 68; see also Boer, 'Restating,' 9.

161 See Chapter 3 of this book on the different positions.

162 Waxman, 'Cyber-Attacks,' 435. For the sake of completeness, it is necessary to give the whole quote: "Along a spectrum of alternatives, at one end, one might take a very legally restrictive view of cyber-attacks. Although I am not aware of any serious proposal that cyber-attacks categorically could *never* constitute 'force' or an 'armed attack,' some legal experts have suggested that to so qualify a cyberattack must produce '*violent* consequences'." See, however, Jurich, 'Cyberwar,' 284–285.

163 Barkham, 'Information Warfare,' 80, emphasis added.

scholars whose work is considered here, constitute force. However, as will be dealt with in the third chapter of this book, the problem in applying the prohibition primarily lies in the second example.[164] Assuming Article 2(4) should or can apply[165], the line between what the prohibition permits and prohibits has to be drawn somewhere.

This final point brings this discussion back to the reasons for the primary focus in this book on the use of force. Precisely because it is so difficult to pin down the point between those cyberattacks amounting to force and those that fall below this threshold, and because Article 2(4) pulls the legal debate into the *jus ad bellum*, from the viewpoint of international legal knowledge construction the prohibition on the use of force is a far more interesting provision than, for example, a state's right to defend itself against an armed attack perpetrated in cyberspace. Some of the questions that arise as a result are, how do scholars argue their way to the boundary of the norm? And on the basis of what do they do so? These questions will be dealt with further on in this book: for now, it is important to note that from the perspective of knowledge construction the relation between Article 2(4) and cyberattacks is of particular interest.

2.3.2 *Solving the Problem of Cyber*

The final part of this chapter provides a general overview of the different suggestions scholars have put forward for 'solving the problem' of cyber, particularly in regard to Article 2(4), and it relates these proposals to the problem-solving attitude described earlier on. Scholars offer a variety of legal solutions to solve the discrepancies between existing law as they reconstruct it in their writing, and the range of (new) possibilities presented by cyberattacks. To some, existing law suffices in dealing with the specific problems caused by cyberattacks ("law-articulators," in Barrie Sander's words); to others, the phenomenon is so unprecedented as to necessitate new law ("law-entrepreneurs").[166] The different assessments of the existence of legal uncertainty also impact the solutions scholars offer: they include

164 See also Watkin, 'Road Ahead,' 496.

165 Some scholars question the applicability of the prohibition, because it arguably doesn't suffice in covering the wide range of effects caused by cyberattacks. This will be discussed in Chapter 3.

166 Barrie Sander, 'Cyber Insecurity and the Politics of International Law' (2017) 6 *ESIL Reflections* 1. He adds a third category of lawyers: "norm-articulators and norm-entrepreneurs," those who turn away from international *legal* solutions proper and instead turn towards "global cyber norms" (7). See also Boer, 'Restating,' 9.

a resort to, for example, treaty or customary law outside of the *jus ad bellum*; others refer to the non-intervention principle as a backup for those situations in which Article 2(4) doesn't suffice.[167] Yet others argue a reinterpretation of Article 2(4). With regard to this last option specifically, three models can be identified in this discourse, each attempting in its own way to account for the specifics of cyberattacks.[168] They are the target-based, the consequence-based and the instrument-based approach; I will briefly discuss all three in turn.[169]

First, those advocating a target-based approach – also referred to as "strict liability"[170] – argue that any cyberattack on a state's critical national infrastructure should be considered a use of force, regardless of the consequences of the action.[171] One of its frequently-cited adherents, Eric Jensen, states that

> once an intruder has shown the intent and capability to pierce the passive defense measures of a critical infrastructure network, he has demonstrated sufficient hostile intent to warrant an action in self-defense, even though he may not yet have consummated his attack.[172]

What Jensen is saying here is that given the importance of these critical national infrastructures to the functioning of society any (attempted) attack on them is a "demonstration of hostile intent" and should therefore be considered as violating Article 2(4).[173] In other words, the "touchstone" of this model is the nature of the target.[174] However, according to its critics the

167 For example, Antolin-Jenkins, 'Defining the Parameters,' 173–174.

168 See also Haataja, 'Cyber Attacks,' 90–93. Weissbrodt contrarily states that two models exist for assessing a violation of Article 2(4): the one designed by Michael Schmitt and a "broad, result-oriented analysis" (360). See Weissbrodt, 'Cyber-Conflict,' 359–360; but see 362–366. Both these models will be discussed in Chapter 3 of this book. The model developed by Schmitt is also designated as a fourth model; see Foltz, 'Stuxnet,' 42.

169 For a discussion of these last two approaches in the context of the interpretive history of Article 2(4), see Boer, 'Echoes,' on the target-based approach see 25.

170 For example by Boris Kondoch, 'Jus ad Bellum and Cyber Warfare in Northeast Asia' (2013) 6 *Journal of East Asia and International Law* 459, 468.

171 Woltag, however, considers it to be part of an effects-based approach; see Woltag, 'Cyber Warfare,' 143–144. On the effects-based approach, see p. 56 below.

172 Eric Talbot Jensen, 'Computer Attacks on Critical National Infrastructure: A Use of Force Invoking the Right of Self-Defense' (2002) 38 *Stanford Journal of International Law* 207, 237 ("the law should evolve to recognize a nation's inherent right of self-defense, including anticipatory self-defense, against a [computer network attack] focused on critical national infrastructure, even if that [attack] does not constitute an armed attack" (229)); see also Matthew Hoisington, 'Cyberwarfare and the Use of Force Giving Rise to the Right of Self-Defense' (2009) 32 *Boston College International and Comparative Law Review* 439, 453–454.

173 Jensen, 'Computer Attacks,' 236; Foltz, 'Stuxnet,' 42.

174 See also Hoisington, 'Cyberwarfare,' 453–454; for the use of the word "touchstone" see Silver, 'Computer Network Attack,' inter alia 88 (though not in relation to this particular model).

problem with this approach is that it does not take into account the different levels of severity of the attack and could, therefore, lead to erosion of the rule. In the words of Reese Nguyen, "it is dangerously overbroad."[175] Another critique of this model, voiced by Michael Gervais, is that "the effects of cyber attacks may be indiscriminate and uncontrolled once unleashed. Cyber attacks do not always intentionally target the critical infrastructure that they eventually disrupt."[176] As this model would, in Gervais's understanding, include attacks on financial systems, it "collaps[es] the distinctions between armed violence, coercion, and interference."[177] Finally, Vita Antolin-Jenkins argues that

> without an international consensus identifying particular electronic infrastructures as so critical they should be sacrosanct, coupled with international agreement that any disabling attack on those systems constitutes a "use of force" under the UN Charter, states might use a definitional means to broadly rationalize a large number of actions.[178]

Antolin-Jenkins points out here the possibility of abuse of labeling something 'critical national infrastructure,' which risks 'rationalizing a large number of actions' that follow violations of Article 2(4).[179] She ends up arguing, inter alia, that a treaty prohibiting cyberattacks on specific kinds of critical national infrastructure might be helpful.[180]

Gathering these critiques it seems that even though this model is fairly frequently referred to as being part of the debate, there seem to be few adherents. The model is 'out there' but it is unclear on the basis of whose support: its continued existence seems to result from its invocation more than from its actual adoption. This is not to say states do not explicitly mention the protection of their critical national infrastructures from cyberattacks[181]: the point is that in the *scholarly* debate its critics far outweigh its supporters.

175 Reese Nguyen, 'Navigating *Jus ad Bellum* in the Age of Cyber Warfare' (2013) 101 *California Law Review* 1079, 1120; see also Michael Gervais, 'Cyber Attacks and the Laws of War' (2012) 30 *Berkeley Journal of International Law* 525, 538; and Hollis, 'Why States Need,' 1042. Briefly, Boer, 'Echoes,' 25.

176 Gervais, 'Cyber Attacks,' 538.

177 Ibid. This critique is also voiced by Jason Barkham, but against the effects-based approach; see Chapter 3 of this book.

178 Antolin-Jenkins, 'Defining the Parameters,' 166; similarly Nguyen, 'Navigating,' 1121.

179 Antolin-Jenkins, 'Defining the Parameters'; similarly Foltz, 'Stuxnet,' 42.

180 Specifically, as violations on the non-intervention principle; see Antolin-Jenkins, 'Defining the Parameters,' 174; see also Hoisington, 'Cyberwarfare,' 453.

181 See GGE Report (2015), specifically paras. 5, 13, 16; see also Antolin-Jenkins, 'Defining the Parameters,' 166 note 124.

The target-based approach does appear, however, in combination with an effects-based approach.[182] Katharina Ziolkowski, for example, suggests that next to inflicting bodily harm or physical destruction, cyberattacks that target critical national infrastructures specifically and in so doing create "[m]assive, medium to long-term disruption" should similarly be considered as violating Article 2(4).[183] This seems to be a response to the criticism levelled at the target-based approach, as it imposes a threshold level of severity while at the same time acknowledging that given the vulnerability of critical national infrastructures to cyberattacks they merit special protection. Similarly, Reese Nguyen argues that

> cyber attacks constitute armed attack [*sic*] when they are intended to cause irreversible disruption or physical damage to a cyber-physical system ... Depending on the severity of the effects, these attacks may instead be considered an illegal use of force under Article 2(4).[184]

So, the translation of cyberattacks to the prohibition – even those that do not resemble traditional uses of force – seems to need a reference to severity in order to gain traction. This brings the discussion to the second, consequence-based approach. In the words of Herbert Lin,

> [e]ffects-based analysis suggests that the ambiguities are fewest when cyber attacks cause physical damage to property and loss of life in ways that are comparable to kinetic attacks and traditional war ... The ambiguities multiply in number and complexity when a cyber attack does not cause physical damage or loss of life though there may be other negative effects to the nation.[185]

What Lin explains here is that a consequence-based view on the prohibition on the use of force facilitates, at the very least, the inclusion of those cyberattacks that 'cause physical damage to property and loss of life.' The question is whether it can do more than that: in other words, cyberattacks raise the question what counts as a consequence and what constitutes 'harm.' The issue is, to paraphrase Michael Schmitt, 'severity in terms of what?'[186] The next chapter will dive deeper into this problem.

182 On this combination of approaches, see also Haataja, 'Cyber Attacks,' 90.
183 Ziolkowski, 'Ius ad Bellum,' 299.
184 Nguyen, 'Navigating,' 1125; for her definition of a "cyber-physical system" see 1084.
185 Lin, 'Cyber Operations,' 73; see also Boer and Lodder, 'Cyberwar,' para. 11.4.
186 Schmitt says this in the context of his critique on a severity-only approach: "Undesirable consequences fall along a continuum, but how could the criteria for placement [of the boundary of force – LB] along it be clearly expressed? In terms of severity? Severity measured by what standard of calculation? Harm to whom or what?" See Schmitt, 'Normative Framework,' 911, and Chapter 3 of this book for a more elaborate discussion of his approach.

The third, instrument-based approach is not always part of these overviews, which perhaps has something to do with the outcome of applying it to cyberattacks when defined in a particular way. Reese Nguyen understands it as follows:

> The more analogous a new weapon is to conventional forms of military force, the more likely its operation will constitute a "use of force" or "armed attack" . . . force means traditional, military armed force to the exclusion of other forms of coercion.[187]

By extension, she says, under this model cyberattacks can never be considered a use of force "because the instrument used – computer code – is neither physical nor a form of conventional military force."[188] This brings "[m]ost commentators," in the words of Andrew Foltz, "[to] reject this strict interpretation because of the potential widespread destabilizing consequences of cyber operations."[189] In other words, the idea that Article 2(4) would have absolutely nothing to say about cyberattacks because of the nature of the instrument is unacceptable to 'most commentators.'[190] It makes Matthew Waxman say (as already cited above) that he is "not aware of any *serious* proposal that cyber-attacks categorically could *never* constitute 'force'."[191] This, in the minds of these scholars unacceptable outcome, might explain why the instrument-based approach is understood so fundamentally differently by different authors. Todd Huntley understands 'instrumentality' to refer to whether a "weapon" has been used: "[I]f so," he says, "its use would be considered a use of force." The problem here is that the 'cyber weapon' in question may have "multiple uses" besides the hostile one; and this, he states, precludes the application of Article 2(4) to cyberattacks *as such*.[192] Alternatively, Boris Kondoch understands the instrument-based approach as asking "whether cyber operations have the traditional characteristics associated with armed force and whether critical infrastructure has been hit"[193] – but that seems to be close to the definition of the target-based approach and furthermore, it is not clear what 'the traditional characteristics associated with armed force' are exactly. Michael Gervais explains the instrument-based model as that

187 Nguyen, 'Navigating,' 1117–1118.
188 Ibid., 1118.
189 Foltz, 'Stuxnet,' 42.
190 See also Huntley, 'Controlling,' 24.
191 Waxman, 'Cyber-Attacks,' 435, emphasis added for "serious."
192 Huntley, 'Controlling,' 24; see for a slightly different analysis with a similar outcome, Woltag, 'Cyber Warfare,' 153.
193 Kondoch, 'Jus ad Bellum,' 468.

> cyber weapons are categorized by the specific method of delivering an attack on an adversary. Whether it is a virus, worm, network intrusion, or some other cyber attack, this model prohibits cyber attacks based on how they are executed. The severe damage that particular types of cyber attack can inflict worldwide relative to the limited effects of narrowly designed exploits provides the basis for this approach. Of course, certain cyber weapons are inherently more destructive and dangerous than others.[194]

In the above quote, what starts out as a definition of an instrument evolves into a standard of damage: 'particular types of cyber attack' should be prohibited under Article 2(4) as they 'are inherently more destructive and dangerous than others.' Johann-Christoph Woltag explains this model in terms similar to those used by Reese Nguyen when he says that

> [t]he classical definition of armed force concentrates on the *type of instrument used* for coercion rather than the consequences of the action. This instrument is regularly taken from the field of *military weaponry*. Proponents of the so-called instrument-based approach see those [cyberattacks] falling under the prohibition if they are *comparable to "traditional" military weapons*.[195]

In his conclusion he elaborates on this:

> As international law does not provide for a conclusive definition of the term military weaponry, the instrument-based approach is ultimately dependent on the interpretation thereof. It is this interpretation which makes [this] approach able to consider the effects of an operation, showing that the alleged differences between the approaches are artificial.[196]

The definition of 'military weaponry' basically implies, Woltag says, "the *effects* of the means utilized, namely those that are capable of causing death, injury, damage or destruction."[197] This brings him to conclude that the instrument- and effects-based approach are basically the same – but as he acknowledges himself, this collapse of the two models is facilitated by defining one in terms of the other.[198]

194 Gervais, 'Cyber Attacks,' 538.

195 Woltag, 'Cyber Warfare,' 142, emphases added.

196 Ibid., 152.

197 Ibid. For alternative understandings of what constitutes a weapon see Silver, 'Computer Network Attack,' 84; Roscini, 'World Wide Warfare,' 106–107; Benatar, 'Cyber Force,' 388–389; Harrison Dinniss, 'Cyber Warfare,' 68–70; see also Wingfield, 'Information Conflict,' 99–100, 365, who discusses this in the context of non-military physical force (the infliction of harm by the breaking of dams, setting forests on fire, etc.).

198 See also Boer, 'Echoes,' 22–23 and references.

Whether scholars argue the 'regulability' of cyberattacks by means of Article 2(4) or whether they resort to other treaty or customary rules to provide legal certainty, the logic is the same.[199] Jason Barkham, for example, after first pointing out the difficulties in applying Article 2(4), and subsequently describing the difficulties involved in a treaty on the subject, still concludes his article by stating that "it is very likely that international law will need new tools and conceptual categories in order to address these new weapons."[200] Similarly, even though he states that "[t]here is no perfect method for analyzing cyber attacks with current technology" and that this "is only one of many hurdles for decision makers," Michael Gervais ends his article on a comforting note: "States may continue to rely on the existing regime of international law to regulate cyber attacks," he says, "while they await the international community's response to this modern form of waging battle."[201] This, then, is what 'application-orientation' looks like: a faith in the regulatory capacity of international law, even when after having spent an entire article or book chapter on analyzing its adaptability to cyberattacks many scholars conclude that, at the very least, it is a very uneasy fit. What is left is often merely a vague reference to the necessity of treaty or customary law to develop on the subject, or the specification of existing rules – but it remains unclear what these rules would have to look like in order for them to effectively curtail the threat posed by cyberattacks, and why these new rules would be any better than the old ones in doing so.

There are those, however, who occupy a completely opposite position. According to some, the problem of attribution and the anonymity of cyberattacks heavily problematize, or even preclude, the possibility of regulating them. Rather than claim that existing law applies or that new laws should be adopted – and thus assume that law, as such, is capable of mitigating the threat posed by cyberattacks[202] – these scholars argue that the characteristics of cyberattacks preclude their regulation under international law.[203] There are not many who do so, but their arguments may serve as a contrast to what Shklar refers to as the 'rule-oriented thinking' displayed by most scholars. For example, Jack Goldsmith identifies similar uncertainties as the ones already outlined in this chapter: the problems of attribution and anonymity. But contrary to the move made by most scholars, in his conclusion he

199 On the "logic of legalism" in the cyberwar debate, see note 94 above.
200 Barkham, 'Information Warfare,' 113.
201 Gervais, 'Cyber Attacks,' 541, 579.
202 See also Shklar, 'Legalism' (1964), 131.
203 Similarly Efrony and Shany, 'Rule Book,' 589.

expresses skepticism on the ability of international rules to circumvent this problem:

> There are many reasons for scepticism, but the main one is the problem of attribution. The laws of war would not be nearly as efficacious or have the same level of normative salience, if the nations that violated the laws could not be identified and publicly shamed. Norms cannot get much purchase in a world without serious attribution; anonymity is a norm destroyer.[204]

Thus, according to Goldsmith, the anonymity of cyberattacks and the subsequent difficulties in attribution preclude the possibility of regulation. Similarly, Michael Preciado states that

> [a]ssuming a comprehensive international treaty is agreed upon to specifically govern cyber warfare, nations will continue to use cyber warfare regardless of the treaty. Nations will reserve cyber warfare as part of their military operations because: (1) attributing responsibility for cyber attacks is problematic; (2) cyber warfare regulations cannot be enforced; (3) the decentralized nature of the Internet fosters cyber exploitation; (4) most cyber attacks go unreported; (5) the entry costs of cyber warfare is [*sic*] minimal; (6) cyber warfare can be used to coerce superior military forces into asymmetric warfare; and (7) attacking a nation's critical infrastructure destroys the victim state's internal operational viability.[205]

He ends up suggesting that the "[US] government should implement active computer defenses" as well as "monitor critical infrastructure networks," both public and private.[206] In a somewhat similar fashion Marco Benatar ends his article by stating that "the cyber wars of tomorrow will not be put on hold as a result of their ambiguous legality."[207] He is doubtful as to the possibilities of even regulating this phenomenon. Having first interpreted the prohibition on the use of force, and subsequently having discussed scholarly approaches to how it applies to cyberattacks, two-thirds into his piece he states how "there simply is no analogy to be made" between cyberattacks and the "type of armed, political or economic force" that is part of traditional legal frameworks. "This

[204] Goldsmith, 'How Cyber Changes,' 136; see also Goldsmith, 'Skeptical View'; and more recently, Goldsmith, 'Don't Get Too Excited.' For the debate on the (im)possibility of regulating cyberspace see note 39 above.

[205] Preciado, 'Cyber Peace,' 142.

[206] Ibid., 151–153. Someone who occupies the middle ground is David Weissbrodt, who argues that a treaty on cyberattacks would be unenforceable because of monitoring issues; see Weissbrodt, 'Cyber-Conflict,' 385–387. With regard to Article 2(4), however, he stays closer to the mainstream; see ibid., 375–376.

[207] Benatar, 'Cyber Force,' 396; see for a somewhat similar argument Huntley, 'Controlling,' 39–40.

begs the question," he says, "does the uniqueness of cyber attack preclude it from being regulated by article 2(4)?"[208] In other words, Benatar argues that 'this is neither like force, nor is it like coercion as we know it.' This, in turn, raises doubts as to the feasibility of *any* form of regulation.

The language used by Goldsmith and a few others is markedly different from that used by the majority of legal scholars in this debate. A lot of them may doubt the sufficiency of Article 2(4) in covering all possibilities presented by cyberattacks, but this does not result in any kind of pessimism about the ability of international law, as such, to regulate them.[209] Though the capabilities of non-state actors and the problems of attribution and anonymity are almost always part of this discourse, with one or two exceptions these do not impact the *legal* analysis. Only a few commentators leave their audience with a sense of the limits of law in responding to the problems presented by cyberattacks.[210]

Ultimately, this suggests that there is nothing inevitable or self-evident about looking at the world – about considering the threat of cyberattacks – through the lens of international law.[211] This is significant in understanding the 'application-orientation' of these scholars as it exposes the scholarly 'reflex' observable in this discourse: that there has to be *some* international legal response to cyberattacks, even though they have particular characteristics that, according to others, defy or at least severely complicate any attempt at regulation. As this chapter has shown, for a long time scholars had to come up with these legal solutions in the absence of state practice or *opinio juris*, let alone treaty law (though this situation has arguably been changing over the last few years). Yet, as Gregor Noll was quoted as saying earlier in this chapter, in the absence of formal declarations of law it is nonetheless important to continue practicing (the) discipline: 'discipline prepares for revelation to come.'

The next three chapters make up the core of this book. They present three close-ups of the cyberwar discourse: Chapter 5 analyzes the conference

208 Benatar, 'Cyber Force,' 391. I will briefly return to his work in Chapter 3.

209 For more insight in this viewpoint see Martha Finnemore and Duncan B. Hollis, 'Constructing Norms for Global Cybersecurity' (2016) 110 *American Journal of International Law* 425, 456–462.

210 Leaving aside radically different proposals: Fleur Johns and Annelise Riles suggest looking at the DNC hack from the lens of private, rather than public international law; Samuli Haataja suggests an "informational approach" to cyberattacks which focuses on the level of entropy they cause to a system, rather than adhering to traditional notions of force and coercion. See Fleur Johns and Annelise Riles, 'Beyond Bunker and Vaccine: The DNC Hack as a Conflict of Laws Issue' (2017) 110 *AJIL Unbound* 347; Haataja, 'Cyber Attacks,' chapter 8.

211 Shklar, 'Legalism' (1964), 2–3, 8–9.

presentations of Michael Schmitt; Chapter 4 scrutinizes claims to consensus made by legal scholars, and how these claims are substantiated. First, however, the next chapter gives a detailed portrayal of how scholars create legal meaning at the boundaries of Article 2(4) when applying the prohibition to cyberattacks. It describes specific argumentative junctions scholars take in their writing, and how the turns they take at these junctions set them on a particular trajectory towards their conclusions. The aim is to offer a close description of legal reasoning, and by juxtaposing these different arguments to present scholarly writing as a creative act: that which, through a sequence of argumentative turns, brings about legal knowledge about Article 2(4).

3

"Not 'Armed Force' in the Literal Sense"

In 2001, the *European Journal of International Law* published one of its first pieces on cyberattacks and international law. Its authors, Christopher Joyner and Catherine Lotrionte, inquire into a wide range of legal issues involved in the use of cyberattacks in international relations. As they discuss the meaning of the prohibition on the use of force, they state the following:

> Arguably, [Article 2(4)] applies only to "armed force". Yet, a use of force implies unlawful violence threatened or committed against persons or property, and, if cyber-force qualifies as a form of violence, it involves swift, injurious impacts on a targeted facility. The critical point is this: *though perhaps not "armed force" in the literal sense*, resort to cyber-force may be viewed as a form of intervention that can produce certain harmful or coercive effects in other states.[1]

Joyner and Lotrionte point out that the comparison between 'armed force in the literal sense' and cyberattacks is not always easy. As they discuss a range of scenarios, from cyberattacks on another state's digital infrastructure to attacks on the New York Stock Exchange, to those on a state's nuclear power facilities, they ultimately conclude that

> computer-based information operations in one state could destroy lives and damage property in other states ... such activities should [therefore] be prohibited as a "use of force" under UN Charter law ... Less clear is ... the disruption of a financial or social security system ... which produces no human injuries or property damage.[2]

[1] Joyner and Lotrionte, 'Information Warfare,' 849, emphasis added. Prior publications on 'cyber' in EJIL include pieces by Franz Mayer (2001, vol. 12) and a symposium on unilateralism in vol. 11(1), with contributions by Yochai Benkler, Franz Mayer and Jack Goldsmith. On the genesis of this chapter see Chapter 1 notes 127 and 129.

[2] Joyner and Lotrionte, 'Information Warfare,' 849–850.

Though this last group of attacks "clearly intrude into the internal affairs of another state," they "do not exceed any visible threshold of harm": it is doubtful whether they would violate the prohibition on the use of force.[3]

As explained in the previous chapter, the problem here lies not so much in those cyberattacks that bring about death and destruction: according to most of the scholars whose work is considered here these would undoubtedly constitute a use of force.[4] The legal challenge cyberattacks present is their potential to inflict disturbance on a massive scale. As Daniel Silver says,

> [i]f [a computer network attack] in all its manifestations easily could be assimilated to armed force, further discussion would be superfluous, since Article 2(4) indisputably encompasses armed force. Neither every form of [computer network attack] nor every purpose for which [it] can be used, however, readily can be analogized to armed force.[5]

Precisely those cyberattacks that operate in the "gray area"[6] between force and coercion present a problem to legal scholars. The more cyberattacks manifest themselves in their "novel"[7] form, the less self-evident the application of the prohibition on the use of force becomes.[8] As these two imageries – of what constitutes force, and the cyberattack in question – become increasingly dissimilar, scholars' conclusions about the ability of Article 2(4) of the UN Charter to regulate them also start to diverge. For example, whereas Marco Roscini claims that existing rules "seem to be flexible enough"[9] to be applied to cyberattacks, Duncan Hollis rather stresses the novelty of hostilities in cyberspace: "Neither kinetic force nor political or economic sanctions can

3 Ibid., 850.

4 The idea that the prohibition applies in these 'obvious' cases is least explicit in the work of Duncan Hollis; I will elaborate on his work further on in this chapter.

5 Silver, 'Computer Network Attack,' 80. See also Lin, 'Cyber Operations,' 73 and Haataja, 'Cyber Attacks,' 2–3.

6 Huntley, 'Controlling,' 26.

7 Benatar, 'Cyber Force,' 391; Hoisington, 'Cyberwarfare,' 454; Hollis, 'Why States Need,' 1042; Ido Kilovaty, 'Rethinking the Prohibition on the Use of Force in the Light of Economic Cyber Warfare: Towards a Broader Scope of Article 2(4) of the United Nations Charter' (2015) 4 *Journal of Law and Cyber Warfare* 210, 221.

8 Lin, 'Cyber Operations,' 73; Nguyen, 'Navigating,' 1117; Haataja, 'Cyber Attacks,' 3. On analogous reasoning see Friedrich V. Kratochwil, *Rules, Norms, and Decisions: On the Conditions of Practical and Legal Reasoning in International Relations and Domestic Affairs*, Cambridge University Press 1989, 223–227; in the context of new technologies, see also Duncan B. Hollis, *The Fog of Technology and International Law*, on 'Opinio Juris,' May 15, 2015.

9 Roscini, 'World Wide Warfare,' 130. This is reminiscent of d'Aspremont's description of the "interventionist posture"; see the discussion of and references to his work in the previous chapter.

disable an entire stock market or banking system the way information operations can – immediately and without casualties or physical destruction."[10]

This not to say that this 'gray area' between force and coercion has been exposed only by cyberattacks, or that the norm is clear everywhere but in its application to cyberattacks[11] – it is to say cyberattacks present a challenge for the meaning and boundary of 'force.' Concretely, in this chapter I look at those scholarly works in which this boundary is related to the exercise of economic coercion.[12] In these pieces the use of (armed) force and economic coercion function as opposite ends in an argument which seeks to place the kind of 'amorphous' cyberattacks described above somewhere in between. It presents a particularly difficult case of "legal line drawing"[13] as throughout its interpretive history economic coercion has been the 'next-door neighbor' of the prohibition on the use of force. Debates on whether massive economic sanctions do not, in fact, very closely resemble – or occasionally even surpass – the effects of 'conventional' force, have been raging ever since Article 2(4) was drafted.[14] For example, in the 1970s OPEC instituted an oil embargo in response to Western support of Israel in the 1973 Yom Kippur war. The embargo caused massive oil shortages in these Western countries, and led legal scholars to debate yet again whether economic coercion really did not constitute force.[15] To cite Matthew Waxman, "where one stands on

[10] Hollis, 'Why States Need,' 1042. Hollis's use of the phrase "information operations" rather than the more common 'cyberattacks' is significant; I will elaborate on this further on in this chapter.

[11] See for a similar comment, Woltag, 'Cyber Warfare,' 154; Foltz, 'Stuxnet,' 42; Aldrich, 'Information Age,' 231; and Gervais, 'Cyber Attacks,' 527; but see Schmitt, 'Normative Framework,' 908; Nguyen, 'Navigating,' 1084; and Waxman, 'Cyber-Attacks,' 431. Similarly, but in a different vein, Boer, 'Echoes.'

[12] Briefly, Boer, 'Echoes,' 17–19.

[13] Waxman, 'Cyber-Attacks,' 422. This is also one of the subheadings of this chapter.

[14] Similarly, Silver, 'Computer Network Attack,' 80. For a revision of the debate on the effect of the economic sanctions imposed against Iraq in the 1990s see Tim Dyson and Valeria Cetorelli, 'Changing Views on Child Mortality and Economic Sanctions in Iraq: A History of Lies, Damned Lies and Statistics' (2017) 2 *BMJ Global Health* 1.

[15] See, for a sample of the debate, Derek W. Bowett, 'Economic Coercion and Reprisals by States' (1972) 13 *Virginia Journal of International Law* 1; Richard B. Lillich, 'Economic Coercion and the International Legal Order' (1975) 51 *International Affairs* 358; James A. Delanis, 'Force under Article 2(4) of the United Nations Charter: The Question of Economic and Political Coercion' (1979) 12 *Vanderbilt Journal of Transnational Law* 101; Jordan J. Paust and Albert P. Blaustein, 'The Arab Oil Weapon – A Threat to International Peace' (1974) 68 *American Journal of International Law* 410; Yehuda Z. Blum, 'Economic Boycotts in International Law' (1977) 12 *Texas International Law Journal* 5; J. Dapray Muir, 'The Boycott in International Law' (1974) 9 *Journal of International Law and Economics* 187. For a more recent discussion, see Cassandra LaRae-Perez, 'Note: Economic Sanctions as a Use of

interpreting Articles 2(4) and 51 has historically depended on one's share of global resources and power."[16]

Therefore, scholars can hardly avoid dealing with this issue when discussing cyberattacks: ever since the creation of the prohibition economic coercion has been hovering at its edges; sometimes included, sometimes excluded from the scope of 'force.' The form it frequently takes on in the cyberwar debate is the example of a cyberattack on the New York Stock Exchange: a recurring event in this chapter as, in the words of Kenneth Watkin, the differing views on its permissibility under Article 2(4) "go to the heart of the discussion of regulating force in the cyber domain."[17] The question is "whether [it] more closely resembles economic ... coercion," or, given the enormous impact it would have, whether it is more like force?[18] According to some scholars, to think of those cyberattacks that have a non-physical result as force entails the risk of, in the words of one of them, "definitional creep."[19] The risk here is an expansion of the notion of force to include economic coercion; in other words, something is at stake in guarding the boundaries of the prohibition. Cyberattacks, in that sense, are merely the next chapter in this interpretive history: "[C]ompeting interpretations ... echo past interpretive disputes."[20]

By juxtaposing at a microlevel the different arguments on this issue this chapter shows what legal knowledge construction at Article 2(4)'s edges looks like. As the opening chapter clarified, this book understands international law as being made in the practice of its 'doers': judges, academics, state legal advisers, etc. Legal writing 'creates what it claims to find':[21] rather than "found or recognized" law is made in the "everyday" doings of those working with it.[22] The aim of this chapter is to show *how* this works exactly: how, for example, the 'flexibility' assigned to these rules by Marco Roscini results from international legal writing as a creative act. I do so by portraying scholarly work on

Force: Re-evaluating the Legality of Sanctions from an Effects-Based Perspective' (2002) 20 *Boston University International Law Journal* 161.

16 Waxman, 'Cyber-Attacks,' 449.

17 Watkin, 'Road Ahead,' 496. Watkin speaks here specifically of the discussion on this kind of attack in the first *Tallinn Manual*; see Schmitt (ed.), 'Tallinn Manual,' 56.

18 Silver, 'Computer Network Attack,' 82; see also Preciado, 'Cyber Peace,' 131–137; his work is discussed in greater detail in Chapter 2. This question is also discussed by Michael Schmitt and Tim Maurer, *Protecting Financial Data in Cyberspace: Precedent for Further Progress on Cyber Norms?*, on 'Just Security,' August 24, 2017.

19 Antolin-Jenkins, 'Defining the Parameters,' 134.

20 Waxman, 'Cyber-Attacks,' 426.

21 As paraphrased from Ingo Venzke, who writes that "interpretations contribute to creating what they find." See Venzke, 'Interpretation,' 54.

22 For "found or recognized" see ibid., 29; on "everyday" doings see Adler-Nissen, 'Why IR needs Bourdieu.' On law's 'doers' see Schlag, 'Problem of the Subject.'

cyberattacks as a dialogue by letting scholars 'respond' to each other through the juxtaposition of arguments across different texts. I point out the turns a scholar takes at specific junctions in her or his text, and by means of contrasting these turns with those taken in other texts show how "it could have all turned out differently."[23]

This chapter identifies two argumentative junctions in particular scholars take in their reconstructions of the meaning of the norm.[24] First, they set its boundaries; the inside and outside of force. The question here is whether there is any room at the edges of the prohibition for the 'hard-to-grasp' cyberattacks: can we conceive of a notion of force that encompasses them? This part of the chapter contrasts scholars' different, or similar, starting positions, and subsequently demonstrates how these lead to different, or similar, conclusions as to the suitability of the norm in regulating cyberattacks. It shows how a diagnosis as to its (in)sufficiency – because it covers too much, too little, or whether it works well[25] – follows an argumentative turn made previously in the article or chapter. The second junction relates to the qualification of the phenomenon Article 2(4) is supposed to regulate. The turn scholars make here is whether to qualify a cyberattack as simply another form of coercion (or force), or to argue the novelty of the phenomenon, and thereby point out the necessity of new, or better, law.[26] So the question here is how they write about these kinds of cyberattacks: are they simply a new means with which to inflict similar kinds of harm, or should we think of them as possessing "novel features"[27], in need of new or adjusted laws? Thus, the second junction pertains to the classification of the threat: either as 'business as usual' or as a phenomenon requiring separate treatment – whether by means of a reconsideration of existing law, or by the development of new laws.

[23] Mansfield Park (1999), Miramax Films, BBC Films and Intermedia Films in association with The Arts Council of England, written and directed by Patricia Rozema, at 1.42.42; similarly Musil, 'The Man Without Qualities,' 11. See also Boer, 'Narratives of Force,' section 4.

[24] On interpretations as reconstructions, see Koskenniemi, 'Apology to Utopia,' specifically chapter 8 and the Epilogue, and Venzke, 'Interpretation,' chapters 1 and 2.

[25] On (the room for) decisions and the over- and underinclusiveness of rules, including the prohibition on the use of force, see Koskenniemi, 'Apology to Utopia,' 590–596; see also Venzke, 'Interpretation,' inter alia 29, 54–55, 60; see, however, Susan Marks, 'False Contingency' (2009) 62 *Current Legal Problems* 1, also cited in this context in Martti Koskenniemi, 'The Politics of International Law – 20 Years Later' (2009) 20 *European Journal of International Law* 7, 9.

[26] Hollis, 'Why States Need,' 1042, section V; see also Waxman, 'Cyber-Attacks,' 431. This is not to say this is the only problem involved in the relation between law and cyberattacks (see, for example, Nguyen, 'Navigating,' section C.), but it *is* the focus of this chapter.

[27] Benatar, 'Cyber Force,' 391. This phrase also used for one of the subheadings of this chapter.

This chapter proceeds as follows. It starts by showing how scholars sketch the rough outlines of Article 2(4).[28] It draws on just under thirty scholarly works,[29] which, given the focus of this chapter, all relate Article 2(4) in some form or fashion to economic coercion. Sometimes this happens very elaborately, by means of the tools for interpretation provided in the *Vienna Convention on the Law of Treaties*; in others, more briefly, with the mere statement of the boundaries of force.[30] So, these articles are not all just devoted to an analysis of Article 2(4) and cyberattacks; some, for example, talk of force in the context of countermeasures (as is the case in Anders Henriksen's piece); others use this discussion to argue against analogous reasoning, as in the case of the pieces by Preciado and Hollis. The point is that in these articles, meaning is assigned to the prohibition as it relates to cyberattacks.

About half of these pieces are then used in the second part of the chapter, as they more specifically or elaborately deal with the problem described above.[31] This is not to say that they are the only ones to deal with this problem; what this part of this chapter seeks to show is what happens when their arguments are compared to and contrasted with each other. The space these authors devote to "navigating"[32] the gap between force and coercion, differs: sometimes, an entire article is spent on it, as is the case in Ido Kilovaty's piece; in others, it is a very small part of, for example, an argument in favor of a treaty on cyberattacks – as in the work of Duncan Hollis. The choice to narrow down the

[28] For a different treatment of the function of these 'rough outlines' see Boer, 'Echoes.'

[29] Most of these can be found via HeinOnline's Law Journal Library by entering the search terms 'cyber & "article 2(4)" & charter' (May 2020). The resulting list is as follows: Antolin-Jenkins, 'Defining the Parameters'; Aldrich, 'Information Age'; Barkham, 'Information Warfare'; Benatar, 'Cyber Force'; Gervais, 'Cyber Attacks'; Henriksen, 'Lawful State Responses'; Hoisington, 'Cyberwarfare'; Hollis, 'Why States Need'; Huntley, 'Controlling'; Jensen, 'Computer Attacks'; Jurich, 'Cyberwar'; Kondoch, 'Jus ad Bellum'; Kilovaty, 'Rethinking'; Erki Kodar, 'Computer Network Attacks in the Grey Areas of *Jus ad Bellum* and *Jus in Bello*' (2009) 9 *Baltic Yearbook of International Law Online* 133; Lin, 'Cyber Operations'; Nguyen, 'Navigating'; Preciado, 'Cyber Peace'; Roscini, 'World Wide Warfare'; Silver, 'Computer Network Attack'; Schmitt, 'Normative Framework'; Watkin, 'Road Ahead'; Waxman, 'Cyber-Attacks'; Weissbrodt, 'Cyber-Conflict.' I have furthermore included two (sections from) book chapters, one from Wingfield, 'Information Conflict,' chapter 6, and Woltag, 'Cyber Warfare,' section 2.2, and four articles: Delibasis, 'Right of States'; Foltz, 'Stuxnet'; Goldsmith, 'How Cyber Changes'; Joyner and Lotrionte, 'Information Warfare.'

[30] For example Goldsmith, 'How Cyber Changes,' 133.

[31] The pieces used for this part of the chapter are those by Aldrich, Antolin-Jenkins, Barkham, Benatar, Gervais, Hollis, Kilovaty, Lin, Roscini, Schmitt, Silver, Waxman, Woltag and Wingfield. On two occasions, I have resorted to other pieces by the same authors: this was done in the case of the work of Schmitt and Roscini in order to clarify their views.

[32] See also Matthew Waxman, who likewise talks of how to "navigate" existing law and the new possibilities created by cyberattacks; Waxman, 'Cyber-Attacks,' 425; similarly, the title of Reese Nguyen's article is '*Navigating* Jus ad Bellum *in the Age of Cyber Warfare*.'

scope of this part of the chapter to a limited number of pieces is deliberate. As explained in the first chapter of this book, the aim here is to closely describe legal knowledge construction. This chapter uses the questions asked on the first couple of pages of this book to come to that description: which words are used; where in these texts are they used; who is using these words; and what does it do to use these, rather than others? To be able to understand what happens if arguments are juxtaposed at this level, it is necessary to restrict the amount of arguments presented. As a result it becomes possible to pin down the contingency as well as the determinacy of legal reasoning in these texts. With 'contingency' and 'determinacy' I do not mean to refer to the contingency or determinacy of international law at large.[33] Instead, I mean to refer to the twists and turns of an individual piece of scholarly writing: the visibility of the scholar in the text who somehow lets one argument prevail over another. In this manner, the construction of legal knowledge about Article 2(4) is made visible.

3.1 SETTING THE STAGE: THE "PARAMETERS" OF FORCE

Chapter 2 of this book discussed the 'application-orientation' of the scholars whose work is considered here. Part of this orientation, as stated in that chapter, is the idea that the application of law can be performed in a structured fashion.[34] For the debate on cyberattacks and Article 2(4) this structure translates into several "reference points"[35] that can be identified in this discourse, which means that those making an argument about the meaning of force largely refer to similar material. These shared reference points in legal argumentation are painted here in broad strokes. It is not an exhaustive list, and not all scholars refer to all these sources all the time[36], and the order in which they do so differs.[37] It is intended to give some of the common

[33] On this question some of the most prominent works include Koskenniemi, 'Apology to Utopia'; David Kennedy, 'Theses about International Law Discourse,' in: *German Yearbook of International Law*, Jost Delbrück, Rainer Hofmann and Andreas Zimmermann (eds.), Duncker & Humblot 1980, 354–391; Marks, 'False Contingency.'

[34] See Chapter 2 notes 82–85.

[35] The phrase "reference point" is taken from Venzke, 'Interpretation,' for example at 27; though he also uses it to indicate those points scholars *have to refer to* in legal argument (at 27, 48). This is not the case for all these points or claims. I therefore use this phrase somewhat differently than Venzke does.

[36] For a somewhat different approach see Goldsmith, Lin, Jensen and Kodar (who only briefly address the norm before applying it); and Hollis, whose discussion of the prohibition serves as an example of how existing law is insufficient in regulating cyberattacks.

[37] See, for example, Kilovaty, 'Rethinking.'

denominators in the material scholars refer to; what results is an image of the boundaries of force.

Scholarly interpretations of the prohibition largely track the interpretive tools provided for in the *Vienna Convention of the Law of Treaties*, either implicitly or explicitly. The Convention provides that "[a] treaty shall be interpreted in good faith in accordance with the ordinary meaning to be given to the terms of the treaty in their context and in the light of its object and purpose." This 'context' includes, inter alia, a treaty's Preamble; also "taken into account" are, among other things, "any subsequent agreement between the parties" as well as "subsequent practice in the application of the treaty." Moreover, "[r]ecourse may be had to supplementary means of interpretation, including the preparatory work of the treaty and the circumstances of its conclusion."[38]

Therefore, the first thing to assess is the 'ordinary meaning' of force, and, inter alia, the 'object and purpose' of the Charter. The ordinary meaning of force can point in the direction of an extensive prohibition on many different kinds of force including, for example, political and economic coercion.[39] To most scholars, however, the object and purpose of the Charter – assessed on the basis of the Charter's Preamble, or the historical context within which it was created – point (most of the time) in a different direction: that Article 2(4) was drafted with military or armed force in mind.[40] Other textual references to force in the Charter are taken as confirmation of this conclusion: Article 41 talks of "measures not involving the use of armed force," which most take as a sign that the word 'force' in Article 2(4) likewise refers to armed force.[41] Roscini points out, however, that "[t]he opposite argument could . . . also be made": "[I]f the drafters had intended," Kerschischnig adds, to insert the word 'armed' in the text of Article 2(4), "they would have done so."[42] According to Michael Schmitt, the fact that the Preamble uses *armed* force means that the 'force' of Article 2(4) can never be interpreted more expansively than that: "After all," Schmitt says, "the Charter's articles are designed to effectuate its

38 *Vienna Convention on the Law of Treaties*, May 23, 1969, 1155 UNTS 331, Articles 31 and 32. For an example of the use of the *Vienna Convention* in the interpretation of the prohibition, see Benatar, 'Cyber Force,' 381 et seq.

39 See, for example, Gervais, 'Cyber Attacks,' 536; Kilovaty, 'Rethinking,' 230; Kondoch, 'Jus ad Bellum,' 467; Roscini, 'World Wide Warfare,' 104–105.

40 Gervais, 'Cyber Attacks,' 536; Kondoch, 'Jus ad Bellum,' 467; Roscini, 'World Wide Warfare,' 105; Woltag, 'Cyber Warfare,' 136; but see Wingfield, 'Information Conflict,' 89. See also Boer, 'Echoes,' 22–23.

41 UN Charter, Article 41. For an alternative interpretation see Aldrich, 'Information Age,' 240–241. His work is discussed further on in this chapter.

42 Roscini, 'World Wide Warfare,' 105; Kerschischnig, 'Cyberthreats,' 106; see also Wingfield, 'Information Conflict,' 89 and Boer, 'Echoes,' 11–12.

preambular aspirations. Thus, preambular terminology is logically interpreted more broadly than that contained in the articles."[43]

Furthermore, the negotiating texts of the Charter show that a Brazilian amendment to extend the prohibition to include economic coercion was rejected. To most of the scholars involved, this implies that the drafters did not intend to maintain a broad interpretation of force. Additionally, some scholars refer to the *Nicaragua* Judgment of the International Court of Justice, in which the Court distinguished between "the mere supply of funds" (not force) and the "arming and training of the *contras*" (force).[44] "It would seem," Daniel Silver concludes from this, "if financing an armed insurrection is not force, that, *a fortiori*, other economic measures that have a less direct nexus to armed violence would not be either."[45] Moreover, in its Advisory Opinion on the use of nuclear weapons the International Court of Justice stated that concepts such as the use of force "do not refer to specific weapons. They apply to any use of force, regardless of the weapons employed."[46] As a final example of the reference points used, some argue that the General Assembly's *Friendly Relations Declaration* maintains a similar distinction between armed force and economic coercion.[47]

From the above the outlines of the meaning of the prohibition emerge.[48] This doesn't mean that scholars do not express uncertainty with regard to the meaning of force: some of them start their analysis with an identification of the "ambiguous wording" of Article 2(4), allowing for "radically opposed understandings of the concept of force," or they explain how the absence of definitions in the UN Charter has led to "50 years of debate" on the interpretation of (among other things) force.[49] Yet, though they might be unable to pin down the exact meaning of force, at least its far ends can be drawn with some certainty. In the words of one of them, "[w]hile the precise definition of what constitutes the

43 Schmitt, 'Normative Framework,' 904. Further on in his article, however, Schmitt does extend these boundaries; see ibid., 908.

44 *Nicaragua* case, para. 228; for the use of this case see for example Weissbrodt, 'Cyber-Conflict,' 358.

45 Silver, 'Computer Network Attack,' 81.

46 *Legality of the Threat or Use of Nuclear Weapons, Advisory Opinion, ICJ Reports 1996, p. 226* (1996), para. 39. For the use of this Advisory Opinion, see for example Kondoch, 'Jus ad Bellum,' 468.

47 See for example, Nguyen, 'Navigating,' 1114; and Woltag, 'Cyber Warfare,' 136.

48 Aldrich and Wingfield draw different conclusions on the basis of the same material; see below.

49 Benatar, 'Cyber Force,' 383; Antolin-Jenkins, 'Defining the Parameters,' 150. See also Foltz, 'Stuxnet,' 42; Hoisington, 'Cyberwarfare,' 440–441; Huntley, 'Controlling,' 15; Kondoch, 'Jus ad Bellum,' 467; Lin, 'Cyber Operations,' 71; Nguyen, 'Navigating,' 1113; Schmitt, 'Normative Framework,' 904; Weissbrodt, 'Cyber-Conflict,' 357; Woltag, 'Cyber Warfare,' 135, 150; for a more firm view, see Wingfield, 'Information Conflict,' 82–83.

use of force is unclear, some of the parameters are well known"; another states that "[t]he paradigm examples at the core of Article 2(4) are relatively clear."[50] These 'parameters' generally consist of two 'knowns' with regard to force: that the prohibition includes armed force (and perhaps a little bit more), and that economic coercion is excluded from its purview – most of the time.[51] With regard to the first, it should be noted that the word 'armed' is almost always inserted, and in these writings it indicates the immediate infliction of physical harm or destruction. Not all authors, however, concern themselves very deeply with the distinction between force and armed force; their interpretation often starts with an instant narrowing down of the scope of the prohibition to armed force.[52] With regard to the second – the exclusion of economic coercion – it was already explicated in the introduction of this chapter that the articles used for this chapter were specifically selected for their treatment of force *in relation to* economic coercion (however brief). There are scholarly works on the prohibition that do not mention economic coercion at all[53] but as explained above, this selection was made due to the focus of this chapter. It should be noted, however, that many pieces on the use of force (whether they deal with cyberattacks or not) do talk of economic coercion, simply because it has been such a contentious issue ever since the drafting of the Charter.

Thus, Marco Benatar talks of how "the structure and language of [the General Assembly's Declaration on the Non-Use of Force] implies a separation of coercive measures with armed force *on the one hand* and other types of pressure *on the other hand*"; taking stock halfway through his article, he states that "[i]t is apparent from this analysis that the UN Charter adopts a clear-cut approach to force by distinguishing three types: armed, economic and political."[54] Michael Gervais likewise talks of economic coercion being "explicitly exclud[ed]" and how "the determination of whether a nation has used force . . . focuses only on military instruments."[55] Daniel Silver, who, unlike

50 Barkham, 'Information Warfare,' 70 (which was also used in the header of this section); Nguyen, 'Navigating,' 1113; see also Weissbrodt, 'Cyber-Conflict,' 358.

51 But see note 48 above.

52 For exceptions see Schmitt, 'Normative Framework,' 904–908; and Aldrich, 'Information Age,' 238 et seq.

53 See for example, Raboin, 'Corresponding Evolution.'

54 Benatar, 'Cyber Force,' 385, 386, emphases added. See for examples of a similar distinction, Schmitt, 'Normative Framework,' 909 et seq., but see the caveat in note 52 above; Silver, 'Computer Network Attack,' 82; Antolin-Jenkins, 'Defining the Parameters,' 153; Goldsmith, 'How Cyber Changes,' 133; Hoisington, 'Cyberwarfare,' 447; Hollis, 'Why States Need,' 1040; Woltag, 'Cyber Warfare,' 138, Joyner and Lotrionte, 'Information Warfare,' 846–848 (though they express doubts about "massive economic sanctions" (848) being permissible under Article 2(4)).

55 Gervais, 'Cyber Attacks,' 537.

Marco Benatar, argues by analogy, nevertheless uses a similar imagery: "Lacking any directly applicable precedents or other sources of international law, the status of [cyberattacks] under Article 2(4) only can be predicted by drawing analogies to *other phenomena whose status is better established*"; he proceeds to draw these lines by means of economic coercion (not force) and non-military physical force (the intentional spreading of cross-border forest fires, etc.), which would constitute force.[56]

However, this does not tell us what else these categories, concretely, may or may not entail. It does not answer the question how to deal with those attacks that do not have a result similar to those caused by traditional uses of force.[57] The issue is whether the prohibition allows for the inclusion of attacks that do not have a direct physical effect: "The boundary [of force] falls somewhere in the wide gray expanse between exercises of traditional forms of military power and soft power coercion or passive intrusions."[58] "The goal here," Marco Benatar writes, "is to determine whether we can conceive of a new notion of force, cyber force, which fits within article 2(4) *without stretching the provision to its breaking point*"; similarly, Herbert Lin states that "the application of . . . U.N. Charter principles may not be as straightforward as when kinetic weapons are involved."[59] Michael Gervais states that "treating all forms of cyber attack as a use of force would require an implausibly broad reading of Article 2(4) that includes non-physical damage. A *more nuanced approach* is needed."[60]

The following pages show how scholars navigate their way to this 'more nuanced approach.' Specifically, it shows the importance of specific argumentative junctions in concluding whether Article 2(4) suffices in regulating cyberattacks. As stated, I identify two in this discourse: first, decisions with regard to the boundaries of the norm; second, decisions with regard to the 'novelty' of the phenomenon. The next few pages discuss both.

3.2 "LEGAL LINE DRAWING"

3.2.1 *Junction 1: The Boundaries of the Norm*

Above, I elaborated on how the majority of the scholars considered here would argue that economic coercion is excluded from the scope of the prohibition. It

56 Silver, 'Computer Network Attack,' 79–80, emphasis added.

57 For a similar comment see Jurich, 'Cyberwar,' 285.

58 Nguyen, 'Navigating,' 1114.

59 Benatar, 'Cyber Force,' 381, emphasis added; Lin, 'Cyber Operations,' 73.

60 Gervais, 'Cyber Attacks,' 537, emphasis added; similarly Nguyen, 'Navigating,' 1084; Silver, 'Computer Network Attack,' 80.

also became clear, however, that there are some exceptions to this position. One of the scholars arguing otherwise is Richard Aldrich. He starts his interpretation of force with a question: whether "the use of force envisioned in the Charter only prohibit[s] the use of physical force?" His answer to this question is 'yes, it probably does'; and as part of this response he acknowledges the "prevailing view" on the exclusion of economic coercion.[61] Then, however, he takes the argument into a different direction. Aldrich points out that "[t]here are … significant examples of non-physical uses of force"; for example, the use of chemical and biological weapons.[62] So maybe, he says, the word 'force' does *not just* refer to physical force. What is more, with regard to economic coercion he states that it is "unclear … whether economic sanctions can ever constitute a use of force."[63] At this point he reverts back to those arguments listed previously in this chapter. He acknowledges that the text of the Charter probably excludes the notion of economic coercion as force, and so does the rejection of the Brazilian amendment to the original draft of the Charter. Yet, there is some historical evidence pointing in the other direction. Specifically, Aldrich points out the difference of opinion between "most Western states" and "[t]he communist bloc and most Third World countries [who] still averred that economic coercion was within the scope of Article 2(4)."[64] There is one argument Aldrich firmly rejects, however:

> One author has suggested that the broad concluding phrase of Article 2(4) – "or in any other manner inconsistent with the Purposes of the United Nations" – was meant also to serve as a catch all to include economic measures within the ambit of a threat or use of force, though this construction has not been generally accepted, especially among Western countries.[65]

This expression of uncertainty gains particular meaning in light of his discussion of the potential economic harms inflicted by cyberattacks. The title of his article is *How do you know you are at war in the information age?* and one of the causes of confusion, according to Aldrich, lies in a situation in which

61 Aldrich, 'Information Age,' 238. On his use of this "prevailing view" argument, see Chapter 4 of this book.

62 Ibid. Note also how then Prime Minister Theresa May designated the use of Novichok against the Skripal family in Salisbury as a use of force; for a discussion see Marc Weller, *An International Use of Force in Salisbury?*, on 'EJIL: *Talk!*,' March 14, 2018.

63 Aldrich, 'Information Age,' 241. Aldrich seems to use the terms "economic force," "economic pressure" and "economic sanctions" interchangeably (at 238 and 241). On these concepts see Clinton E. Cameron, 'Developing a Standard for Politically Related State Economic Action' (1991) 13 *Michigan Journal of International Law* 218, 220–221.

64 Aldrich, 'Information Age,' 241.

65 Ibid., 246–247. I understood this as Aldrich rejecting this particular interpretation of the last few words of Article 2(4), not as his rejection of the inclusion of economic coercion as such.

"someone were to use an information weapon to take down Wall Street or the Federal Reserve system." If this were to happen, he says, "we may not know whether we are at war, but the effects of the takedown would be devastating."[66] These are precisely the kinds of amorphous attacks Aldrich suggests necessitate a revision of what is currently considered to be force:

> The weapons' effects may not be to produce immediate death and destruction of property, but to innocuously manipulate bits of data . . . to deleterious effect nonetheless . . . Many believe that an "electronic Pearl Harbor" is inevitable. This all requires a serious reevaluation of what constitutes an illegal use of force in the Information Age.[67]

This 'reevaluation,' according to Aldrich, entails that

> what constitutes an illegal threat or use of force must focus more on the actual or potential impact of the attacker's actions than with [*sic*] the technological means used to achieve it . . . we must assess the threat to international peace by assessing the harm that occurs or is threatened.[68]

Similarly, he says that "[i]nformation wars will not be concentrated in 'war zones,' but perhaps more than ever will have impact on civilians through incapacitation of telephone systems, takedown of key electrical grids, or disruption of financial systems. The impact of such operations is likely to be widely felt."[69] In this manner, he appears to advocate – though not explicitly – a very "broad, result-oriented test"[70] to assess violations of Article 2(4) by means of cyberattacks.

According to some authors, however, this approach has some unforeseen consequences – and this is where, in their mind, the problem in applying the prohibition to cyberattacks comes in. Discussing the different kinds of effects cyberattacks can have, Jason Barkham refers to those scholars – such as Aldrich – who think 'overall results' should matter, rather than merely the physical effect of an attack. This "result-oriented test," he says, eliminates "the existing distinction" between what is thought of as force, and (economic) coercion: "[O]nce the analysis focuses on the results rather than the physical impact," he says, "it becomes difficult to preserve the distinction between uses of force, which typically have an instantaneous impact, and acts of coercion, which do not":[71]

66 Ibid., 231, 232.
67 Ibid., 225.
68 Ibid., 261.
69 Ibid., 235.
70 Barkham, 'Information Warfare,' 86.
71 Ibid., 86, 84, 88. For a similar point see Weissbrodt, 'Cyber-Conflict,' 360 and Woltag, 'Cyber Warfare,' 142.

> [Information warfare's] potential applications create serious problems for the existing distinction between force and coercion under Article 2(4). Including all IW actions within the use of force would require a major expansion of Article 2(4) . . . [This] would make it very difficult to continue to exclude acts of coercion from Article 2(4) because international law would have to distinguish IW acts that do not cause physical damage, such as electronic incursions and blockades, from acts of economic and political coercion, such as economic sanctions, which traditionally and specifically have been excluded from Article 2(4), but which often have the same effect . . . One potential alternative framework would be a broad, result-oriented test. The problem with the result-oriented approach to electronic actions is that it would blur the distinction that excludes economic coercion from the use of force. If the time requirement were expanded, the destruction caused by some economic actions might suggest that they also should be included in Article 2(4).[72]

Barkham points out a few things here. Prior to this paragraph he has, like many others, argued that economic coercion has been excluded from the scope of the prohibition ever since the drafting of the Charter. Given this exclusion, Barkham says, we get into trouble when considering cyberattacks under Article 2(4). He states we can go two ways, both of which are problematic. One option is to consider all cyberattacks as 'force,' regardless of their consequences; to include them under the headings of the prohibition, as such. But this, he points out, eliminates the distinction between force and economic and political coercion – both can have limited, non-physical effects, but the one (cyber) would be included, whereas the other (economic and political coercion) would be excluded. The alternative is to only include those cyberattacks that surpass a certain threshold level of 'harm.' However, if we do that, and what is more, also let go of the idea that the impact of the use of force has to be immediate, the distinction between force and coercion likewise disappears.

This is what a focus on overall result does, according to Barkham, to the distinction between force and coercion. He points out that this problem goes way back: in 1963, Ian Brownlie made the case for the inclusion of chemical and biological weapons under the prohibition, in his *International Law and*

[72] Barkham, 'Information Warfare,' 84–85, 86. Barkham explains he understands information warfare as "computer network attack" (cf. the broad definition employed by Duncan Hollis, see below); see ibid., 60. He mentions several other problems in analogizing cyberattacks with 'conventional' uses of force; for example, besides the delay in effects he questions the permissibility of the "destruction of data," "electronic blockades" and whether data constitutes property. See ibid., 87–93.

the Use of Force by States.[73] As also explained by Barkham, in this book Brownlie discusses an extension of the prohibition on the use of force to include chemical and biological weapons. He acknowledges that these weapons don't resemble kinetic force; but they *are* very harmful.[74] His argument in favour of extending the prohibition is based on "the fact that these weapons are employed for the destruction of life and property, and are often described as 'weapons of mass destruction.'"[75] Brownlie's reorientation on the meaning of force basically entails a shift in focus from "kinetic impact" to the overall result of an attack.[76] As pointed out by Jason Barkham this one phrase in Brownlie's book is essential, not only as an argument to include biological and chemical warfare under the heading of 'force,' but moreover, to extend the scope of the prohibition to cyberattacks.[77] For if "results rather than . . . physical impact"[78] matter to assessing a violation of Article 2(4), *any* weapon can be incorporated under Article 2(4).[79] The importance of Brownlie's thinking for the work of some of these scholars is such that, in the words of one of them, he "established a new juridical basis" for assessing the meaning of 'force.'[80]

So, according to Barkham, Brownlie's reasoning creates a problem: a focus on overall result eliminates the distinction between force and coercion. After all, considered over a longer period of time economic coercion can be as harmful as the use of armed force.[81] What we end up with is a deadlock, Barkham says: "Either [cyber]attacks must be divided into acts of force and coercion, or the definition of force must be expanded significantly to encompass all [cyber]attacks. Neither solution seems satisfactory. Either similar means or similar results must receive different

73 Ian Brownlie, *International Law and the Use of Force by States*, Oxford University Press 1963.

74 This is the argument made by Aldrich (who also refers to Brownlie), above: that there are examples of non-kinetic harm, and that the prohibition should be interpreted so as to entail this broader notion.

75 Brownlie, 'Use of Force,' 362. He also considers that biological and chemical weapons "are commonly referred to *as* 'weapons' and as forms of 'warfare'," but finds the second argument (quoted in the body text) to be "[m]ore convincing" (362, emphasis added).

76 Barkham, 'Information Warfare,' 72; see also Boer, 'Echoes,' 20.

77 Ibid., 87–88.

78 Ibid., 88.

79 The reasoning is basically similar to that of the International Court of Justice in its *Nuclear Weapons* Advisory Opinion, which therefore might suffer from a similar problem. See the discussion at the beginning of this chapter and Chapter 2 notes 197–198.

80 Benatar, 'Cyber Force,' 389. A discussion of the significance ascribed to Brownlie's work is outside the scope of this chapter; it is interesting, however, how one single (scholarly) argument can impact very foundational considerations on a particular norm.

81 Barkham, 'Information Warfare,' 87–88; d'Aspremont, 'Cyber Operations,' 586.

treatment."[82] In other words, viewed like this the prohibition becomes either under- or overinclusive.[83]

A similar anxiety as Jason Barkham's about the non-physical impact of cyberattacks is reflected in the work of Vita Antolin-Jenkins. She says that "[o]ne of the gravest dangers in cyberwar is destruction of or interference with information infrastructure in such a manner as to cause devastating economic harm to a State."[84] We have a "choice," she says, either "to revaluate inclusion of 'economic aggression' in the accepted international legal definition of 'use of force' under customary and conventional international law or to create a completely new analytic framework to regulate cyberwar."[85] She confronts herself with the same deadlock as Jason Barkham does in his piece:

> Cyberspace operations for the most part do not meet the criteria for "use of force" as currently defined in international law. Defining the parameters of proportional response through analogy is possible, but creates clear dangers of definitional creep into other areas of international relations that have been the subject of long and contentious debate . . . Defining attacks on economic centers of gravity as "use of force" under the current international regimes has grave potential for unintended and undesirable legal consequences. Incorporating cyber attacks on critical economic infrastructures into the definition of "use of force" cannot be done with sufficient precision to exclude other state economic policies which have long been defended as necessary tools of foreign policy, and deliberately excluded from the international definition of "use of force," particularly by market-based democracies.[86]

A few things stand out here. First, in order to use the phrases 'definitional creep' and 'force as currently defined' there has to be a preconceived notion of the boundaries of force; moreover, it carries the idea that at its edges the definition might be expanding due to cyberattacks. More importantly, this expansion is a hazardous thing: cyberattacks mess with the boundaries of force, and expanding them has 'grave potential for unintended and undesirable legal consequences.' In this case, these 'undesirable legal consequences' entail the

82 Barkham, 'Information Warfare,' 94; for an extended take on this contradiction see Boer, 'Echoes.' Preciado assumes a similar dichotomy; see Preciado, 'Cyber Peace,' 134–135; Herbert Lin makes a slightly similar point, though his conclusions are less radical than those of Preciado; see Lin, 'Cyber Operations,' 80–82. As will be discussed below, there are attempts to draw a more detailed line between force and coercion, for example by Michael Schmitt and Ido Kilovaty.

83 Barkham, 'Information Warfare,' 94–95, who also uses the word "underinclusive."

84 Antolin-Jenkins, 'Defining the Parameters,' 134–135.

85 Ibid., 135.

86 Ibid., 134–135.

inclusion of those measures that 'have long been defended as necessary tools of foreign policy,' that is, economic coercion. The idea of previously fixed and firmly drawn lines is reinforced by the reference to 'economic policies *deliberately excluded*' from the scope of the prohibition, as well as the notion that lines have to be drawn with 'sufficient precision.' So, in this one paragraph we find a diagnosis, a warning and a reminder that things cannot be as they once were.

There is nothing inevitable, however, about either Barkham's or Antolin-Jenkins' conclusions. Barkham's idea of under- or overinclusion, as well as Antolin-Jenkins' idea of 'definitional creep' are contingent on the prior establishment of an 'inside' and 'outside' of force. They start their analysis with the firm boundaries drawn between armed force and economic coercion. However, by subsequently wanting to place cyberattacks in one of the two categories they get themselves into argumentative trouble. For example, Antolin-Jenkins discusses the following hypothetical:

> [W]here the attack is on economic infrastructures, such as financial markets and banks, destruction of national wealth can paralyze the state with a devastating effect on the state's ability to maintain independence. The issue which arises is whether the use of a cyber attack on the economic operations within the target nation fits more clearly into the definition of economic coercion or whether it can fit into armed attack.[87]

The 'definition of economic coercion,' however, is given its boundaries in the text. In other words, the problem Barkham and Antolin-Jenkins identify is not a given but results from the argument they themselves make – something which emerges from the contrast with Richard Aldrich's work, described above. Under the broader harm-principle he suggests, the choice to consider cyberattacks either as force or as economic coercion does not appear to be such a binary one as suggested by Antolin-Jenkins and Barkham. Aldrich's argument suggests that, with a different starting point, the diagnosis might also change. Even though, at least as far as the pieces here are concerned, the idea of the exclusion of economic coercion seems to have the upper hand there are some who argue the exact opposite: that the norm itself allows for the inclusion of at least *some* kinds of economic coercion. This can be further explained by looking closer at the work of Thomas Wingfield, who argues something similar to Richard Aldrich, but does so more elaborately.

Like Aldrich, Thomas Wingfield acknowledges the 'prevailing view' on armed force (more on this in the next chapter), and lists the different

87 Ibid., 155.

arguments for adhering to this position. And like Aldrich, he then proceeds by questioning the veracity of this claim.[88] To each and every argument made in favor of the predominant position, he opposes another one. For example, "[m]ost of the developing countries and the former Eastern bloc countries . . . have repeatedly claimed that Article 2(4) also prohibits political and economic coercion."[89] With regard to the rejection of the Brazilian amendment to include economic coercion, Wingfield points out that "[o]ther scholars, however, have also reviewed the working documents of the drafters of the Charter, and concluded that they 'do not indicate that the phrase ["use of force"] applied only to armed force.'"[90] "More importantly," in Wingfield's view,

> the preamble and the purposes of Article I describe a Charter that is concerned with far more than simply the use of armed force. The Charter is concerned with human rights, social progress, justice, standards of life, tolerance, and living together in peace as good neighbors.[91]

His view of 'force' is that a violation of the prohibition occurs on a "spectrum"[92] of intentional infliction of harm. Speaking specifically of economic measures that potentially violate the prohibition, he concludes that "Article 2(4) . . . does not include coercive political and economic sanctions that are intended to influence another state's policy or actions . . . In contrast, political or economic aggression is a use of force within the meaning of Article 2(4)."[93]

Wingfield subsequently applies this broad standard to a hypothetical cyberattack, in which "State B completely jams all electronic transmissions into, out of, and within State A."[94] He then discusses a series of effects caused by this "virtual blockade":[95] no communication is possible within State A, and medical care cannot be properly given; moreover,

88 See also the discussion of the work of Walter Sharp in the next chapter.

89 Wingfield, 'Information Conflict,' 88. It is interesting to note the language scholars use to point out these opposing views; see for example Silver, 'Computer Network Attack,' 82.

90 Wingfield, 'Information Conflict,' 88, second set of brackets in original. It should be noted that here, Wingfield refers to pages 361–362 of Ian Brownlie's book on the use of force. However, Brownlie himself asserts that "whilst it is correct to assume that [Article 2] paragraph 4 applies to force other than armed force, it is very doubtful if it applies to economic measures of a coercive nature." See Brownlie, 'Use of Force,' 362. This is also the part referred to by Wingfield, but he seems to draw opposite conclusions.

91 Wingfield, 'Information Conflict,' 89.

92 Ibid., 90.

93 Ibid.

94 Ibid., 91.

95 Ibid., 92.

> [n]o financial transaction can occur electronically within State A or between anyone in State A and someone in another state. The volume of imports and exports has dropped sharply 95% from the previous month ... Without a single shot being fired, State A has effectively been brought to its knees ... [this] is a use of force within the meaning of Article 2(4).[96]

Wingfield even concludes this example would constitute an armed attack.[97]

More variations on this are possible, however. Above, I stated that with a different starting point, one's diagnosis might also change. Likewise possible, however, is a completely different starting point with a similar outcome. Marco Roscini, who was already cited in the introduction of this chapter, also argues that a cyberattack on the New York Stock Exchange would be a use of force; but he also argues, much more firmly, that economic coercion is excluded from the scope of the prohibition. He does make allowance for the argument that other references in the Charter to armed force should not necessarily be taken to mean that 'force' in Article 2(4) should likewise be read as 'armed force.' Roscini and Wingfield read the ambition of the Charter very differently, however: whereas Roscini emphasizes the Preamble's reference to "sav[ing] succeeding generations from the scourge of war," and thus not extending to "all forms of coercion," Wingfield argues the Charter "is concerned with far more."[98] Moreover, Roscini *does* read the rejection of the Brazilian amendment as narrowing down the prohibition to armed force, contrary to Wingfield – ultimately arguing that the prohibition only pertains to armed force, to the exclusion of economic coercion.[99] Subsequently comparing cyberattacks to conventional weaponry, he argues that

> [i]t is true that the indirect effects of cyber attacks are often more important than the direct effects, but that could well apply to many kinetic attacks as well ... if the Stock Exchange or other financial institutions were to be bombed and the markets disrupted as a consequence, this would certainly be considered a use of armed force, and not economic coercion, even though

96 Ibid., 92. Notably, Wingfield discusses the 'New York Stock Exchange' example in the context of non-military physical force; that is as another example of the infliction of harm via non-military means; see ibid., 99–100, 114.

97 Ibid., 92. He ends by suggesting the approach taken by Michael Schmitt (at 120–127), adjusting it slightly – but given Wingfield's consideration of "political or economic aggression" (90) as force, whereas Schmitt rejects this extension outright, a difference between the two ideas has to be assumed.

98 Roscini, 'World Wide Warfare,' 105; Wingfield, 'Information Conflict,' 89.

99 In support of his conclusion he furthermore adds the 1970 *Friendly Relations Declaration* (General Assembly Resolution 2625), the 1987 Declaration on the Non-Use of Force (General Assembly Resolution 42/22), and several scholarly pieces. See Roscini, 'World Wide Warfare,' 105–106 and 106 note 96.

> the economic consequences of the action would by far outweigh the physical damage to the buildings: one cannot see why the same conclusion should not apply when the Stock Exchange, instead of being bombed, is shut down by a cyber attack.[100]

This is part of his discussion of indirect effects, in which he also says that "a series of unauthorized military incursions into the territory of another state that produce no material damage but have the indirect effect of destabilizing the country would still amount to a violation of Article 2 para. 4."[101] Given this outcome, it is ultimately unsurprising that Roscini concludes that "the provisions contained in the UN Charter and in customary international law ... seem to be flexible enough to be extended to warfare that did not exist when they were conceived."[102]

Similarly, Herbert Lin argues that "economic competition or sanctions, and economic and political coercion do not rise to the threshold of a use of force, regardless of the scale of their effects."[103] Yet, a little further on in his article, he posits a hypothetical in which

> [a] cyber attack temporarily disrupts Zendia's stock exchanges and makes trading impossible for a short period ... In this case, the cyber attack may be less likely to be regarded as a use of force than a kinetic attack with the same (temporary) economic effect, simply because the lack of physical destruction would reduce the scale of the damage caused. However, a cyber attack against the stock exchanges that occurs repeatedly and continually, so that trading is disrupted for an extended period of time, for days or weeks, would surely constitute a use of force or even an armed attack, even if no buildings were destroyed.[104]

Considering these arguments, one can almost hear Jason Barkham in the background pointing out the difficulties involved in such a broad notion of 'force.' He would probably state that if this is indeed the reasoning employed with regard to cyberattacks, it becomes very difficult, for legal purposes, to tell the difference between a cyberattack on the New York Stock Exchange and crippling economic sanctions.[105]

100 Ibid., 107–108.

101 Ibid., 107; see the body text below for an elaboration of his views. The issue of indirect (economic) effects is also addressed in Kondoch, 'Jus ad Bellum,' 468; Lin, 'Cyber Operations,' 68, 73; Waxman, 'Cyber-Attacks'; 445; Nguyen, 'Navigating,' section C.1., 1099 note 133; Silver, 'Computer Network Attack,' 87–88.

102 Roscini, 'World Wide Warfare,' 130, as already quoted in the introduction of this chapter.

103 Lin, 'Cyber Operations,' 72.

104 Ibid., 74.

105 These "inconsistencies" are acknowledged by Lin, see ibid., 80; see also Antolin-Jenkins, 'Defining the Parameters,' 134–135.

What this points at, is Roscini's as well as Lin's different delineation of the boundaries of force, where the emphasis doesn't lie so much on the effects caused by an attack but on its characteristics.[106] First, Roscini would probably argue that a cyberattack on the New York Stock Exchange is simply another example of a non-kinetic use of force – similar to the use of biological and chemical weapons. To make this point, Roscini refers to the inclusion of chemical and biological weapons as discussed above, as well as the *Nuclear Weapons* Opinion of the International Court of Justice.[107] Furthermore, he states that "[m]ilitary or other hostile use of environmental modification techniques have also been considered a weapon." Finally, he refers to the ICJ's *Nicaragua* Judgment, in which the Court stated that "the arming and training" of guerrillas in another state constitutes a use of force.[108] "There is then no reason," Roscini says, "why weapons should necessarily have explosive effects or be created for offensive purposes only."[109] His second argument is that "several states have included cyber technology in their military doctrines"; in other words, the 'frame' of cyberattacks is that they are part of warfare.[110] This is not the case for economic coercion, Roscini implies; thus, the first merits consideration under Article 2(4), the second does not. Moreover, according to Roscini *opinio juris* suggests that "cyber force is a type of armed force."[111] States have apparently decided that these kinds of cyberattacks can potentially qualify as force. So, however illogical[112] the distinction between non-physical cyberattacks (as force) and economic coercion may be to Jason Barkham, the level of harm inflicted simply is not the primary touchstone of Roscini's definition of force.[113]

In a 2014 book, Roscini offers some more clarification on why the 'stock exchange example' would qualify as force, and not as coercion:

> First, economic coercion does not have a specific target, while the cyber attack would be undertaken against an identifiable infrastructure. Secondly, while economic coercion, such as an oil embargo, employs the economy as

106 See also Lin, 'Cyber Operations,' 74.

107 *Nuclear Weapons* Opinion, para. 39, cited by Roscini, 'World Wide Warfare,' 106.

108 Roscini, 'World Wide Warfare,' 106 note 100.

109 Ibid., 106.

110 Ibid., 107. For this argument, Roscini relies on Brownlie (at 106), see the body text above. For a similar argument see Silver, 'Computer Network Attack,' 84; see, however, Chapter 2 note 25 of this book.

111 Roscini, 'World Wide Warfare,' 108, 106–108.

112 See the reference to Barkham in note 136 below, for the use of the word '(il)logical' in this context. See also Boer, 'Restating,' 10.

113 This also emerges from one of Roscini's points of critique on the framework of Michael Schmitt; see below.

> a *means* of pressure, in a cyber attack that incapacitates the financial market or cripples a state's banking system the economy is rather the *target*, while the means employed is malware.[114]

In other words, as long as the target is specific and the means employed are not economic, a cyberattack on a stock exchange can constitute a use of force. I will return to this notion of 'economic targets' in the discussion of the second junction.

The above does not mean, however, that Roscini is unaware of the difficulty of making the distinction between force and coercion. In one of his footnotes he refers to a model developed by Michael Schmitt, which aims to differentiate between "cyber attacks that do not directly cause physical damage or injury ... [and] other forms of coercion not amounting to the use of force."[115] Schmitt's model addresses precisely the problem defined by Jason Barkham: in case of non-physical cyberattacks, how to distinguish between force and coercion? Schmitt suggests the Charter's actual concern lies with the consequences of coercive acts, but that "it would prove extraordinarily difficult to quantify or qualify consequences in a normatively practical manner."[116] This is similar to the positions adopted by Aldrich and Wingfield, outlined above. However, it is also problematic, Schmitt says, because how do we measure severity? "Severity measured by what standard of calculation? Harm to whom or what?" he asks.[117] This also means he objects to the general harm-principle espoused by inter alia Aldrich and Wingfield as, he argues, "[i]t would constitute a new standard."[118] Instead, he argues that the Charter contains a "prescriptive short-hand" by focusing on the weapon used, rather than on the consequences caused.[119] This brings about the division between armed, economic and political coercion – the same division as used by others. The first category (armed coercion) is assumed to potentially cause the greatest level of harm; the second and third, less so – something Schmitt refers to as "consequence-instrument congruence."[120]

114 Roscini, 'Cyber Operations,' 62. He raises these two points with regard to the exact same example he mentions in the 2010 article.

115 Roscini, 'World Wide Warfare,' 108 note 104.

116 Schmitt, 'Normative Framework,' 911. Schmitt explicitly positions his work as a reinterpretation of the Charter, not as a proposal entailing new laws; see Chapter 5 of this book for a more elaborate treatment of this claim. See also d'Aspremont, 'Cyber Operations,' 579, section 3 and Boer, 'Echoes,' 15–16.

117 Schmitt, 'Normative Framework,' 911.

118 Ibid., 917.

119 Ibid., 911.

120 Ibid., 911, 915; see also Boer and Lodder, 'Cyberwar,' para. 11.4.

The problem with cyberattacks, he moves on to point out, is that they "span[...] the spectrum of consequentiality": unlike the weapons we already know, the consequences of cyberattacks range from mere inconvenience to severe harm. So, to facilitate the comparison between a concrete cyberattack, and what we 'know' to be force, Schmitt looks for that dividing line between force and (economic) coercion.[121] This dividing line, he suggests, is made up of seven "criteria": severity, immediacy, directness, invasiveness, measurability, the presumptive legitimacy of the attack and state responsibility.[122] Apply these to a concrete cyberattack, he says, and you will know whether the attack in question is a use of force, or whether it "resemble[s]" (economic) coercion. "By this scheme," Schmitt says, "one measures the consequences of a computer network attack against the commonalities to ascertain whether they more closely approximate consequences of the sort characterizing armed force or whether they are better placed outside the use of force boundary."[123]

In this way, Schmitt attempts to reinterpret the existing paradigm so as to facilitate the inclusion of cyberattacks. In that sense, it is a response to the problem defined by Barkham and Antolin-Jenkins, as well as to the harm standard espoused by Wingfield and Aldrich. The impact of his model for the cyberwar debate can hardly be overestimated: it is referred to by other scholars as the "Schmitt Analysis," and in the words of one of them, it is "one of the most academically rigorous and frequently cited frameworks for characterizing cyber operations."[124]

This does not mean, however, that it is not subject to criticism. Reese Nguyen, for example, argues that the criteria can be applied in fundamentally different ways for the same case: they "can be too easily manipulated to create

121 Ibid., 912 et seq. I explored this part of his work and its inclusion in the Manuals in greater depth in Boer, 'Restating,' 10 et seq.; briefly Boer, 'Echoes,' 15–16.

122 Schmitt, 'Normative Framework,' 914–915; Michael N. Schmitt, 'Cyber Operations and the *Jus Ad Bellum* Revisited' (2011) 56 *Villanova Law Review* 569, 575–577. This is also the framework included in the *Tallinn Manuals*, which added "military character"; it furthermore changed "state responsibility" to "state involvement" and "presumptive legitimacy" to "presumptive legality"; see Schmitt (ed.), 'Tallinn Manual,' 48–51; Schmitt (ed.), 'Tallinn Manual 2.0,' 334–336. Schmitt himself has clarified he was not involved in the drafting of this part of the Manual; see Chapter 5 note 49 and the accompanying body text of this book. For a 'mathematical application' of Schmitt's criteria, see James B. Michael, Thomas C. Wingfield and Duminda Wijesekera, 'Measured Responses to Cyber Attacks Using Schmitt Analysis: A Case Study of Attack Scenarios for a Software-Intensive System' (2013) *2013 IEEE 37th Annual Computer Software and Applications Conference* 621.

123 Schmitt, 'Normative Framework,' 916, 915.

124 Foltz, 'Stuxnet,' 41 (capitals for 'Schmitt Analysis' in original). It also has its own Wikipedia page; see Wikipedia, 'Schmitt Analysis.'

results supporting the geostrategic goals of the nation conducting the inquiry."[125] Similarly, Daniel Silver argues that

> examination of the criteria suggests that virtually any event of [computer network attack] can be argued to fall on the armed force side of the line, except perhaps as regards the criterion of severity, and ... the criterion of severity in effect is just another way of articulating the observation that, for an event of [computer network attack] to be considered a type of force under Article 2(4), it must produce (or at least threaten to produce) personal injury or property damage similar to that caused by military weapons.[126]

Michael Gervais, moreover, states that "extending [the] principles outside the regime of cyber weapons introduces measures of coercion not traditionally included in the prohibition on force, such as economic, diplomatic, or ideological coercion."[127] Gervais's critique is that the application of these factors only works for cyberattacks. Apply them to economically coercive measures, he says, and these might as well fall on the 'force' side of the line.

Schmitt himself would probably disagree. In his article, he elaborates on the distinction between the use of force and economic coercion. Force, Schmitt says,

> usually results in some form of physical destruction or injury, whereas economic ... coercion seldom does. Additionally, the risk of an escalating conflict from a use of force ordinarily exceeds the risk from economic or political coercion ... An even more basic problem is pinning down the cause and effect relationship when applying economic ... coercion ... intervening factors may enter the picture without which the consequences would not have occurred.[128]

This is basically the conceptual framework underlying his proposal for the seven factors, outlined above. What Schmitt is saying, is that force is qualitatively different from economic coercion. Gervais is not convinced, however, and the difference between their approaches can be clarified by resorting once again to the example of a cyberattack on the New York Stock Exchange. In another piece than the one just referred to, Schmitt cites a report that put forward the possibility of "a cyberattack against the stock exchanges that occurs repeatedly and continuously, so that trading is disrupted for an extended

[125] Nguyen, 'Navigating,' 1124.

[126] Silver, 'Computer Network Attack,' 89; see also Roscini, 'World Wide Warfare,' 108 note 104. For more elaborate criticism see Ziolkowski, 'Ius ad Bellum'; see also Boer, 'Restating,' 12 note 95; Boer, 'Echoes,' 15–16.

[127] Gervais, 'Cyber Attacks,' 540; see also Boer, 'Echoes,' 16 note 55.

[128] Schmitt, 'Normative Framework,' 911–912.

period of time." This, Schmitt says, "would likely qualify as [a use] of force."[129] Gervais disagrees. In his reading, this kind of cyberattack constitutes economic coercion and, he says, "[a]s previously mentioned, Article 2(4) did not categorize economic coercion as a prohibited use of force . . . In practice, economic coercion is an accepted tactic in international relations."[130]

With regard to Schmitt's model, Gervais has another idea altogether – and this brings us to the discussion of the second junction in legal argument. "An alternative approach," he says, "might be to scrap the Schmitt model altogether when the targets are economic, diplomatic, and ideological instruments of the state."[131] This is a new approach to the argumentative exclusion of economic coercion altogether. What Gervais suggest, is to place the boundary of force firmly with those attacks that target the economy, whatever the instrument used. It presents a different kind of argumentative turn – one that is concerned not so much with the substance of the norm, but with putting a full stop on substantively considering expansion of the prohibition. What it signifies, is a second junction in legal writing.

3.2.2 *Junction 2: The (Not So) "Novel features" of Cyberattacks*

Among the works here considered, a fundamentally different way of speaking of cyberattacks can be discerned. These scholars argue that there is nothing new about these kinds of cyberattacks;[132] that – at least where these kinds of "economic cyber-attacks" are concerned – this is business as usual.[133] This way of thinking facilitates a radical posture toward those cyberattacks that target the economy. Consider the following fragment from a chapter in Johann-Christoph Woltag's book on cyberwar:

> Most authors see a need to establish an approach which on the one hand encompasses those computer network operations which in their effects are comparable to conventional weapons while on the other hand preventing economic coercion from likewise being encompassed. This concern is explicitly voiced by the critics of the effects-based approach who fear lack of

129 Schmitt, 'Cyber Operations,' 604, quoting National Research Council, *Technology, Policy, Law, and Ethics Regarding U.S. Acquisition and Use of Cyberattack Capabilities*, William A. Owens, Kenneth W. Dam and Herbert S. Lin (eds.), The National Academies Press 2009, 255. It is unclear, however, how this use of force is different from economic coercion.

130 Gervais, 'Cyber Attacks,' 551.

131 Ibid., 540.

132 Cf. d'Aspremont, 'Cyber Operations,' 579, 581.

133 The phrase "economic cyber-attacks" is also used by Kilovaty, 'Rethinking,' 215; though I do not necessarily use it here as understood by him.

> distinction between economic and armed coercion. The history of the prohibition of Article 2(4) UN Charter does not necessitate this, however. Today it is generally settled and accepted that economic coercion is not to be considered as force, making concerns that the effects-based approach would lead to an expansion of the interpretation of the notion of force in order to include [cyberattacks] somewhat superfluous.[134]

What Woltag says here, is that 'this is what we already know.' It is completely contrary to the concerns expressed by Barkham and Antolin-Jenkins, cited above, who warned of 'definitional creep' and the 'grave potential for unintended and undesirable legal consequences' emanating from the inclusion of cyberattacks. Woltag then adds,

> [c]onfirming the applicability of a rule to a new circumstance through interpretation does not mean that disputes generally deemed to be settled automatically need to be reconsidered ... The particular use and effect of a [cyberattack] is decisive. If it is used to disrupt production in a factory, this might be done under the pretence of an economic coercion; but there is a difference between economic coercion on the market and an intrusive operation directly destroying a production line. While the goal might be the same, only the latter qualifies as a use of force, in that it has destructive effects, thereby shifting the key aspect away from economic and towards armed force.[135]

This fragment is crucial to Woltag's view of whether there is actually a problem in that 'grey area' between force and coercion. What he is saying here, is that even if new situations – such as cyber – present themselves, there is no reason to revisit already established standards, regardless of "logical"[136] problems. He ends this part of his discussion by arguing that the standard for violating Article 2(4) is the "destructive effect" caused by an attack, which would include destructive yet indirect effects – but then adds the caveat that "not every remote consequence needs to be taken into consideration."[137] Economic coercion, however, is excluded from the scope of the prohibition, period, and there is no need to reconsider that position.

This is a fundamentally different way of speaking about the relation between economic coercion, cyberattacks and force, compared to the

[134] Woltag, 'Cyber Warfare,' 153–154.

[135] Ibid., 154.

[136] Barkham uses this word specifically during his discussion of a categorical *inclusion* of *all* cyberattacks under the headings of 'force'; see Barkham, 'Information Warfare,' 84–85. For a logic similar to the one maintained by Woltag, see for example Schmitt (ed.), 'Tallinn Manual,' Rule 11. See also Boer, 'Echoes,' 16–17.

[137] Woltag, 'Cyber Warfare,' 154.

uncertain terms in which Antolin-Jenkins and Barkham express themselves. Similarly, Woltag steps away from the harm-principle espoused by Aldrich and Wingfield. Instead, he proposes a much narrower idea of what would constitute force: "[O]nce the [cyberattacks] are used to destroy economic targets," he writes, "one can no longer speak of economic coercion, as the key aspect shifts to the forceful destruction of property."[138] Thus, physical destruction constitutes the boundary between coercion and force. This also means that, similar to Gervais, Woltag doesn't consider an attack on a stock exchange to constitute force.[139] His final thoughts on the subject constitute a balancing act:

> Finally it must plainly be admitted that there is no crystal clear dogmatic framework available that would resolve the question of from which point on [computer network operations] are to be definitely qualified as armed force. This is however *not unique* to the new technology but has gone along with the interpretation of the prohibition of the use of force since its incorporation in Article 2(4) UN Charter.[140]

Like Woltag, Daniel Silver doesn't see how the 'economic' possibilities presented by cyberattacks are new ones. This is simply a new "form," Silver says, "another manifestation of . . . economic and political coercion."[141] He is firm in his refusal to even consider the inclusion of those cyberattacks that only have an effect in the "economic sphere," as he calls it.[142] He argues that

> [a computer network attack] that produces effects (even if direct and foreseeable) that are only of an economic or political nature is not likely to be held to be within the scope of Article 2(4). Thus a program of [computer network attack] that crippled the financial infrastructure of a target State would not be a use of force under Article 2(4). Even if angry investors rioted and tore down the stock exchange, that physical damage would not be direct and foreseeable.[143]

The "underlying principle" of force, Silver says, is that 'force' in Article 2(4) is any kind of force that "causes physical injury or property damage that is recognizably similar to that produced by instruments generally identified as weapons."[144] In other words, the effects one should take into account when

138 Ibid., 151, see also 154.
139 Ibid., in a different part of his chapter: 124.
140 Ibid., 154, emphasis added.
141 Silver, 'Computer Network Attack,' 82.
142 Ibid., 82.
143 Ibid., 85, parentheses omitted.
144 Ibid., 87, 91.

assessing a potential violation of the prohibition, are the physically destructive ones. Silver contrasts two hypothetical situations here, to clarify his point. Suppose, he says, that a state was to "cut a fiber-optic cable on which essential financial information is transmitted," thereby blocking trade in the target state. This, Silver says, would constitute force. The same economic effects, however, might be achieved by feeding false information into the market, which would also lead to severe disruption of trade. "These seem to be quintessential measures of economic coercion," Silver says, "and it is very unlikely that scholarly opinion would sustain the view that such acts constituted force under Article 2(4)."[145] Woltag and Gervais would probably agree.

This example clarifies that what distinguishes Silver's view from, for example, Wingfield's, is how one places the boundaries of force. In case of Silver, the relevant effects are the physically destructive ones; in case of Wingfield, the standard of harm is much broader. Again, this doesn't mean that Silver doesn't see the problem in distinguishing between cyberattacks as force, and cyberattacks as coercion: it means that he doesn't consider economic coercion – by whatever means – to be force. He ends his article by arguing – as does Woltag – that the infliction of "physical injury or property damage" violates Article 2(4) but adds – contrary to Woltag – that, at the very least, this has to be the "direct and foreseeable consequence of the [computer network attack]."[146] The rest is uncertain, Silver says – but I will return to that conclusion, below.

There is a different turn to take at this junction, however. Rather than argue that these cyberattacks that occur in-between force and coercion are not new, others emphasize their "novel features."[147] They escape the confines of either category, these scholars argue, and therefore require a thorough reconsideration either of the norm itself; of the way these attacks should be regulated; or even, of the desirability or possibility of regulating them by means of international law. All three turns will be discussed in the remainder of this chapter.

Novel Features: Reconsidering the Norm

First, in his 2015 article Ido Kilovaty specifically focuses on the possibilities of economic coercion brought about by cyberattacks. His starting point is to highlight the distinction between what he refers to as "economic force," versus economic coercion. The latter concept refers to a situation in which

145 Ibid., 88.
146 Ibid., 92.
147 Benatar, 'Cyber Force,' 391. This phrase is used in the header of this section.

"an economically superior state exerts its economic power over another state to affect certain political choices of the latter state."[148] Economic force is different, Kilovaty argues: it "is the effort of one actor to disrupt or harm the economic activities of a state, for the sole purpose of injury to that state."[149] In the era of cyberattacks, this distinction becomes pertinent once again, and in this context he refers to "economic cyber-attacks" which "can cause tremendous economic harm to victim states, and the perpetrators ... exercis[e] power for purposes of revenge, hatred, reprisal or just to escalate or support existing armed conflicts."[150] One of the examples he mentions is an attack on a state's stock exchange. Under the current use of force paradigm, this would probably not be considered force, Kilovaty says, due to the different means involved and, possibly, the particular context within which the attack takes place.[151]

Kilovaty argues that this needs to change. What we need to do, he says, is "distinguish between economic coercion, which is a form of permissible act in international relations, and economic force, which ought to be prohibited under international law."[152] So, like Michael Schmitt, Kilovaty comes up with a series of criteria to assess whether a particular 'economic cyberattack' violates the prohibition, which include the "effects magnitude" and the "[a]bsence of alternative explanation[s]" for the economically deleterious situation.[153]

Novel Features: New Forms of Regulation

The argument presented here by Kilovaty is based on the novelty of the threat: his emphasis on the 'tremendous economic harm' that can be caused by cyberattacks, and the fact that "cyber warfare adds a 'new slice' of effects to the continuum [of effects]"[154] highlights the necessity to come up with a new interpretation of the rule. The kinds of 'novel' cyberattacks referred to by Kilovaty are also invoked by Duncan Hollis – but very briefly.[155] I refer to it

148 Kilovaty, 'Rethinking,' 218.
149 Ibid.
150 Ibid., 214–215, 219.
151 Ibid., 226.
152 Ibid., 236.
153 Ibid., 237–242. The difference being that Schmitt explicitly situates his work in existing law; see pp. 84–85 above.
154 Ibid., 222.
155 Hollis uses Article 2(4) to demonstrate the "translation problems" involved in trying to apply existing law to cyberattacks; other examples include how to distinguish civilian(s) (objects), and the notion of perfidy, both based in the *jus in bello*. See Hollis, 'Why States Need,' 1039 et seq. As stated in the introduction of this chapter, all scholars whose work is used in this section

here because of what its juxtaposition with the other arguments outlined in this chapter reveals. His point is that the prohibition on the use of force cannot account for the whole range of possibilities presented by cyberattacks;[156] he approaches this problem in the following way.

First, and tellingly, Hollis doesn't refer to 'cyberattacks,' as this new phenomenon that requires regulation: instead, he refers to "information operations" (IO). He argues against a narrow definition of cyberattacks, which only focuses on their offensive uses. Instead, Hollis states, we need to look at the bigger picture: at the range of possibilities presented by IO. Referring to the definition maintained by the US Department of Defense, he understands IO to refer to those operations that aim "to influence, disrupt, corrupt, or usurp adversarial human and automated decision making while protecting [one's] own."[157] Such a definition includes, for example, "'psychological operations' . . . that convey information . . . with the aim of manipulating the views of foreign governments, organizations, or individuals."[158]

This broad understanding of what exactly requires regulation, also relates to the problem central to this chapter:

> Neither kinetic force nor political or economic sanctions can disable an entire stock market or banking system the way IO can – immediately and without casualties or physical destruction. Do we treat IO as outside the U.N. Charter whenever its effects differ from kinetic force? Or, do we include it under the prohibition where its effects have an immediacy not seen in economic or political coercion that may generate more civil disturbances or disruption?[159]

So, similar to Kilovaty, Hollis points out that these kinds of attacks simply do not allow for regulation under Article 2(4). The very novelty of information operations, including these kinds of economic cyberattacks, means "the existing system suffers from several, near-fatal conditions: uncertainty . . .

argue that, at least, cyberattacks that cause physical damage or destruction are prohibited under Article 2(4). Compared to the other works used here this is least explicit in the work of Hollis. Yet, as he discusses the different models that scholars have developed to facilitate the translation of the prohibition to cyberattacks (discussed in the previous chapter), he critiques them for being either over- or underinclusive. The notion of over- and underinclusion, in turn, suggests an idea of there being a core meaning to force, and given the examples he mentions this core consists of attacks that lead to death and destruction. Hence, the inclusion of his work here.

156 Ibid., 1040–1042.

157 Ibid., 1030, quoting from Joint Chiefs of Staff, U.S. Department of Defense, Joint Publication 3-13, *Information Operations*, ix (2006).

158 Ibid. Though not a dominant view during the heyday of the cyberwar debate, recent events may just prove Hollis right. See also Chapter 2 note 25.

159 Ibid., 1042, as also cited in the introduction of this chapter.

complexity . . . and insufficiency."[160] Rhetorically, he presents his reader with the same two options as Jason Barkham does in his piece: do we conceive of these kinds of attacks as force, or should they be understood as coercion?[161] "To redress these deficiencies," Hollis says, "I propose that states adopt a new set of rules – an international law for information operations, or 'ILIO.'"[162] He is not very specific as to what such a treaty, concretely, would look like: he does emphasize, however, that it would remedy the flaws of the existing legal paradigm.

Novel Features: Not Necessarily a Bad Thing

There is a third option, however, next to the arguments put forward by Kilovaty and Hollis. To some scholars, the uncertainty surrounding the legal analysis of cyberattacks is not necessarily a bad thing. Marco Benatar, for example, argues that cyber weapons are more precise and bring about less death and destruction than traditional weapons. He ends his article with a statement of legal uncertainty about the sufficiency of existing law to regulate cyberattacks. But, he says, there is an upside to this:

> The inability to definitively outlaw cyber force is not necessarily a reason for disillusionment. Maybe it is better as a matter of policy not to integrate cyber force in the *jus ad bellum*. Using computer warfare to achieve military aims has the advantage over conventional weapons of being highly efficient and less prone to cause any loss of life. Why then would we want computer operations to be subject to the highly stringent conditions for using force?[163]

In other words, if attacks can be very precisely targeted, and if the outcomes are less physically destructive, why regulate this possibility in the first place, under 'the highly stringent conditions for using force'? Yet, even to Benatar this seems to be going too far out on a ledge. Before the possibility of nonregulation has fully sunk in, Benatar reverts back to the limits imposed by existing law:

> [O]ne could argue that there is already sufficient law to regulate interstate cyber conflict. After all, as mentioned in the pages above, even if a cyber attack does not amount to a use of force, it is still an intervention, which constitutes a violation of international law.[164]

160 Ibid., 1029, emphases omitted; see ibid., 1039–1046 for the "translation problems" involved in existing law, and 1046–1053 for its "insufficiency" and "complexity."

161 He similarly talks of the problems of over- and underinclusion, referred to by Barkham. See ibid., 1041–1042, 1053; see also note 155 above, for his idea of the 'core meaning' of force.

162 Ibid., 1029.

163 Benatar, 'Cyber Force,' 395.

164 Ibid.

He proceeds to outline other legal remedies that could be developed against the threat posed by "cyber force."[165] However, the very last line of his article issues a warning, which after all seems to express skepticism as to the mitigating function of international law: "[T]he cyber wars of tomorrow," he says, "will not be put on hold as a result of their ambiguous legality."[166] This final argument is reminiscent of the positions outlined in the previous chapter. Not only does Benatar fundamentally question the ability of international law to regulate cyberattacks; his conclusion also highlights that the absence of law may encourage states to do *more* in cyberspace, not less.[167]

Daniel Silver likewise questions the evils of legal uncertainty. He initially concludes his article by stating that it is uncertain how Article 2(4) will apply, exactly, and that "[t]his conclusion appears highly unsatisfactory, leaving the law in a state of uncertainty."[168] Yet, this is followed by the somewhat rhetorical question, "but does it really matter that much?"[169] After all, other laws might fill the gaps left by Article 2(4), Silver posits, and states might be more concerned with their right to self-defense than with possible violations of the prohibition. Furthermore, chances of a cyberattack occurring as a single event rather than as part of a larger military operation are slim, and in that case, current debates will turn out to have been moot. Finally, he says, "worrying about the status of [cyberattacks] under Article 2(4) may be fiddling while Rome burns."[170] The Charter system has been decaying for a while now, Silver argues, and thus it might just be "that over time a set of understandings as to the lawfulness of [computer network attacks] will evolve outside the Charter framework."[171] He does not seem too satisfied with this conclusion himself, however: the very last few lines of his article contain a proposal for treaty regulation, and for "global legal cooperation in fighting [computer network attacks] perpetrated by non-State actors, by making such action criminal under domestic laws."[172] This is legal problem-solution in action: the faith that legal solutions will be found (and are necessary) to remedy deficiencies in the existing legal fabric. In that sense, the argument presented by Daniel Silver

[165] He uses this phrase in the title of his article, as well as on, inter alia, 395.
[166] Benatar, 'Cyber Force,' 396.
[167] Benatar's article was also mentioned at the end of Chapter 2; his conclusion contains both the point elaborated on there and the argument outlined in this particular section. On the absence of law see Chapter 2 note 50.
[168] Silver, 'Computer Network Attack,' 93.
[169] Ibid.
[170] Ibid., 93.
[171] Ibid., 94.
[172] Ibid., 93–94.

on these last few pages of his article seems to be more of a thought experiment than an outright acceptance of legal uncertainty.

In sum, the above shows that to point out the novelty or normalcy of cyberattacks sets the writer on a trajectory toward a conclusion about the (in)sufficiency of existing law. The dynamic is similar to the one demonstrated earlier in this chapter: these lines are drawn in the course of an argument, and bring about a particular conclusion as to the (in)sufficiency of the norm. With regard to the first turn identified here, the question asked by those scholars is what kind of boundaries Article 2(4) calls for, in relation to, for example, the Charter Preamble or other references to force it contains. The contingency of these turns was demonstrated by juxtaposing them with the alternatives; different routes taken by other scholars in other pieces of academic work. Secondly, the classification of the threat matters to the sense of urgency a scholar displays with respect to legal change: to some scholars, cyberattacks present a previously unknown threat; one that escapes the set boundaries of Article 2(4). To others, any changes to the law are unnecessary.

The question as to what to include and exclude from the scope of the prohibition on the use of force, is raised as a result of one of the characteristics of cyberattacks: their wide range of effects. These kinds of cyberattacks escape easy grasp as they challenge pre-constructed notions of what force is, and what it is not. The aim of this chapter was to show through close description how legal knowledge at the edges of Article 2(4) is constructed in relation to those cyberattacks these writers situate in-between economic coercion and the use of force. The attempt here was to make these scholars 'talk' to each other and in so doing, show how the sequence of turns made in legal reasoning bring about solutions to the problem presented by cyberwar. This shows what precedes the argument for more, new, different or the same laws, and how specific argumentative turns result in these legal outcomes. This is the first close-up of legal knowledge construction in the cyberwar discourse.

The themes discussed in this chapter are also reflected in the next two chapters. In Chapter 5, 'giving answers' to legal problems takes center stage. It resonates with the attitude described as the undercurrent of this chapter, as it examines the self-positioning of Michael Schmitt as the one doing precisely this, in the cyberwar discourse. The next chapter, however, is still – at least partially – concerned with the substance of legal reasoning; the 'what' of the construction of legal knowledge. The first part of this chapter already mentioned how scholars set the parameters of force. Taking a step closer to the text we see that these interpretive claims are accompanied by claims that this interpretation is shared by the majority of scholars. Chapter 4 refers to these claims as 'consensus claims' and in its first half, examines their function in an individual scholarly argument. Halfway through the chapter, focus shifts to the footnotes following these claims. In the Appendix accompanying this chapter it is shown how most of the time scholars refer to the same people in order to substantiate their consensus claim. In other words, it shows that it seems to matter who we cite to support these consensus claims; that we do not cite randomly.[173] The second half of the chapter inquires into why this happens, and what the function is of these particular footnotes. In this way the fourth chapter shifts the focus in this book from the 'what' to the 'who' of legal knowledge construction; this is then further pursued in Chapter 5.

173 Nigel Gilbert, 'Referencing as Persuasion' (1977) 7 *Social Studies of Science* 113.

4

"The Greater Part of Jurisconsults"*

In the summer of 1920, the President of the Committee of Jurists charged with drafting the Statute of the Permanent Court of International Justice, took the floor at one of the Committee's sessions. After extensively dealing with the composition of the Court, the Jurists had arrived at a discussion of the law to be applied by it. The President, Baron Descamps, argued largely in line with proposals made by states with regard to the sources the Court could use to come to its judgment.[1] However, a few minutes into his speech Descamps made an additional suggestion. A mere reliance on treaties, custom and jurisprudence, he argued, "leaves the judge in a state of compulsory blindness," even though "a perfectly just solution is possible" in cases lacking either three of these sources, or where their contents proved to be insufficiently clear. A judge should have the possibility to resort to "objective justice," Descamps said, "allow[ing] him to consider the cases that come before him with both

* This chapter was previously published as Lianne J. M. Boer (2016) '"The Greater Part of Jurisconsults": On Consensus Claims and Their Footnotes in Legal Scholarship,' *Leiden Journal of International Law*, 29(4), 1021–1042 © Foundation of the Leiden Journal of International Law 2016, published by Cambridge University Press. Reproduced with permission. Though large parts of the text remain unchanged, the chapter presents a somewhat edited version of the article.

[1] None of the state proposals included a reference to the use of scholarly work by the Court; see The Secretariat of the Advisory Committee of Jurists, 'Advisory Committee of Jurists, Documents presented to the Committee relating to existing plans for the establishment of a Permanent Court of International Justice,' 103, point 28(a). The proposals to which this point refers (such as the Scandinavian and German ones) can be found elsewhere in the same document; see its Table of Contents on page iii. For a more extensive treatment of the Jurists' discussion of Article 38(1)(d), and a similar account of this part of their deliberations see Peil, 'Scholarly Writings,' 138–140; on the drafting process see Spiermann, 'Who Attempts Too Much,' on sources specifically section V. At the time of writing, Luíza Leão Soares Pereira is finishing her PhD dissertation at Cambridge University on this topic; see Leão Soares Pereira, 'International Lawyers as Lawmakers.'

eyes open." Elaborating on his proposal, he specified that this 'objective justice' consisted of both "the legal conscience of civilised nations" and "the concurrent teaching of the authors whose opinions have authority." After all, Descamps said,

> when the greater part of jurisconsults agree upon a certain rule – the presumption in favour of that rule becomes so strong, that only a person who makes a mock of justice would gainsay it.[2]

Baron Descamps's invocation of the views of 'the greater part of jurisconsults' can, in fact, still be found in scholarly writing. These kinds of appeals come in different shapes and sizes: scholars refer to a "majority view," they reference a "generally accepted" interpretation of the norm, or they state how their interpretation is "consistent with mainstream thought." Others talk of how "the jurists seem unanimous" or of what the "prevailing view" holds with regard to Article 2(4).[3]

This chapter examines these kinds of 'consensus claims,' as I call them, as they are made in the discourse on cyberattacks and Article 2(4) of the UN Charter.[4] Consensus has been studied in different contexts: for instance, as

[2] All quotes from this paragraph are taken from the Permanent Court of International Justice, 'Procès-Verbaux of the Proceedings of the Committee,' Annex No. I to the 14th Meeting on July 2, 1920, 323. On Article 38 more generally, see for example, Alain Pellet and Daniel Müller, 'Article 38,' in: *The Statute of the International Court of Justice: A Commentary*, Andreas Zimmermann et al. (eds.), Oxford University Press 2019 (3), 819–962; they point out that the inclusion of scholarly work was originally proposed by Root and Phillimore (para. 337).

[3] Benatar, 'Cyber Force,' 385 ("majority view"); Buchan, 'Cyber Attacks,' 212, 216, and Stephen Moore, 'Cyber Attacks and the Beginnings of an International Cyber Treaty' (2013) 39 *North Carolina Journal of International Law & Commercial Regulation* 223, 236 and Paul Ducheine et al., 'Towards a Legal Framework for Military Cyber Operations,' in: *Cyber Warfare: Critical Perspectives*, Paul Ducheine, Frans Osinga and Joseph Soeters (eds.), T.M.C. Asser Press 2012, 101–128, 116 ("generally accepted"); Stephen J. Cox, 'Confronting Threats through Unconventional Means: Offensive Information Warfare as a Covert Alternative to Preemptive War' (2005) 42 *Houston Law Review* 881, 899 ("consistent with mainstream thought"); James N. Bond, 'Peacetime Foreign Data Manipulation as One Aspect of Offensive Information Warfare: Questions of Legality under the United Nations Charter Article 2(4)' (MA, Naval War College 1996), 78 ("unanimous"); Antolin-Jenkins, 'Defining the Parameters,' 152; Aldrich, 'Information Age,' 238; Georg Kerschischnig, *Cyberthreats and International Law*, eleven international publishing 2012, 110; Sheng Li, 'When Does Internet Denial Trigger the Right of Armed Self-Defense?' (2013) 38 *Yale Journal of International Law* 179, 184; Sharp, 'CyberSpace,' 88 and Woltag, 'Cyber Warfare,' 136 ("prevailing view").

[4] Rhetoric distinguishes between "appeals to common knowledge" and "ad populum arguments"; see David M. Godden, 'On Common Knowledge and *Ad Populum*: Acceptance as Grounds for Acceptability' (2008) 41 *Philosophy & Rhetoric* 101. On the distinction as well as on the difference with the question asked here see also notes 15 and 40 below.

a decision-making tool in the UN;[5] how it may bring about international law;[6] and how it is pursued by the US Supreme Court.[7] "Consensusing" has also been examined as a societal practice,[8] and the function of public consensus in judicial decision-making has similarly been scrutinized.[9] This chapter, however, studies *claims* to consensus: how they function in a scholarly argument and how they are substantiated.[10] Specifically, it considers claims that there is a consensus that 'force,' in the UN Charter, means *armed* force, rather than that it constitutes an all-encompassing prohibition on both military and economic or political coercion.

These consensus claims appear alongside the other "knowledge claims"[11] made in this debate, some of which were mentioned in the previous chapter. Next to, for example, scholarly references to the rejection of the Brazilian amendment to the original UN Charter text and interpretations of the *Friendly Relations Declaration* – as discussed in Chapter 3 – these texts contain appeals to consensus, majority opinion, general acceptance, unanimity, etc. Though

5 Arnold N. Pronto, 'Some Thoughts on the Making of International Law – Review of Boyle, Alan and Chinkin, Christine. The Making of International Law. New York: Oxford University Press, 2007. Pp. 288. $95. ISBN: 9780199248193' (2008) 19 *European Journal of International Law* 601; Giuseppe Sperduti, 'Consensus in International Law' (1976) 2 *Italian Yearbook of International Law* 33.

6 Anthony d'Amato, 'On Consensus' (1970) 8 *Canadian Yearbook of International Law* 104.

7 Richard S. Markovits, 'Learning from the Foreigners: A Response to Justice Scalia's and Professor Levinson's Professional Moral Parochialism' (2003) 39 *Texas International Law Journal* 367; Youngjae Lee, 'International Consensus as Persuasive Authority in the Eighth Amendment' (2007) 156 *University of Pennsylvania Law Review* 63.

8 Maja Horst and Alan Irwin, 'Nations at Ease with Radical Knowledge: On Consensus, Consensusing and False Consensusness' (2010) 40 *Social Studies of Science* 105.

9 Shklar, 'Legalism' (1964), 12–13. Some further examples include Katharine G. Young, 'The Minimum Core of Economic and Social Rights: A Concept in Search of Content' (2008) 33 *Yale Journal of International Law* 113; Eyal Benvenisti, 'Margin of Appreciation, Consensus, and Universal Standards' (1999) 31 *New York University Journal of International Law and Politics* 843; Weal B. Hallaq, 'On the Authoritativeness of Sunni Consensus' (1986) 18 *International Journal of Middle East Studies* 427; Kristin Henrard and Elaine Mak, 'The Use of Consensus Arguments in Transnational Judicial Decision-Making: Confirming or Jeopardising Universal Human Rights,' June 2014, at SSRN.

10 Cf. Koskenniemi, 'Apology to Utopia,' 532 et seq., 596–599. For discussions of consensus *arguments* in law and legal writing see, for example, Olivier Corten, 'Formalization and Deformalization as Narratives of the Law of War,' in: *New Approaches to International Law: The European and the American Experiences*, José María Beneyto and David Kennedy (eds.), T.M.C. Asser Press 2013, 251–272, 253–255 (very briefly); Chiara Degano, 'Dissociation and Presupposition in Discourse: A Corpus Study' (2007) 21 *Argumentation* 361; Ahmed Sahlane, 'Argumentation and Fallacy in the Justification of the 2003 War on Iraq' (2012) 26 *Argumentation* 459; Douglas Walton and Fabrizio Macagno, 'Common Knowledge in Legal Reasoning about Evidence' (2005) 3 *International Commentary on Evidence* 1.

11 Hyland, 'Disciplinary Discourses,' 8; see also Chapter 1 of this book.

scholars may use different words, the function in an argument of words such as 'majority' and 'unanimity' is the same:[12] they make the reader think of interpretations as fixed,[13] regardless of how the author in question subsequently relates to this interpretation (for example, in a neutral or opposing fashion). In other words, these kinds of claims construct legal knowledge as much as, for example, an appeal to the meaning of the Preamble of the UN Charter does. Consensus claims are very much part of scholars' (re)construction of the norm and as such, they have a part to play in what we know the law to be in this particular debate.[14]

This chapter consists of two parts. In the first half I consider the use and function of consensus claims in a scholar's argument and what is invoked, exactly, when consensus is appealed to.[15] Specifically, I discuss how consensus claims (temporarily) fix the meaning of force, and how they have a seemingly empirical character – as if the scholar making the claim has made his or her own inquiry into the majority opinion of scholars. However, I will proceed to argue that the strength of a consensus claim lies precisely in its elusive character: consensus seems to evaporate the moment we attempt to substantiate it. This brings to the fore the question of the 'origins' of consensus: Section 4.3 shows that these claims on the boundaries of 'force' were made fairly soon after the creation of the prohibition. Furthermore, this section shows how consensus is the outcome of its repeated invocation – referred to here as meta-consensus – as well as of the combined *interpretive* claims of the scholars whose work is considered for this chapter.

The second half of the chapter changes focus to the seemingly "mundane"[16] practice of footnoting. Of twenty-six consensus claims made in the cyberwar

[12] Though 'majority' and 'general agreement' indicate different group sizes, I argue in this chapter that the difference is irrelevant to the function of the claim in a scholar's argument. Cf. Douglas Walton, *Appeal to Popular Opinion*, Pennsylvania State University Press 1999, 27, referred to by Emma van der Deijl, '*Argumentum ad Populum*: Classificatie, Beoordeling en Presentatie van de Populistische Variant' (MA, Leiden University 2017), 14. For the use of specific verbs that can similarly indicate consensus, see Thomas and Hawes, 'Reporting Verbs,' 144–146.

[13] Kessler and Werner similarly refer to the "fixation of meaning"; see Kessler and Werner, 'Expertise,' 794 note 4; for a similar dynamic with regard to expert opinions, see ibid. 805–806.

[14] On interpretations as reconstructions, see note 130 in Chapter 1 of this book.

[15] I avoid the term ad populum here so as not to suggest consensus claims are fallacious arguments, because this is not the question this chapter is concerned with. Instead, this chapter deals with another question: what these kinds of arguments 'do' in an individual paragraph. So I refer to argumentative theory and rhetoric only on occasion as a way of speaking about consensus, keeping in mind that the question asked here is a different one. See also note 4 above and note 40 below.

[16] Johns, 'Unruly Law,' 23.

debate, the references in the accompanying footnote have been noted down.[17] For example, the phrase "the *prevailing and commonly accepted view* put forward by scholars is that the force referred to in Article 2(4) is limited to armed force," is followed by a footnote, in which the claim that this is, indeed, 'the prevailing and commonly accepted view,' is substantiated.[18] In the (online) Appendix of this chapter this 'primary reference' has been 'track-backed,' in order to find out to which sources this footnote, itself, refers (the 'secondary references'). This process has then been repeated once over ('tertiary references').[19]

What the Appendix shows is that the footnotes following these claims most of the time consist of references to largely the same, limited set of scholars. Simply put, in order to support their consensus claim, scholars largely refer to the same authors. In other words, it seems like here, we don't cite randomly.[20] In order to explain how this works and what it signifies, I draw on a combination of applied linguistics, sociology of science and information science.[21] What this allows for, as explained by Howard White, is an

17 The works used are Antolin-Jenkins, 'Defining the Parameters'; Aldrich, 'Information Age'; Barkham, 'Information Warfare'; Benatar, 'Cyber Force'; Bond, 'Foreign Data Manipulation'; Buchan, 'Cyber Attacks'; Cox, 'Confronting Threats'; Ducheine et al., 'Legal Framework'; Handler, 'New Cyber Face'; Harrison Dinniss, 'Cyber Warfare'; Hathaway et al., 'Law of Cyber-Attack'; Kerschischnig, 'Cyberthreats'; Li, 'Internet Denial'; Moore, 'Cyber Treaty'; Todd A. Morth, 'Considering Our Position: Viewing Information Warfare as a Use of Force Prohibited by Article 2(4) of the UN Charter' (1998) 30 *Case Western Reserve Journal of International Law* 567; Titiriga Remus, 'Cyber-Attacks and International Law of Armed Conflicts: A "Jus Ad Bellum" Perspective' (2013) 8 *Journal of International Commercial Law and Technology* 179; Schmitt, 'Normative Framework'; Sharp, 'CyberSpace'; Silver, 'Computer Network Attack'; Matthew J. Sklerov, 'Solving the Dilemma of State Responses to Cyberattacks: A Justification for the Use of Active Defenses against States Who Neglect Their Duty to Prevent' (2009) 201 *Military Law Review* 1; Tsagourias, 'Tallinn Manual Commentary'; Waxman, 'Cyber-Attacks'; and Woltag, 'Cyber Warfare.' In three cases, two consensus claims were taken from the same piece: Buchan, 'Cyber Attacks,' 212, 216; Harrison Dinniss, 'Cyber Warfare,' 41, 43; and Kerschischnig, 'Cyberthreats,' 106, 110. See also Chapter 1 note 129.

18 Harrison Dinniss, 'Cyber Warfare,' 41, emphasis added.

19 As also done by Urška Šadl in her 'trackbacking' of an ECJ decision. See Šadl, 'Case-Law'; on the ICJ's references to itself see Alschner and Charlotin, 'Growing Complexity.' The Appendix of this chapter can be found online as supplementary material to the article published with the *Leiden Journal of International Law*; see p. 97 above.

20 See Gilbert, 'Referencing,' and the second half of this chapter. On the history of the role and function of "bibliographic citations," see Raymond G. McInnis and Dal Symes, 'David Riesman and the Concept of Bibliographic Citation' (1988) 49 *College & Research Libraries* 387 and Anthony Grafton, *The Footnote: A Curious History*, Harvard University Press 1997.

21 Howard D. White, 'Citation Analysis and Discourse Analysis Revisited' (2004) 25 *Applied Linguistics* 89, 89–90. On analyzing discourse by using "mixed methods" see Markus Rheindorf, *Revisiting the Toolbox of Discourse Studies: New Trajectories in Methodology, Open Data, and Visualization*, Palgrave Macmillan 2019, specifically section 1.1.

understanding of the "rhetorical choices" involved in preferring one author over another when citing, the link between the knowledge claim and the reference given in support of it, and the effect of repeated invocation of the same reference for the same claim.[22] I first elaborate on the function and effect of the footnotes supporting consensus claims, and what the effect is of the repeated use of the same authors. Specifically, I use Henry Small's idea of "concept symbols" to point out how, through sheer repetition, the publicists that scholars refer to in order to support their consensus claim turn into the bearers – or 'concept symbols' – of majority opinion.[23] Though in an individual piece of writing one single reference can appear to be quite harmless, when considered as a more widespread practice of self-referentiality[24] it seriously impacts who gets a say in this discourse. By means of footnotes, what we know to be law is solidified and the authority to speak is distributed.[25] Put differently, the individual scholar's in- or exclusion of particular voices has an impact on what we 'know' to be law[26] – and this chapter shows how that happens.

This chapter thus presents a tipping point in the focus of this book: halfway through it redirects attention from the 'what' to the 'who' of legal knowledge construction in the cyberwar discourse. The first half of the chapter takes a closer look at what consensus claims signify in legal argument, and thereby scrutinizes what scholars say exactly as they attempt to give meaning to the prohibition on the use of force. The second half of the chapter looks at how these claims are supported, and in so doing concludes on who is allowed to do the saying in this discourse; who is given a voice in assessing 'what the law is.' This focus on having the authority to speak, is then continued in Chapter 5.

A note on the scholarly works used for this chapter is in order. They have all been screened for the use of consensus claims on the meaning of the word 'force'; a more extensive discussion of the approach taken toward these claims can be found on the cover page of the online Appendix of this chapter. The number of claims 'trackbacked' was limited by practical considerations: given

22 White, 'Citation Analysis,' 89–90.

23 Small, 'Concept Symbols,' specifically 329 (where he explains his use of the words "concept" and "symbol"); on repetition see inter alia 329 et seq. and the body text of this chapter, below.

24 This term is also used by Šadl, 'Case-Law,' 208 and by Skouteris, 'New Tribunalism,' 334 (where he writes how "[t]he self-referential nature of … discourse forges and solidifies the impression of the existence of a common professional knowledge").

25 Hyland, 'Disciplinary Discourses,' 20–21 and chapter 2 of his book; Gilbert, 'Referencing,' 117; see also the last part of this chapter and its references to Hyland's work.

26 Ken Hyland refers to "knowledge and knowing as social institutions … something collectively created through the interactions of individuals." Hyland, 'Disciplinary Discourses,' 7, see also 8 et seq.

the extensive nature of the trackback table, it was only possible to examine a limited number of claims. Moreover, the extent to which the pieces used here deal with Article 2(4) varies greatly. Some deal only with Article 2(4) and cyber and extensively go into its history, General Assembly Resolutions on the subject, and the meaning given to the prohibition by the International Court of Justice. In other works, Article 2(4) is mentioned only sideways, as part of a discussion of, for example, countermeasures or Article 51 of the UN Charter. However, I have understood all consensus claims on Article 2(4) as part of its construction – however minor its part may be in a scholar's overall argument.[27]

4.1 "WRITERS HAVE GENERALLY CONCLUDED"

In the first chapter of her book titled *Cyber Warfare and the Laws of War*, Heather Harrison Dinniss describes how "[t]he world in which we live and fight"[28] has changed over the last few decades. The possibilities presented by cyberattacks, Harrison Dinniss says, require a scholar "to examine the current legal regulation of armed conflict and consider how it can be applied to computer network attacks," as well as "to return to the underlying principles for those laws."[29] Thus, as part of her inquiry Harrison Dinniss sets out to find out how, given the threat of cyberattacks, we should assess a violation of Article 2(4) of the UN Charter.[30] It brings her to reconstruct the meaning of 'force,' and as discussed in Chapter 3 of this book, as part of this reconstruction she reaches back into the interpretive history of the prohibition:

> The *travaux préparatoires* of Article 2(4) detail a proposal by the foreign minister of Brazil to specifically extend the prohibition to the threat or use of "economic measures" which was firmly rejected.

Following this reference to the drafting of the UN Charter, Harrison Dinniss proceeds by outlining two positions with regard to what the rejection of this Brazilian amendment means for the interpretation of Article 2(4):

> Although Randelzhofer has cited this as evidence that military force is the only intended concern of the prohibition, David Harris states that it is unclear from the texts whether the rejection of the Brazilian amendment is proof that

27 See also notes 128–129 below and the accompanying body text, on consensus claims that remain unsubstantiated.

28 Harrison Dinniss, 'Cyber Warfare,' 1. This is the title of her first chapter.

29 Ibid., 8.

30 See Chapter 3 of this book; though Harrison Dinniss's work is not part of the analysis presented there. For a discussion of her work as it relates to Article 2(4) and cyberattacks see Boer, 'Echoes.'

> the Article was not intended to prohibit economic force, or that the term force in Article 2(4) was thought sufficient to cover it without specific mention. The latter view appears to stem from the Belgian delegate's comments regarding Brazil's proposed amendment and the phrase "or any other manner".

Concluding on these different views, she writes that "[d]espite this, writers have *generally concluded* that the better view is that Western states were not prepared to admit anything other than armed force."[31]

Opposing the view of Randelzhofer to that of David Harris, Harrison Dinniss thus concludes that we should read the *travaux* as limiting the prohibition on the use of force to 'armed' force, and at the end of her chapter we have been presented with a comprehensive argument for a particular interpretation of force. But something more is happening here. What remains unexplained, is how she has come to find Randelzhofer's view to be the 'general conclusion of writers.'

As a start, it is worth inquiring into the role played by these claims on the level of the individual paragraph of which they are part. Consider another example, taken from a piece by Oona Hathaway et al. They argue that

> [t]he precise scope of the international prohibition on the threat or use of force has been the *subject of intense international and scholarly debate*. Weaker states and some scholars have argued that Article 2(4) broadly prohibits not only the use of armed force, but also political and economic coercion. Nonetheless, *the consensus* is that Article 2(4) prohibits only armed force.[32]

This paragraph is fairly similar to the one from Harrison Dinniss's piece. It starts with an assessment of 'intense international and scholarly debate' – in other words, there is uncertainty about what the prohibition means exactly. Hathaway et al. proceed by stating the position held by 'weaker states and some scholars,' which entails a broader interpretation of force.[33] Despite the existence of these other views they nevertheless identify a 'consensus' on force as meaning armed force. As in Harrison Dinniss's chapter, the function of the consensus claim is to present a sense of certainty on what 'force' *is*. One question that could be asked following their statement is how much room actual consensus really leaves for *other* views, put forward by 'weaker states and some scholars'; but that is not the main point here. What the consensus claim

[31] These three quotes are all taken from Harrison Dinniss, 'Cyber Warfare,' 43, emphasis added for "generally concluded."

[32] Hathaway et al., 'Law of Cyber-Attack,' 842, emphases added.

[33] On the different views held by "weaker states" and the more powerful ones, see Waxman, 'Cyber-Attacks,' 449–450; see also my comment in Chapter 3 note 89.

does here is present a point from which to position or move on to the rest of the interpretive effort: it is "an unambiguous point of departure"; part of the "material starting points regarding the premises of the discussion."[34] In short, a consensus claim offers a point from which the argument can move forward.[35]

A similar argumentative move from the ascertainment of debate and/or the sketching of opposing views, to a statement about consensus is found in other pieces as well (though the sequence of these moves can differ).[36] Though these authors might, to a larger or lesser extent, provide an analysis of why this interpretation is the right one, the appeal to majority opinion – its particular function, and why it is invoked in the first place – remains somewhat mystifying. The point is not that the consensus claim is the only support given for the interpretation in question – though something really close to this happens occasionally.[37] For example, Todd Morth points out that the majority view is based on, in his words "historical context and state practice."[38] This could be critiqued for verging on an *ad populum* argument, in which the only support given for a particular claim is that it is accepted by the majority of a particular group.[39] However, my point is not that because appeals to general acceptance can never be persuasive evidence for the knowledge claim in question, the invocation of consensus is fallacious.[40] Scholars can be very elaborate in

34 Frans H. van Eemeren, *Strategic Maneuvering in Argumentative Discourse: Extending the Pragma-Dialectical Theory of Argumentation*, John Benjamins 2010, 44; see also Van der Deijl, 'Argumentum ad Populum,' 15–16.

35 As illustration, see Tsagourias's consensus claim in his discussion of the *Tallinn Manual*'s treatment of force in Tsagourias, 'Tallinn Manual Commentary,' 22.

36 See the pieces by Moore, 'Cyber Treaty'; Antolin-Jenkins, 'Defining the Parameters' (who adds some more disclaimers to her interpretation at 152–155); Benatar, 'Cyber Force' (who claims a "majority view" and a *contra* opinion in the footnote); Kerschischnig, 'Cyberthreats' (at 110); Silver, 'Computer Network Attack' (with immediate application to cyberattacks); Barkham, 'Information Warfare'; Woltag, 'Cyber Warfare'; Harrison Dinniss, 'Cyber Warfare' (at a different point in her chapter than the one cited earlier); and Ducheine et al., 'Legal Framework,' 116.

37 Remus, 'Cyber-Attacks'; Li, 'Internet Denial'; Sklerov, 'Solving the Dilemma.' On the lack of support provided for "the basic premises of an argument" see Godden, 'On Common Knowledge,' 101.

38 Morth, 'Considering Our Position,' 593. He elaborates somewhat on this position, but only slightly.

39 Godden, 'On Common Knowledge,' 104–105.

40 This is presuming (1) that these are ad populum arguments (which are considered fallacious) rather than appeals to "common knowledge" (which, contrarily, "can serve as grounds for the acceptability of [a] claim, at least in a prima facie manner"; see ibid., 104) and (2) that the distinction is clear and can be made in the first place. On this issue see Van der Deijl, 'Argumentum ad Populum'; Godden, 'On Common Knowledge'; and Walton and Macagno, 'Common Knowledge.' See also notes 4 and 15 above.

piecing together the evidence to argue that force is, indeed, supposed to be read as armed force – but that too is beside the point. Rather, I seek to emphasize that consensus claims are very much part of this interpretation, with a specific function in the argument. In other words, the question here is what kind of "work"[41] these different arguments are doing. Consider this paragraph taken from Russell Buchan's piece on the subject, worth quoting in full:

> In light of these [previous] observations, it is therefore apparent that there is textual support within the Charter to support an interpretation of Article 2(4) that includes political and economic force on the one hand and an interpretation that is restricted to armed force on the other. Article 32 [of the *Vienna Convention on the Law of Treaties*] provides that if after the application of Article 31 the meaning of the term or provision is still ambiguous recourse can be had to the preparatory materials of the treaty. This is significant in the context of Article 2(4) because the preparatory materials reveal that the Brazilian delegation proposed that Article 2(4) expressly prohibit "the threat or use of force and the threat or use of economic measures in any manner inconsistent with the purposes of the Organization". As is well known, this proposal was vetoed by the drafting committee. As a result, "the *travaux preparatoires* also reveal that the drafters did not intend to extent the prohibition to economic coercion and political pressures". Thus, the *generally accepted* interpretation is that the term force within Article 2(4) is limited to *armed* force.[42]

Buchan refers here to both 'textual support' and the Charter's *travaux préparatoires* to argue that force equals armed force. In his final sentence, however, he suddenly shifts gear: we move from interpretation, to a claim that this interpretation is the 'generally accepted' one. A few pages prior to this claim, Buchan also states that

> [t]he *generally accepted* interpretation of Article 2(4) is that only those interventions that produce physical damage will be regarded as an unlawful use of force. Consequently, according to positive international law those cyber attacks that do not produce physical damage will not constitute a violation of Article 2(4).[43]

Though it is clear that the argument is contingent on an analysis yet to follow further on in his article, the jump from general acceptance to positive law is

41 Godden, 'On Common Knowledge,' 119.

42 Buchan, 'Cyber Attacks,' 216; emphasis added for "generally accepted."

43 Ibid., 212, emphasis added.

striking; nor do we know the origins of his majority claim. A similar mechanism can be found in other works as well.[44]

A completely contrary way of invoking consensus can be seen in a book written by Walter Sharp. He affirms the existence of majority opinion on the interpretation of 'force,' but proceeds to argue against it: "A more balanced, contextual interpretation of Article 2(4)," he writes, "concludes that political and economic sanctions may indeed be ... an unlawful use of force ... in violation of Article 2(4)."[45] This ultimately brings him to the conclusion that "any state activity in CyberSpace that intentionally cause [*sic*] *any* destructive effect within the sovereign territory of another state are [*sic*] an unlawful use of force."[46] Similarly, like Walter Sharp, Richard Aldrich refers to a "prevailing view" (that force equals physical, or armed force) but he is unsure how to qualify economic coercion.[47] Though this is not exactly the same thing as arguing against majority opinion – he would only be doing so, if he were to argue that the majority claims that economic coercion is not armed force, and that he disagrees with that qualification – most claims under review here do precisely that: the interpretation of force as armed force is mentioned in the same breath as the exclusion of economic coercion.

However formulated, the claims described in this section have one thing in common: they fix the meaning of force – even if only temporarily, as is the case with Sharp's argument – and offer the scholar the opportunity to build the argument from there. Going back to the basic question how 'force' is made known and where in these texts this is done exactly, the above shows that consensus claims are just as much part of the construction of an argument as are the other elements taken from the interpretive history of the prohibition. In other words, the invocation of consensus is in that sense similar to, say, a conclusion on the meaning of the rejection of the Brazilian amendment to the original Charter text.

Yet, there is a qualitative difference between the two kinds of arguments. In his discussion of the search for consensus by US courts Frederick Schauer points out that "[i]t is the *very actions* of the other nations, and not their

44 In the works of Waxman, 'Cyber-Attacks,' Kerschischnig, 'Cyberthreats' (the first consensus claim in his work, at 106) and Schmitt, 'Normative Framework.'

45 Sharp, 'CyberSpace,' 90. He refers to the "prevailing view" at 88. This is described by Crawford Camiciottoli as "disalignment"; see Belinda Crawford Camiciottoli, 'Collective and Individual Identities in Business Studies Lectures,' in: *Commonality and Individuality in Academic Discourse*, Maurizio Gotti (ed.), Peter Lang 2009, 141–162, 153–154; see also the next part of this chapter.

46 Sharp, 'CyberSpace,' 102.

47 Aldrich, 'Information Age,' 238, 242. See also the elaborate discussion of his work in Chapter 3 of this book.

justifications for those actions, that add weight to the Court's conclusion."[48] Schauer points here to an important distinction: that between the claim to consensus and the support for the interpretation on which consensus is claimed to exist. One can take issue with a scholar's conclusions drawn from the rejection of the Brazilian amendment – for example, one can instead claim that the Charter is open to evolving interpretations[49] – but it is much harder to argue against claims to majority opinion. For example, Harrison Dinniss's chapter on cyberattacks and Article 2(4) contains an elaborate interpretation of force (though this is not the case for all the pieces considered here). We can assess the validity of the arguments she presents for thinking force equals armed force, but it is far more difficult to check whether this is in fact what 'writers have generally concluded.'[50] Considered as such, the invocation of consensus is to some degree 'empty,' as it does not rely on substantive conviction but on a leap of faith that the interpretive claim in question is shared by the majority:[51] "Authority implies at least relative content-independence."[52] Those arguing against majority opinion, such as Walter Sharp, don't argue against *the existence* of a majority view: they take issue with what the majority thinks the law is.

The next section further explores the elusive nature of consensus by asking whether this typology is fitting. It deals in greater depth with what is appealed to, when scholars invoke consensus on force as *armed* force, and argues that the strength of a consensus claim may lie precisely in its elusive nature.

4.2 THE ELUSIVENESS OF CONSENSUS

Whether a scholar agrees with a majority interpretation, or argues against it – as in the case of Walter Sharp – the consensus claim presents a certain interpretation as something to which the scholar working with it will have to relate. To be more precise, by posting the claim the scholar has maneuvered him- or herself into a position where relating to this majority view becomes inevitable. The effect of invoking consensus resembles what Horst and Irwin

48 Frederick Schauer, 'Authority and Authorities' (2008) 94 *Virginia Law Review* 1931, 1944, emphases added.

49 For a development of this argument in the debate on economic coercion see Delanis, 'Force under Article 2(4),' inter alia 109, 116.

50 Van der Deijl, 'Argumentum ad Populum,' 19–20; Godden, 'On Common Knowledge,' 112, 122.

51 This is similar to Ingo Venzke's discussion of authority; see Venzke, 'Understanding Authority,' for example at 383 and the introduction to Chapter 5 of this book.

52 Ingo Venzke in reference to Hart; see ibid., 395, more extensively 394–396. Schauer similarly refers to Hart; see Schauer, 'Authority and Authorities,' 1935 note 13.

describe as "closure":[53] it "represents a point of stabilization . . . where, typically, certain arguments and forms of evidence are ruled 'in' and others 'out'."[54] The "dividing line"[55] in this particular case is made up of, plainly put, the power of numbers.[56] To appeal to consensus is to invoke what Young refers to as "nose-counting authority,"[57] regardless of the function of the claim for the author's argument.

Yet these numbers are difficult to grasp in academic writing, for what would this look like?[58] As far as the consensus claims studied here are concerned it is not always clear "whose consensus"[59] is claimed to exist: occasionally it appears to be that of states, but most of the time the claim pertains to the ruling opinion of scholars; rarely, both to that of scholars and states.[60] To push this point a little bit further, a thought experiment would be to ask what we would demand of the evidence to prove the existence of consensus. What would we consider as proof, in an individual piece of scholarly work? Would it suffice to list the support of ten, twenty or maybe fifty writers in a footnote? The trackback table shows a few authors providing a footnote containing what we could consider a 'list,' a substantiated consensus claim (but more on this later). What such a list does, however, is that it provides support for a particular interpretation – it does not prove the existence of consensus, *as such*. The difference between the two – between an interpretive and a consensus claim – can be illustrated by the following phrase from one of the most cited works in this debate, by Albrecht Randelzhofer: "[T]he fundamental notion of 'force' is not undisputed. The term does not cover any possible kind of force, but is, *according to the correct*

53 As part of their introduction to "consensusing" as a community practice; see Horst and Irwin, 'Nations at Ease,' 107–110. Though written in a completely different context, I invoke their work here anyway as the process they describe fits what a consensus argument does in scholarly work.

54 Ibid., 110.

55 Ibid.

56 Lee refers to the "'Wisdom of Crowds' argument"; Lee, 'International Consensus,' 101–102.

57 Ibid., 77 note 47, quoting Ernest A. Young, 'Foreign Law and the Denominator Problem' (2005) 119 Harvard Law Review 148, 153.

58 Vilfredo Pareto, *The Mind and Society, volume I*, Harcourt, Brace and Company 1935, 359.

59 Young, 'Minimum Core,' 148; Godden, 'On Common Knowledge,' 106. Note, however, that Young describes a problem of sources: where we *should* be looking for consensus. The question as to 'whose consensus' is similarly raised by those who have studied it in different contexts: see Horst and Irwin, 'Nations at Ease,' 117; Thomas and Hawes, 'Reporting Verbs,' 145–146; Laurence R. Helfer, 'Consensus, Coherence and the European Convention on Human Rights' (1993) 26 *Cornell International Law Journal* 133, 139 (for a list of sources used); Kanstantsin Dzehtsiarou, *European Consensus and the Legitimacy of the European Court of Human Rights*, Cambridge University Press 2015, chapter 3.

60 For examples of all of these, see the Appendix of this chapter.

and prevailing view, limited to armed force."[61] What Randelzhofer is saying here, is that his view of Article 2(4) is not only the right one but, moreover, the one adhered to by the majority of scholars. It is something described by Crawford Camiciottoli as "alignment with other experts in the field in order to reinforce [one's] own expertise" or in rhetorical terms, a "bandwagon" argument.[62] Randelzhofer is invoking the power of numbers, reinforced by subsequently listing thirteen authors in a footnote that support this interpretation.

But however large this list – a scholar might list 100 authors in a footnote – it would still fail to capture what a consensus claim *does*. I do not mean to imply that consensus is false and that it does not exist.[63] What I mean to point out is its character as being quite distinct from the empirical nature it seems to have when invoked by scholars as part of their argument. This makes sense if we consider a consensus claim to be more than the sum of its parts – its character exceeds what we might successfully grasp in a footnote. However contradictory, consensus seems to evaporate the moment we attempt to substantiate it. Consensus evades capture; and this might be precisely where its strength lies. This view of consensus would account for the phraseology found in some footnotes: those that start with 'see, for example,' followed by the works of a few scholars.[64] These 'examples,' then, function as reference points, touchstones or placeholders for the elusive consensus that exceeds them.

But regardless of what consensus does, is its mystical character really that mystical? One might respond that, taken together, among this group of scholars at least, there is general agreement on the interpretation of force. Consensus, in that case, follows from the *mass* of consensus claims: what we have at the end of the twenty-six consensus claims under scrutiny here, is consensus on the existence of consensus. What results is a meta-consensus, if you like, on the idea of 'force' as *armed* force. After all, if everyone says it is there – the majority opinion on force as armed force – might we not, at some point, simply assume that this is apparently the interpretive framework within which we design and create our arguments? The result might arguably be the

61 Albrecht Randelzhofer, 'Article 2(4),' in: *The Charter of the United Nations: A Commentary*, Bruno Simma (ed.), Oxford University Press 2002, 112–136, 117, emphasis added.

62 Crawford Camiciottoli, 'Business Studies Lectures,' 153. She refers here to previous work done by James R. Martin and Peter R. R. White, *The Language of Evaluation*, Palgrave 2005, 1, inter alia 95 et seq. On bandwagoning see Thomas S. Vernon and Lowell A. Nissen, *Reflective Thinking: The Fundamentals of Logic*, Wadsworth Publishing Company 1968, 148 as also referred to by Van der Deijl, 'Argumentum ad Populum,' 12.

63 See the references above to fallacies; see also Horst and Irwin, 'Nations at Ease,' 109–110.

64 See the Appendix for an example. Nimis likewise refers to the "'see also' formula," see Steve Nimis, 'Fussnoten: Das Fundament der Wissenschaft' (1984) 17 *Arethusa* 105, 125.

same as when we were to organize a referendum among scholars as to the most appropriate interpretation of force. There is something to be said for this argument, but some notes are in order.

The image that is evoked by the scholars making these claims is that consensus is the result of some empirical inquiry into the dominating opinion among scholars.[65] The fact that these claims are substantiated makes the reader think the empirical support for this claim lies with the authors referred to in a footnote. Similarly, Pareto states that "oftentimes the consensus is not based upon direct observation, but is merely taken for granted on the basis of certain sentiments held by the person asserting it."[66] I do not consider the consensus claims studied here as based on sentiments only; but Pareto does point out their empirical appearance.[67] Consensus is supposedly 'out there,' brought into the argument by an individual scholar. This, in turn, raises the question whether 'actual consensus' precedes its being claimed, or whether the chain of causality works in exactly the opposite way? Does the postulation lead to actual consensus through the performativity of the claim and by creating the meta-consensus, described above – or is there no postulation without an actual consensus preceding it?[68] In other words, the question is whether consensus merely results from its postulation in the debate, or whether it also precedes it. The next section elaborates on this issue, by inquiring whether consensus is 'real,' and what substantiated consensus in a scholarly argument would look like.

4.3 'BUT SURELY CONSENSUS EXISTS'

This brings us to the chronology of consensus. Supposedly, someone, at some particular point in the interpretive history of Article 2(4), was the first to claim consensus on the idea that force equals armed force, calling consensus to life for the first time. We could assume that at this point in the history of scholarly thinking on the prohibition, consensus *resulted* from the debate, and did not

65 Cf. Van der Deijl, 'Argumentum ad Populum,' 19, referring to Christopher W. Tindale, *Fallacies and Argument Appraisal*, Cambridge University Press 2007, 107–108.

66 Pareto, 'The Mind and Society,' 355.

67 See ibid., 355–359, also referred to by Chaïm Perelman and Lucie Olbrechts-Tyteca, *The New Rhetoric: A Treatise on Argumentation*, University of Notre Dame Press 1969, 33.

68 Thanks to one of the anonymous reviewers of the article originally submitted to the *Leiden Journal* for pointing out the need for clarification on this point. On performativity see *inter alia* John Austin, *How to Do Things with Words: The William James Lectures Delivered at Harvard University in 1955*, Clarendon Press 1962; Judith Butler, *Bodies that Matter: On the Discursive Limits of 'Sex,'* Routledge 2011, xii; Cynthia Weber, 'Performative States' (1998) 27 *Millennium* 77, 82.

precede it. All we would arguably need after this point, is many repetitions of the claim that consensus exists: at this tipping point in history, consensus also becomes performative. One of the findings of the trackback table, however, is that consensus is claimed to exist very early after the creation of Article 2(4) in 1945. This makes it difficult to consider consensus only as the outcome of some collective scholarly deliberation, but suggests it also approaches something like the invocation of a fairly magical 'out there.'[69] To illustrate, what follows below is an example of the trackback of a footnote following an interpretive claim, made by Russell Buchan in the debate on cyberattacks. The starting point is a claim made by Buchan on increasing support for a particular approach to cyberattacks; the authors he cites to support his claim discuss the meaning of force. If one traces the footnotes these authors use, back to their origin – back to that one author that does not use a footnote anymore, or where the 'trackback chain' stops – one finds a consensus claim as early as 1952. This claim, in turn, reaches back to an *interpretive* claim made on the meaning of force in 1949.

Russell Buchan, in a 2012 article in the *Journal of Conflict and Security Law* states the following:

> In order to ensure that [chemical, biological and nuclear weapons] fell within the use of force prohibition, the definition of Article 2(4) moved ... towards the effects that the weapon produced ... This effects-based approach *has since gained considerable traction* in international legal literature, particularly in the context of cyber war.[70]

In support, he cites a 2001 article by Christopher Joyner and Catherine Lotrionte on cyberattacks. In their article, on the page referred to by Buchan, they write:

> This fundamental proscription against the use of interstate force is *traditionally regarded* as being confined to the use or threat of "armed" force, meaning the possible resort to a violent weapon that inflicts human injury.[71]

69 The word 'magical' in reference to consensus is similarly used by Fleur Johns, in her chapter on the work of the Intergovernmental Panel on Climate Change as it is depicted in international legal scholarship. The latter, Johns writes, treats the scientists involved in the IPCC as 'one community' speaking with 'one voice,' that is as putting forward a consensus on the science involved in climate change. "[T]his consensus," she writes, "tends to have a *magical, found quality* in much international legal scholarship in which it appears." See Johns, 'Unruly Law,' 177, emphasis added.

70 Buchan, 'Cyber Attacks,' 217, emphasis added in the last sentence; omitted in the first.

71 Joyner and Lotrionte, 'Information Warfare,' 845, emphasis added.

To support this claim, they cite books by Ian Brownlie and Derek Bowett, respectively. On the page referred to by Joyner and Lotrionte, Brownlie says that force "is commonly understood to imply a military attack," but points out that this does not necessarily imply the involvement of a state's "military and other forces."[72] On the next page Brownlie is more specific about why force should be understood as armed force – but this is not the one referred to by Joyner and Lotrionte.[73] Also cited by Joyner and Lotrionte, Derek Bowett argues that

> [i]n the absence of authoritative decisions on the meaning of [Article 2(4)] it becomes necessary to discuss its interpretation in the light of accepted rules of construction. Taking the words in their *plain, common-sense meaning*, it is clear that, since the prohibition is of the "use or threat of force", they will not apply to economic or political pressure but only to physical, armed force.[74]

Bowett, in turn, refers to Waldock's 1952 work in the *Hague Recueil*:

> This general prohibition of the use of force is, however, qualified ... by the fact that the word "force" in Article 2 (4) undoubtedly covers only armed or physical force ... There seems to be *general agreement* on this point.[75]

Ultimately, Waldock refers to a 1949 book dealing, inter alia, with the meaning of force:

> While the paragraph is not explicit on the point, the discussions at San Francisco, other provisions of the Charter and common usage strongly suggest that the word "force" is to be understood in the sense of "physical force" or "armed force".[76]

These quotes combined show that at no point in this entire chain of references is the general acceptance of the interpretation of force as armed force actually attested – it is stated. This suggests that consensus does not merely precede the debate: it is likewise confirmed by its invocation.[77] This would explain how it

[72] Brownlie, 'Use of Force,' 361.

[73] For the trackback of Brownlie's page 362, see the Appendix of this chapter.

[74] Derek W. Bowett, *Self-Defence in International Law*, Manchester University Press 1958, 148, emphasis added.

[75] Claud H. M Waldock., 'The Regulation of the Use of Force by Individual States in International Law' (1952) 81 *RCADI* 455, 492, emphasis added. Bowett refers to chapter 3 of Waldock's work; the only page relevant to Bowett's interpretation, in the sense that it is itself also footnoted, is 492. In the same footnote, Bowett also refers to the Brazilian amendment to the Charter.

[76] Leland Goodrich and Edvard Hambro, *Charter of the United Nations*, Stevens and Sons Limited 1949, 104.

[77] See also Johns, 'Unruly Law,' 176 ("the realisation of ... consensus must always pre-date its registering in international legal writing") and 178 (discussing the knowledge-generating

is possible for one of the contributors to the debate, Todd Morth, to argue in his article that "the *general consensus* of scholars is that economic coercion ... does not violate Article 2(4)," at the same time adding in the accompanying footnote that Belatchew Asrat has, contrarily, "argu[ed] that *no clear consensus exists* on the prohibition of economic force."[78] At the same time, there is no denying the existence – at least, as far as the empirical material here allows – of meta-consensus. Thus, the answer to the question of the causality between consensus and its invocation seems to be, 'both.'[79] Consensus appears to result from its invocation as much as it precedes the works of those making these claims.

The next section takes a closer look at how the consensus claims used for this chapter are substantiated by those scholars making them. Following the above, it explores a scholar's attempt to grasp consensus in an individual piece; in other words, how the struggle to grasp the elusive character of consensus materializes in a footnote.

4.4 "CONCEPT SYMBOLS": ON THE BEARERS OF MAJORITY OPINION

The introduction of this chapter already briefly addressed the way the analysis for this piece came about.[80] To reiterate, for those twenty-six claims used here I have listed the references given in the footnote; the same then has been done, twice over – resulting in a table of primary, secondary and tertiary references. What this shows is that most writers, most of the time, refer to mostly the same set of scholars. (Which, of course, is also a majority claim. It is based on the trackback table, and is therefore based on a discrete number of cases. I cannot claim that this practice of self-referentiality extends beyond what I have found

power of invoking consensus); Riles, 'New Agenda,' 999–1000. Horst and Irwin similarly talk of "the performativity of consensus," but their interest lies in what "consensusing" as a societal practice is "productive of," and they refer to consensusing as "generating shared identities and understandings." See Horst and Irwin, 'Nations at Ease,' 107, 118.

78 Morth, 'Considering Our Position,' 593 and 593 note 169, emphases added; Marco Benatar similarly refers to a contrary opinion (on the interpretive level, not on that of the consensus claim itself) in the footnote following his consensus claim; see Benatar, 'Cyber Force,' 385 note 48.

79 See also Christian Bueger and Felix Bethke, 'Actor-Networking the "Failed State": An Enquiry into the Life of Concepts' (2014) 17 *Journal of International Relations and Development* 30.

80 Cf. ibid.; Danette Paul, 'In Citing Chaos: A Study of the Rhetorical Use of Citations' (2000) 14 *Journal of Business and Technical Communication* 185, particularly 201 et seq.; Debra L. Casey and G. Steven McMillan, 'Identifying the "Invisible Colleges" of the Industrial & Labor Relations Review: A Bibliometric Approach' (2008) 62 *Industrial & Labor Relations Review* 126.

here, though, given findings in citation analysis, it may be expected that it does.)

The convergence on the names of a very few can best be demonstrated by means of one of the most cited works in the table, which is Albrecht Randelzhofer's chapter on the use of force, in Bruno Simma's *Commentary* on the UN Charter. A very basic count of the number of times he is cited in the footnotes of those twenty-six claims under scrutiny here shows that in the 'primary references' column he is mentioned seven times out of a total of thirty-nine references.[81] How this happens, is illustrated in Table 4.1 below.

The rows given here are a sample from the trackback table; the consensus claim itself, as well as the primary and secondary references for three separate consensus claims are presented. In bold are those authors whose work – not generally, but one work in particular – reappears throughout the trackback table, though there are variations in the number of times they are cited; Dinstein, for example, is cited more frequently than Singh. This also includes different editions of the same work; for instance Cot and Pellet's book was published in 1985; a new edition appeared in 1991.

The first row tells us that for this particular claim, a reference is given to a book by Yoram Dinstein, to be specific, to his *War, Aggression and Self-Defence* (the fourth edition, published in 2005). The second column shows that Dinstein himself refers to, inter alia, Randelzhofer's chapter in Simma (the second edition, published in 2002).

The second row shows that this claim is substantiated by reference to an article by Daniel Silver; he himself refers to, inter alia, the same Dinstein book cited in the first row – only this time, the reference is to an earlier edition (the second, 1994 edition). Daniel Silver also refers to Albrecht Randelzhofer; again, this concerns a previous edition (1994) of the same chapter in Bruno Simma's *Commentary* to the UN Charter.

The third row indicates that this particular consensus claim is substantiated by reference to Randelzhofer's chapter in Bruno Simma's book; Randelzhofer himself, in turn, refers to thirteen other scholars. One of these is Dinstein's *War, Aggression and Self-Defence*; the 1988 edition.

A couple of specific observations emerge from this snapshot, as well as from the trackback table generally.

[81] As stated above, three authors appear twice in the trackback table. These numbers pertain to references to the specific page or paragraph in which Randelzhofer makes his own consensus claim; see the Appendix of this chapter.

TABLE 4.1 *Excerpt trackback table*

Consensus claim	Primary references	Secondary references
"Today it is a *general agreement* in doctrine that the 'use of force' covers 'armed force' and not economic or psychological pressure. [11]"[82]	1) Dinstein (2005/4) 86 [11]	1(a) **Kearney and Dalton** (1970) 534–535 [16] 1(b) Randelzhofer (2002/2) 117–118 [17] 1(c) **Wehberg** (1951) 69 [18]
"[T]he *consensus* is that Article 2(4) prohibits only armed force. [90]"[83]	1) Silver (2002) 80–82 [90]	1(a) **Dinstein** (1994/2) 81 [24] 1(b) **Randelzhofer** (1994) 112 [24] 1(c) Schmitt (1999) 904–908 [26, 27, 31, 34] 1(d) **Gordon** (1985) no page nrs. [28] 1(e) Friendly Relations Declaration [29] 1(f) General Assembly Resolution 42/22 (1988) [30] 1(g) ICJ: *Nicaragua* case [32, 33]
"The *prevailing view*, according to one authoritative text, is that Article 2(4) does not prohibit 'any possible kind of force, but is . . . limited to armed force.[218]'"[84]	1) **Randelzhofer** (1994) 112 [218]	1(a) **Virally in Cot and Pellet** (1991/2) 122–123 [25] 1(b) **Goodrich, Hambro and Simons** (1969/3) 49 [25] 1(c) **Verdross and Simma** (1984/3) para. 476 [25] 1(d) Kelsen and Tucker (1966/2) 86 [25] 1(e) Brownlie (1963) 362 [25] 1(f) Bowett (1958) 148 [25] 1(g) **Khare** (1985) 27–28 [25] 1(h) **Singh** (1984) 212 [25] 1(i) **Dahm** (1962) 49 [25] 1(j) **Schindler** (1986) 14 [25] 1(k) Malanczuk (1987) 244 [25] 1(l) **Dinstein** (1988) 84 [25] 1(m) **Derpa** (1970) 26fn71 [25]

82 Remus, 'Cyber-Attacks,' 181, emphasis added.

83 Hathaway et al., 'Law of Cyber-Attack,' 842, emphasis added.

First, consensus claims are hardly substantiated in individual cases: writers resort to the work of one or a few individual scholars.[85] The list of cited authors expands significantly with the trackback for Randelzhofer's work, but if we trace the secondary and tertiary references for his consensus claim the same thing happens – to some extent – as well. The column listing the tertiary references for his claim, for example, contains six separate entries for the 1949 book by Goodrich and Hambro (their 1969 book with Simons, referred to by Randelzhofer himself, is the revised edition of the same book). Furthermore, the trackback table shows that several authors cited by Randelzhofer are likewise cited by others; for example Virally's chapter in Cot and Pellet's book; the 1969 book by Goodrich, Hambro and Simons (as well as its first, 1949 edition); Brownlie's 1963 *International Law and the Use of Force by States*; Bowett's 1958 book, and Derpa's book on the use of force.

Most striking is the cross-referencing between Yoram Dinstein's several editions of his *War, Aggression and Self-Defence*, and Randelzhofer's chapter in Bruno Simma's edited volume. For his claim that force equals armed force (2005, fourth edition), Dinstein refers to Randelzhofer's chapter in Simma's *Commentary*; the 2002 edition. In this 2002 edition, for his consensus claim that force means armed force, Randelzhofer refers to thirteen scholars, including Dinstein's *War, Aggression and Self-Defence* of 2001. On the page referred to by Randelzhofer, Dinstein himself refers to the previous, 1995 edition of the same chapter by Randelzhofer in Simma's *Commentary*. In that 1995 edition, on one of the pages indicated by Dinstein, Randelzhofer refers, inter alia, to the previous, first edition of Dinstein's *War, Aggression and Self-Defense* of 1988. Strikingly, even though Randelzhofer and Dörr in the 2012 edition of Simma's commentary still refer to Dinstein (in this case the fifth edition of his *War, Aggression and Self-Defence* of 2012), Dinstein himself ceases referring to Randelzhofer's chapter in this fifth edition of 2012. This could be related to his changed definition of 'force' compared to his fourth edition. Whereas in 2005 (fourth edition) he argues that "the term 'force' in Article 2(4) must denote armed – or military – force"; in 2012 (fifth edition) he states that "the term 'force' in Article 2(4) must denote *violence*."[86]

85 See notes 128–129 and the accompanying body text below, for those writers who leave their claims unsubstantiated.

86 Compare Yoram Dinstein, *War, Aggression and Self-Defence*, Cambridge University Press 2005 (4), 86, with *War, Aggression and Self-Defence*, Cambridge University Press 2012 (5), 88, emphasis added. For a discussion of "violence" as a criterion for 'force' (as used by Dinstein) see Waxman, 'Cyber-Attacks,' 435–436. For a discussion of similar dynamics in terms of linguistic and national communities of legal writers, see Roberts, 'International Law,' 101–104.

This practice of what J. S. Watson refers to as "mutual cross-citation" is not particular to this debate, nor to the discipline of international law.[87] In 1979 Watson wrote a critique of legal reasoning on human rights in international law, and with regard to academic writing he argued that

> [i]n articles advocating the international protection of human rights one usually finds that initial reference is made to Lauterpacht's *International Law and Human Rights* ... After citing Lauterpacht, writers usually allude to the works of any of a large group of colleagues who, in varying degrees, have reached conclusions similar to Lauterpacht's: Cassin, Humphrey, McDougal, Robertson, Schwelb, Sohn, and others ... this tendency ... can develop into mutual cross-citation.[88]

Watson states that "it is much easier to cite authors who have already reached [a similar] conclusion ... the writer does not need to concern himself with a full explanation of his argument."[89] His critique is aimed at the "discrepancy" between what he refers to as "the reality of state practice" and "advocacy in an academic context," and the use of secondary rather than primary sources: he argues that "it is crucial ... not to confuse the snowballing acceptance of a rule by academics with snowballing acceptance by states."[90] In that respect it is interesting to note that the Appendix of this chapter shows that, even though writers do cite some judgments of the International Court of Justice as well as General Assembly Resolutions, the majority of footnotes contain references to other scholars. The practice of mutual cross-citation Watson observes is similar to the one under scrutiny here – and it has been observed elsewhere.[91] Part of it might be explained through the "Matthew effect," "which predicts that authors who are already well-cited will get a disproportionate share of additional citations."[92]

87 J. S. Watson, 'Legal Theory, Efficacy and Validity in the Development of Human Rights Norms in International Law' (1979) 1979 *University of Illinois Law Forum* 609, 637; see also Arthur Austin, 'Footnote Skulduggery and Other Bad Habits' (1990) 44 *University of Miami Law Review* 1009, 1022 note 87, quoting Frederick C. Thorne, 'The Citation Index: Another Case of Spurious Validity' (1977) 33 *Journal of Clinical Psychology* 1157, 1160.

88 Watson, 'Legal Theory,' 636–637, see generally 635 et seq.

89 Ibid., 636; Watson is referred to by Godefridus J. H. van Hoof, *Rethinking the Sources of International Law*, Kluwer Publishing 1983, 178, which is how I came across this part of his work.

90 Watson, 'Legal Theory,' 610, 641, 637; see also Friedrich Kratochwil, *The Status of Law in World Society: Meditations on the Role and Rule of Law*, Cambridge University Press 2014, 114–116 .

91 Thorne, 'Citation Index,' 1160, as also referred to by Austin, 'Footnote Skulduggery'; see note 87 above.

92 White, 'Citation Analysis,' 110.

A blogpost on the subject phrased the individual scholar's thinking as follows: "[I]f so many people cite it, it must be a reasonable paper to cite."[93]

Something more might happen here, though, which might be clarified by asking what it is a footnote is supposed to *do*. In his work on footnotes and the sociology of science, Henry Small writes how

> [i]n the tradition of scholarship, the references are the "sources" which the author draws upon to give further meaning to his text. Reversing this view ... the author is imparting meaning to his "sources" by citing them ... Referencing viewed in this way is a labelling process ... In citing a document an author is creating its meaning, and this ... is a process of symbol making.[94]

Small writes how this "symbolic content is shared among a number of citing authors": "[T]he uniformity with which these works are used," he writes, indicates their status as a "concept symbol."[95] Referring to his work, Danette Paul describes how "citations ... act as a discipline's shorthand for certain ideas."[96] What Small is saying, is that certain sources acquire meaning through the citation process. Of course, this meaning cannot be detached from what the source says, but Small points out that there is a process of identification, where the source comes to represent a certain idea (a relation Small describes as metaphoric as well as potentially metonymic).[97] If this is repeated a sufficient amount of times between "citing author[s]" – between those involved in a similar debate – these sources turn from one author's "private symbols" to "standard symbols" for those involved.[98] Something similar is described by Gilbert when he discusses the use of citations:

> [I]n citing certain papers, the author can be seen to be making an assertion about his own opinion concerning the validity of the findings of the cited papers, and is thus contributing, albeit only in small measure, to the *overall consensus* of his research area, a consensus which is also continually being re-established through the choices of references in his fellow participants' own publications.[99]

The kind of consensus Gilbert refers to here is similar to the process of an emerging 'meta-consensus' identified in this chapter. What he seeks to point

93 Douglas Kell, 'The Matthew Effect in Science – Citing the Most Cited.'
94 Small, 'Concept Symbols,' 328.
95 Ibid., 329, 334, 337.
96 Paul, 'Citing Chaos,' 196; see also Gilbert, 'Referencing,' 117.
97 Small, 'Concept Symbols,' 329, 338.
98 Ibid., 328, 329. On repetition, see notes 103–104 and the accompanying body text below.
99 Gilbert, 'Referencing,' 117, emphasis added; see also Riles, 'New Agenda,' 999.

out, is the emergence of a shared idea on the 'validity of the findings of the cited papers.' Something similar is pointed out by Ken Hyland when he writes how

> [t]he importance of citation as a constitutive element of the modern academic paper can be seen in its increasingly prominent role in the ways writers seek to construct facts through their communicative practices.[100]

Translating Small's idea to consensus claims and their footnotes, we might think of frequently cited authors such as Randelzhofer as 'concept symbols,' representing the idea of 'consensus.' Or, in Small's words, "[r]ecurring patterns of terminology used by citing authors when referring to these documents show that they have become standardized in their usage and meaning."[101] The 'recurring pattern of terminology,' in this case, is the word 'consensus,' 'majority,' etc. The claims under scrutiny here are by no means *proof* of how this process has taken place, as Small acknowledges: he denies any claims to knowing "how a document is transformed" into a concept symbol.[102] However, he does refer to, as just cited, 'recurring patterns of terminology,' 'uniformity of usage' and 'standardized terminology,' which means that he understands this as simply a matter of repetition (though we still wouldn't know what started this process).[103] The idea of repetition is the point where we might link the Matthew effect – those who are cited often, will be cited more often – with Small's idea of 'concept symbols.' Phrased differently, a concept symbol comes into being through its repeated use; and the more it is used, the more it *will* be used. Mahbuba and Rousseau likewise make this connection, when they state that

> articles or journals considered as concept symbols become the hard-to-ignore default citation value. This is exactly the Matthew effect at work: the highly visible and highly cited become even more visible and cited, while the less known disappear completely from the "citation" radar.[104]

So, it might be helpful to understand these clusters of references in the way understood by Small. "Meaning," as Small says, "[is] conferred through

100 Hyland, 'Disciplinary Discourses,' 21, and, generally, the second chapter of his book; see also the concluding pages of this chapter and their references to his work.

101 Small, 'Concept Symbols,' 337. Bueger and Bethke refer to "obligatory passage points"; see Bueger and Bethke, 'Actor-Networking,' 40, 50.

102 Small, 'Concept Symbols,' 329, see also 338.

103 Ibid. On the role of repetition in the construction of international law, see Wouter G. Werner, *Repetition and International Law*, Cambridge University Press 2021, forthcoming.

104 Dilruba Mahbuba and Ronald Rousseau, 'The Matthew Effect and a Relation with Concept Symbols and Defaults' (2011) 58 *Annals of Library and Information Studies* 335, 337.

usage,"[105] and thus, symbols come into being. As described above, 'proving' the existence of consensus is extraordinarily difficult, precisely because of what it purports to convey, and what – in the same move – is almost impossible to grasp. The elusive nature of consensus forces scholars to resort to the work of largely the same set of scholars, who become the figureheads of consensus; and in their wake we find – and this is an implicit part of the substantiation of the claim – many more scholars whose opinion converges around this particular interpretation. So rather than listing in a footnote all the support they can find, most scholars[106] resort to those publicists they identify as being the 'bearers' of this majority opinion; in and of themselves these cited scholars represent a larger body of work.

Another way to approach this is by asking (following the work of Anthony Grafton) whether we think of footnotes as sources, or as authority.[107] "The historian," Grafton writes, cites sources, in which he "explains the methods and procedures used to produce the text."[108] This is different from the function of a footnote as authority, which "list[s] . . . the great writers who sanction a given statement or whose words an author has creatively adapted."[109] Rodgers makes a similar point, as he distinguishes between a footnote's "evidentiary" and its "authorising function." "Through their authorising functions," he writes,

> citations legitimize the text and establish the author as trustworthy in the discourse community. Evidentiary functions . . . may justify claims of causality, explain terms or experimental operations, or provide evidence in an argument.[110]

Whereas we might think of the footnotes accompanying consensus claims as 'evidence' or sources, the fairly consistent reference to the same people makes them more closely resemble claims to authority. The authority of the footnote, then, is based on its value as a concept symbol: the community of scholars an author engages with by means of his or her text recognizes the source given as one that represents a certain idea. As stated by Paul, "naming indicates a sense of community. It indicates that the author believes the readers will recognize the

105 Small, 'Concept Symbols,' 338.

106 As discussed in this section, and as the Appendix shows, this practice significantly expands with Randelzhofer's references.

107 Grafton, 'Curious History,' 33.

108 Ibid., 32–33; see also 16.

109 Ibid., 33. It is necessary to add the context of Grafton's statement here: he refers to the practice of "theologians and lawyers of the Middle Ages and the Renaissance" (33).

110 Rodgers adds a third, "mapping" function, which I have not included here as it is not directly to the point. See John Rodgers, 'Whose Citations Are They?' (2010) 9 *Journal of Medical English Education* 94, 95.

name and its value."[111] In this way, the name of the cited author and a particular idea collapse into each other,[112] to the point where what they say becomes indistinguishable from who is doing the saying. A reference to a single author can thus start to lead a life of its own, and become an "institutional function."[113]

Small's work describes what citations can signify; and to speak of the authority of footnotes inevitably leads to a discussion on *why* an individual scholar would cite Randelzhofer, or one of the other frequently cited scholars. The literature on citer motivations is enormous, and the basic question is whether it is possible to assess a scholar's reasons for citing in the first place.[114] Susan Cozzens has argued that the citation following particular knowledge claims serves either a "rhetorical" or a "reward" function.[115] The first are the means "through which scientists try to persuade each other of their knowledge claims"; the second, as the one "through which credit for achievement is allocated."[116] Danette Paul eventually argues that a citation is both, "simultaneously."[117] Given what consensus claims are used for, it seems that the first motivation – citation as rhetorical device – at least in this case, is much more likely. Consensus claims carry the weight of collective scholarly authority. To invoke consensus is an attempt to evoke a sense of certainty about the substance of the law[118] – even if a scholar, like Walter Sharp, ultimately argues against it. As was shown above, the consensus claims studied here serve as a stepping-stone to move the argument further. Persuasion of the reader, then, can only spring from an identifiable substantiation of the claimed consensus. In this instance, to quote Gilbert, "referencing is essentially a device for persuasion ... certain references will vary in their power of persuasion according to the opinions and concerns of those who are to be persuaded."[119]

111 She is talking specifically about science citations; see Paul, 'Citing Chaos,' 199.

112 Paul describes something similar in natural sciences, but in the context of the "obliteration phenomenon"; see ibid., 202–203 and note 129 below.

113 Nimis, 'Fussnoten,' 131. Related to this, and pointed out by Small, is that a scholar cannot control the way in which her or his work is taken up by the discipline. See Small, 'Concept Symbols,' 338.

114 Blaise Cronin, *The Citation Process: The Role and Significance of Citations in Scientific Communication*, Taylor Graham 1984, 57. For an example see Terrence A. Brooks, 'Private Acts and Public Objects: An Investigation of Citer Motivations' (1985) 37 *Journal of the American Society for Information Science* 34.

115 Paul, 'Citing Chaos,' 187, quoting Susan E. Cozzens, 'What Do Citations Count? The Rhetoric-First Model' (1989) 15 *Scientometrics* 437, 440.

116 Ibid.

117 Ibid., 196.

118 See also Kessler and Werner, 'Expertise,' inter alia 805–806, about attempts to silence dissent.

119 Gilbert, 'Referencing,' 119; see also Janet B. Bavelas, 'The Social Psychology of Citations' (1978) 19 *Canadian Psychological Review/Psychologie canadienne* 158, 160. In engaging with

Whether we rely on authority explicitly, or are simply lazy, or not familiar enough with a particular field to cite lesser-known works, we cite so others will recognize.[120] In other words, this is not a casual practice: when it comes to supporting consensus claims we do not just cite anybody; we cite those we believe to be holders or representatives of the majority view.[121] Thus, references used to support the invocation of majority opinion tend to converge on the names of a very few, sometimes by direct reference to their work, at others via the work of less known scholars.

But what are we to make of those authors who *do* cite a long list of scholars? Because, whereas many references converge around the work of Randelzhofer, references given by Randelzhofer himself – especially if we focus on the secondary and tertiary references – fan out over a large range of authors. As shown in the trackback table, this means that if we do a similar trackback for his claim, the list of cited authors and works in support of his interpretive, as well as consensus claim, expands. The first, primary references given in the trackback table present a rather bleak view on the substantiation of consensus claims; the list of works cited is short. This list expands as we move to the secondary and tertiary references, especially following the work of Randelzhofer: we come to see a large body of work stretching out over several decades. We could understand these lists as supportive of the interpretation argued; that force equals armed force. The next section offers a few reflections on this.

4.4.1 *The "Single Monster Footnote"*

I have addressed the notion of 'meta-consensus,' above; but what are we to make of one single footnote containing a 'list' of references, such as in Derpa's book? To revert once again to analyses done in the field of citation analysis, the question is what these lists are *for*. John Budd, for example, argues that these citations appear in the text without explicating how exactly they support the knowledge claim made. In other words, there is no contextualization: "There is no discrimination among the cited works," Budd writes, "they are simply

Gilbert's work on citer motivations Henry Small claims "citation as a symbol for an idea" to be "more nearly universal"; but he does consider "[t]he concept symbol interpretation of citation practice" as "complementary" to other citer motivations. See Small, 'Concept Symbols,' 337; see also 338. For a critique of Gilbert's work see White, 'Citation Analysis,' 108–111.

120 Paul, 'Citing Chaos,' 199, as already cited above; Gilbert, 'Referencing,' 116, 119; more explicitly, Skouteris, 'New Tribunalism,' 334. Thanks to one of the anonymous reviewers of the article originally submitted to the *Leiden Journal* for pointing out the need for clarification on this point.

121 Gilbert, 'Referencing,' 117.

accorded bibliographic mention."[122] He later adds the caveat that "an author cannot possibly provide textual evidence of epistemic links to *every* potentially relevant piece of previous work" but this comment does not specifically pertain to a 'list' of references.[123] Steve Nimis, in a scathing critique of the way footnotes are used in classicism, refers to the "single monster footnote," the problem with which, he says, is that it "has the character of a 'pile,' a collection of opinions which is *ahistorical*: not because dates are not given, but because the judgments recorded are 'reified' knowledge."[124]

This notion of 'ahistoricity' can be illustrated by again taking a closer look at the work of Albrecht Randelzhofer. What is striking about the continuous reference to his work is that the works he himself cites in support of his consensus claim are virtually unchanged between the 1994, 2002 and latest, 2012, edition of the chapter; and all cited works, save one, predate 1992. The only change between the 1994/1995 and the 2002 edition is an update to the 2001 third edition of Dinstein's *War, Aggression and Self-Defence*. The same has been done for the 2012 *Commentary* which refers to the 2012 fifth edition of Dinstein's book. Moreover, the 2012 edition of Simma's *Commentary* omits Virally's chapter in Cot and Pellet as well as the 1962 article written by Dahm. In effect, this means that a contemporary reference to this particular consensus claim in Randelzhofer constitutes a reference to works most of which are over twenty years old. Put differently, if a scholar (such as Yoram Dinstein) were to inquire into the meaning of force in 1994 and would thereby refer to Randelzhofer, he would be referring to the exact same works Heather Harrison Dinniss would be referring to, almost twenty years later. This brings us back to the critique voiced by Steve Nimis: the claim based on Randelzhofer's work – that force as *armed* force is the generally accepted interpretation – is presented as 'given' or as 'reified knowledge.'[125]

In that sense, a list of footnotes might even make the argument *less* persuasive. In *Laboratory Life*, Latour and Woolgar describe different levels of certainty with which knowledge claims are presented in a text. This ranges from a "type 5 statement," where "readers are so persuaded of the existence of facts that no explicit reference is made to them"[126], to "type 1 statements"

[122] John M. Budd, 'Citations and Knowledge Claims: Sociology of Knowledge as a Case in Point' (1999) 25 *Journal of Information Science* 265, 270.

[123] Ibid., 271.

[124] Nimis, 'Fussnoten,' 118, 119.

[125] Ibid., 119. For a possible explanation see Lowell L. Hargens, 'Using the Literature: Reference Networks, Reference Contexts, and the Social Structure of Scholarship' (2000) 65 *American Sociological Review* 846.

[126] Latour and Woolgar, 'Laboratory Life,' 76; see also Paul, 'Citing Chaos,' 199–200.

containing multiple expressions of uncertainty ('X has suggested that perhaps - ...').[127] With regard to the footnotes supporting consensus claims, it is interesting to note that some authors (as can be seen in the Appendix) do not substantiate their consensus claim at all: a "type 4 statement," which signifies "tacit knowledge that is written down, with no reference to origin."[128] So, rather than think of this lack of footnotes as a weakness, we could also think of consensus as – at least in the minds of these authors – being such common knowledge that there is no need to support it.[129]

Ultimately, both a plethora of references and a complete lack of them fail to catch what a consensus claim does to a reader: the 'mythical out there' still stands, however many – or few – authors we might find to support a particular claim.[130] Writing in a different context, but describing a similar dynamic Ken Hyland states that

> [t]he ways that [disciplinary] discourses represent reality, express probability, and enact social relations play an important part in establishing how we perceive the world. Many ... features ... work to disguise what is contingent, competitive and contentious in academic debate [such as] citing previous work ... drawing on shared understandings, and boosting collegiality are strategies of rhetorical persuasion with peers, but they also act to erase most traces of conflict and division with them.[131]

Consensus claims might actually be one of the ways in which a 'shared understanding' can be identified, but simultaneously raise the question what kind of 'conflict and division' they cover up or 'erase.' This is not to say there may not be a 'shared understanding' about the meaning of the prohibition on

[127] Latour and Woolgar, 'Laboratory Life,' 79; on these expressions of uncertainty see Paul, 'Citing Chaos,' 218 (Appendix C).

[128] Latour and Woolgar, 'Laboratory Life,' 77–78; Paul, 'Citing Chaos,' 217. Latour and Woolgar add that a footnote can signal two contradictory things: it could either leave the impression that the knowledge claim in question is 'man-made' and thereby less "objective"; alternatively, it "lends weight to a statement which otherwise appears to be an unsupported assertion." Which one of these two applies, is context-dependent. See Latour and Woolgar, 'Laboratory Life,' 80.

[129] Though reminiscent of the "obliteration phenomenon," where the author of an idea is no longer cited as the idea itself has become common knowledge, this does not apply here: Randelzhofer or any other of the frequently cited authors are not the 'creators' of the idea of consensus. See Paul, 'Citing Chaos,' 203 referring to Eugene Garfield, 'The Articles Most Cited in Science from 1961 to 1982. Another 100 Citations Classics: The Watson-Crick Double Helix Has Its Turn.' *Essays of an Information Scientist* 8 (1985) 187–96, 188; White, 'Citation Analysis,' 104; Rodgers, 'Whose Citations?,' 95.

[130] See also Grafton, 'Curious History,' 104.

[131] Hyland, 'Disciplinary Discourses,' 162; somewhat differently see Venzke's reference to "genuine agreement"; Venzke, 'Interpretation,' 62.

the use of force among these scholars, but it does bring to light how these kinds of certainties about 'what the law is' are constructed in legal discourse.

Concluding, this chapter has, first, brought to the fore the use of a particular kind of argument in legal reasoning; secondly, it has pointed out the particular part played by referencing practices.[132] The first half inquired into the use of consensus claims as part of legal reasoning; into their particular function in the scholar's argument and what it is exactly that is invoked when a scholar refers to majority opinion. In the second part, this chapter looked at the substantiation of these consensus claims, and wondered what it is these footnotes do and what they represent. The image that emerges is that of a practice of self-referentiality: an intricate web of cross-references between authors such as Randelzhofer and Dinstein; between first, second and third editions of the same titles. By means of consensus claims particular interpretations are brought to the fore; but it also elevates those we use to substantiate these claims to be bearers of majority opinion. On the level of the single academic piece this might appear to be fairly innocent. Yet the individual scholar merely pointing out in a footnote where consensus might be found, is also a participant in a larger practice that impacts who is given a voice in the debate – and by implication, whose voice remains in the dark.[133] The practice of self-referentiality, or in Watson's terms, mutual cross-citation, brings a select group of scholars to the forefront of the legal academic community. Ken Hyland describes how "[t]he social interactions in the writings of academics ... help to produce and sustain status relationships [and] exercise exclusivity."[134] When viewed as 'social interaction' academic writing is more than a contribution to a specific debate: it is also a platform by means of which writers decide whose work to 'bring into the piece' and whose work to leave aside.

In other words, this chapter has shown how legal knowledge results from what is said, as well as from who is given the floor in this exchange. The next chapter continues this focus on the 'who' of the cyberwar discourse. It deals with the presentations given by the leading scholar in the cyberwar debate, Michael Schmitt. By closely considering the words he uses at these public performances, the chapter demonstrates how he discursively positions himself as occupying the center of the debate; how, linguistically, he occupies a position from which he can pronounce not only what we know to be law, but also, on who is allowed to do the saying.

132 See Hyland, 'Disciplinary Discourses,' chapter 2.
133 See also ibid., 156 and Gilbert, 'Referencing,' 117.
134 Hyland, 'Disciplinary Discourses,' 168; see also note 26 above.

5

"Call Me Again If You're Ever Ready to Begin Answering the Questions"

This book opened with the *Tallinn Manuals*, the international legal handbooks on cyber operations written by a group of legal experts. Commissioned by NATO's Cyber Defence Centre (the CCDCOE) they list the "black-letter rules" of state behavior in cyberspace.[1] Both *Tallinn* projects were directed by Michael Schmitt, the leading scholar in the cyberwar debate and chairman of the International Law Department of the US Naval War College at the time the first Manual came out.

Over the years, Schmitt has given numerous presentations on the *Tallinn Manuals*, detailing their rules, the interpretive difficulties involved and the composition of the group of experts. On one of these occasions, he related the story of how he came to be the director of the project. He told the audience how the CCDCOE had called him to extend an invitation to speak at one of their conferences, but that he had declined, responding as follows:

> We bring a bunch of lawyers together and they appear to impress the audience by telling [them] how truly hard cyber is. How about if we start answering the questions? ... Call me again if you're ever ready to begin answering the questions.[2]

The rest, really, is history. The CCDCOE *did* call again, and three years later the first *Tallinn Manual* was published by Cambridge University Press.

By means of the words quoted above, Schmitt explicitly positions himself as the 'go-to scholar' for the provision of legal answers, and this is precisely the positioning this chapter investigates. Specifically, it is concerned with how, by means of the words he uses, Schmitt places himself at the heart of the cyberwar

1 Schmitt (ed.), 'Tallinn Manual,' front matter.

2 CyCon 2012 (I), 0.35. All quotes given in this chapter can also be found in the Appendix; the times indicated in both, however, may differ. This is because the quotes given in the Appendix sometimes are the more extensive ones, also providing a broader context to what Schmitt says.

debate; as the one 'giving the answers' on cyber and international law. As such, the quote that serves as the title of this chapter is the ultimate expression of "application-orientation,"[3] for not only is he – like the other scholars whose work was considered in the previous chapters – concerned with the solution of legal problems, he explicitly positions himself as the one being able to solve them. Given the overarching concern of this book with the construction of legal knowledge in the cyberwar debate, this self-positioning by Schmitt as 'knowledge-producer' merits closer scrutiny. This chapter is the last of the three close-ups of this discourse, and continues the inquiry started in the previous one: the distribution of the authority to speak.[4]

The kind of prominence as enjoyed by Professor Schmitt in the cyberwar debate is neither particular to this discourse, nor to the field of international law. Other disciplines have their own more or less well-known figures, though the visibility of these "personalities" differs.[5] Some of the most famous international lawyers featured in, for example, Koskenniemi's *Gentle Civilizer of Nations*, and a couple of years ago the *Leiden Journal of International Law* dedicated two special issues to the work of Alejandro Álvarez and Taslim Olawale Elias.[6] However, this chapter is not concerned with Schmitt's place in the history of ideas, nor is the approach taken here biographical.[7] Instead, I ask what his words 'do' in terms of how they impact what we think international law on cyberwar is, and how he situates himself in relation to those "knowledge claims."[8] The reason for studying *his* words in particular so closely is that, in the cyberwar debate, his position is unrivalled by that of any other, and he has left an indelible mark on the direction the law has taken in this field. He directed the groups of experts that drafted the *Tallinn Manuals*, and as explained in Chapter 3, his work on Article 2(4) and cyberattacks is referred to as "one of the most academically rigorous and frequently cited frameworks for characterizing cyber operations."[9] When speaking in public he is introduced as "the number one expert on cyberwar in the world" and as "[o]ne of the ... world's top experts on the laws of war in general ... When I have

3 As adopted from Noll, 'Analogy at War,' 210; see Chapter 2.

4 I am fully aware of the performativity of labeling Schmitt a pivotal figure in the debate, as well as the writing of this chapter as a whole. Some examples of the way others refer to him are given in this introduction.

5 Hyland, 'Disciplinary Discourses,' 35.

6 Koskenniemi, 'Gentle Civilizer'; the *Leiden Journal* special issues are volume 19, issue 4 (2016) (on Álvarez) and volume 21, issue 2 (2008) (on Elias) respectively.

7 On *Gentle Civilizer* as a history of ideas see ibid., 2.

8 On the "relationships between people, and between people and ideas" see Hyland, 'Disciplinary Discourses,' 1; for "knowledge claims" see ibid., 8.

9 Foltz, 'Stuxnet,' 41.

a question I'm not sure about it, Mike is the guy I call, and I say 'what's the answer to this?'"[10]

Importantly, these last couple of quotes also show that the kind of authority Schmitt claims and enjoys is not unidirectional: its exercise depends on a recipient granting it.[11] Authority, in other words, is contingent on the "voluntary recognition" of one's audience: if the audience withdrew its support, so to speak, there would be no authority left to claim.[12] This does not mean that Schmitt's work is not subject to critique: examples of this were provided in Chapter 3 of this book, and the reception of the *Tallinn Manuals* has likewise not been uncritical.[13] What I'm trying to point out here is the necessity of the recognition and acceptance of Schmitt's authority and for that, complete "substantive agreement" with what he says is not required.[14] Crucially, authority is – at least to some degree[15] – freely granted: it hinges on an audience's (quiet) acquiescence with its exercise.[16]

This chapter looks at those places where, in fact, Schmitt's "audience is physically present":[17] his presentations. Over the years, he has been a guest speaker or panelist on many different occasions, and here he talks about, for example, the way the group of experts was assembled, and how the first *Tallinn*

10 LENS Conference 2013 | Michael N. Schmitt, The Law of Cyberwar: The Tallinn Manual (hereafter: LENS 2013), 13.57 (this introduction is by one of his former teachers, which Schmitt explains later on in the presentation); PILAC 2015, 3.41.

11 This (very brief) discussion of authority is based on Venzke, 'Understanding Authority,' specifically 382–387; see also Ingo Venzke, 'Semantic Authority,' in: *Concepts for International Law: Contributions to Disciplinary Thought*, Jean d'Aspremont and Sahib Singh (eds.), Elgar 2019, specifically 1, 10 and Venzke, 'Interpretation,' 63–64.

12 Venzke, 'Understanding Authority,' 383 (in reference to Hannah Arendt). Bruce Lincoln refers to "the trust of the audience"; see Bruce Lincoln, *Authority: Construction and Corrosion*, The University of Chicago Press 1994, 8. The phrase "authority claims" in relation to the Manual is also used by Kessler and Werner, 'Expertise,' 806.

13 Examples include Tsagourias, 'Tallinn Manual Commentary'; Fleck, 'Searching'; Dinah PoKempner, 'Squinting Through the Pinhole: A Dim View of Human Rights from Tallinn 2.0' (2017) 95 *Texas Law Review* 1599; Christian Schaller, 'Beyond Self-Defense and Countermeasures: A Critical Assessment of the *Tallinn Manual*'s Conception of Necessity' (2017) 95 *Texas Law Review* 1619. See pp. 85–87 above for a discussion of the critique aimed particularly at Schmitt's work on Article 2(4).

14 Venzke, 'Understanding Authority,' 383.

15 Venzke refers to "a minimal degree of voluntary recognition"; see ibid., 384.

16 That is, I view an audience as having a functional relation to the speaker. Cf. Perelman and Olbrechts-Tyteca, 'The New Rhetoric,' 19 and the different notions of "discourse community" discussed by Sally Burgess, 'Packed Houses and Intimate Gatherings: Audience and Rhetorical Structure,' in: *Academic Discourse*, John Flowerdew (ed.), Pearson Education Limited 2002, 196–215, 200–203.

17 Shirley Carter-Thomas and Elizabeth Rowley-Jolivet, 'Analysing the Scientific Conference Presentation (CP): A Methodological Overview of a Multimodal Genre' (2003) 39–40 *ASp* 59, 60.

Manual deals with issues such as 'use of force' and 'armed attack' in cyberspace.[18] I attended several of these events, and this chapter was born out of an attempt to give language to the sense that they mattered to his construction of authority in this field. These constructions pertain to, not only, claims with regard to what the law is, but, what is more, to whom he considers eligible for making those claims. The turn to description as enacted in this book means that I ask which words he uses at these events; where he uses them; and what it does to use these words rather than others.[19] Concretely, for the purposes of this chapter I have looked at eight of his presentations, on the first *Tallinn Manual* in particular as well as on cyberwar and international law in general.[20] They are publicly available recordings of presentations[21] given between 2012 and 2015, to audiences ranging from computer scientists to a mixed group including legal scholars and students; they vary in length between about twenty minutes to a little over an hour and a half. Five out of those eight are conference presentations; two are university lectures with Schmitt as a guest speaker; and one is a panel presentation, followed by a brief discussion between the panelists. The full answer to the first two questions – which words does he use, and where does he use them – can be found in the Appendix at the back of this book: it provides more detail on which presentations were used and shows how I categorized his words, and as such forms the empirical backbone of this chapter. The question as to the *effect* of these words – what does it do to use these, rather than others – is answered here.

In asking these questions, rather than situated in a history of ideas or biographical work this chapter is in fact closer to (socio)linguistic analyses of individual speech and writing.[22] The core question shared by these kinds of inquiries is how individual writers and speakers "convey their meaning" to an

18 On the use of capitals when referring to the *Tallinn Manuals*, see Chapter 1 note 5.

19 See Chapter 1 for an explanation of these questions.

20 The research for this chapter took place between summer 2015 and late spring 2016. As the second *Tallinn Manual* had not been published at the time, the presentations analyzed here only deal with the first *Tallinn Manual*. The ones I attended that were used in this chapter were those given at CyCon 2012. The Appendix further accounts for the other choices made here.

21 Except for the presentation at CyCon 2014, which was available at the time of researching this chapter but now no longer is; see the Appendix.

22 Examples include Ken Hyland, '"Small Bits of Textual Material": A Discourse Analysis of Swales' Writing' (2008) 27 *English for Specific Purposes* 142 (though his is a quantitative analysis); Julia Valeiras Jurado, 'A Multimodal Approach to Persuasion in Conference Presentations,' in: *Multimodal Analysis in Academic Settings: From Research to Teaching*, Belinda Crawford Camiciottoli and Inmaculada Fortanet-Gómez (eds.), Routledge 2015, 108–132; M. Noelia Ruiz-Madrid and Inmaculada Fortanet-Gómez, 'A Multimodal Discourse Analysis Approach to Humour in Conference Presentations: The Case of Autobiographic References' (2015) 173 *Procedia – Social and Behavioral Sciences* 246.

audience and what (in case of speech) is the combined effect of their words, intonation, gestures or other modes.[23] Specifically, I use Ken Hyland's work on "stance and engagement" – which I will elaborate on in the relevant sections, below – and that of Carmen Konzett on identity constructions during Q&A sessions at academic conferences, which similarly will be dealt with further on.[24] Both help to explain what words 'do' in a text: what happens when Schmitt adds words like 'absolutely' or 'very important,' or how the use of particular pronouns can be used to include or exclude one's audience. For example, Konzett's analytical frame helps to clarify how an "in-group" and an "out-group" can be linguistically created through the use of specific words, and how this creates a gap between a speaker and their audience.[25] Conference presentations, in this view, are "social event[s]":[26] they allow for "the construction of ... professional selves" and are a form of "self-presentation."[27] In other words, this chapter operates under the presumption that on these stages, Schmitt is performing one or more professional roles.

Ultimately, what this chapter presents is a view of these presentations as involving a kind of map-drawing: a creation of gaps between Schmitt and several 'others.'[28] The first part of the chapter shows how he relates to 'time' and international legal thinking; the second, how he constructs a spatial map of the field within which he functions. With regard to time, section 5.1 shows how Schmitt positions himself as well as the Manual squarely within the history of international legal thinking, both on international humanitarian law generally as well as cyberwar in particular. He furthermore expresses a fidelity to and certainty about "the law as it is today"[29] which, as will be shown further on, comes tantalizingly close to the religious. Lastly, he prophesies the possible futures of international law on cyber. The second part of the chapter, in section 5.2, shows how he draws a map of the professional world he

23 Valeiras Jurado, 'Multimodal Approach,' 108.

24 Ken Hyland, 'Stance and Engagement: A Model of Interaction in Academic Discourse' (2005) 7 *Discourse studies* 173; Carmen Konzett, *Any Questions? Identity Construction in Academic Conference Discussions*, Walter de Gruyter 2012.

25 Konzett, 'Any Questions?,' para 7.4.3., 383–385.

26 Ventola, Shalom and Thompson, 'Introduction,' 9; see also Neil Gross and Crystal Fleming, 'Academic Conferences and the Making of Philosophical Knowledge,' in: *Social Knowledge in the Making*, Charles Camic, Neil Gross and Michèle Lamont (eds.), The University of Chicago Press 2011, 151–179, 152 et seq.

27 Konzett, 'Any Questions?,' 1, 6, more elaborately 53–57. Though she writes about Q&A sessions, the same may be said of conference presentations.

28 Thanks to Jessica Lawrence for suggesting 'map-drawing' as a metaphor. See also Anna Duszak, 'Us and Others: An Introduction,' in: *Us and Others: Social Identities across Languages, Discourses and Cultures*, Anna Duszak (ed.), John Benjamins 2002, 1–28, 8.

29 CyCon 2012 | Michael Schmitt: Tallinn Manual Part III (hereafter: CyCon 2012 (III)), 28.28.

inhabits. By means of the words that he uses he positions himself vis-à-vis several 'others': first, nonlawyers; second, other(s) (lawyers) who, in his view, misinterpret international law as well as those he refers to as "pure academics";[30] third, the group of experts, involved in the composition of the *Tallinn Manual*; and, finally, himself in the third person. Looking at the map as a whole, we see Schmitt at the heart of the debate, and to some extent also the group of experts with whom he drafted the Manual. In this manner it becomes clear how he constructs his authority in these presentations: as the one holding the key, not only to what we know to be international law, but what is more, to who is eligible to make those claims.

A few notes on the text are in order. This chapter only focuses on the words Schmitt speaks, whereas a conference presentation is a "multimodal" event: meaning is conveyed not just through words, but through gestures, intonation and PowerPoint slides (to name a few).[31] However, I have assumed Schmitt's words to contain sufficient meaning in and of themselves to merit this particular focus.[32] This also means that I draw on analyses of both academic speech and academic writing, though these two differ in the sense that "the constraints governing the two events are radically different and this has an obvious impact on the precise choice of content, structure, language and semiotic resources brought into play."[33] In other words, the "context" of both 'events' is very different and structures what is said and how.[34] Academic speech is also

30 Brown 2013, 1.04.38.

31 Valeiras Jurado, 'Multimodal Approach,' 113–114. See also Teresa Morell, 'International Conference Paper Presentations: A Multimodal Analysis to Determine Effectiveness' (2015) 37 *English for Specific Purposes* 137, who understands modes as "ways of representing and communicating meaning" (137); Miguel F. Ruiz-Garrido, 'Intensifying Adverbs in Academic Spoken Discourse: A Contrastive Study Between English and Spanish,' in: *Multimodal Analysis in Academic Settings: From Research to Teaching*, Belinda Crawford Camiciottoli and Inmaculada Fortanet-Gómez (eds.), Routledge 2015, 61–82. On the relation between words and (what are usually thought of as) paralinguistic features see Alan Cienki, 'Language as a Prototype Category: Cognitive Linguistics meets Multimodal Communication,' Inaugural Lecture Vrije Universiteit Amsterdam, September 14, 2015; Alan Cienki, 'The Dynamic Scope of Relevant Behaviors in Talk: A Perspective from Cognitive Linguistics' (extended abstract), *Proceedings of the 2nd European and the 5th Nordic Symposium on Multimodal Communication* 2015, 6; Alan Cienki, 'Spoken Language Usage Events' (2015) 7 *Language and Cognition* 499.

32 For a similar choice as the one made here see Konzett, 'Any Questions?,' chapter 5, specifically 107; but see Cienki, 'Spoken Language,' 502–503.

33 Carter-Thomas and Rowley-Jolivet, 'Analysing,' 60 (comparing conference presentations to articles submitted to conference proceedings). See also Ruiz-Garrido, 'Intensifying Adverbs,' 61–63; Ventola, Shalom and Thompson, 'Introduction,' 10. For other examples of this crossover see note 60 below.

34 Carter-Thomas and Rowley-Jolivet, 'Analysing,' 60; see also John M. Swales, 'Evaluation in Academic Speech: First Forays,' in: *Academic Discourse: New Insights into Evaluation*,

more 'casual'; it "is much more like conversation than it is like academic prose."[35] What this means for this chapter is that the analysis is based on what I have considered to be patterns across the different presentations; where this is less obvious, I have explicated this in the relevant section.[36] Throughout the chapter I have furthermore attempted to give as faithful an account as possible of these words and the context within which they are said; words were only deleted when they did not radically change the meaning of a phrase. The quotes used here also contain some words in bold to highlight specific parts; this is not an indication of Schmitt's own emphasis. Where I wanted to convey this I have italicized his words. In addition, as the same quote can be relevant to different sections of this chapter, some quotes appear more than once. Lastly, I should point out that as a Western European I am situated in a different rhetorical as well as (legal) academic tradition than Schmitt, which surely impacts the way I listen to his presentations (and thereby, what I think these presentations do to an audience). Moreover, as a self-identified New Haven scholar (which may in part account for his focus on 'giving answers') his view of international law likewise differs from my own.[37]

5.1 TIME: SETTING THE STAGE

In this section I detail, first, how Schmitt invokes the past to point out that both the Manual, as well as he himself, are part of a 'lineage' of international legal thinking; secondly, this section brings to the fore his claim of a firm grasp on existing law. As the Appendix shows, these expressions of certainty with regard to *lex lata* are the ones that are most frequent (as are those about the group of experts; see the second part of this chapter). This part of the chapter concludes with a discussion of the way he prophesies the future of international law.

Gabriella Del Lungo Camiciotti and Elena Tognini Bonelli (eds.), Peter Lang 2004, 31–54, 49–50.

35 Ibid., 32.

36 As also the Appendix shows, these statements are most explicit and elaborate with regard to his level of conviction about the substance of existing law, and when he discusses the group of experts involved in the drafting of the Manual.

37 Orford refers to the New Haven school's "problem-solving focus"; Anne Orford, 'Scientific Reason and the Discipline of International Law' (2014) 25 *European Journal of International Law* 369, 371; see also Lung-chu Chen, 'Perspectives from the New Haven School' (1993) 87 *American Society of International Law Proceedings* 407, specifically 408–409. For his own statement on the New Haven school see Michael N. Schmitt, 'The "Use of Force" in Cyberspace: A Reply to Dr Ziolkowski,' in: *4th International Conference on Cyber Conflict*, Christian Czosseck, Rain Ottis and Katharina Ziolkowski (eds.), NATO CCD COE Publications 2012, 311–317, 315. For a comparative study of the education and publication patterns of international law academics, see Roberts, 'International Law,' chapter 3.

5.1.1 *Bridging the Past and the Present*

Schmitt relates to the past in a couple of different ways. First, he positions the *Tallinn Manual* in a long-standing tradition of manuals, invoking both nineteenth-century international law manuals as well as more recent ones in which he himself was involved as a legal expert. The "long lineage" of manuals is, for example, expressed by him in a presentation in 2013, when he says that "it was a **long lineage** of doing manuals. For the legal historians ... the Oxford Manual, the Brussels Manual, from the nineteenth century, and so forth."[38] By invoking these previous manuals, the *Tallinn Manual* becomes part of this lineage. It suggests a place for this particular Manual in the history of international law, in which it constitutes the most recent addition to an existing tradition of international legal handbooks. In Schmitt's words, "we wanted to do a new Manual ***like those previous ones***."[39] Drawing on more recent history, in the same part of this presentation Schmitt emphasizes his own involvement in the drafting of these 'previous manuals':

> **This Manual is not the first of its kind.** You have heard the term San Remo Manual on the law of naval warfare ... There was a NIAC Manual ... **that I did** with Yoram Dinstein of Israel and Charles Garraway of the United States. And then most recently there was a product that was called ... [the] Air and Missile Warfare Manual that was done by a group of forty experts and then ultimately drafted **by myself** and Wolff von Heinegg and Bill Boothby was involved ... We all got together and we drafted the Commentary.[40]

He repeats this reference to his experience a little later in the same presentation, when he says that "we had **a lot of experience** in the group, people like Wolff who'd been involved in all these projects, **and myself.**"[41] Similarly, in

38 LENS 2013, 26.07. The Oxford Manuals date back to 1880 and 1913, the Brussels Declaration to 1874; see International Committee of the Red Cross, 'Treaties, States Parties and Commentaries.' On this claim see Petrov, 'Expert Laws,' section 1.3. I first took the idea of these invocations of history as part of authority constructions from Sofia Stolk, '"The Record on Which History Will Judge Us Tomorrow": Auto-History in the Opening Statements of International Criminal Trials' (2015) 28 *Leiden Journal of International Law* 993.

39 CyCon 2012 (I), 3.08.

40 Ibid., 2.09. During this presentation Schmitt does state that this Manual is different from other manuals in the sense that it pertains to a phenomenon yet to take place; see ibid., 17.30. For these other manuals see inter alia Yoram Dinstein, *Commentary on the HPCR Manual on International Law Applicable to Air and Missile Warfare*, Program on Humanitarian Policy and Conflict Research, Harvard University 2010; Michael N. Schmitt, Charles H.B. Garraway and Yoram Dinstein, *The Manual on the Law of Non International Armed Conflict With Commentary*, International Institute of Humanitarian Law 2006.

41 CyCon 2012 (I), 4.02. Schmitt is referring here to Wolff Heintschel von Heinegg; see also Section 5.3.2.

a 2015 presentation, he refers to his previous participation in the ICRC's study into direct participation in hostilities.[42] These are appeals to experience that also signal his own part in the more recent history of international law.[43] For example, in the spring of 2015 he gives a lecture at Harvard University, which starts as follows:

> Let's start at the beginning. The beginning is actually in the 1990s ... **we began** to look at the issue of cyber in war colleges around the world, most notably the war college in Newport, the Naval War College, **I was then a student, an Air Force officer going through the program there**, and cyber, everyone was talking about cyber, *everyone* was. And so there was an, an, an **initial conference** there, in 1998, held by the law department ... a book was produced, **I was the editor of the book.**[44]

Thus, a little over a minute into this lecture,[45] we are informed that Schmitt was there, both in terms of time as well as place – the Naval War College – when the debate on cyber and international law began. This matters to his positioning of himself as part of the "in-group."[46] Elsewhere, he likewise refers to himself as "one of the, the old guys, who started dealing with cyber a long time ago."[47] So, Schmitt does not only historicize the Manual; he also historicizes his own position. In 2013, when talking about anticipatory self-defense against imminent cyberattacks, he says the following:

> **[A] number of us in the aftermath of 9/11 started looking at this problem, and I will tell you what I came up with,** and my view is ... This has been, **this has developed into** what is **now known** as the 'last window of opportunity test,' the United States government has, I, **I called it in my article back in 2003, we now start to see US government documents and speeches coming out**, talking about 'last window of opportunity,' it's my *last* window of opportunity to defend myself.[48]

42 PILAC 2015, 39.31.

43 On experience as part of an expert/authority claim, see also Konzett, 'Any Questions?,' section 7.1.2.1, 370–372, 384; on the effect of the claims to experience in the *Tallinn Manual* see Kessler and Werner, 'Expertise,' 802–807.

44 PILAC 2015, 7.56; see also LENS 2013, 24.32.

45 Schmitt starts the lecture at PILAC 2015 at 6.28.

46 Konzett, 'Any Questions?,' 383–385.

47 Michael N. Schmitt, CyCon 2012 | Michael Schmitt: Tallinn Manual Part II (hereafter: CyCon 2012 (II)), 21.25. It should be noted Schmitt says this in a different context; see ibid., 20.25 et seq.

48 Brown 2013, 47.18, continued at 48.00. The article Schmitt refers to is Michael N. Schmitt, 'Preemptive Strategies in International Law' (2003) 24 *Michigan Journal of International Law* 513, specifically 535.

One thing to take away from this is that Schmitt points out how his previous work has been adopted by others – in this case, through US *opinio juris*: an idea he launched in an article in 2003 has made its way to 'US government documents and speeches.' Similarly, in another presentation in the same year he discusses the lack of consensus among the experts involved in the *Tallinn Manual*, with regard to the threshold level for violating the prohibition on the use of force. Ideas on the subject as expressed by him in a 1999 article (and discussed in the third chapter of this book) were acknowledged – though not fully adopted – by the group of experts, who, in the Manual, suggest it for use by states. Though Schmitt himself emphasizes that he was not part of the experts' discussions on Article 2(4)[49] – and is therefore not the one who suggested or is responsible for the reference to his work in this area in the Manual – the very fact that his work *is* included shows his influence in this particular area. With regard to this framework he said in a 2011 article, that it had "generally withstood the test of time."[50] The same 'bridging' movement from past to present goes for the group of experts as a whole, when he refers to the then-upcoming second *Tallinn Manual* and says that

> [w]hat we are doing is we're looking at cyber issues what we call 'below the threshold,' **a term that has caught on**. 'Below the threshold' referring to cyber operations that don't rise to the level of a use of force or an armed attack in the context of the UN Charter.[51]

This also happens when he says that "**I've suggested before**, that what y'ought to be looking at" (on organized armed groups in a non-international armed conflict); and, "something **I thought up in an article a long time ago** and the jury is out on whether this is true"[52] (on the protection of particular data under international humanitarian law). In these last few examples, Schmitt does not present himself as the *only* one providing the answers. But what he *does* do, is bring to the fore that he is very much part of the group of people giving them. Ingo Venzke likewise points out how an invocation of having been right in the past, is part of the construction of "semantic authority": "An actor has the capacity of finding acceptance for its statements about international law,"

49 Brown 2013, 32.38; see also LENS 2013, 40.25 et seq.

50 Schmitt, 'Cyber Operations,' 575; Brown 2013, 31.19 et seq., and Schmitt, 'Normative Framework,' 914–915; see for its recurrence in the *Tallinn Manual*, Schmitt (ed.), 'Tallinn Manual,' 48–51.

51 PILAC 2015, 17.13. The second *Tallinn Manual* also deals with peacetime cyber operations.

52 ILD 2012 | Panel Discussion: Cyber Conflict and the Law of Armed Conflict (hereafter: ILD 2012), 17.57 and CyCon 2012 (II), 13.26. This raises the question who 'the jury' is. In Schmitt's view, there are probably two answers to this: states, in case of new law, or in case of existing law, other lawyers.

Venzke says, "if it has been right in the past and if it can present those statements as consistent with tradition … Having been right in the past supports an actors' [*sic*] semantic authority."[53]

Moreover, the effect of placing himself in the history of the debate is that we come to think of him as part of the 'in-group': as one of the people who have been concerned with these questions for a long time. And, as discussed more elaborately in the next section, he implies that legal problems inevitably move towards their resolution – in other words, "there is nothing … the law cannot cover."[54] There might be legal uncertainty, and the expert group may not have been able to solve every issue with which they were confronted – but it is only a matter of time before 'the jury' decides. For example, when discussing the definition of 'attack' in international humanitarian law, "this question that everyone seemed to be **struggling with ten years ago**, has been **asked**, and **answered**, and you **need not concern yourself** with it any further";[55] or, speaking some time before the publication of the Manual,

> [the notion of] [a]ttack, we had brutal, bloody battles, thank god we are friends, over the issue of 'what does an attack … mean today?' However, I think in the last couple of, of literally weeks, the [International Committee of the Red Cross] and those who are on the other side **are coming to an accommodation** that the international law community will find acceptable. **So I think that one's gonna be resolved by the Manual.**[56]

The emphasis here lies on the resolution of legal problems; and Schmitt positions himself as one of those able to solve them. Concomitant to this is his way of speaking of the law, which conveys a high sense of certainty with regard to its substance. The next section deals with these expressions of legal certainty.

5.1.2 *"The Answer Today Is Absolutely 'Yes' … There's Absolutely No Question"*

Listening to Schmitt's presentations, one gets a sense that he is in firm control of the substance of the law. Consider the following extract from a 2012 presentation:

53 See Venzke, 'Semantic Authority,' 10; this is part of his discussion of Weber's "classic tripartite division of authority's character." Ibid., 8.
54 Werner and Boer, 'Imageries of Cyberwar,' 50; see also 46.
55 CyCon 2012 (II), 8.59.
56 CyCon 2012 (I), 21.18.

> So, over and over, particularly in the early days of cyber, the **question** was 'does this rule apply to cyber operations?' The **answer today** is **absolutely** 'yes' . . . there's **absolutely no question** whatsoever, **anyone who argues this point doesn't know what they're talking about**. Because there's **almost unanimity** on this point. **You should not worry** about the fact that the *means* are not violent, **you have to focus** on the consequences of the operation. It's not the nature, it's the consequences.[57]

A few things emerge from this quote that are relevant to Schmitt's construction of his own authority, and several of its elements resonate throughout this chapter. As the claim to there being 'almost unanimity on this point' was extensively dealt with in the previous chapter, it will not be discussed any further here.

First, Schmitt again emphasizes the nature of legal problems as questions requiring an answer. In this case, the question 'in the early days of cyber' was whether 'this rule' (he is speaking here of the notion of 'attack' in *jus in bello*) applied at all.[58] Most notably, his positioning as 'answering questions' directly translates to how he phrases this issue: 'the question was . . . the answer is.'[59] Moreover, he is extremely direct here: to ask this question is basically to disqualify oneself as a lawyer (I will return to this in the second part of this chapter). Secondly, the level of conviction is also expressed by his use of the phrase that 'there's **absolutely** no question' that this is the right answer. Thirdly, he ends with an instruction to his audience: what they 'should not worry about' and what, instead, they 'have to focus on.'

Schmitt very frequently uses these elements in his speech, and here it is useful to look at linguistic analyses of these kinds of phrases to consider what they *do*. I use Ken Hyland's linguistic work on "stance and engagement" here, where stance denotes the speaker's positioning towards particular knowledge claims: whether the speaker, for example, conveys a high or low level of conviction with regard to the particular claim he is making. 'Engagement' refers to the interaction with or involvement of the audience.[60] I will elaborate on these terms, below.

57 CyCon 2012 (II), 7.59.

58 See also the discussion in Chapter 2 of Jean d'Aspremont's concept of "interventionism," signifying claims that existing law applies to cyberattacks. See d'Aspremont, 'Cyber Operations,' 578.

59 See also Brown 2013, 29.08.

60 Hyland, 'Stance and Engagement,' specifically 176 on "engagement." Though Hyland's "model" is applied by him to academic writing rather than speech, it can also be used for the latter 'genre.' For an example of such use see Wenhsien Yang, 'Stance and Engagement: A Corpus-Based Analysis of Academic Spoken Discourse Across Science Domains' (2014) 5

Starting with Schmitt's instructions to his audience as to what they should or should not focus on, worry about, or look at, other examples include, "**[i]f you're starting with a [law of armed conflict] analysis, start here**."[61] Or, on the word 'attack' in international law, "there are *two* legal meanings, and you **must not confuse** the two legal meanings, because they're **very very very** distinct";[62] or, "you **should commit this to memory** if you are an attorney."[63] As a final example, "[t]here are **two more things you need to worry about.** The next one is, for the Germans in the audience, this is ***überimportant.*** **Pay attention, write this down. Ok**?"[64] (The 'ok?' at the end of this sentence is a "tag question." Schmitt uses it on more than one occasion, and its effect is to invite a response from the listener – but in this case, both possible responses to this 'question' place the listener in an uncomfortable position. If the response to 'ok?' is 'yes,' it leads to an asymmetrical relation, where the listener submits to the speaker's claim. However, if the answer is 'no,' the situation becomes very confrontational.[65])

The various phrases listed here are known as "directives," which "instruct the [listener] to perform an action or to see things in a way determined by the [speaker]."[66] The kinds of directives we find in Schmitt's speech are what Hyland refers to as "physical" and "cognitive" acts, directing the audience to particular "kinds of activity." Physical acts are directions as to "how to carry out research processes or to perform some action in the real world"; cognitive acts "guide readers through a line of reasoning, or get them to understand a point in a certain way."[67] Plainly put, through these statements Schmitt tells his audience what to do or think: he tells them what they have to 'start with,' should not 'confuse,' or 'worry about' – and even, to 'pay attention' and 'write down.' There is more to these instructions than telling people what to do,

LSP Journal 62, specifically 64. Yang refers to Hyland's work as the "'stance and engagement' model," see ibid., 63.

61 ILD 2012, 4.24.

62 CyCon 2012 (III), 3.32.

63 CyCon 2012 (II), 5.06.

64 Michael N. Schmitt and Bernhard Blumbergs, Active Cyber Defense Case Studies (hereafter: CyCon 2014), 11.58.

65 Thanks to Alan Cienki for explaining this to me. On tag questions generally, see Maria Josep Cuenca, 'Form-Use Mappings for Tag Questions,' in: *Discourse and Perspectives in Cognitive Linguistics*, Wolf-Andreas Liebert, Gisela Redeker and Linda Waugh (eds.), John Benjamins 1997, 3–20; on inviting a response specifically, 3.

66 Hyland, 'Stance and Engagement,' 184. Elsewhere, Hyland explains how he "borrow[ed] the term from the speech act literature where it is used to denote a broad category of illocutionary acts proposing an action to be carried out by the reader." See Ken Hyland, 'Directives: Argument and Engagement in Academic Writing' (2002) 23 *Applied Linguistics* 215, 216.

67 Hyland, 'Stance and Engagement,' 184–185.

however. By speaking authoritatively the chances that someone is believed increase: "[A]n authoritative rhetorical effect helps display an undisputed command of [the] subject."[68] Following Hyland, it could be argued that precisely because Schmitt is so firm – the 'authoritative rhetorical effect' – he is convincing.[69]

The second element mentioned above, is that of Schmitt's use of the word 'absolutely.' As the Appendix of this chapter shows, he uses this kind of firm language more often, for example when he says with regard to a particular case, "that's **clearly, clearly** a breach of [state] B's sovereignty."[70] Or, "[t]here is this belief that civilians cannot engage in hostilities, **that's completely wrong, that's completely wrong,** it's perfectly acceptable for civilians to engage in hostilities, **but what it means** is that there's certain consequences."[71] Moreover, dealing with the law should not be taken lightly. On assessing state responsibility in case of violations of the prohibition on the use of force, he states "[t]his is **very important law**"; elsewhere, the "classification of conflict" "is a **very important topic**."[72]

Resorting again to linguistic tools to explain the use of these words, two things happen here. In the first set of examples, he uses words such as 'absolutely,' 'clearly' and 'completely wrong' as "boosters"[73] in relation to the interpretive statements he makes. A 'booster' is a somewhat self-explanatory term: it emphasizes the level of certainty with which certain claims are made (it should be noted, however, that the setting of a conference presentation might induce the more frequent use of boosters over their opposite, hedges,

68 Hyland, 'Directives,' 226. This quote needs some context: Hyland is speaking here of the frequent use of cognitive acts (see the body text) in textbooks and research articles. Earlier in the same article he explained how, moving from textual, to physical to cognitive acts one finds "[i]ncreasing imposition" (218) of the writer on the audience. He attempts to explain this by stating that "in both genres [textbooks and research articles] writers must ensure that their points are understood and their convictions recognized. For researchers their commitments and authority are important ways of negotiating their ideas and of gaining acceptance for the priority of their claims. For textbook authors *an authoritative rhetorical effect helps display an undisputed command of their subject*." Ibid., 226 (emphasis added). So in fact, Hyland is speaking here of the different functions cognitive acts may have for textbook authors and research article writers. In both cases, however, the point is that these kinds of directives convey a sense of authority; in this context Hyland speaks of "authorial intervention in a discourse" and "implied authority." See ibid., 232, 233.

69 See also Hyland, 'Stance and Engagement,' 180.

70 CyCon 2014, 40.43.

71 PILAC 2015, 37.03; see also CyCon 2012 (II), 0.52. For a similar process see Ken Hyland, 'Constraint vs Creativity: Identity and Disciplinarity in Academic Writing,' in: *Commonality and Individuality in Academic Discourse*, Maurizio Gotti (ed.), Peter Lang 2009, 25–52, 38–39.

72 LENS 2013, 46.00; ILD 2012, 4.13.

73 Hyland, 'Stance and Engagement,' 179.

where claims are clothed in expressions of uncertainty, such as 'maybe').[74] "Boosters," writes Hyland,

> allow [speakers] to express their certainty in what they say and to mark involvement with the topic and solidarity with their audience. They function to stress shared information, group membership, and engagement with readers.[75]

In the quote provided at the beginning of this section, Schmitt acknowledges an opposite view, but by dismissing it so assuredly – 'absolutely yes, there's absolutely no question' – he 'boosts' the claim he is making about the 'right view.'[76]

The second set of examples – 'very important law,' a 'very important topic' – indicate how Schmitt relates to the law generally, rather than that he expresses certainty with regard to particular substantive claims. The distinction between the above two sets is described by Hyland as one between an "epistemic" and an "affective attitude."[77] Both indicate how the speaker relates to the claims s/he is making; and, in this case, Schmitt's claims with regard to the substance of the law, as well as those with regard to the importance of this law, are very strong. His continuous oaths of allegiance to law create the impression that, when he is certain, there is no room for uncertainty in others; vice versa, when he is unsure about the meaning of a certain legal concept, there is no room for absolute certainty in others.[78] The point is not that he is certain about every aspect of law: he expresses uncertainty, for example, about the concept of direct participation in *jus in bello*, and how it applies to activities in cyberspace.[79] Several of his presentations elaborate on those legal issues the group of experts involved in the drafting of the Manual struggled with, and those they did not 'solve.'[80] The point is that Schmitt, in these moments, discursively 'decides' when the meaning of a concept is fixed, and when it is not. For example, during a panel presentation

74 See Carter-Thomas and Rowley-Jolivet, 'Analysing,' 61.

75 Hyland, 'Stance and Engagement,' 179. Note that Hyland is speaking of academic writing; for an analysis of the use of boosters in academic speech see Yang, 'Academic Spoken Discourse,' 68 et seq.

76 For a description of a similar move see Hyland, 'Constraint,' 38–39.

77 Hyland, 'Stance and Engagement,' 180; he describes this second set as "attitude markers."

78 A similar dynamic is described by Kessler and Werner with regard to the Manual's occasional references to a lack of consensus among the experts. Anyone claiming legal certainty on a subject on which the experts weren't sure, will have to fight this 'authoritative assessment of uncertainty.' See Kessler and Werner, 'Expertise,' 805–807, 810 (using similar wording).

79 See his discussion at PILAC 2015, 40.52 et seq.; see also the same presentation at 29.43 and LENS 2013, 34.34, and 1.11.41: "The one place where we struggled a little bit . . . We disagreed on this issue"; see also Brown 2013, 23.21.

80 Which he does at, for example, LENS 2013, very explicitly at 36.54; see also the previous footnote. At these points Schmitt 'hedges' (qualifies) his statements, rather than boosting them; see the body text, above.

he discusses the notion of perfidy with another panelist, who expresses doubts as to its application to a particular case. Schmitt responds by saying,

> [i]**t is certainly perfidious, it is certainly *not* perfidy.** And the war crime is perfidy and requires perfidious conduct in, in connection with an intent to kill, wound, or, if you're a Protocol party, capture.[81]

The Appendix of this chapter is rife with expressions similar to those noted here.[82] To put it plainly, when Schmitt is sure, he is very sure – and when he is unsure, the possibility of certainty in others is discursively excluded.

Moreover, he continually stresses the importance of taking these things seriously. In this respect, one moment in these presentations stands out and deserves separate mention here. In 2014, Schmitt copresents with a technical expert, who elaborates on a hypothetical cyber incident, at which point Schmitt responds by giving a legal analysis. The presentation starts as follows:

> We selected three [scenarios] that we would like to present to you and show you how, how a lawyer would go through the **legal stations of the cross** if you will, with respect to understanding a particular scenario.[83]

There is no irony or humor here: the view of the profession laid out here, is that lawyers approach problems so methodically and structured that it can be equated to religious ritual. Each step of law-application, in this view, has its own hallmarks, and is followed by a next step which is already similarly laid out. The legal work, perhaps, is something to have faith in.

Finally, the quote at the beginning of this section highlighted another element of Schmitt's speech: the use of questions and answers.[84] I want to emphasize it here because it is such a tangible display of his self-identification with lawyers as the ones giving answers – as was already reflected in the quote which serves as this chapter's title. Consider the following few phrases, in which Schmitt discusses how the expert group did not definitively solve the question of where the boundary of a 'use of force' lies. In response to a question by an audience member, he says the following:

81 ILD 2012, 1.13.27; the exchange starts at 1.13.01.

82 Under this particular heading in the Appendix ('Expressions of (un)certainty') I have included a broad range of similar statements, to give a comprehensive image of the way Schmitt speaks. As stated on the cover page of the Appendix, to provide a more balanced image I have also included some statements of uncertainty by Schmitt. As explained in this chapter, however, these expressions of uncertainty do not detract from the idea presented here: that these are uncertainties on the road towards legal answers; that they will be solved, and that no one can be sure in this regard until they are.

83 CyCon 2014, 0.12.

84 Hyland, 'Stance and Engagement,' 185–186.

> [I]f the policy maker is looking at me as the legal adviser, what he or she wants to know is, 'was that a violation of international law?' You know. And if it was, 'what are my remedies? What can I do in response?' And, and I have to say to ... him or her, I have to say, 'well, you know, it kind of looks,' and that's, you know. **That's why policy makers hate lawyers, ok, so. 'On the one hand, on the other.' The answer is always, 'it depends'** ... And that's why this is the greatest disappointment, I believe, in the, in the project. **Because I can't answer your question and I *should* be able to.**[85]

This is very telling with regard to how Schmitt perceives his own role as a lawyer: that he should be able to answer the questions put to him by policy makers. In a similar vein, he says

> [u]nfortunately, or fortunately for lawyers and law professors the term [armed attack] is not defined in international law anywhere, in any authoritative place in international law. **But we have some clues.**[86]

The Appendix of this chapter shows other examples of how this positioning finds its way to the words he uses. Most explicitly, in the presentation he gives jointly with the technical expert, he suggests what the audience should be writing down if they were answering these questions as law students taking an exam.[87] In response to one of the case studies presented by the technical expert Schmitt says, "'[d]oes state C have an obligation to do something ... ?' **Answer**: we weren't sure, we weren't sure." And, "[i]s it ok? Answer: yeah. It's ok as a what? As a countermeasure. It's ok as a countermeasure."[88] This is the presentation where Schmitt goes through several 'cyberattack scenarios' to assess their legality, and therefore, it can be expected that his words are more instructive. Yet, given other examples of a similar kind, this last one is likewise telling with regard to the 'giving of answers.' It is something Esther Pascual refers to as "fictive interaction," where a speaker interacts with an imagined 'other' while speaking. Crucial here, is that the interaction *could* have happened, and is therefore not entirely fictional – but not entirely real, either: they are "illustrations of actual language usages."[89] It happens in Schmitt's speech more often:

> First of all, the big question that was asked ... 'well ... does an armed attack have to be kinetic? ... Because of the word 'armed.' And therefore, does it

85 Brown 2013, 37.27. He ends this section by saying that the group decided Stuxnet was a use of force.
86 CyCon 2012 (III), 6.39.
87 CyCon 2014, 17.04, and 19.11.
88 Ibid., 5.35, 40.13.
89 See Esther Pascual, *Imaginary Trialogues: Conceptual Blending and Fictive Interaction in Criminal Courts*, LOT 2002, 13; more elaborately, 13–20. On "[f]ictive interaction in oral, legal discourse" see ibid., 146–155.

> exclude cyber stuff?' **The answer is 'no.'** The International Court of Justice has answered this question in the Nuclear Weapons Case . . . it matters what the consequences are. And in fact state practice supports this, **this should be no epiphany . . . This is a question asked by scholars that need not be asked, this question has been asked and answered, this is settled law.**[90]

Here, we similarly find an example of 'fictive interaction' in the first few lines of this quote: 'does it exclude cyber stuff? The answer is no.' Its effect, in Pascual's terms, is that it "has the power of turning addressees into cognitive co-constructors of discourse."[91] Something similar is described by Ken Hyland with regard to the kinds of questions asked by Schmitt: they "invit[e] engagement and [bring] the interlocutor into an arena where they can be led to the writer's viewpoint"; these questions "encourage the reader to explore an unresolved issue with the writer as an equal . . . following where the argument leads."[92] What both Pascual and Hyland point out, is how the use of this kind of fictive interaction draws the audience into the argument, which makes it seem as if the conclusion follows naturally. Thus, we find Schmitt at the end of this quote saying, 'this is a question that has been asked, and answered, this is settled law.'

The above has elaborated on the different elements of Schmitt's speech that place him firmly in control of existing law, and as the one in a position to be providing the answers. The next section details why this positioning matters in light of the goals of the *Tallinn Manual*, and how these statements extend into the future of international law.

5.1.3 *"Let Me Tell You What Mike Schmitt Thinks the Future Is Going to Be"*

In Schmitt's own words, he is "in the business of finding what the law is today."[93] The distinction between existing law and the law as it will, or should be, is crucial for the *Tallinn Manual*, as it purports to provide existing law as normative guidance for states.[94] Thus, Schmitt himself describes the Manual as

> **a *restatement* of the law. It does *not* make law. There is no effort to progressively develop the law.** This was an attempt to say 'we now have

[90] CyCon 2012 (III), 6.51; this follows his previous statement, see also note 86 above. This is an example of what Pascual would refer to as an "imaginary trialogue," see Pascual, 'Imaginary Trialogues,' 130–131.

[91] Pascual, 'Imaginary Trialogues,' 148; relatedly, 190.

[92] Hyland, 'Stance and Engagement,' 185. Note that Hyland is referring to academic writing here – hence, the reference to "the writer."

[93] CyCon 2012 (III), 13.19. For the copyright notice of this section see p. vii above.

[94] Schmitt (ed.), 'Tallinn Manual,' 3, 5–6. But see Tsagourias, 'Tallinn Manual Commentary,' 40 and Boer, 'Restating'; see also note 102 below.

> cyber, how does the law of bellum and in bello, how does that body of law apply in the cyber context?'[95]

This emphasis on the distinction between *lex lata* and *lex ferenda*, which follows from Schmitt's repetition as well as his emphasis (in italics), makes sense if we consider that any reference in the Manual to what kind of rules states *should* abide by, would defeat its object and make it useless as a handbook.[96] So, Schmitt says, the group of experts was "**slave to *lex*** [***lata***]" and "**wanted to maintain fidelity to the law as we believe states would interpret it on *that* date**";[97] they "did not want to go **out on the ledge**"; "**let's make sure** we are **in no way** trying to suggest **what the law should be.**"[98] Similarly, in 2015, Schmitt says that the experts "**swore on a stack of Bibles in front of ten bishops** that we would **never never never** delve into ***lex ferenda***, that we would be **strictly tied to *lex lata*.**"[99] It is said jokingly, and the audience laughs in response, but two things emerge from this and similar statements. First, Schmitt describes the boundary between *lex lata* and *lex ferenda* as one that is *possible* to draw.[100] What is at stake with this strong emphasis on *lex lata* is that "[a]ctors trying to win any legal dispute need to base their arguments 'on the law as it is,' everything else would defeat their claims from the outset."[101] The Manual, in that sense, also has a comforting effect: regardless of the legal uncertainty one may think cyberwar creates, the law can still be said to function properly.[102] The point here is not to assess whether Schmitt and the group of experts are right in their assessment of the substance of *lex lata*: the point is to bring to the fore the continued emphasis on as well as the function of maintaining this distinction.[103]

95 CyCon 2012 (I), 3.12.

96 See note 101 below; see also Boer, 'Lex Lata,' for an elaboration.

97 PILAC 2015, 55.26, 52.52. Schmitt in fact misspeaks at 55.26 and says the experts were "slave to *lex ferenda*," but it is obvious from the context as well as from his other presentations that this is the opposite of what he intends to say. I have therefore changed it in the body text.

98 LENS 2013, 26.53, 1.06.41.

99 PILAC 2015, 47.14.

100 This is based on Wouter G. Werner, 'International Law: Between Legalism and Securitization,' in: *Security: Dialogue Across Disciplines*, Philippe Bourbeau (ed.), Cambridge University Press 2015, 196–218, 196 note 1; see also Koskenniemi, 'Apology to Utopia,' 470–471, pointing this out in the context of customary law.

101 Venzke, 'Interpretation,' 17, as well as his reference to Stanley Fish on that page.

102 See also Werner and Boer, 'Imageries of Cyberwar,' 43, 46, 54. For a somewhat different view on parts of 'the law' in the Manual, see Watkin, 'Road Ahead,' 494; see also Michael J. Adams, *A Warning About Tallinn 2.0 … Whatever It Says*, on 'Lawfare,' January 4, 2017.

103 He does something similar in his article on the application of the prohibition on the use of force, discussed in Chapter 3; see Schmitt, 'Normative Framework,' 917–918; see also Boer, 'Restating,' 14 and Boer, 'Lex Lata,' 76–77.

Secondly, it is not only *possible* to draw this boundary: it is also *necessary* to do so. Schmitt even implies the danger involved in not adhering to it, by saying that, as for the group of experts suggesting what the law should be, would be 'going out on the ledge.' The danger in confusing *lex lata* and *lex ferenda* lies in the Manual not being used: the only way Schmitt and the expert group can ensure the Manual is actually used by its 'customers,' is by pointing out that the legal obligations outlined in the Manual are nothing new; that they are, basically, what states are already subject to – but, this time, in cyberspace.[104] The purpose of the Manual's emphasis on its adherence to existing law might be the same: to increase the chances of its use.[105] This is the background against which we have to understand Schmitt's references to the Manual as a "product," intended for "customers," who are, predominantly, states and their legal advisers.[106] It therefore makes sense that Schmitt, in response to a question by an audience member on a substantive point, says that "your point is . . . a very very good one, it's just we were *very* hesitant about getting out ahead of **where we thought states would** [go]."[107] This doesn't mean, however, that he does not think the law might change: "If you ask me what armed attack *lex ferenda* is **you'll get a different answer** than what we put in the Manual. Because we asked **'what is the law *now*?'**"[108] So, Schmitt says, "my **mission** is to find **what the law *is today***."[109] Again, this shows Schmitt's belief in the possibility of drawing the distinction; put differently, his belief that the substance of current law can be firmly assessed – and, moreover, that he is able to draw this line. This boundary even comes with a date: "Our goal is to say, **'what is the law, *right* now,'** it was **June 2012,** that was the date. In **June 2012, 'what is the law today?'**"[110]

The awareness that the law might evolve emerges at several points during Schmitt's presentations. He frequently pronounces on these developments, in a manner exemplified in the header of this section: "Let me tell you what Mike

104 Kessler and Werner, 'Expertise,' 805, and Werner and Boer, 'Imageries of Cyberwar,' 40. See also Boer, 'Lex Lata,' specifically 78.

105 See notes 58 and 101 above.

106 CyCon 2012 (I), 1.48, 11.37; see also Brown 2013, 1.04.45, where Schmitt talks about the "audience" of the Manual, and PILAC 2015, 53.00. He also refers to an earlier manual as a product at CyCon 2012 (I), 2.35. On the notion of the *Tallinn Manual* as a manual proper see Werner, 'Absence, Restatement.' See also Boer, 'Lex Lata,' 78.

107 PILAC 2015, 48.28. Schmitt doesn't finish this sentence, so I have inserted the word 'go' here at the end of it.

108 CyCon 2012 (I), 14.01; see also LENS 2013, 1.06.23 and PILAC 2015, 52.18.

109 CyCon 2012 (II), 20.42.

110 LENS 2013, 1.06.46. Note that this date shifts to August 2012; see CyCon 2012 (I), 14.11; see also Boer, 'Lex Lata,' 78.

Schmitt thinks **the future is going to be**"[111] (I will return to this at the end of this chapter). For example, during one presentation he shows a slide titled "Vectors," on which he lists several elements of international humanitarian law (IHL), the interpretation of which he thinks will change.[112] Occasionally, these predictions extend from the past to the near future, for example when he expresses an expectation that a particular kind of test he referred to a little earlier in that presentation is about to be adopted in the final version of the Manual (as also discussed above).[113] Schmitt expresses the same expectation with regard to an instrument-based view of, again, the concept of 'attack' in the *jus in bello*. In one presentation he elaborates on the views of some who claim that to "**shoot cyber at civilians** ... then that's a violation of international humanitarian law **irrespective of the consequences,**" because the targeting of civilians is, as such, prohibited under these laws. Schmitt states that "**this view is fading away,** but there's still a few **dinosaurs** out there that hold it."[114] By referring to those who still maintain this view as 'dinosaurs,' the imminent prevalence of the opposite view – where consequences, rather than the "status of a target,"[115] determine whether IHL has been violated – is prophesied (I return to his use of the word 'dinosaur' below). Schmitt expects the same development of legal norms with regard to the use of force in taking countermeasures. He states we should "**watch this space,** because this wasn't horribly important when *Oil Platforms* came out, it's **überimportant** today, because of cyber warfare."[116]

Schmitt's predictions also relate to changes occurring in the next couple of years. These predictions concern very specific rules of international law, inter alia, the notion of armed attack ("I think that law will be different **in seven years**"),[117] data as an object under international humanitarian law ("I will tell you that I anticipate that **in five years**, that will change"),[118] an organized armed group in cyberspace ("we **won't see** a lot of that")[119] and the classification of

111 CyCon 2012 (II), 20.22.

112 PILAC 2015, 42.38.

113 He states that "I think we're [the group of experts] about to put this debate to rest" at ILD 2012, 10.22. He refers to this imminent resolution (of the same issue) a couple of times in the earlier, 2012 presentations; see for example CyCon 2012 (I), 21.28; CyCon 2012 (II), 16.13.

114 CyCon 2012 (II), 19.35.

115 Ibid., 18.46.

116 LENS 2013, 51.26. Schmitt refers here to the *Oil Platforms* case before the International Court of Justice; one of the questions raised there pertained to the lawfulness of forceful countermeasures. See Oona A. Hathaway, 'The Drawbacks and Dangers of Active Defense,' in: *Proceedings of the 6th International Conference on Cyber Conflict*, Pascal Brangetto, Markus Maybaum and Jan Stinissen (eds.), NATO CCD COE Publications 2014, 39–50.

117 CyCon 2012 (I), 21.14.

118 PILAC 2015, 52.42.

119 Ibid., 38.58.

a state's economy as a civilian object ("I do believe that economies will be seen as a civilian object, **over, *over* time**").[120] Given Schmitt's continuous emphasis on the Manual's focus on *lex lata*, it makes sense that his predictions are often accompanied by caveats: that this is not "the law today,"[121] but rather, his expectation as to how the law will evolve. Likewise, in 2013, he states that more rules that are laid down in the Manual, are going to change:

> I will tell you, that **I am a firm believer that this body of law will evolve, it will evolve quickly through state practice**, because some of the Rules that we came up with that we say are the law, we believe they're the law, **states are not going to be willing to accept** ... Armed attack is a good example. I am **absolutely convinced** that if the United States were to suffer a massive cyberattack that caused no damage or injury but massively disrupted our way of life, we would consider that an armed attack. I'm *absolutely* convinced.[122]

The above statement shows that this anticipation of the law developing is tied here to state will – something Schmitt explicates in the lines following this predictive statement. So, though the experts give states the law they are currently bound by, states might change their mind on what they think this law to be. Alternatively, he prophesies:

> **Where's the future going?** I gave you ***lex lata***, the law as it is today. **Where do I anticipate the future's going?** There are two possibilities ... But that's *not* today, **that's seven, eight, nine years from now** when state practice begins to crystallize.[123]

Though he is skeptical about the development of specific treaties on cyber, "**we may see state practice**."[124] There is a similar dynamic at play here as the one described above, on Schmitt bridging the gap between the past and the present. That section dealt with how legal problems progress towards their answers, and how Schmitt positions himself as part of the group of people who have dealt with these issues in the past. Similarly, in these statements just

120 CyCon 2012 (II), 21.53.
121 LENS 2013, 1.06.52; CyCon 2012 (III), 14.56; CyCon 2012 (II), 18.38.
122 LENS 2013, 1.06.54; see also Boer, 'Lex Lata,' 79–80.
123 CyCon 2012 (III), 28.25, continued at 29.16; see also LENS 2013, 45.38.
124 PILAC 2015, 36.22; see also Brown 2013, 1.28.56. At one of these presentations Schmitt responds to the criticism on the group's lack of geographical spread and states that "[i]t's our sense that that international participation should come in the form of treaty negotiations, or whatever, but we were just twenty academics and practitioners that were trying to solve a problem." This seems to be more of a casual remark, however, than a serious expectation that a treaty on the subject will develop – especially given Schmitt's firm statements that this will not happen, elsewhere. See LENS 2013, 1.05.04.

cited, though there might be a sense of uncertainty, there is no sense of rupture: the experts provided *lex lata*, but if circumstances or states require differently, this will be solved within the boundaries of the law. This brings us back to Koskenniemi's explanation of what legal problem-solution entails: that "the legal system itself is coherent."[125] Whatever is 'legally' unresolved at present, will be resolved in the future.

As Schmitt positions himself in the history of international doctrinal legal thinking, and occasionally shows how he has been right before, he creates the idea that he might also be right about the direction the law will take in the future. What the statements described in this first part of the chapter do – dealing with the past, present and future of international law – is discursively place Schmitt in the 'in-group' of those able to answer these questions.[126] The next, second part of this chapter first briefly introduces this positioning, and subsequently elaborates on the several groups of 'others' Schmitt refers to.

5.2 SPACE: (DIS)QUALIFYING OTHERS

As portrayed above, by means of the words that he chooses Schmitt comes to personify the bridge between the past and present; between *lex lata* and *lex ferenda*, and between the present and future of international law. In this part I seek to account for what the map of that world looks like, following Schmitt's drawing of boundaries between himself and several 'others.' Ken Hyland refers to the "discursive power ... that enables individuals to exercise control over participation in disciplinary discourses."[127] Though Hyland is speaking here of academic writing, the same kind of 'discursive power' can be witnessed in (academic) speech, and this part of the chapter explores its manifestations in the presentations under scrutiny here.[128] In addition, writing about academic conferences specifically, Carmen Konzett states the following:

> In academic conference situations, where most participants are to some extent experts in the (general) subject matter, while coming across as expert is one of the key aims of conference participation ... discussants and presenters routinely do two different things: they construct selves as *at least as much expert* as the others, but they also try to display self as *more expert* than

[125] Koskenniemi, 'Apology to Utopia,' 62.

[126] Ingo Venzke similarly speaks of "semantic authority" as "above all the product of discursive construction." See Venzke, 'Semantic Authority,' 10.

[127] Hyland, 'Disciplinary Discourses,' 167–168; see also the discussion in Section 5.2.3 on Foucault's "orders of discourse."

[128] As explained in this chapter's introduction, I use the word 'authority' rather than 'power' here.

> others . . . participants have to negotiate to what degree they are each entitled to claim authority in a certain area of knowledge.[129]

This specific part of her analysis is based on those situations where the presenter and the audience can both claim expertise on a specific subject.[130] This is not always the case in the presentations analyzed here; Schmitt also sometimes addresses a 'lay' audience (something described by Konzett as "lay-expert interactions").[131] The point here is that these presentations, regardless of the composition of the audience, are places where authority is negotiated; in other words, there is something to be gained vis-à-vis the audience. So, Konzett says, "each presentation of self implies an image of the other, while presentations of other imply images of the self."[132]

To put it very simply, the way Schmitt discursively relates to others has a particular function: authority is negotiated and constructed here. This doesn't mean his authority is not already acknowledged the moment he steps onto the stage: it means that he himself plays a very particular part in claiming it. The boundaries as drawn by his words are created through three moves. The first, exclusionary move, is the one by means of which he divides the world into lawyers and nonlawyers, dealt with in the next section. Within the remaining 'lawyer category,' he furthermore distinguishes between "pure academics"[133] – those who are lawyers, but have not given legal advice to governments – as well as lawyers who do, and those who do not, properly understand the law. The notion of distance is furthermore implied in the act of *including* those lawyers who, though not part of the group of experts, Schmitt still considers to be "world class":[134] Schmitt decides who is in, and who is out of this inner circle – as happened with the composition of the group of experts involved in the *Tallinn Manual*, as Schmitt was the one asking them to join (along with a few others).[135] Once formed, however, there is no need for Schmitt to distinguish between the group of experts and himself – on the contrary. Thus, when all partitions have been put up we find Schmitt and the group of experts at the center of the map – those lawyers he affiliates with and

[129] Konzett, 'Any Questions?,' 167–168; see also Michael Lynch, 'Circumscribing Expertise: Membership Categories in Courtroom Testimony,' in: *States of Knowledge: The Co-Production of Science and the Social Order*, Sheila Jasanoff (ed.), Routledge 2004, 161–180, 161.

[130] Konzett, 'Any Questions?,' 104.

[131] Ibid.; see, for example, Schmitt's presentation at Brown University.

[132] Ibid., 135, followed by a list of different "strategies" to do so (135–136); see also 367, on "creating a contrast between self and other," and Duszak, 'Us and Others,' 1–28.

[133] Brown 2013, 1.04.38.

[134] CyCon 2014, 0.48, 4.40.

[135] LENS 2013, 30.52; see also note 218 below and the accompanying body text.

whom he draws towards himself. In a final act of construction, Schmitt distances himself from his *professional* self, by referring to himself in the third person.[136] As a result, 'Michael Schmitt' turns into a stand-alone reference point in the debate.

5.2.1 *On "Lay Folks" and "Lawyers' Speak"*

As Schmitt occasionally addresses an audience which, at least for some part, consists of nonlawyers, it makes sense that it is sometimes inevitable to draw the boundary between those who are, and those who aren't, lawyers. For example, when presenting at Brown University in 2013 he addresses an audience that seems to consist mostly of computer scientists and international relations scholars. As the Appendix of this chapter shows, this is also the presentation in which the distinction between lawyers and nonlawyers is emphasized most frequently by Schmitt. For example, at one point, he elaborates on the notion of an 'armed attack' in cyberspace. As he portrays the different views on *lex lata* held by the group of experts, he gets a question from an audience member:

Audience member:	[D]o you include the imminent threat of an armed attack?
Schmitt:	Absolutely. This is – are you a lawyer?
Audience member:	Eh, I guess I let that slip.
Schmitt:	Yeah ok [laughter from the audience]. It's a very good lawyer question.[137]

The fact that the audience member uses the phrase 'imminent armed attack,' signals to Schmitt that this is a lawyer asking a 'lawyer question.' There is nothing unusual about his highlighting those points at which he is 'speaking law' in front of a nonlegal audience; explaining these legal terms may even constitute an effort to bridge the two worlds.

The boundary drawing as done in these presentations, however, may be said to be doing something else as well. Hyland describes "how the expert use of specialist language defines someone as belonging to an exclusive group which,

136 For a similar phraseology, see S. Viswanathan, '"Illeism With a Difference" in Certain Middle Plays of Shakespeare' (1969) 20 *Shakespeare Quarterly* 407, 411, and the last pages of this chapter for further references.

137 Brown 2013, 45.25. Schmitt doesn't draw the distinction at all in the presentation at CyCon 2012. This makes sense, as there he addresses the composition of the group of experts.

in turn, helps to form the individual's identity and exclude others who do not have the same experience and training."[138] Similarly, Konzett writes how "by strategically employing specific and vague lexical references" someone can create an "image ... [of] himself as a professional in contrast to lay people."[139] She moreover describes this as distancing oneself from "[a] present other,"[140] a situation in which a member of the public is linguistically placed in the 'out-group' by the speaker. In this manner, an "in-group" and "out-group" are created.[141] The phrases Schmitt uses to identify *legal* language or even the legal world as separate from the nonlegal one, are an illustration of this moment when "an image of self can be constructed as the opposite of the image of *other*."[142] The example he uses himself, is the use of the word 'attack,' which makes "**lay folks** normally think of computer network attack ... But that's not at all **the world according to the lawyers**."[143] When talking about the *Corfu Channel* Case, he states that "the United Kingdom had a right to pass through that strait in **what we would call** transit passage."[144] This, in Schmitt's terms, is "**lawyers' speak**."[145] In the same presentation at Brown University, Schmitt refers to anticipatory self-defense being "**a legal term**," necessity being "a **technical legal thing**" and that "for some **technical legal** reasons" Additional Protocol I is binding on the United States, even though it is not a signatory to the Protocol.[146] Moreover, he uses phrases such as "that is a ***legal*** **term of art . . . legally known as**" and "**in the legal sense**."[147] Though, 'in the legal sense,' the word 'attack' indeed means something very specific, by consistently emphasizing the different languages as well as the 'technicalities' involved, Schmitt contributes to the boundaries between, in his own words, "the nonlawyer and the lawyer community,"[148] and highlights that a 'world according to lawyers' is not the same as the one inhabited by 'lay folks.'

138 Hyland, 'Disciplinary Discourses,' 157.
139 Konzett, 'Any Questions?,' 384.
140 Ibid., section 7.4.3.4.
141 Ibid., 374, more extensively, 374–377; she points out this can also work in reverse, when an audience member asking a question places the speaker in the 'out-group.' The example she discusses, however, is much more adversarial than the situation described here.
142 Ibid., 367.
143 CyCon 2012 (III), 0.22. Konzett points out a similar dynamic, in a different context: "How can participants display the fact that they have privileged access to knowledge on a particular topic or sub-topic? Those conference delegates who give a presentation usually achieve this task in their oral communication, when they inform the audience about some new research, thus casting self in the role of expert and the audience in the role of non-expert." Konzett, 'Any Questions?,' 168.
144 CyCon 2014, 4.30.
145 Brown 2013, 42.04.
146 Ibid., 46.42, 53.04 and 55.03.
147 ILD 2012, 7.31; CyCon 2012 (II), 0.15.
148 CyCon 2012 (III), 1.02.

The existence of these different communities is further emphasized by Schmitt's use of the pronoun 'we,' which he occasionally uses to distinguish between 'lawyers' and 'others.' The use of this pronoun in general is not necessarily exclusionary (also referred to as an "exclusive-we"); it can also work in an inclusive fashion (or "inclusive-we") but this depends on the "context" within which it is used.[149] For example, at CyCon 2014 Schmitt says "[this is] all **we'll** be talking about today," referring to the audience and himself in an inclusionary way.[150] His reference to lawyers specifically, however, often works the other way around. For example, he states that "because **we're lawyers we** have to argue," or, "the question that **we lawyers** have not gotten our arms around," or, "as **lawyers we** have to ask."[151] Additionally, "as **lawyers we're** particularly upset about the use of the word 'attack'"; "you can fashion what **we call** a colorable argument."[152] This reference to 'we' sometimes refers to lawyers generally, and sometimes to the group of experts involved in the *Tallinn Manual* (which I will return to, below). The use of the word 'we' achieves several things at once: first, it establishes a group, and secondly – and more importantly – in one swing it both turns Schmitt into a "member of this group," by those means "excluding others"; specifically, nonlawyers.[153] By means of a different choice of words something similar happens when, speaking in 2013, Schmitt specifically addresses "the lawyers in the audience" to explain a particular point with regard to the use of force. A few minutes on in the presentation, he repeats this.[154] Likewise, in 2012 he disagrees with a previous presentation by another legal scholar, who appears to be seated in the audience; after briefly addressing the disagreement he states, "[b]ut **the rest of the audience is bored, this is something two law professors argue about**."[155]

As a final illustration of the boundary-drawing between lawyers and nonlawyers, consider an exchange taking place at Brown University in 2013, when

149 Inmaculada Fortanet, 'The Use of "We" in University Lectures: Reference and Function' (2004) 23 *English for Specific Purposes* 45, 48, 46, 63(see also Chapter 6 of this book); see also Pascual, 'Imaginary Trialogues,' 148–149.

150 CyCon 2014, 1.26.

151 LENS 2013, 57.44; CyCon 2014, 5.11; PILAC 2015, 22.01.

152 CyCon 2012 (II), 0.04; Brown 2013, 39.09.

153 Johannes Helmbrecht, 'Grammar and Function of *We*,' in: *Us and Others: Social Identities across Languages, Discourses and Cultures*, Anna Duszak (ed.), John Benjamins 2002, 31–49, 31. Helmbrecht mentions another element, namely that the use of the word 'we' makes no sense unless the group to which it refers is already known to the audience. In the text, above, I have added the qualifier 'most importantly' myself; Helmbrecht does not particularly highlight this.

154 LENS 2013, 38.22, 42.55.

155 CyCon 2012 (III), 19.17.

Schmitt discusses ceasefires during armed conflicts. He starts by saying that "[a]s a matter of law, a ceasefire does not end a conflict." He then turns to an audience member on the front row who, judging from what follows, must be a lawyer. Addressing this person, Schmitt says "I know it was called something else, but, the terminology's changed." Turning his attention back to the audience, he explains this intermission by saying, referring to the person on the front row, "**I'm getting a lawyer look**."[156] Schmitt signals here, to the audience member he has identified as a lawyer,[157] that he is aware of the 'change in terminology' with regard to ceasefires. He then proceeds by portraying this exchange towards the audience as one among lawyers – he got 'a lawyer look.' Again, allowance has to be made for the fact that Schmitt addresses a primarily 'nonlawyer' audience here; moreover, this exchange appears to be done in jest. At the same time, it also signals to the audience that the 'lawyer world' is different from the nonlawyer one. As in the 2012 presentation, where the audience must have been 'bored,' the exchange happens between two lawyers: something from which the audience is excluded.

The explicit kind of exclusionary moves made here by Schmitt, serve to emphasize how he is part of the "in-group" vis-à-vis those who are not; Anna Duszak states that "by aligning with some we also detach ourselves from others."[158] It is reminiscent of the way Weber refers to the legal profession, as was discussed in Chapter 2: "[R]ules are created by the use of highly specialized forms of thought which allow the construction of an intellectual system which can be applied only by *trained professionals*."[159]

In contrast, at one of these presentations Schmitt occasionally explicitly *includes* the audience when he addresses a predominantly legal audience, which includes more well-known lawyers such as Yoram Dinstein.[160] In response to a point made by another panelist, he states this was already addressed in previous expert meetings and, while pointing at the audience, states that "a number of **us** were [t]here."[161] What this shows is "alignment" rather than "disalignment"; an identification with a particular group, rather

156 Brown 2013, 1.20.59.

157 I do not know whether Schmitt and the lawyer in question know each other.

158 Konzett, 'Any Questions?,' 335; Duszak, 'Us and Others,' 2.

159 Trubek, 'Max Weber,' 736, emphasis added.

160 Note that the audience at PILAC 2015 probably also mostly consists of lawyers, but these are most likely students – as opposed to the more well-established legal scholars present at ILD 2012. There is at least one professor of international law present at PILAC 2015.

161 ILD 2012, 1.17.52. Schmitt refers here to the ICRC's DPH-guidance; the Appendix provides more detail on his participation in this process. For a similar reference to "a number of us" see LENS 2013, 26.40.

than an emphasis on its exclusive nature.[162] At this point in the presentation the distinction between lawyers and nonlawyers disappears. Instead, another distinction emerges: one between those 'who were there,' and those who were not.

The distinction between lawyers and nonlawyers is not the only difference Schmitt emphasizes, however. The next section considers a second and third one: between Schmitt or the group of experts, academics, and those who do not properly understand the law.

5.2.2 *On "Dinosaurs" and "Pure Academics"*

As the Appendix shows, Schmitt's references to other people who do not properly understand the law, as well as to academics, are far less frequent than those to nonlawyers. However, when they do occur, they appear in such terms as to merit separate mention here. The first distinction already briefly appeared earlier in this chapter, as part of the discussion of Schmitt's grasp of *lex lata*. By dismissing the views of others as those held by 'dinosaurs' or people who 'don't know what they're talking about' (as discussed on the next page), he affirms his own position as being in control of legal knowledge. The second reference, to academics, appears in two contradictory ways. Schmitt refers to them at those points where he wants to emphasize that those involved in the drafting of the Manual had practical experience, and were not "**pure academics** who might not be able to contextualize as well as people who had **actually given legal advice**, because we knew who our audience was."[163] In its second, opposite form, however, the reference to academics serves either to emphasize that the Manual does not *make* law, as legal scholars – the experts involved – cannot do that; or, to deflect specific kinds of critique. I will briefly elaborate on this, below.

First, this chapter already briefly referred to the way Schmitt on occasion talks about those holding contrary views. Talking about the word 'attack' in international humanitarian law in a 2012 presentation, he states how

> over and over, particularly in the early days of cyber, the question was 'does this rule apply to cyber operations?' The answer today is **absolutely 'yes,'** it's, there's **absolutely no question** whatsoever, anyone who argues this point **doesn't know what they're talking about**. Because there's **almost unanimity** on this point.[164]

162 Crawford Camiciottoli, 'Business Studies Lectures,' 153–155. She refers here to the work of Martin and White; see Chapter 4 note 62 of this book.

163 Brown 2013, 1.04.38.

164 CyCon 2012 (II), 7.59, also discussed in Section 5.1.2.

A little later in the same presentation, he discusses different views held with regard to this same notion of 'attack.' Speaking about those that maintain that any cyber operation aimed at civilians or civilian objects is a violation of *jus in bello*, he argues "I think this view is fading away, but there's still a few **dinosaurs** out there that hold it."[165] Something similar happens at Duke University in 2013, when Schmitt talks about the composition of the group of experts. Pointing at a slide, listing their names, he says the following:

> These were the experts, unusual mix of people. We wanted people who understood use of force issues, and we wanted people who understood warfare. **We were joking about a scholar, who will remain nameless, in the hallway, who has written an outrageous article and we were joking about it because the guy just simply doesn't understand** the context of warfare. So in this group what we did was we picked people who in some way, form or fashion kind of *got* conflict.[166]

Half an hour later in the same presentation, when Schmitt discusses several substantive points from the Manual, he states something similar:

> Ok, a lot of people are always asking questions about, 'what about civilians?' 'Cause you know, today, civilians are cyberwarriors. We did not struggle very much with that. I add this only because there appears to be in the press and so forth a lot of talk about this. In our view, and the view of the group I mean this was the uniform view of the group, the whole group agreed with this, there's absolutely no prohibition in humanitarian law, the law of war, on civilians participating in hostilities. **This is a myth invented by somebody, not a lawyer, that knows anything about humanitarian law. There's no prohibition on civilians participating in hostilities, whether it's cyber or kinetic, ok?** ... What happens though, is when that civilian participates in the hostilities, they, there are several consequences.[167]

Though these kinds of dismissals do not appear very frequently, the reason for highlighting them here is the specific wording with which Schmitt delivers them. He does not simply portray the differences in interpretation as points of substantive disagreement; rather, these people don't know what they are talking about, they 'don't get the context of warfare,' or they are 'dinosaurs.'

165 Ibid., 19.35.

166 LENS 2013, 28.43. The audience's response here might be some laughter, but it's not completely audible. The scholar in question is not identified by Schmitt; for an analysis of this kind of "bashing" in academic writing see Eija Ventola, 'Interpersonal Choices in Academic Work,' in: *Linguistic Choice Across Genres: Variation in Spoken and Written English*, Antonia Sanchez-Macarro and Ronald Carter (eds.), John Benjamins 1998, 117–136, particularly section 2.2.

167 LENS 2013, 1.00.14.

With regard to this dismissal of those who 'do not know what they're talking about,' Ken Hyland (in reference to Foucault) writes how

> [t]he doctrinal knowledge of a field does more than define allegiance to a body of truths and practices; it also, by raising issues of heresy, controls topics of discourse, and so defines who might speak with credibility and who has public authority.[168]

In other words, these people cannot be taken seriously in the debate; they are disqualified from participating by virtue of the views they hold.

The second distinction discussed here, is the one Schmitt draws between academics and the group of experts. As previously stated, the Manual's target audience was not (at least not primarily) an academic one:

> **[O]ur audience was not, academic, was not a law student or a professor,** our audience consisted, our intended audience were legal advisers and ministries of foreign affairs, ministries of defense, militaries, private companies that might engage in cyber operations, NGO's, practitioners, and **they need to know, not theoretically 'does this make sense?' but 'what, what's going to be the call?'**[169]

The different kinds of focus displayed by 'pure academics' versus those with 'practical experience,' also emerges in a 2012 presentation:

> We also wanted to pick people who had **practical experience, we did not want this to be a group of eggheads**, exploring the **mysteries** of the International Law Commission's Articles on State Responsibility . . . So we wanted to get people who had **been there, done that**, have thought through these problems in a **practical sense.**[170]

It's obvious from the above that there is a very concrete purpose to making the distinction: "We did not want **pure academics** who might not be able to contextualize as well as people who had **actually given legal advice,**" Schmitt says, "because we knew who our audience was"[171] (as already cited, above). He repeats this distinction several times, for example when he states that the experts involved "had to have **experience** as a . . . **practicing legal adviser** . . . people who had *done* this" – adding, that "if you were **just purely** an academic" you were not deemed suited to join the expert group.[172] The

168 Hyland, 'Disciplinary Discourses,' 170.

169 PILAC 2015, 52.59.

170 CyCon 2012 (I), 10.49. Though Schmitt does not explicitly mention academics here, I have understood the reference to 'eggheads exploring the mysteries of the Articles on State Responsibility' as such.

171 Brown 2013, 1.04.37.

172 PILAC 2015, 15.26.

practical experience of the experts is further emphasized when Schmitt once again explains that the Manual deals with *lex lata*, not *lex ferenda*: "I emphasize, that it is ... *lex lata* ... we asked, 'what is the law *now?*' ... [i]n August 2012, what's the law, not, where is the law going, **that's for scholars to write about**."[173]

The qualifier 'academic' sporadically also works in an opposite way. In these instances, it doesn't serve to emphasize the practical experience of the group of experts versus 'pure academics'; it rather serves here to tone down, so to speak, the ambitions of the Manual. For example, again with reference to the difference between *lex lata* and *lex ferenda* maintained in the Manual, Schmitt emphasizes that "states make law, not **law professors**"; elsewhere he says that

> everyone wanted us to emphasize that we were speaking only in our personal capacity. Because no one wanted **a bunch of academics** to steal their discretion. You know what I mean, if you're the Air Force General Counsel the last thing you want is some **academic** at the Naval War College determining what your cyber rules of the game were. **So this is a, a purely an academic exercise, twenty folks trying to figure out what *they* believe the law to be.**[174]

Similarly, responding to criticism that the nationality of the experts was not sufficiently geographically spread and that these were "the usual suspects"[175] (which I will return to, below), Schmitt acknowledges the criticism, but also argues that

> we were **just twenty academics and practitioners** that were trying to solve a problem, or trying to figure out what the law was in an area that no one seemed to know any answers [to].[176]

Alternatively, as shown in the Appendix, he occasionally refers to academia jokingly, for example when he presents his own idea on prohibited targets in cyberspace, and refers to it as "a very transparent **attempt by a scholar to try and get his gig out there**, 'ah it's the Schmitt idea.'"[177] On the one hand, one

173 CyCon 2012 (I), 13.54. At his Harvard presentation, he somewhat jokingly states that "if you were just purely an academic you didn't make the cut ... If there are purely academics, I do respect you, ok?," which is followed by some laughter from the audience. See PILAC 2015, 15.45. On the June/August date shift see also note 110 above; see CyCon 2012 (I), 14.11.

174 Brown 2013, 1.06.01; LENS 2013, 28.12.

175 LENS 2013, 1.04.18.

176 Ibid., 1.05.12; Schmitt doesn't finish this sentence, I have added the word 'to.' It should be noted that elsewhere Schmitt dismisses this critique; yet the expansion of the expert group with the second Manual could be understood, in part, as a response to this criticism. See also PILAC 2015, 15.02, and Section 5.2.3 below.

177 PILAC 2015, 35.57.

could argue that these different references to 'academics' result from Schmitt's addressing the audience from the perspective of different roles: at times as a professor of international law, at others as director of the *Tallinn Manual*. However, these references to 'a bunch of academics' and that this was 'just twenty academics,' also seem to have the effect of downplaying the ambitions of the Manual ("[s]o this was **twenty independent scholars** ... This is twenty guys ... **that's all it is. Twenty scholars, it's our view, and nothing more than that.**")[178] rather than to make a distinction between academics and those who have given 'practical advice.'[179]

The two exclusionary moves made by Schmitt discussed here further contribute to his positioning at the heart of the debate. The next section focuses on the major *in*clusionary move of these presentations: the way Schmitt refers to the group of experts. Contrary to the other groups discussed in this chapter, he aligns himself with that group of experts.[180] What this section also shows, is how this 'selection' of who is in, and who is outside of this 'inner circle,' extends beyond those involved in the drafting of the *Tallinn Manual*.

5.2.3 *The Group of Experts*

This chapter started with narrating how Schmitt came to be asked to be director to the group of experts. In the same presentation, Schmitt explains how the group came about:

> I got a phone call ... and the phone call basically said ... 'we're ready to start answering these questions, we'll give you as much money as you need in order to answer the questions and **you can design your own group**.'[181]

Judging from what Schmitt says in another presentation, he, Wolff Heintschel von Heinegg (who was also involved in the drafting of previous manuals), and several others,[182] subsequently decided who should be part of the group of experts. Schmitt explains the criteria for inclusion into the group as follows, worth quoting in full:

> So what we were trying to do was bring together people that had **three characteristics. They had to be really really good international lawyers to make the team. The second characteristic is, they also had to have some**

[178] Brown 2013, 14.35.
[179] Konzett refers to "[p]erforming ... multiple professional identities" including specifically the combination of practitioner and academic. See Konzett, 'Any Questions?,' 334 et seq.
[180] On "alignment" and "disalignment" see note 162 above.
[181] CyCon 2012 (I), 0.56.
[182] LENS 2013, 30.52; see also note 205 below.

> **affiliation, with not the military, but with people who dealt with the battlefield** ... they had to be people who had provided *actual* legal advice about conflict situations. **We did not want pure academics who might not be able to contextualize as well as people who had actually given legal advice, because we knew who our audience was.** And the third is, is that we we needed to, we needed to pick people who liked each other and got along and played well together because we would go to Estonia when it was thirty-five degrees below zero and be locked in a room together.[183]

The second criterion – that the experts had to 'have given actual legal advice' – has been elaborated on in the previous section. The first characteristic – that the experts had to be 'good international lawyers' – signals how Schmitt draws the group of experts towards him, as opposed to the other moves discussed in this chapter. His references to the experts all are along the same lines: they are "international world class experts"; "smart people" and "brilliant."[184] These claims to authority also extend to those functioning in an advisory role to the project. Stating his and/or the other experts' ignorance on technical issues, Schmitt explains how there was a "technical team"[185] advising them; moreover, several observers participated in the project, but did not vote on the substantive rules of the Manual.[186] When talking about these observers – one from the International Committee of the Red Cross (ICRC), one from US Cyber Command and one from NATO – Schmitt says with regard to the first, that they are "always spectacular attorneys" and that "no one knows humanitarian law better."[187] On the observer from US Cyber Command, Schmitt says that he was asked to participate "because he was the one we felt that was most likely to know what the challenging legal issues were."[188] Elsewhere, Schmitt phrases this in a more interesting way, when he says that the purpose of Cyber Command's participation was "**to keep us honest, because we wanted to make sure we were dealing in the realm of** ... **the real**, and ... that individual was the one that knew **what was really happening**."[189] A similar phraseology is used by Schmitt when he talks about the technical experts involved in the

183 Brown 2013, 1.04.05. See the Appendix for similar descriptions of these criteria.

184 CyCon 2014, 4.54; CyCon 2012 (I), 1.57 and 10.35. On the authority claims as pertaining to the experts, see also Kessler and Werner, 'Expertise,' section 3.1.

185 Brown 2013, 19.08; see also PILAC 2015, 16.19 and CyCon 2012 (I), 12.18.

186 CyCon 2012 (I), 11.59.

187 PILAC 2015, 16.44 et seq. and CyCon 2012 (I), 11.41. Schmitt is less clear about the reason for inclusion of the NATO representative; see PILAC 2015, 16.46; Brown 2013, 25.17 and CyCon 2012 (I), 11.47.

188 Brown 2013, 20.44.

189 PILAC 2015, 16.27.

Manual: "[T]hey kept us **honest** throughout, they explained when we were getting off track."[190] Similarly, he says that

> [i]n addition to the group of experts we had a group of observers ... because we wanted, we wanted to have entities represented in the room that could, that could, could provide ***realism*** to how our customers would react. **And so the ICRC is a good example, no one knows humanitarian law better than the ICRC, Cyber Command, no one's doing this more than Cyber Command, ACT, sponsor of the CCDCOE.**[191]

The 'dealing in the realm of the real' echoes Schmitt's emphasis on the experts' practical experience; the focus of the Manual on *lex lata* and the idea of the Manual as a 'product' for certain users.

There are a few ways in which the authority of the experts finds its way to decisions about the substance of the law. Consider the following quote, when Schmitt addresses criticism of the Manual:

> There are some assertions that are fair ... one of them is that we in virtually every Rule indicate our opinion as to whether or not a Rule is customary in nature or it's simply treaty-based ... some of the criticism is 'but you guys didn't review state practice.' We did look at state practice but not in a comprehensive way ... **my reply is, 'yes, but we've looked at, we were twenty people that are fairly senior**, and we looked at all of the previous efforts to identify state practice, **so if there was a consensus view in the community that something was in fact customary** we simply were restating what the consensus view in the community [was].'[192]

Schmitt responds here to criticism of the Manual; specifically, that the assessment of customary law was done in a somewhat haphazard fashion. If we look at the customary law sources as listed in the Manual itself, it states that "of particular importance" to the identification of customary law were the ICRC Customary IHL Study, the Air and Missile Warfare (AMW) Manual, and the Non-International Armed Conflict, or NIAC Manual.[193] Though Schmitt, in the quote provided above, portrays this 'restatement' of customary law as a simple rendition of a consensus view – similar to the dynamic described in the fourth chapter of this book – the introduction of the Manual as well as statements made by Schmitt elsewhere, suggest a much more active role played by the experts. The Manual itself states that

[190] CyCon 2012 (I), 8.45.
[191] See ibid., 11.17.
[192] LENS 2013, 1.03.10. Schmitt doesn't finish this sentence; I have added the word 'was.'
[193] Schmitt (ed.), 'Tallinn Manual,' 7–8.

> all of the aforementioned sources were persuasive, but not dispositive, evidence of a norm's status as customary law. Ultimately, **the professional knowledge, experience, and expertise of the Experts** form the basis for the *Tallinn Manual*'s conclusions as to the customary status of a Rule.[194]

Similarly, in a 2012 presentation, with regard to the same issue Schmitt argues that

> [w]hat we said, was that, 'it is customary law, or is applicable in [non-international armed conflict] or [international armed conflict], in, **in accordance with *us*.**' In other words, ***we* are the authority, we have twenty high-speed people here, through our years and decades of experience**, we are agreeing that this is customary, we are agreeing this is applicable in IAC or applicable in NIAC.[195]

So, rather than a 'simple restatement' of a consensus view,[196] the experts were crucial in assessing the substance of law here – on the basis of their 'years and decades of experience.'[197] Something similar is described by Frédéric Mégret when he writes about moments of fundamental change in international humanitarian law. At these points of potential rupture, the "grand old men" of the discipline come forward, Mégret says, and proclaim what the law is. They "are the ones whose pronouncements come closest to 'speech acts' ('the law is as it is because I say it is')."[198]

Something more is to be said about this, however, pertaining to the sources used by the experts in their assessment of customary law. In one particular presentation Schmitt mentions several sources, largely similar to those mentioned above: first, some states' military manuals; second, the ICRC's study of customary international humanitarian law; third, the ICRC commentaries to the Geneva Conventions and the Additional Protocols; and fourth, the Air and Missile Warfare Manual and the NIAC Manual.[199] With regard to the latter, he says the following:

> [Other sources included] the Air and Missile Warfare Manual and the NIAC Manual because those are both **restatements of customary law** as well, again we weren't *bound* by those, but it was persuasive evidence **because of the caliber of the people that were involved in those projects**.[200]

194 Ibid., 8.
195 CyCon 2012 (I), 14.31.
196 See Chapter 4 of this book; on 'restatements of the law' see Werner, 'Absence, Restatement.'
197 For a similar critique of this point see Kessler and Werner, 'Expertise,' 804.
198 Mégret, 'Thinking About,' 282.
199 CyCon 2012 (I), 14.54 et seq. For a more elaborate list of sources see Schmitt (ed.), 'Tallinn Manual,' xiv–xix.
200 CyCon 2012 (I), 16.25.

However, there is some overlap between the 'people involved in those projects'; some overlap between those involved in the AMW, NIAC and *Tallinn Manual* specifically. The NIAC Manual was drafted by Schmitt himself, together with Yoram Dinstein and Charles Garraway; Garraway also served as a peer reviewer for the *Tallinn Manual* (though not as a member of the 'core' group).[201] Wolff Heintschel von Heinegg was part of the "Core Group of Experts"[202] of the AMW Manual (as was Charles Garraway) and participated in the "Editorial Committee" of the *Tallinn Manual*; Bill Boothby had the same two functions; and Kenneth Watkin was an expert in both these groups.[203] Finally, Yoram Dinstein was similarly part of the core group of experts of the AMW Manual.

The purpose of this enumeration is not to repeat in full the 'trackback exercise' underlying the fourth chapter of this book; it does suggest, however, that perhaps a similar dynamic may be at play here. Schmitt himself acknowledges this criticism and says that those involved in the *Tallinn Manual* were "the usual suspects"; elsewhere he similarly states that "[w]e had a bunch of lawyers together, ok, we – most of us knew each other. I knew most of these people."[204] What this means is that Schmitt (and a few others) selected people for participation in the *Tallinn Manual*[205] at least some of whom Schmitt had worked with before; subsequently, the work they had previously done together was used as one of the sources they drew on 'because of the caliber of the people involved.' There is, at least to some extent, a similar self-referentiality to this process as the one described in the previous chapter.

Moreover, consider the third characteristic mentioned at the beginning of this section – that Schmitt wanted to 'pick people who liked each other and played well together.' Schmitt repeatedly emphasizes the importance, in a project such as the *Tallinn Manual*, of coherence among the group members:

> Just wanted to show you who the groups of, group of experts were. This was *critical* because we needed to pick people – I, I've been through a number of these processes and listen, the most important . . . rule is, don't, **not to get the**

201 For the function of the peer reviewers see Schmitt (ed.), 'Tallinn Manual,' 10.

202 Dinstein, 'AMW Manual (With Commentary),' 8 et seq.

203 The experts involved in the *Tallinn Manual* are listed in Schmitt (ed.), 'Tallinn Manual,' x-xiii; those involved in the AMW Manual in Dinstein, 'AMW Manual (With Commentary),' appendix I (this is the document referred to in the *Tallinn Manual*); those involved in the NIAC Manual can be found at Schmitt, Garraway and Dinstein, 'NIAC Manual,' i.

204 LENS 2013, 1.04.18; Brown 2013, 1.25.55; see also Section 5.1.1 and Petrov, 'Expert Laws.'

205 CyCon 2012 (I), 4.20; LENS 2013, 30.51.

> **smartest people in the room, but you wanna get people that can play well together because they're gonna be with each other for a *long, long, long* time** ... So the number one criterion is to get people who were ***nice***. But fortunately there were **lots and lots and lots** of ***brilliant***, nice people around. **And so then, we picked people who we knew were a specialist in the field, who really knew IHL or the *jus ad belllum* in a *very, very, very* deep sense.**[206]

Similarly, a little earlier in the same presentation, Schmitt explains how the start-up process of the Manual proceeded; he states how "we spend a little time saying 'who are the **best people in the world** that we think would **form a cohesive group** to attack these problems?'"[207] Given his previous, less fortuitous experience with other expert-based projects,[208] the idea that the experts had to 'play well together' in order for the project to finish makes sense: his own experiences in the creation of manuals may be one explanation for his urge to create coherence.[209] At one point he recognizes the criticism[210] on the lack of geographical representation of the group; and for example in 2013 responds to it by saying that

> [t]he other thing is is that I have to be honest with you, for those of you who've been through these sorts of efforts, **if you have three years, we had three years, period, three years**, we had cash for three years, I was the project director ... we were gonna finish in three years, and the problem is, **the broader, the more diverse the representation, the more impossible it becomes to move forward, at all, so we picked people that we knew could stay focused** ... in order to meet the three year window.[211]

He states here that his aim was to meet the deadline set by the CCDCOE, and in order to do so, the project had to 'move forward' with people who 'could stay focused.' Elsewhere, he expresses himself in different terms with regard to this criticism:

> How did we do it? We brought twenty experts from around the world, **a very politically incorrect group of experts**, because we knew we were doing this for **the first time**, so we **really didn't care if we had geographical distribution**, etcetera etcetera, we took the **twenty best people we could find.**[212]

206 CyCon 2012 (I), 9.45, continued at 10.27.
207 Ibid., 4.21.
208 For his comments on the DPH-guidance see, for example, Brown 2013, 1.05.01.
209 See LENS 2013, 30.46 et seq.; Brown 2013, 1.04.50.
210 At some points he acknowledges this as "a fair criticism" (for instance, LENS 2013, 1.04.30), at others, he speaks more casually of the composition of the group being geographically skewed; see also note 176 and the accompanying body text above.
211 Ibid., 1.05.45.
212 PILAC 2015, 15.02.

Ultimately, what we are to conclude from the above is that, first, only senior people are able to tell what (the consensus view on) customary law is in the *Tallinn Manual*, secondly, that Schmitt and only a couple of others decide who these senior people are, and thirdly, that coherence of the group is crucial for its success.[213] Wanting to meet a deadline is nothing unusual, and it may simply be healthy project management: what is more interesting here is that it shows Schmitt's pivotal role in assembling this group of people. Foucault writes how "control of discourses" can be exercised by

> imposing a certain number of rules on the individuals who hold [these discourses], and thus of not permitting everyone to have access to them. There is a rarefaction ... of the speaking subjects; none shall enter the order of discourse if he does not satisfy certain requirements or if he is not, from the outset, qualified to do so. To be more precise: not all the regions of discourse are equally open and penetrable; some of them are largely forbidden.[214]

This notion of admittance to the inner circle emerges from Schmitt's statements about the experts as those "that **made it** onto what we called the international group of experts"; or, with regard to those lacking practical experience, they "**didn't make the cut**."[215] Schmitt is really functioning as a gatekeeper here, where, in admitting some, he leaves out others.[216] Seen in this light, his judgments of other lawyers also become more poignant. This goes not only for those who, according to him, should not be taken seriously (as described earlier in this chapter); it also works the other way around. In July 2014, Schmitt speaks at CyCon 2014 and refers to presentations given by other lawyers earlier that day:

> This morning you had, no kidding, a *masterclass* in international law. You had two scholars who are **truly at the world class level** and then you had a young scholar who is **clearly moving in that direction**.[217]

In one way, he is decreasing the distance between himself and these 'others' by referring to them as 'world class lawyers.' At the same time there is a similar relation of dependency to those who are not, in the sense that Schmitt (in this

213 See also Kessler and Werner, 'Expertise,' 805.

214 Foucault, 'Order of Discourse,' 61–62. I was drawn to this particular part of Foucault's work by Hyland; see Hyland, 'Disciplinary Discourses,' specifically 157–158.

215 PILAC 2015, 15.23 and 15.47. Kessler and Werner add that "the selection of experts is very important in light of the statement that the group of experts has sought to 'capture all reasonable positions for inclusion in the Tallinn Manual's Commentary.'" See Kessler and Werner, 'Expertise,' 805.

216 Ken Hyland similarly speaks of "gatekeepers"; see Hyland, 'Disciplinary Discourses,' 157.

217 CyCon 2014, 0.48.

case discursively) decides the level at which these lawyers are functioning. As identified by Konzett with regard to a particular panel exchange she herself reflects on:

> By taking on an evaluative stance [the speaker] positions himself as an assessor ... Producing an assessment means that a speaker displays knowledge about the matter assessed, which raises his authority in the discussion.[218]

Overall, both in the case of the composition of the group of experts, as well as when Schmitt qualifies other lawyers as 'world-class' or, alternatively, as 'not knowing what they're talking about,' the audience is presented with an imagery or map of the legal profession, as arranged by him.

The final section of this chapter discusses Schmitt's references to himself in the third person.

5.2.4 *"Let Me Tell You What Mike Schmitt Thinks the Future Is Going to Be" – Revisited*

There are a few moments in these presentations when Schmitt refers to himself in the third person, also known as "illeism."[219] The way Schmitt does this is frequently jokingly, or somewhat apologetically, for example as done halfway through his presentation at Harvard University in 2015:

> **I have suggested in, in a couple of articles that maybe what we will see happen**, is we will see the emergence of a new customary norm over time. And my, my idea is, is that we should not be able to conduct military operations against something that is related to what I call 'essential civilian functions.' This is a completely undeveloped idea, it's a very transparent **attempt by a scholar to try and get his gig out there, 'ah it's the Schmitt idea.'**[220]

The audience laughs in response, and the Appendix of this chapter shows other examples of similar jokes, and those moments when he refers to others who have labeled particular parts of his work 'the Schmitt-test,' all the while emphasizing he didn't come up with the term.[221] The title of this section

[218] Konzett, 'Any Questions?,' 384.

[219] Matthew Harris, 'Metafiction in New Zealand From the 1960s to the Present Day' (PhD, Massey University 2011), 162 note 19. He cites an article similarly referring to this phenomenon; the author calls this self-reference to one's proper name "illeism with a difference." See Viswanathan, 'Illeism,' 407.

[220] PILAC 2015, 35.28; see also p. 158 above.

[221] See, for example, Brown 2013, 31.18.

presents one instance at which Schmitt refers to himself in the third person seriously. Similarly, when presenting three 'case-studies' in 2014, with regard to the third he states that

> this scenario, at least as the facts given to us ... **would not meet the Mike Schmitt test of intervention**, it would meet the test of some other people.[222]

In another presentation, one of the slides has a bullet point, stating "**Schmitt view**"; when talking about the difficulty in applying *levée en masse* to cyber-space, he says that

> the whole population, like **Mike Schmitt**, I'm not capable of spontaneously rising up against any invader. Why? 'Cause I wouldn't know how to fire a virus if, if, if it fell down in front of me.[223]

And, finally, the header of this section: "**Let me tell you what Mike Schmitt thinks the future is going to be.**"[224]

These references bring to the fore that Schmitt, besides being the person speaking at this or that particular event, is also very much a prominent player in the debate; it "create[s] a sense of distance and framing."[225] In Foucauldian terms, Schmitt may be said to attempt to create his own authorship.[226] Foucault writes how "the name of an author is not precisely a proper name among others";[227] in other words, when Schmitt is referring to 'Schmitt' he is not just referring to a proper name: he is referring to something more than that. Foucault indicates what this 'something more' is: the name of an author, unlike a proper name, is irreplaceable – it matters whether Shakespeare wrote those sonnets, Foucault says, or whether it was someone else altogether.[228] In other words, it matters whether Schmitt declares something to be 'the law,' or whether someone else does exactly the same thing. Moreover, it is precisely in the "scission"[229] of his professional self from the particularities of the speaker that Schmitt's authorship emerges: in the same moment, multiple versions of "self" are present.[230] Thus, "it gestures to a difference between [his] public and

222 CyCon 2014, 37.46.
223 PILAC 2015, 23.13; CyCon 2012 (I), 20.16.
224 CyCon 2012 (II), 20.22.
225 Harris, 'Metafiction,' 162.
226 Michel Foucault, 'Authorship: What is an Author?' (1979) 20 *Screen* 13.
227 Ibid., 18.
228 Ibid., 18–19.
229 Ibid., 23; see also Viswanathan, 'Illeism,' 414.
230 Foucault, 'Authorship,' 23; Viswanathan similarly speaks of "detach[ing] [one]self from [one] self"; see Viswanathan, 'Illeism,' 409, see also 414.

private selves"; it "clarif[ies] identity and objectif[ies] the subjective."[231] He simultaneously dissociates, as well as associates, himself with a particular view: his views exist in the field and are recognized by others as carrying his name – and it matters that they do. Talking about himself in the third person, then, is the final act of cartography: it turns him into a stand-alone reference point in the debate.[232]

The introduction of this chapter stated that Schmitt's self-positioning constitutes the ultimate act of application-orientation. Not only does Schmitt phrase these legal issues as questions requiring answers, he moreover discursively positions himself as the one able to give them. This chapter described the ways in which this is achieved: by positioning himself as well as the *Tallinn Manual* in the history of international law; by expressing firm control over the substance of *lex lata*; and by pronouncing on the (possible) future(s) of international law. Secondly, he construes distances between himself and several others: between lawyers and nonlawyers; between those who properly understand the law, and those who misunderstand it; and between those with and without practical experience. The opposite happens when Schmitt refers to the group of legal experts involved in the drafting of the *Tallinn Manual*: the words he uses when referring to them evoke an image of proximity rather than distance. Finally, this chapter described how he refers to himself in the third person, and suggested a possible reading of these referrals.

In this way this chapter has attempted to give language to what these words 'do': how this authority to speak is constructed by Schmitt as he places himself not only in a position to say what the law is, but moreover, to control access to this debate. This control is exercised in a very material way through his decisions as to whom to include and exclude from the group of experts; but in a more discursive sense something similar happens by means of the way he speaks of others. This is not to say that the 'who' of legal argument is all-important; my aim was not to show that, when authority speaks, anything goes.[233] What both this chapter as well as the previous one do demonstrate, however, are the different ways in which the 'seats at the table' can be discursively assigned.[234]

231 Harris, 'Metafiction,' 163, 162; on public and private selves see also Viswanathan, 'Illeism,' 409–412.

232 As stated earlier in this book, Venzke speaks of "authoritative reference points" as those points "[interpretive] claims have to be argumentatively tied to." This is about the making of interpretive claims, however, not about individual legal scholars. See Venzke, 'Interpretation,' 48.

233 Venzke, 'Semantic Authority,' 10; see also Venzke, 'Understanding Authority,' 395–396.

234 See also Hyland, 'Disciplinary Discourses,' 167–168.

In the next, concluding chapter of this book, I briefly summarize and then elaborate on what results from the three close-ups of the cyberwar discourse presented here. The conclusion subsequently builds on these close-ups by elaborating on what, in the introduction, was proposed as the main point of this book: to argue a new "way of seeing" international legal scholarship.[235] This way of seeing, I conclude, results in a specific form of theorizing about law: one which attends closely to international legal texts, and in so doing also reflects back on its own knowledge practices. Ultimately, the "turn to description"[236] as performed here results in a view of international legal scholars as engaged – in a very literal, textual, tangible sense – in the writing of international law.

[235] Johns, 'Unruly Law,' 21.
[236] Orford, 'Description,' 609.

6

In Conclusion: International Law As We Know It

The basic question lying at the heart of this book was 'how do we know what we know, in the academic discourse on cyberwar and international law?' In order to answer it, this book looked at doctrine as a (socio)linguistic practice and showed how individual words and phrases bring about this international legal knowledge on cyberwar. By means of three close-ups it attended to that which is so ingrained in scholarly practice, so much part of the "everyday" that it is not usually considered relevant to the construction of doctrine.[1] Though these individually spoken and written words may appear to be trivial and to do very little on the level of individual legal scholarship, it has been precisely the aim of this book to show how they matter to the knowledge generated within this discourse. Chapter 3 did so by juxtaposing the different turns taken in individual pieces of writing; arguments made at specific junctions in the text by means of which the writer sets her- or himself on a trajectory towards a particular conclusion. Taking a step closer to these texts, Chapter 4 detailed the use of consensus claims in legal writing, and by looking at their footnotes asked how scholars know this consensus exists. Footnotes are placed in the margins of the body text and in a smaller font size: everything suggests this is peripheral to the "real work"[2] of legal scholarship. As Chapter 4 showed, however, these seemingly minor features of a text are actually relevant to what we know international law to be; what is more, they are a way of assigning the authority to speak. Chapter 5 turned its attention to the presentations given by Michael Schmitt and asked which exact words he uses to claim, not only what we know international law to be, but what is more, who is eligible for making those claims.

[1] Foucault in Orford, 'Description,' 617 (see Chapter 1 note 21 of this book); for "everyday" see Adler-Nissen, 'Why IR needs Bourdieu.'

[2] Koulen, 'Blind Justice,' 97.

In other words, all three close-ups considered how, at the level of their individual writing and speaking, the scholars involved in this discourse construct what we know to be law, and how through these words they assign the authority to speak to others or themselves.[3] By answering its questions in this way this book proposed a new "way of seeing" international legal scholarship; a way of seeing that operates under the basic presumption that the mundane and the usually overlooked matter to what we know international law to be.[4] In this last chapter, my aim is to revisit this approach as outlined in the Introduction, and to consider its implications for our theorizing about law.[5] Three conclusions in particular follow. First, as stated in Chapter 1 of this book, that which is "hidden in plain sight" only comes into view by changing the way we read, see or listen.[6] This change entails a willingness to attend to international law's texts. As I elaborate on in the next section, attending to these texts means to spend time with them and to 'stay seated' throughout the attempt at reading or hearing them differently. In turn, the willingness to engage in this way follows from an attitude of "curiosity" rather than "suspicion"; of "intimacy" rather than "distance."[7] What results is a way of theorizing about law that moves 'from the ground up,' allowing "for a more careful understanding of the many unnoticed aspects" of the making of international legal knowledge.[8] Second, considering others' knowledge practices this closely spills over into a closer consideration of one's own. As explained in the Introduction, this is what follows from the sociological approach taken here, which goes back and forth between an internal and an external perspective on law. By showing what forms this (self-)reflection may take on, I argue that the scrutiny of those involved in the cyberwar discourse is not limited to doctrinal work. Third, and finally, looking at international legal scholarship in this way also reveals the presence of its writers. In writing *about* international

3 Aalberts and Werner refer to "micropractices," see Aalberts and Werner, 'International Law,' 41.

4 Johns, 'Unruly Law,' 21. As explained in Chapter 1, the words "mundane" and "overlooked" are part of an assembly of words describing *where* this kind of inquiry thinks to look. See Chapter 1 note 108.

5 Cf. Valverde, 'Non-Legality,' 963 et seq.

6 Ibid., 964; for 'seeing' in particular see Sofia Stolk and Renske Vos, 'International Legal Sightseeing' (2020) 33 *Leiden Journal of International Law* 1.

7 Anne Orford, 'Epilogue: Critical Intimacy and the Performance of International Law,' in: *Backstage Practices of Transnational Law*, Lianne J. M.Boer and Sofia Stolk (eds.), Routledge 2019, 174–178, 175; Anne Orford, 'Critical Intimacy: Jacques Derrida and the Friendship of Politics' (2005) 6 *German Law Journal* 31, 32, referring to Gayatri Chakravorty Spivak, *A Critique of Postcolonial Reason: Toward a History of the Vanishing Present*, Harvard University Press 1999, 425.

8 Riles, 'Collateral Knowledge,' 14.

law its scholars distance themselves from it; and in so doing we come to see that there is, in fact, a writer at work. What results is a view of scholars as engaged in 'writing law' in a very literal, textual, tangible sense.

6.1 ATTENDING TO INTERNATIONAL LEGAL TEXTS

Recounting the process of writing her book on the responsibility to protect, Anne Orford writes how she

> gradually began to understand the responsibility to protect concept as a means of rationalizing and integrating already-existing practices of executive rule, [but] when I tried to convey this, I was invariably frustrated by the response ... I realized that part of the problem was the structure of my argument, which only talked about practices of protection very late in the piece ... [T]he form of my argument had to reflect its substance. It would be necessary to restructure the argument around what I had found in the archives ... So while initially I had planned to move from an abstract discussion of the grounding of authority on protection ... to an analysis of the practices of protection, the book now has the reverse form – it starts with practices and then moves on to their systematization and articulation in the form of the responsibility to protect concept.[9]

Orford's account of her writing process starts by detailing how she made her argument 'work'; how she managed to be properly understood by her audience. She writes how she discovered that, rather than move from the abstract to the concrete, the story had to be told the other way around. In order to convincingly show how 'already existing practices' together were made to mean the 'responsibility to protect,' her narrative had to start with a description of those practices – not with the responsibility to protect. Importantly, however, she also points out that this "problem of writing"[10] is more than a matter of tailoring one's narrative to its target audience. To move from the description of practices to their 'systematization and articulation' in other terms is, in fact, an ordering mechanism tied into "a way of doing science."[11] 'What we find in the archives' and how we subsequently write down our findings are intimately linked in a specific way of theorizing about

9 Orford, 'Description,' 615–616.
10 Ibid., 615.
11 Ian Hacking, '"Style" for Historians and Philosophers' (1992) 23 *Studies in History and Philosophy of Science* 1, 2; also referred to by Fleur Johns, 'From Planning to Prototypes: New Ways of Seeing Like a State' (2019) 82 *The Modern Law Review* 833, 838 note 19. For description as style see Marcus, Love and Best, 'Better Description.'

law: this is "theory close to the ground . . . build[ing] up its analytical categories at close proximity to . . . practice."[12] In other words, the reason the argument works when written down as emerging from practice is because that is the place where it first came into view.[13]

Equally, this book is not a case study of the cyberwar discourse – quite the contrary. It 'builds up its analytical categories at close proximity' to the practice of legal academic writing and speech. But how do we theorize from the ground up; how does that which is 'hidden in plain sight' suddenly jump off the page?[14] I initially set out to explore how, given the uncertainties around cyberwar, legal scholars nonetheless attempted to make sense of it in terms of international law. Over time, a different understanding of exactly the same question began to emerge: I had the growing suspicion that 'making sense' happened in ways *other* than the ones usually assigned to the realm of international legal reasoning proper.[15] As it turned out, international law on cyberwar was made in places I had failed to look the first time around.[16] But to start noticing that which initially escaped notice it is necessary to attend to these texts more closely: to stay put and sit with them for a while. To 'attend to' something is "to stretch to [it] . . . to listen, apply oneself; to watch over, minister to, wait upon, follow, frequent; to wait for, await, expect."[17] In the case of this book, paying "careful" and "closer attention" meant to read and listen to these texts over and over again, and in so doing develop what may best be described as "exceedingly extended acquaintances" with them.[18] Looking

12 Riles, 'Collateral Knowledge,' 14, in-text quotation marks omitted; see also Johns, 'Unruly Law,' 21–22; Orford, 'Description,' 615; Orford, 'Epilogue,' 176.

13 Bigo, 'Pierre Bourdieu,' 232; also referred to by Orford, 'Epilogue,' 176.

14 For a similar question see Riles, 'New Agenda,' 1018; see also note 24 below and the accompanying body text.

15 Cf. Foucault, 'Order of Discourse.' On changing research questions see Sarah M. H. Nouwen, '"As You Set out for Ithaka": Practical, Epistemological, Ethical, and Existential Questions about Socio-Legal Empirical Research in Conflict' (2014) 27 *Leiden Journal of International Law* 227, 236; Riles, 'Collateral Knowledge,' 12.

16 See also Riles, 'Collateral Knowledge,' 12 and Constable, Volpp and Wagner (eds.), 'Looking for Law.'

17 "attend, v.," Oxford English Dictionary Online; see also Marcus, Love and Best, 'Better Description,' 14.

18 The phrases "careful" and "closer attention" are used by Annelise Riles, 'Models and Documents: Artefacts of International Legal Knowledge' (1999) 48 *International and Comparative Law Quarterly* 805, 810 and by Johns, 'Unruly Law,' 215, respectively. See also Orford, 'Description,' 622–625 and 'Epilogue,' 175–176. The links between this book and their work are explained in Chapter 1. "Paying attention" is the title of an essay by Clifford Geertz, see Clifford Geertz, 'On Paying Attention,' in: *Fine Description: Ethnographic and Linguistic Essays by Harold C. Conklin*, Joel Kuipers and Ray McDermott (eds.), Yale University Press 2007, 27–30. Geertz also refers to building up "acquaintances"; see Geertz, 'Interpretation,' 318.

at (reading, listening) international law's texts "with curiosity rather than suspicion" allows for the mundane to come into view and start to 'mean' something else; it allows for it to become pertinent.[19] From this curiosity a kind of intimacy with these texts follows.[20] In his book about descriptions of landscapes – woods, water, mountains and countryside – Robert Macfarlane writes that "[t]o exercise a care of attention towards a place ... is to achieve a sympathetic intimacy with it."[21] Macfarlane refers to the landscape writers he puts forward in his book as "us[ing] words exactly and exactingly when describing landscape and natural life," one of whom in particular "was absorbed by what lay hidden in plain view," applying a "method ... based on long-term and patient acquaintance, and on careful observation" to make it visible.[22] Description, in this account, becomes a means by which we can "direct [our] attention," as it forces us to look more closely at and to be more precise in writing down what we see.[23] This is the point, moreover, at which linguistics may come in, for allowing a meticulous reading of texts and in so doing also expanding the scope of inquiry beyond what would be covered by a doctrinal reading.[24] In sum, where we think to look follows from *how* we look. What this kind of looking will reveal about what or how exactly it matters is, at the outset, uncertain.[25] But the basic presumption underlying it is that "something interesting and surprising" can be uncovered when we theorize about law in this way.[26]

One of the hallmarks of looking at international legal scholarship like this is that, somewhat "inevitably," it starts to reflect back on itself.[27] Taking a closer look at others' knowledge practices raises questions about one's own; for example, what one's conference presentations are like or what kind of beliefs

[19] Orford, 'Epilogue,' 175; Valverde, 'Non-Legality,' 963; see also Bigo, 'Pierre Bourdieu,' 232 and Renske Vos, 'Europe and the Sea of Stories: Operation Sophia in Four Absences' (PhD, Vrije Universiteit Amsterdam 2021).

[20] Orford, 'Epilogue,' 175; Orford, 'Critical Intimacy,' 32, discussing Derrida's work and Spivak's commentary; similarly, Johns, 'Data, Detection,' 66.

[21] Robert Macfarlane, *Landmarks*, Penguin 2016, 211.

[22] Ibid., 1, 238–239.

[23] Marcus, Love and Best, 'Better Description,' 12, 14, 19 note 14; Johns, 'Data, Detection,' 66; Geertz, 'Interpretation,' 318; Johns, 'Unruly Law,' 21–22.

[24] For an alternative suggestion see Riles, 'New Agenda,' 1018.

[25] In similar wording, Orford, 'Critical Intimacy,' 32.

[26] Riles, 'Collateral Knowledge,' 13; Johns, 'Data, Detection,' 66 (in reference to Orford).

[27] Wouter Werner uses the word "inevitably" in describing this balancing act between two perspectives; see Werner, 'Use of Law,' 305. On this reflection feeding back into its own knowledge construction see Bueger and Gadinger, 'Play of Practice,' 457 and Chapter 1 of this book; see also Nouwen, 'As You Set Out,' 233–234 ("[r]eflexivity brings the author back into the story").

about public international law my teaching conveys. This is actually to be expected: it follows from the sociological approach taken in this book. In the Introduction I highlighted how sociological analyses of law "waver between the internal and the external perspective."[28] There is a constant back and forth between recognizing the particularities of legal reasoning and reflections on what, for instance, results from the normalization of those particularities through practice.[29] This kind of hovering around the boundaries of law also means, however, that it is not possible to be fully detached from the knowledge practices one studies; it also implies a reflection on one's own.[30] A panel presentation at a conference with a critical orientation, for example, might well display features similar to the ones given by Michael Schmitt. It may sound different, and there may be a different choice of words, but for the past two decades or so (socio)linguists have considered academic conferences precisely in this light: that these are places where professional identities are constructed.[31] Even though a critical audience is unlikely to identify with the "application-oriented"[32] scholars involved in the cyberwar discourse, the practices the latter group employs are used across the board. This also accounts for the use of the pronoun 'we' in this book, including in its title. As explained in Chapter 5, linguists refer to it as an "inclusive-we," which brings "the hearer or audience in its reference scope."[33] What I mean to say is that the practices studied in this book are not 'out there,' employed by others, but are part of the discipline of international law broadly speaking.[34]

This extended reflection on knowledge practices may materialize, as suggested, in a closer consideration of one's own conference presentations, but something similar happens in my teaching. For example, my class on

28 As explained by Werner, 'Use of Law,' 305. As others have noted this specific dichotomy between the internal and external comes with its own set of problems; see Kendall, 'Academic Production,' 619, 622.

29 See Chapter 1 note 64 for the appropriate references.

30 On "introspection" turning into "narcissism" see Bueger and Bethke, 'Actor-Networking,' 33.

31 Which is the basic premise of Carmen Konzett's book; see Konzett, 'Any Questions?,' specifically 135; more generally, Duszak, 'Us and Others,' introduction. For a critique on academic conferences and some more points raised, see Christy Wampole, 'The Conference Manifesto,' *New York Times Opinionator*, May 4, 2015 and Pierre Schlag, 'The Faculty Workshop,' *University of Colorado Law School Legal Studies Research Paper Series, Working Paper Number 11–12*, June 3, 2011; see also Boer and Stolk, 'Backstage Practices,' chapter 1.

32 Noll, 'Analogy at War,' 210.

33 Fortanet, 'Use of "We",' 48. For examples of similar uses see David Kennedy, 'The Politics of the Invisible College: International Governance and the Politics of Expertise' (2001) 5 *European Human Rights Law Review* 463, 496–497 and Anne Orford, *Reading Humanitarian Intervention: Human Rights and the Use of Force in International Law*, Cambridge University Press 2003, 78.

34 See also Chapter 1 of this book, and Bueger and Gadinger, 'Play of Practice,' 457.

international legal personality for second-year law students includes a discussion of the ICJ's *Reparation for Injuries* Advisory Opinion. There, the Court concludes that the personality of the United Nations under international law "arises by necessary intendment out of the Charter." Elsewhere in the same Opinion, the Court argues that "[i]t is difficult to see how [[t]he 'Convention on the Privileges and Immunities of the United Nations' of 1946] could operate except . . . as between parties possessing international personality." The intent of the drafters and subsequent practice, the Court moreover claims, provide the UN with "functions and rights which can only be explained on the basis of the possession of a large measure of international personality."[35] When reading these phrases with my students, the (socio) linguistic work undertaken in this book finds its way into a class discussion of what these words *do*: what happens when the Court says that something 'arises by necessary intendment,' 'can only be explained' in a particular way and 'is difficult to see' otherwise.[36] Moreover, the closer we look the more difficult it becomes to say which parts of the text are doing what exactly for the justification of the Court's conclusion; to differentiate between what these phrases *do* in relation to the 'doings' of the legal arguments put forward by the Court. So, as with this book, to look this closely at legal writing raises questions about how we know international law when we read or hear it, and what is involved exactly when we claim to speak (for) it.[37]

From this approach to legal knowledge construction the sense emerges that there is a difference between teaching students how to make an international legal argument, versus instilling in them a faith that their future speaking as

[35] *Reparation for Injuries Suffered in the Service of the United Nations, Advisory Opinion, ICJ Reports 1949, p. 174* (1949), 184, 179.

[36] Far more extensively: Laura E. Little, 'Hiding with Words: Obfuscation, Avoidance, and Federal Jurisdiction Opinions' (1998) 46 *UCLA Law Review* 75.

[37] Charlotte Peevers, *The Politics of Justifying Force: The Suez Crisis, the Iraq War, and International Law*, Oxford University Press 2013, 12 ("Justification involves a claim to authority, which itself represents a claim to speak the law, bringing it into being and manifesting itself as lawful authority."); Edwin Bikundo, 'Review of *The Politics of Justifying Force: The Suez Crisis, the Iraq War, and International Law* by Charlotte Peevers (2013) Oxford University Press, 288 pp, ISBN 9780199686957' (2014) 36 *Sydney Law Review* 727, 728. See also Costas Douzinas, 'Speaking Law: On Bare Theological and Cosmopolitan Sovereignty,' in: *International Law and its Others*, Anne Orford (ed.), Cambridge University Press 2006, 35–56, 42–44; Gregor Noll, 'Theorizing Jurisdiction,' in: *The Oxford Handbook of the Theory of International Law*, Anne Orford, Florian Hoffmann and Martin Clark (eds.), Oxford University Press 2017, 600–617; Shaunnagh Dorsett and Shaun McVeigh, *Jurisdiction*, Routledge 2012, 4, referring to Peter Rush, 'An Altered Jurisdiction – Corporeal Traces of Law' (1997) 6 *Griffith Law Review* 144, 150; similarly but in a different style, Matthew Craven et al., 'We Are Teachers of International Law' (2004) 17 *Leiden Journal of International Law* 363, 366.

legal professionals is done not on their own behalf, but on behalf of something else; on behalf of the law.[38] A different way of saying this, is that how we write and speak law determines what is possible to do with it. The contributors to the cyberwar discourse, for example, ask whether Article 2(4) 'allows' for the inclusion of cyberattacks, or "whether we can conceive of a new notion of force" that incorporates this phenomenon "without stretching the provision to its breaking point."[39] These phrases suggest that the limits of the law are something the writer will ultimately bump into; something to inevitably come across at some point in the writing process. Similarly, in a chapter discussing whether cyberspace can be regulated by means of international law at all, another contributor claims that it can, concluding that "a *non liquet* has been avoided; a finding that is of a substantive or interpretative gap in international law."[40] Here, too, the writer suggests that he has only limited power over what his answers will look like – over what he will 'find.'[41] In other words, these phrases suggest a distance between the writer and the law s/he writes *about*. But in writing about law as taking place somewhere else, these phrases do not just create a scission between the law and its writer; they also reveal that there is, in fact, a writer at work.[42] To consider international legal texts as individual acts of writing changes not just how we look at legal knowledge construction; it also reveals the presence of its writers.[43]

This book is based on a belief in the value of looking at legal scholarship on the level of its individual contributors. That is why, for example, its footnotes

38 Cf. Craven et al., 'We are Teachers'; Koskenniemi, 'Apology to Utopia,' 16, denying there is such a thing as a "specifically legal discourse"; Koskenniemi, 'Commitment and Cynicism'; similar to the point made here is Nouwen, 'As You Set Out,' 233.

39 Benatar, 'Cyber Force,' 381.

40 Nicholas Tsagourias, 'The Legal Status of Cyberspace,' in: *Research Handbook on International Law and Cyberspace*, Nicholas Tsagourias and Russell Buchan (eds.), Edward Elgar Publishing 2015, 13–29, 28; see also Boer, 'Narratives of Force,' 15–16, 17.

41 Schlag, 'Problem of the Subject,' 1633–1634, 1647; Philadelphoff-Puren and Rush, 'Fatal (F)laws,' 195, 201; Nouwen, 'As You Set Out,' 233; see also Chapter 1 note 37.

42 On words creating this scission see among others Schlag, 'Problem of the Subject,' specifically 1658, 1646 note 70; Constable, 'Our Word,' chapter 2; Winter, 'Transcendental Nonsense,' 1208, referring to Robert M. Cover, 'The Supreme Court, 1982 Term – Foreword: Nomos and Narrative' (1983) 97 *Harvard Law Review* 4, 45. I explore this scission and its relation to grammar more fully in Lianne J. M. Boer, '"Article 51 Authorizes": Writing International Law,' in: *Constructing the Authority of International Law*, Gleider Hernández and Giedre Jokubauskaite (eds.), submitted (on file with the author).

43 On law as writing see Orford, 'Critical Intimacy,' 32 (about Derrida); referring to Philadelphoff-Puren and Rush, 'Fatal (F)laws,' 202. See also Schlag, 'Problem of the Subject,' 1629, 1642. On the presence of the writer in the text see Boer, 'Narratives of Force'; for a linguistic take on this see for example Hyland, 'Disciplinary Discourses,' chapter 6 and Anna Mauranen, *Cultural Differences in Academic Rhetoric: A Textlinguistic Study*, Peter Lang 1993, chapter 6.

give a scholar's full name when referring to her or his work for the first time: in so doing I sought to underline that there is indeed a writer to these ideas.[44] If the aim is to show how international law comes about at the level of its individual writing and speaking, it matters that this writing and speaking is made as tangible and concrete as possible, and it matters *who* speaks or writes.[45] At the level of the individually spoken and written word many things happen that, if we do not take the trouble of looking this closely, run the risk of being overlooked. Such an approach is key to understanding what happens on the everyday level of legal scholarship, and, moreover, to grasp how these individual contributions bring about international law as we know it.

44 Hyland, 'Disciplinary Discourses,' 1, 12, 33 et seq. (in relation to citations).

45 See also Matilda Arvidsson, 'The Subject in International Law: The Administrator of the Coalition Provisional Authority of Occupied Iraq and its Laws' (PhD, Lund University 2017); Schlag, 'Problem of the Subject.'

Appendix Chapter 5

This Appendix forms the empirical backbone to Chapter 5. Its aim is to account for the way I categorized Schmitt's words; specifically, as also outlined in the introductory chapter, to highlight which words he uses exactly; by assembling them to uncover "regularities" and, essentially, to be able to point at the text and say 'where they are.'[1] By presenting them in this way I seek to make Schmitt's words as concrete and tangible as possible: my aim is "to make visible" what we already hear when listening to his presentations.[2] In other words, by means of this Appendix it becomes possible to call attention to the specific words he uses, and in so doing to account for what these words do.

The following pages first explain how I analyzed these presentations, followed by an overview of which presentations were used exactly; where, when and to whom they were given, and what merits their grouping together here. A summary of the presentations is given in the first table on pp. 185–186 below. The second table shows which quotes from these presentations were assigned to each category (time – past, present, future – and space; the creation of gaps between himself and several others).

APPROACH AND ANALYSIS

The basic question underlying Chapter 5 – how do Schmitt's words construct his authority in his presentations on cyber and international law? – determined the way I approached these presentations.[3] As stated, the assumption under

[1] Johns, 'Unruly Law,' 21–22, quoting Wolcott; see Chapter 1 note 107.

[2] Orford, 'Description,' 617, quoting and translating Foucault; see Chapter 1 note 21.

[3] In comparison, consider Konzett's method: she analyzes roughly four hours of spoken interaction, looking for specific "linguistic devices and interactional strategies" by means of which a range of "professional identities" are constructed. See Konzett, 'Any Questions?,' 109, 135, 137 and chapter 7 of her book in general.

which I did so was that these were sites at which authority was constructed: for example, I had noticed the level of certainty with which he expresses himself about existing law, the direct manner in which he addresses the audience and the way he refers to (the views of) others. During the first viewing of all eight presentations, I transcribed those parts that I considered to play a role in this authority construction. Following this transcription, the outlines of the categories as described in Chapter 5 emerged: how Schmitt positions himself in the past, present and future of international legal scholarship, and how he discursively creates gaps between himself and several others. This was followed by a repeated viewing of all eight presentations. The point of viewing them several times was to complement and check the existing 'time' and 'space' categories. For example, once I had identified several invocations of the past by means of which Schmitt constructs the 'lineage' of the Manual, I would check all presentations again for similar invocations of history I may have missed on a previous viewing. This would lead both to the inclusion of some quotes and to the elimination of others. An example of the latter is when Schmitt talks about the range of sources used by the experts. This particular section of his presentation is not part of the construction described here and has therefore been left out – though I had initially written it down as relevant.[4]

As stated in Chapter 5, the (socio)linguistic work used there helped to explain what these words do exactly. First and foremost, however, it accounted for considering academic speech as a distinct form of speech and academic discourse (as compared to, for example, academic writing as analyzed in Chapter 4). Linguists working in the field of English for Academic Purposes (or EAP, see also the Introduction of this book) started paying attention to "spoken academic discourse" a little over twenty years ago, following an extensive and already well-established body of literature on academic writing.[5] To these linguists, academic speech is a discrete "event"[6] that merits consideration in its own right. With regard to this book, it allowed for these presentations to be analyzed as a distinct form of knowledge construction in the cyberwar discourse. Where I deviated from EAP was in its aims and its focus on discerning difference. What matters to these linguists

4 CyCon 2012 (I), 14.55 et seq. There has been critique on the use of sources by the experts, see Kessler and Werner, 'Expertise,' 803–804; I similarly address one specific criticism on the experts' use of sources in the second half of Chapter 5.

5 Eija Ventola, 'Why and What Kind of Focus on Conference Presentations?,' in: *The Language of Conferencing*, Eija Ventola, Celia Shalom and Susan Thompson (eds.), Peter Lang 2002, 15–50, 16; Ventola, Shalom and Thompson, 'Introduction,' 9.

6 Ventola, Shalom and Thompson, 'Introduction,' 10.

is, for example, what makes for an effective conference presentation: one of the early writings states that "speakers must . . . be shown how they could/should vary their linguistic and non-linguistic realisations when mode changes are necessary in various speaking contexts."[7] Variance matters when different genres set different demands on communicating effectively with one's audience. The question in Chapter 5 of this book, however, is not one of effectiveness but of effect – and for that, the differences between genres are less relevant (the differences between academic writing and speech that do matter to the analysis are addressed in the introduction of Chapter 5). I will return to this below.

THE PRESENTATIONS

As stated in Chapter 5, for the purposes of this chapter I have used eight presentations, given by Schmitt on the first *Tallinn Manual* specifically as well as on cyberwar and international law in general. My own presence at several of these formed the basis for the writing of this chapter. I participated in the 2012 CCDCOE conference and attended several of Schmitt's presentations given there; they were recorded by the conference organizer and have been included in this chapter. Other events that I attended along the years which were not recorded were excluded from the scope of this chapter. At one of these I was a panelist myself, with Schmitt attending that particular session as an audience member.[8]

All eight presentations that are used here were available online at the time of research; at the time of submitting the manuscript for this book the presentation at CyCon 2014 no longer is.[9] Moreover, when I started researching this chapter these eight presentations were, to my knowledge, the only ones given by Schmitt that dealt with the *Tallinn Manual* and/or the *jus ad bellum* and *jus in bello* in cyberspace, that were available online. However, during the research process I found two more: the first dealt with cyber and international law generally, with some brief references to the Manual. The second dealt with the Manual specifically: its inception, the

7 Ventola, 'Conference Presentations,' 17; see also p. 19 of this book.

8 'The Cyber Warfare Manual: A Detailed Assessment,' December 3, 2014, T.M.C. Asser Institute, The Hague, www.asser.nl/upload/documents/20141022T181409-Draft%20Conference%20Programme.pdf (July 16, 2020). I also attended the GCCS 2015 conference, but this panel presentation was not included in Chapter 5; see note 11 of this Appendix and the accompanying body text below.

9 The manuscript was submitted in July 2020; the research took place between the summer of 2015 and late spring 2016.

composition of the group of experts, and some substantive points of law (including the legality of the Stuxnet attack).[10] These presentations were not included here as I came across them relatively late in the research process. In terms of substance, both are largely similar to what Schmitt talks about in the other eight presentations, with the exception of his extensive comments on the legality of Stuxnet during the second presentation just mentioned. A third (panel) presentation was given in 2015 and may be a boundary case for inclusion here: it deals with sovereignty, due diligence and countermeasures taken in response to violations of due diligence obligations. I have not included this one here, however, as it is substantively too far removed from the focus of the chapter.[11]

A table listing the presentations, date, audience and a brief description can be found below; some general comments are in order. These presentations were given between 2012 and 2015, at a time when the second Manual had not been published – so the presentations analyzed here only deal with the first one.[12] Based on the different venues as well as the way Schmitt addresses the audience, presumably his audience is occasionally exclusively made up of lawyers; on other occasions, there are hardly any lawyers in the room. This matters to the substance of what he says, and how he says it (as also explained in Chapter 5). The majority are conference presentations; two are university lectures; and one is a panel presentation, followed by a brief discussion. In linguistic terms this means that even though these presentations may be said to belong to different genres (conference presentation, panel presentation, a Q&A at a conference) I have grouped them together.[13] The reason for this is that my primary interest was how Schmitt discursively positions himself at

10 Michael N. Schmitt, 'Re-Conceptualizing International Law Frameworks in Response to the Threat of Cyber Warfare,' and Michael N. Schmitt, 'International Law and Cyber Warfare.'

11 For this last presentation, see Michael N. Schmitt, Global Conference on CyberSpace 2015 (GCCS 2015), 3.40.05–3.49.24. There is a Q&A session following all four panelists' presentations, which starts at 4.10.14, during which Schmitt briefly responds to a question on the law of conflict management, but this was not enough to include the presentation here.

12 The first *Tallinn Manual* (2013) was reprinted and included in one bind with the second (2017); see also Chapter 2 of this book. This reprint also allowed for some changes; the introduction of the second Manual states that "[s]everal modifications to the original *Tallinn Manual* rules, including complete renumbering, and commentary have been made and one new rule has been added." See Schmitt (ed.), 'Tallinn Manual 2.0,' 2.

13 For example, academic conferences are a distinct genre and studied as such in applied linguistics. See Ventola, 'Conference Presentations'; Konzett, 'Any Questions?,' 3. Similarly in the sociology of knowledge; Gross and Fleming, 'Academic Conferences,' 152–158 and 153 specifically. The notion of 'genre,' however, is not fixed. As an indication of the definitional difficulties involved, see Inger Askehave and John M. Swales, 'Genre Identification and Communicative Purpose: A Problem and a Possible Solution' (2001) 22 *Applied Linguistics* 195.

the center of the debate on cyberwar and international law. Setting, composition of the audience and length of the presentation therefore mattered less than the fact that he was speaking in reference to this particular debate. Approaching his presentations in this way, means I have identified all statements he makes about the Manual (e.g. with regard to its participants, or the drafting process) as part of the construction of his authority. What I mean to say is that he has never distanced himself from its outcomes or its process – quite the reverse. It is important to emphasize this as the opposite is also possible: Schmitt was one of the legal experts participating in the expert process of the International Committee of the Red Cross with regard to direct participation in hostilities. As no consensus was reached between the ICRC and the experts the final report is an ICRC-only document: the process did not work out as intended. In his own words, Schmitt "withdrew his name upon reviewing the final draft."[14] This means that I have considered all the claims he makes about the *Tallinn Manual* in these presentations as serviceable to his construction of his own authority.

READING INSTRUCTION

The next two pages first list the eight presentations, and give some brief details on their substance and the audience. This is followed by a table containing the quotes used for the purposes of Chapter 5, which shows how I classified them. Not all of these quotes have been used in the chapter, but they do all serve to support its claims. I do not presume to have caught all the quotes relevant to the categories listed here, and some quotes appear in more than one category as they are relevant to several of them. To maintain a certain level of readability I did not always contextualize these statements (though I have added some clarifying comments in brackets); for the same reason, text that is sequential in a presentation is occasionally presented as a distinct 'text block,' and the transcription of Schmitt's words does not include words such as 'eh.' The attempt throughout has been to give as faithful a reflection of his speech as possible. In bold are those parts of the quote I wanted to emphasize as I considered them relevant to the category in question; italicized are those words Schmitt emphasizes and where I thought it relevant to convey this emphasis (as well as Latin phrases such as *lex lata*, and the ICJ cases Schmitt

14 Michael N. Schmitt, 'The Interpretive Guidance on the Notion of Direct Participation in Hostilities: A Critical Analysis' (2010) 1 *Harvard National Security Journal* 5, 6; see also William J. Fenrick, 'ICRC Guidance on Direct Participation in Hostilities' (2009) 12 *Yearbook of International Humanitarian Law* 287, specifically 288.

refers to). The sequence of the categories tracks that of the chapter. First addressed are Schmitt's references to time: past, present (which includes his expressions of (un)certainty) and future. The table also provides, in the 'certainty' section, some of Schmitt's expressions of uncertainty, to make sure the picture here is a balanced one (see also my comments in Chapter 5 on this). Also included in that particular row are expressions of Schmitt's attitude of 'solving legal questions.' Secondly, the table provides his references to space: nonlawyers, other(s) (lawyers) who do not really understand the law, academics, the group of experts and others involved in the drafting of the Manual, and references to himself in the third person.

Finally, as these presentations have different focal points, emphases on the different elements of the 'discursive map' differ per presentation. The fact that they were given over a span of three years, to different audiences, on (somewhat) different subjects, in different settings, of course matters to the substance of what Schmitt is saying. For example, a large portion of a 2012 presentation is devoted to the composition of the group of experts involved in the *Tallinn Manual*; it makes sense that here Schmitt places far less emphasis on substantive points of law. At the same time, the presentations on the *Tallinn Manual* are in some respects very similar, such as when he describes the origins of the project (compare, for example, the first five minutes of the presentation he gives at Brown University and at Duke University, both in 2013, and the one at Harvard University in 2015). This also means that some of these presentations have empty columns under some headings. For example, as Schmitt elaborately discusses the composition of the group of experts at CyCon 2012 (I), it makes sense that he does not address this subject during the other two presentations he gives at the same conference.

Abbreviation	Date	Event name/ location	Brief description	Audience	URL
CyCon (I)	8/6/2012	CyCon is the CCDCOE's annual conference on cyber conflict. This presentation is part of the 'law and policy' track.	The *Tallinn Manual* generally: its drafting, the group of experts, substantive scope.	CyCon attracts both academics and practitioners working in cyber as well as those working in the military. There were three tracks at this conference: a law and policy, strategy and technical track; the audience of this presentation is particular to the law and policy track.	www.youtube.com /watch?v=wY3uEo-Itso
CyCon 2012 (II)	8/6/2012	CyCon is the CCDCOE's annual conference on cyber conflict. This presentation is part of the 'law and policy' track.	'Attack' in international humanitarian law (as applied to cyber operations).	CyCon attracts both academics and practitioners working in cyber as well as those working in the military. There were three tracks at this conference: a law and policy, strategy and technical track; the audience of this presentation is particular to the law and policy track.	www.youtube.com /watch?v=f_TC3y7g4aA
CyCon 2012 (III)	7/6/2012	CyCon is the CCDCOE's annual conference on cyber conflict. This presentation is part of the 'law and policy' track.	*Jus ad bellum* in cyberspace.	CyCon attracts both academics and practitioners working in cyber as well as those working in the military. There were three tracks at this conference: a law and policy, strategy and technical track; the audience of this presentation is particular to the law and policy track.	www.youtube.com /watch?v=iPdLtZEhofc
ILD 2012	The conference took place from 25–27/6/2012	Panel presentation at the Annual Conference of the International Law Department of the US Naval War College.	Schmitt participates as one of three panelists and talks about cyber and IHL, particularly 'the classification of conflict,' and addresses the audience from 3.34 to 24.40. Two other panelists subsequently speak, which is followed by an exchange between the panelists from 1.10.34 to 1.20.25, which is the end of the recording.	As this is the annual conference of the International Law Department at the Naval War College, it may be expected there are mostly lawyers in the room.	www.youtube.com /watch?v=sgIT605YIu4
LENS 2013	The lecture was posted online on 2/3/2013	Presentation at Duke University's Annual Conference on Law, Ethics and National Security	This presentation deals with the composition of the group of experts, as well as with some substantive points of law dealt with in the Manual.	Mostly lawyers; footage of the audience and the Q&A shows that members of the military participate as well.	www.youtube.com/ watch?v=vQBiLBrmJJI Following an introduction Schmitt's presentation starts at 15.00.
Brown 2013	11/4/2013	Guest lecture at the Watson Institute, Brown University.	This presentation deals both with the composition of the group of experts and some substantive points of law dealt with in the Manual.	This appears to be a mixed audience of computer science students and international relations students and scholars (see the introduction to the lecture), as well as at least one lawyer (see the body text of Chapter 5).	https://brown.hosted.panopto.com/ Panopto/Pages/Viewer.aspx?id=1962 891D-B51E-4B88-BB05-A99F011762B4 Following an introduction Schmitt's presentation starts at 3.50.

(continued)

Abbreviation	Date	Event name/ location	Brief description	Audience	URL
CyCon 2014	5/6/2014	Conference presentation at CyCon: the CCDCOE's annual conference on cyber conflict. This presentation is part of the 'strategy & law' track.	Schmitt's presentation is a joint one with a technical expert, where they discuss three hypothetical case studies that all relate to 'active defense' in cyberspace, including countermeasures. The technical expert describes the case, followed by a legal analysis by Schmitt. This also means, as stated in Chapter 5, that his tone is more 'instructive' than in the other presentations. In terms of substance this presentation may be a boundary case for inclusion in this chapter: Schmitt's talk only sporadically touches upon the use of force, e.g. when he briefly talks about forceful countermeasures; the focus here lies mostly on sovereignty, due diligence and countermeasures. I have used it in the chapter nonetheless, as the substance of what he says very frequently borders on use of force issues (much more so than the presentation given at GCCS 2015, which has not been included here; see above) and is in fact part of the *Tallinn Manual*; moreover, he occasionally refers to the opinions held by the experts on specific points addressed in his speech.	CyCon attracts both academics and practitioners working in cyber as well as those working in the military. There were three tracks at this conference: a law and policy, strategy and technical track; the audience of this presentation is particular to the law and policy track.	https://ccdcoe.org /cycon/2014/app.html (13 May 2016) This presentation is no longer available online.
PILAC 2015	3/4/2015	Guest lecture at Harvard Law School.	The Manual itself, as well as cyber and international humanitarian law.	There appear to be both (legal) scholars and students in the audience.	www.youtube.com /watch?v=ZWwrVAMSOT4 Schmitt starts his presentation at 6.30.

	Time							
	CyCon 2012 (I)	CyCon 2012 (II)	CyCon 2012 (III)	ILD 2012	Brown 2013	LENS 2013	CyCon 2014	PILAC 2015
Past	(2.09) "**This Manual is not the first of its kind.** You have heard the term San Remo Manual on the law of naval warfare used several times. That was a 1995 project. Professor doctor Von Heinegg, Wolff Heintschel von Heinegg was instrumental in that. There was a NIAC Manual that was put out also by San Remo **that I did** with Yoram Dinstein of Israel and Charles Garraway of the United States. And then most recently there was a product that was called … [the] Air and Missile Warfare Manual that was done by a group of forty experts and then ultimately drafted **by myself** and Wolff von Heinegg and Bill Boothby was involved … *[here Schmitt mentions some others]* We all	(8.59) "So today, this question that everyone seemed to be **struggling with ten years ago,** has been **asked,** and **answered,** and you **need not concern yourself** with it any further." *[on defining 'attack' in IHL by way of the means, or the consequences]* (13.23) "Data transferrable to tangible objects was something **I thought up in an article a long time ago** and the jury is out on whether this is true, and the example you use is, I take my ATM-card I go down, I stick it in the machine, and a hundred euros pops out. My banking data is immediately directly transferable into a tangible *object* that *can* be damaged. Ok? So if you attack my banking data you're really depriving me of the ability to		(17.55) "As a practical standard, **I've suggested before,** that what y'ought to be looking at, is you look at the act, and you ask yourself 'was that the act of a group?'" *[on earlier work on the criterion of 'organized armed group' for the purposes of NIAC]*	(4.24) "I guess it was about the mid-1990s at the Naval War College at the time I was an Air Force Officer on exchange duty at the Naval War College, we started thinking about cyber warfare, in the law department, in the law department there …. **And in fact we organized a major conference in 1999.** It was the very first conference in the world to consider the subject of the norms, the international law norms, that might govern cyber conflict. We held a conference, it was very successful, produced a book, and then 9/11 happened." (5.24) "And really, **we really forgot about cyber. I mean we really did.** There were a couple of articles written, I wrote one article, in the Review of the Red Cross, but most of us this was not of, of interest anymore. Until 2007." (46.39) "[T]he classic law of anticipatory self-defense, that's a legal term … it generally was understood in, in, in terms of time … this doesn't make sense in the context of, of terrorism … you don't have warning … so **a number of us in the**	(24.32) "You have to understand that we started looking at the law actually at the Naval War College **in 1999** there was a a major conference, the first major conference, **we produced a book** on the subject, everyone was focused on on cyber, I went to War College in 95, we were all talking about cyber, then 9/11 happened, and everyone focused on counterterrorism." (26.05) "We, we decided to do a manual because it was a **long lineage** of doing manuals. For the legal historians … the Oxford Manual, the Brussels Manual, from the nineteenth century, and so forth. There had been manuals recently, the '95 Manual on Naval Warfare … Professor von Heinegg was the rapporteur for that project, was integral to that; the San Remo Manual, **there's a San Remo Manual also on non-international armed conflict that I did with Charles Garraway from the UK and Yoram Dinstein from Israel, there was a Harvard Manual on Air and, Air and Missile Warfare … led by Yoram Dinstein, a number of us were involved** *[points at the audience]* … so we thought a manual might help."		(7.56) "Let's start at the beginning. The beginning is actually in the 1990s … **we began** to look at the issue of cyber in war colleges around the world, most notably the war college in Newport, the Naval War College, I was then a student, **an Air Force officer going through the program there,** and cyber, everyone was talking about cyber, *everyone* was. And so there was an, an, an **initial conference** there, in 1998, held by the law department … a book was produced, **I was the editor of the book** … " (17.13) *[on Tallinn 2.0]* "What we are doing is we're looking at cyber issues what we call 'below the threshold,' **a term that has caught on.** 'Below the threshold' referring to cyber operations that don't rise to the level of a use of force or an armed attack in the context of the UN Charter, **ok?**" (39.31) "There was a **major study** conducted by the **ICRC,** for **five years, I was one of the experts** involved in this, called the, it was a study into the notion of direct participation, where we struggled to, to, to articulate 'what, what, what qualified as direct participation' … "

(continued)

	Time							
	CyCon 2012 (I)	CyCon 2012 (II)	CyCon 2012 (III)	ILD 2012	Brown 2013	LENS 2013	CyCon 2014	PILAC 2015
	got together and we drafted the Commentary." (3.01) "So we had a **lot of experience** in drafting these sort of manuals … so we wanted to do a new Manual ***like those previous ones***." *[he repeats this at (4.02)]* " … we had **a lot of experience** in the group, people like Wolff who'd been involved in all these projects, **and myself**, and so the very first thing we did … "	access tangible stuff. This, and this particular case, **the jury is out.** Fifty percent say 'yes,' fifty percent say 'no no' … " (15.24) "What about the unwitting intermediary? Something that **those of us who were involved in kinetic warfare** never think about, but the cyber folks brought it up." (21.24) **"I was one of the, the old guys, who started dealing with cyber a long time ago**, and the wireheads would come in and they'd go 'hey man, you know what we can do?' … you know, capabilities seek targets, this is a truism of warfare. But I'm hoping the first bullet is more accurate." *[Schmitt refers here to a bullet point on a PowerPoint slide]*			**aftermath of 9/11 started looking at this problem, and I will tell you what I came up with**, and my view is, is that you may act in anticipation of an attack … when I know the other guy has the capability to attack me … *and* I know he has the intention of attacking me … *and* if I don't do something now, I may give up my chance to effectively defend myself, ok? This has been, **this has developed into** what is **now known as the 'last window of opportunity test,'** the United States government has, I, **I called it in my article back in 2003, we now start to see US government documents and speeches coming out**, talking about 'last window of opportunity,' it's my last window of opportunity to defend myself."			

	CyCon 2012 (I)	CyCon 2012 (II)	CyCon 2012 (III)	ILD 2012	Brown 2013	LENS 2013	CyCon 2014	PILAC 2015
Present Expressions of (un) certainty (includes: existing law applies to cyber; questions and answers)	(0.13) "About three and a half years ago I got a phone call from an Estonian … asking me to come and speak at one of these conferences … And my answer to her was 'I'm not interested in coming to any more of those boring conferences on cyber. We bring a bunch of lawyers together and they appear to impress the audience by telling, telling the audience *how truly hard* cyber is. **How about if we start answering the questions? When – Call me again if you're ever ready to begin answering the questions'**." (6.33) " … we focused mostly on what's called 'black-letter' … **because we wanted to make *absolutely sure* we got the law right** … we nailed down what the black-letter looks like in plenary. Every black-letter rule	(0.52) "It's **very very important**, several of the speakers yesterday mentioned the necessity of having an armed conflict before the *jus in bello*, before international humanitarian law applies." (2.21) "So we need to be **very careful**, when we're applying this concept, you **must apply it** either in an international armed conflict, which is pretty easy to identify, or a non-international armed conflict, which isn't so easy to identify." (3.02) "This is the **mother** of all IHL principles. This is the, this is the, **the jewel** in **the crown** of IHL principles … *[smiles]*" (5.04) "It's found in Article 49, you **should commit this to memory** if you are an attorney." (6.04) "The first point up here is violence, and this is **very important** because we're wanting to know 'what does attacks really mean in practice?'." (6.49) "What's our **legal result in the cyber context**? The legal result is that we	(0.00) *[probably in response to him being introduced by a moderator]* "Well I'm one of those people that think the legal stuff matters and it matters a lot." (2.50) "It's a *very* different body of law, and **these two bodies of law are not related in any way** … So when we're playing with the word 'attack,' **we need to be very careful**." *[on the distinction between* in bello *and* ad bellum*]* (3.32) *[on the word 'attack' in international law]* " … there are *two* legal meanings, and you **must not confuse** the two legal meanings, because they're **very very very** distinct." (4.15) " … it's very simple today, today **most lawyers say** 'listen it just means "don't use force"'." (4.34) "This is a **very important provision**, and it's the question most people ***should*** be asking about cyber. Not, 'was it an attack?' **They should be asking** 'was it a use of force?' I attended the media session that the sponsors put on the first day, and all the	(3.48) "**I**, I need to come out of the closet right up front, I'm in the Wolff [Heintschel von Heinegg], Terry [Gill] school of thought. **I do not for a second believe that we need a new body of law**, the very first step we should do is figure out what the international law is and then apply it to this weapon just like we would apply it to any new weapon." (4.14) "And this is **a very important topic**, and it's a very important topic because classification of conflict is the very first step in any LOAC analysis. **If you're starting with a LOAC analysis, start here.** Ask yourself what type of conflict you're in. Why? Because the type of conflict you're in determines what body of law applies. International or LOAC in its entirety, that portion of LOAC	*Overall, Schmitt is a lot less firm in his statements here – he only treats those issues that were very contentious among the group of experts.* (23.22) "Let me talk about the real issues that we struggled with. And, and, although most of the issues we **came to consensus fairly easily**, there were some that were **really really tough** let me tell you what they are." (23.34) "The very first one, the threshold question, is the question of whether the, the, the international law that existed as we started the project, did that apply to cyberspace? A number of scholars and reportedly a number of states have suggested that it does not. **The United States position is that it does, the European Union**	(24.54) "So what happened is … suddenly cyber is big, but **no one knows what the law is."** (34.34) "Let me talk a little bit about the **tough issues, there were many many many**, this is just a sampling." (34.49) "One **of the really really big questions**, was 'when is it that a state may *lawfully* use force?' … The issue for us was use of force … What in the world does use of force mean in the cyber context? I mean, I was in the Air Force, I was a targeting officer, before I was a JAG, I understood use of force, but in the cyber context …" (36.53) "And **we struggled, and we struggled, and we struggled, and we eventually gave up.** We could not come up with a, a, a *firm* line that, sitting in a policy or legal position you could say 'yep, it's over the threshold'. What we said was that, the best we can hope to do given this grey area, given this lack of	(0.12) "We selected three [scenarios] that we would like to present to you and show you how, how a lawyer would go through the **legal stations of the cross** if you will, with respect to understanding a particular scenario." (1.00) "I have to tell you, I thought all three presentations **were on the money one hundred percent**, there was not a flaw in any of them." (1.19) "So let me start **in the beginning**. States have obligations under international law, **that's all we'll be talking about today**, international law. I know the first day here in Tallinn we spend looking at a variety of norms, I'm not talking political norms, I'm not talking sociological norms, I'm not talking ethical norms, I'm talking **hard law** which is found in **only two places**. In treaties, and in customary international law." (1.45) "Now, the first, **the mother of all obligations** in international law, is the obligation to respect, to *respect*, the sovereignty of other states." (1.57) "Now what does sovereignty mean, it's a **mushy** term. **What it means** is that if you're a state, you get to control everything that happens in your state. Almost everything. You get	(6.38) "Actually I found this interesting that the **Secretary** [Albright] **was talking about cyber and saying that there, there really aren't a body of rules, there's not a body of rules for cyber, I think exactly the opposite is true**, and it's been my position for some time now that international law is **rather robust** and international law can be applied to cyber in a way … that's **very logical and meaningful**." (7.30) *[talking about an address at NATO, where he got a sense that the people in the room thought international law didn't apply effectively]* " … **hopefully I dissuaded that group of that,** because I think international law is **pretty good**, *although, although* there are **certain problems, certain difficulties**, and we'll talk about those this afternoon." (14.28) "And so the

(continued)

	CyCon 2012 (I)	CyCon 2012 (II)	CyCon 2012 (III)	ILD 2012	Brown 2013	LENS 2013	CyCon 2014	PILAC 2015
	reflects the opinion of every single member of the group of experts. There's no member of the group of experts that objects to any statement of law that we have in there." (9.12) "That final plenary is for the purpose of saying **'now is everyone absolutely sure we got it right?'** Cause we're going final … " (16.40) "We come up with two things in the Manual, you'll find two things, black-letter law, it's an American term, but it means ***'the law, this is the law,'*** they're usually short, they're usually very very broad because remember they had to represent consensus among the group." (18.34) " … and so you, as users in a state, or a ministry, or a scholar, **this is not a Manual that gives you one answer.** It is a Manual that says 'here's a broad Rule everyone	can say **with great certainty** that an action that is non-violent in character is not governed by the prohibitions on attack. So we're talking espionage and psyops." (7.59) "So, over and over, particularly in the early days of cyber, the **question** was 'does this rule apply to cyber operations?' The **answer today** is **absolutely 'yes,'** it's, there's **absolutely no question** whatsoever, **anyone who argues this point doesn't know what they're talking about.** Because there's **almost unanimity** on this point. **You should not worry** about the fact that the *means* are not violent, **you have to focus** on the consequences of the operation. It's not the nature, it's the consequences." (8.35) " … this is consistent with our interpretation of this term in other contexts. For example, biological warfare isn't really kinetic, but no one in this room would suggest that that's not an attack. Or chemical warfare need not necessarily be kinetic, but no one in	journalists wanted to know was you know, 'Stuxnet, was that an armed attack?' **Doesn't matter** if it was an armed attack! **What it matters**, is whether or not it was a use of force … " (5.10) " … it's recognized as customary international law, and in, indeed, not even regular customary law, but **super duper** customary law, known as *jus cogens*. **The kinda stuff you can never ever never break. Ok? So this is the important prohibition."** (6.11) "And so when we ask, 'is Stuxnet an armed attack?,' the **only relevance of that question, the *only* relevance**, is 'what can the Iranians do?' To whoever launched that attack … Here we're only talking about responses." (6.39) "Unfortunately, or fortunately for lawyers and law professors the term is not defined in international law anywhere, in any authoritative place in international law. **But we have some clues."** *[he proceeds]* (6.51) "First of all, the big question that was	that applies to non-international armed conflicts, or alternatively, human rights law … " (5.11) "The analysis I'm gonna go through **should be** the analysis, **exactly** the analysis you go through in any context. Because when you're looking at cyber operations **it's exactly the same, exactly the same** as operations with a Tomahawk cruise missile … " (5.32) **"Apply the law that already exists, and I think you'll find it serves you well."** (5.37) "Let's talk about cyber conflict. What's unique about it in the classification of conflict context, there are several things that **might appear to be unique."** (6.14) "Now, my going-in premise, and I'm gonna take this off the table right away, is if you're talking about the use of cyber operations during an armed conflict, a kinetic armed conflict,	**position is that it does, and the position of all twenty of the participants is that it does.** And we say that for two reasons." (28.21) *[on Article 2(4)]* "This was the hardest, we did not resolve this. I'm very disappointed **we did not solve this problem."** (37.23) "[T]hat's what's unsatisfactory about the test. Because, if, if , if, if the policy maker is looking at me as the legal adviser, what he or she wants to know is, 'was that a violation of international law?' You know. And if it was, what are my remedies? What can I do in response? And, and I have to say to him in this case, him or her, I have to say, 'well, you know, it kind of looks,' and that's, you know. **That's why policy makers hate lawyers, ok, so. 'On the one hand, on the other'.** The	clarity, the best we can hope to do is to tell policy makers, to look for these sorts of things in determining whether or not an operation they conduct will be deemed a use of force by the international community … these are the sorts of factors the international community will look at." (40.13) "[W]e're gonna have to watch a lot of state practice before we can definitively say we've established a clear threshold for crossing, crossing to, crossing into the 2(4), Article 2(4) realm. **So no clear standard."** (40.51) **"Equally tough** was Article 51." (42.20) "The *Nicaragua*-case told us to look at the scale and effects of an operation to determine if it's an armed attack. And so our Rule … this is the broad, black-letter Rule, I think it's, there's **absolutely no question** that it reflects international law because we're simply taking a scale and effects test … "	to control most of what happens in your state certainly with regard to the cyber infrastructure … " (2.42) *[on violating sovereignty as physical damage or destruction]* "Now I have to tell you, that's something that the international group of experts in the *Tallinn Manual* actually dealt with, that's **the one thing we could agree on.** What we **could not agree on** … " (5.25) "And then the third issue that is **unresolved in international law** … " (5.35) "'Does state C have an obligation to do something … ?' **Answer: we weren't sure**, we weren't sure." (5.55) "[T]he issue we're really concerned with is the issue of attribution. And it's a **very very important** question." (6.21) "So it's **very important** to be able to attribute, there are three cases that **you need to be concerned with."** (8.43) "*However, however,* **you must remember this** … **you must remember** that there is a duty of a state to put an end to harmful activities on its territory." (10.35) "But it need not be the same kind. **So you need to be a little bit careful** when you're talking about countermeasures. The mere fact that you've done something to me in cyberspace doesn't mean I	**question** is, *[refers to slide]*, 'what's the law?' (19.24) *[on international humanitarian law]* "I will tell you, that **it was easier than we thought.** We thought 'oh golly, I mean, this is so new, and how are we gonna do that?' – **it wasn't so hard,** because most of IHL is *adapted*, it's designed to *be* an adapted body of law, it's *designed* for new weapons, **there are *rules* on new weapons for crying out loud."** (19.43) *[about applying IHL]* "So what it meant was that we spent some time interpreting norms in the cyber context, but in many cases we all went 'yeah, ok that makes sense, you know, you you you can't attack medical things, and you probably can't attack medical databases.' **That's hardly a judicial, juridical epiphany. Right?"** (22.00) *[on operations really being 'attacks' for the purposes of international*

agrees on, but in terms of the interpretation of this Rule, you can kinda go through and say, you know, 'that may have been the majority, minority view, among *that* group of scholars, but we in Israel, we think the minority rule is the accurate reflection of law'." *[Schmitt appears to misspeak here: he is not referring to minority rules, but to minority views]*
(19.01) "So the most valuable aspect of this Manual is we did not try to come to consensus on everything. We tried to lay out for the user the various alternatives they had. And we also sometimes simply said, 'it's unclear. I don't know. We thought about this and golly, **it's too hard for this group of twenty people**'."
(21.44) "Blockade was the hardest. We have the world's blockade expert in the audience … literally the

this room would ever suggest that that's not an attack if you conducted such an operation."
(8.59) "So today, this **question** that everyone seemed to be struggling with ten years ago, **has been asked, and answered, and you need not concern yourself with it any further.**"
(10.09) " … the *type* of consequences **you're looking for** are death or injury to individuals, or damage or destruction to property."
(11.02) "**Now we know what it is … It seems to me, that, and most international law scholars and practitioners**, that it *includes*, this concept of attack, includes damage that is not directly caused."
(12.24) "Now the classic example is the one I use up here, everyone likes to use it because it's easy to get your head around, I attack a dam, it causes no damage, all it does is cause the flood, the floodgates to open … **clearly, clearly,** those secondary effects on the civilian population downstream as a result of the flood qualify

asked … 'well … does an armed attack have to be kinetic? … Because of the word 'armed'. And therefore, does it exclude cyber stuff?' **The answer is 'no'**. The International Court of Justice has answered this question in the *Nuclear Weapons* Case … it matters what the consequences are. And in fact state practice supports this, **this should be no epiphany**. State, every state would believe that if you conduct a radiological attack or a chemical attack against another state and it's not kinetic in nature every state would agree that this is an armed attack. **This is a question asked by scholars that need not be asked, this question has been asked and answered, this is settled law**."
(9.56) "So if you're asking 'was Stuxnet an armed attack?' … **you should ask yourself this question**. 'Did people die? Were they injured? In a significant way? Was there significant damage?' And if the answer is 'yes' then you're at the armed attack threshold and

then **it's real easy**. Apply the law that applies to that kinetic armed conflict."
(6.38) "The classic case is Georgia, there were lots of cyber operations that occurred during operations between Georgia and Russia, that was **clearly, unquestionably**, an international armed conflict. Those cyber operations would have been governed by the law of international armed conflict."
(8.01) "And basically what they say, the Commentary to Common Article II and the Commentary to the Protocol, basically what they say is 'intensity and duration, they simply don't matter' … **This happens to be my view, although there are some that would require *some* degree of intensity. But this represents the majority view** *excluding* again truly *de minimis, de minimis*

answer is always, 'it depends'."
(37.54) *[on Article 2(4)]* "And that's why this is the greatest disappointment, I believe, in the, in the project. **Because I can't answer your question and I *should* be able to.** I will tell you, we, we determined that Stuxnet *was* a use of force, we, it was unanimous, everyone agreed that Stuxnet *was* a use of force, because it caused physical damage … "
(40.19) "Now note the words are 'armed attack' … if you're the victim of a cyber armed attack then you can shoot back with cyber uses of force, or you can just use the United States navy … **So it's very very very important.**"
(54.44) "Of course it's **hardly a judicial epiphany** for me to tell you you may engage in cyber operations against the enemy's command and

(46.00) "This is **very important law,** because in the cyber environment, it will often be the case that you don't have a state actor conducting the operations, but they have outsourced, encouraged … so it's **critically important** to get your arms around 'when is an operation going to be a use of force by virtue of the law of state responsibility?'."
(46.34) "These are the Rules we basically came up with, there are three situations … if the CIA … conducts an operation, **clearly**, there is state responsibility, and, **clearly** even if the individuals conduct the operations beyond the scope of their actual duties … listen, if he's at CyberCom headquarters and he's doing this, America's responsible."
(47.53) "[T]he third case is **very important** today … "
(48.43) "**One thing that is often missed** is that the fact that something is not an armed attack doesn't leave a state defenseless."

have to do something unlawful, if I wanna take a countermeasure, in cyberspace."
(11.11) "**Very important. Very important.** There's no **such thing** as collective countermeasures."
(11.58) "There are **two more things you need to worry about.** The next one is, for the Germans in the audience, this is ***überimportant.* Pay attention, write this down. Ok?**"
(12.14) "[N]ecessity says this: listen, if you can engage in unlawful actions, if you need to, in response to something that happens to you, something is happening to you, and it's not something bad, it's something **extraordinarily bad**, it is affecting the essential interest of your state in a way … that, that **has grave and imminent peril. It's really bad.** They're affecting your critical infrastructure for example. In this case, **you can respond** by violating the law *even if, even if*, the, the action by the other state is not unlawful. Moreover, **and this is really important**, you may respond even if the action is not caused by a state. **You should be thinking** 'non-state actor,' **you should be thinking** 'terrorist group' … **You have to be careful**, if there's bleedover effect into other states, **that's ok, but it can't**

humanitarian law]
"So then it begs the question, **as lawyers we have to ask 'what?** So what's *attacks* mean?' **Ok?** Now we know what operations mean, what's attacks mean?"
(26.01) *[talking about the way the functionality test came about]*
"There's a … non-attribution, but a **very brilliant person** working for a certain organization that's dedicated to humanitarian causes, and and and myself, and we're talking by email from different continents, we're both in a hotel late at night … and this person said 'what about focusing on functionality?' And that was, it clicked for me. It it it made sense. So what the majority, *the majority*, here was not a unanimous view, the majority of the experts would say that damage *includes* an operation, that albeit not physically damaging or … destructive affects the functionality of

(continued)

	CyCon 2012 (I)	CyCon 2012 (II)	CyCon 2012 (III)	ILD 2012	Brown 2013	LENS 2013	CyCon 2014	PILAC 2015
	number one guy in the world there, of course, I don't wanna put words in his mouth but he was asserting there's *[no?]* such thing as blockade, we had another guy who said 'you're crazy' we never could resolve cyber blockade. So there's a long commentary on it and then say 'we're not sure'. Ok?"	this as an attack." (14.30) "This, delayed effects, would be included in the effects that are acceptable *[for inclusion]*. **How do we know this? We know this because** when you look at the negotiating history of the Additional Protocol, it tells us that using land mines is an attack. Even though the effect doesn't happen until well down the line. If I go dig a hole out here and put a land mine I've conducted an attack." (15.08) "If I shoot a gun at you, and I miss, I've still attacked you. **It's exactly the same way** in cyber." (17.28) "And I have to be frank, I'm slowly coming around to this view myself, because I'm struggling with the difference between replacing a component and loading an operating system. All I know is I don't how to do either of those … So I'm slowly coming myself around to this view. There is another view … "	that means that the victim of the attack can respond with a cyber operation that rises to the level of force without violating the prohibition on the use of force." (11.29) "We also need to be careful because there are, there is a **little bit of controversy** here, some scholars, the most famous one being Yoram Dinstein, who's former President of Tel Aviv University, he says 'no no, the Court got it wrong'. Ok? The *only kind* of damage that would be excluded, the *only* kind of damage would be absolutely meaningless, not her thing caught, her computer caught on fire, but it was scratched by operation of another state. Ok? But there is a bit of … dispute. **Now what there is *valid* dispute about is that this, this accepted provision of international law has been questioned by a lot of folks because of cyber.** Because cyber can cause consequences that are not death, injury, damage or destruction or serious suffering, that are nevertheless *very very very* severe.	hostilities." (8.53) "[A]rmed *[in the sense of 'armed conflict']* means any operation that amounts to an attack as a matter of law. Again, attack is a legal term of art. I'm using it here in the LOAC sense, in the *in bello* sense, *not* in the Article 51 sense. **All that stuff we've already talked about, forget that. Has nothing to do with what we're talking about here.**" (9.35) "I believe today **it is pretty well accepted** that we can look at *consequences* to determine whether or not something is an attack as a matter of law and thus can qualify it as an armed conflict. **Clearly** everyone agrees death, injury, damage or destruction qualify." (12.13) "This would **obviously** include actions by the armed forces, it would **obviously** include actions by organs of the state, such as intelligence	control facilities. **No kidding.** That's a military objective."	(49.14) "[B]ased on this feedback, we have included sections on a few other options. There are two that are **particularly important** … " (54.12) "So the majority took the position that the word 'operations' in the principle of distinction, which is the **mother of all principles** in LOAC … " (54.56) "Now this was for the group rather problematic because of the word 'violence' *[in the Additional Protocol]* … so we had to dig into the negotiating history of the Protocol and the commentary and so forth and ask 'what did they really mean?' … And what we discovered is, they really weren't talking about the act itself being violence, but rather the consequences being violent. And the example is, is there are repeated references, **and everyone agrees**, that a radiological, or a biological or a chemical operation is an attack. Ok? **Everyone … agrees**	**be** bleedover that affects their essential interests. So, **bleedover is ok, really really** bad ***überbleedover* is not ok. Ok?**" (17.04) "Ok. So let's get rid of, first, what we call the red herring in law. In other words, the fact in the scenario that is here because they wanna trick the student into writing most of the time in the exam on something that has nothing to do with the question … Domestic law has **absolutely nothing whatsoever to do** with the international legal, legal analysis in that case." (18.13) "This is a **mistake that's often made**. People usually think of this in terms of [x] … wowowowowow stop." (19.11) "This is an easy one. If you're a **law student** this is the point at which you should just leave the paper blank … Because there are no international law, legal issues with regard to the misleading information. **Why? Because** … " (20.19) "Don't we *[Schmitt is referring to private companies]* have a right to respond? **The answer is** 'I'm afraid not'. You may like to respond, but a doctrine in law is the tough-noogie doctrine, it means you're out of luck … " (21.15) "Now, next question …. company X was in part state-owned. So you should go 'aha! State-owned! This is the law of attribution! I	the cyber infrastructure against which it is directed. Ok? Now this **was a very very important. Very very important.**" (30.44) "That was our rule, and we could not come to an agreement on this." (37.03) "There is this belief that civilians cannot engage in hostilities, **that's completely wrong, that's completely wrong,** it's perfectly acceptable for civilians to engage in hostilities, **but what it means** is that there's certain consequences … " (37.57) "If you **directly, directly, directly** participate in hostilities you're targetable … " (40.13) "**Let me basically tell you that the rule is:** if you are engaging in cyber operations during an armed conflict, and they hurt the enemy, so you're maybe, probing in … you're probing into my systems to try and find vulnerabilities such that you can then give that information to

The classic example … is bringing down the New York Stock Exchange. Or doing something that undermines the economy of a state. That would have devastating … consequences but have no direct result in terms of death, injury, damage or destruction. Is this an armed attack? **According to the conventional understanding the answer is 'no'**. However, a group of scholars have argued that what you should do is dispense with the idea that … the attack has to be of a particular nature … And that the only question you should ask is 'how severe are the consequences?'" (13.14) "I will tell you that, I mean, this, this approach appeals to me, **but I'm in the business of finding what the law is today** not what the law will be seven years from now, and today, the **predominant opinion** among states and among scholars is **clearly**, death, damage, injury or death. This is the agreed upon interpretation." (15.16) "An interesting

agencies. **In other words, 'is it international if these guys are doing it?' Yes."** (13.55) "There is a different standard – and this is **often missed** – there is a different standard if we're not talking about an organized armed group." (16.17) "So if you're looking for a non-international armed conflict, **you're looking for two things.** First, a particular level of intensity, second, an organized armed group. Ok? So let's look at those." (21.33) "**[P]retty much everyone accepts** this aspect of the Protocol as reflective of customary international law. That's certainly the position taken in the ICC Statute, it is certainly my position … The problem is is although that gives us some hints, we don't have a bright-line test, we don't have a clear threshold … But the **one thing we can be certain of,** is that it's a fairly

with that. So if that's the case, we concluded that attacks as a matter of law must mean an operation that had violent consequences." (56.21) "Some of you should be troubled by this. I mean, this is a pretty high standard … *[continued at 56.46]* We really **struggled** with this …. literally this is a debate that took a couple of years." (58.45) "This is, this is perhaps the most interesting thing to read in the Manual … and we think these are **very real** situations, because on the modern battlefield **you will want to attack** enemy civilian cyber infrastructure for lots of different reasons." (59.02) *[question from the audience: "Do these rules apply to dual use objects?" Response by Schmitt:]* "**Absolutely**. There's absolutely **no doubt, not a scintilla, none**. *[some inaudible comment, laughter]* It became a big issue, that's why I'm … *[continued at 59.40]* The answer is

heard about that this morning … ' **Wrong answer. That's the wrong answer."** (21.50) **"What you look for** in this case, is you ask whether or not the state is in control of the company." (27.18) "This is **critically important** because of the principle of necessity. Because remember what I told you about the principle of necessity. It has to affect an essential interest in a **really really really bad way**. And that's **clearly** the case here." (27.34) "So right now **you should be thinking** in the back of your mind 'hm I wonder if that principle of necessity applies'." (28.11) "And so therefore there's **not a scintilla of doubt** that [state] B is in violation of its obligations owed to [state] A." (28.37) "I would tell you the same thing. That the blank piece of paper with regard to legal issues is the right one. But here there's been a change of fact." (29.30) "So, what do we look for next? Well, we wanna see whether or not there's a countermeasure. We know B is in breach. We know that A … is also now in breach … which remember is ok if it's in the guise of a countermeasure." (30.53) "So the better argument, perhaps the best argument, is necessity. Why

someone else, that's direct participation … " (42.35) "**I don't know the answer to these questions.**" (49.27) "**In IHL you generally don't think about** 'how bad is the harm to the civilian object,' you think, 'I've harmed a civilian object,' you protect certain categories of individuals and certain categories of things, so although there was **great sympathy for your view**, this wasn't the **normal approach** taken in IHL."

(*continued*)

CyCon 2012 (I)	CyCon 2012 (II)	CyCon 2012 (III)	ILD 2012	Brown 2013	LENS 2013	CyCon 2014	PILAC 2015
		prospect is that you mount … an operation, a cyber operation, and the cyber operation has consequences that you did not intend. But those unintended consequences rise to the level of an armed attack. Where the scale and effects are met. What do you do in this situation? Here the community is split. **In my view, which I** ***believe*** **is the prevailing view,** I would say that's nevertheless an armed attack. Because if it's not the state has no way to respond … **So my view** is even unintended consequences can enable a state to respond with its own use of force … " (18.02) "Does it matter who's shooting at you? Yeah **it matters a lot**." (20.19) *[Schmitt renders two different views on armed attacks by non-state actors]* "There is a second view, it's the correct view *[smiles]* ok? *[laughter from the audience]* The correct view is that non-state groups may in fact commit armed attacks … The question here is 'may you resort to measures that are	high threshold." (24.17) "And I think that, I believe that these standards are likely to evolve over time, as we start to see what happens as states become concerned about operations, we'll see them begin to evolve. But you know, **we're not making new law here, this is naturally the way international law evolves every day in in areas other than cyber**." (1.10.57) *[responding to another panelist]* "**I wanna pray that I misunderstood what you said**, that, you said that a commander may have some ethical obligation to place a lawful target on notice that he or she may be endangering the civilian population *[exchange between the panelists, Schmitt continues at 1.12.27]* I, I guess my point would be, I may have the same trouble but the law is pretty well settled with regard to warnings … and with regard to		**absolutely**. The group had **absolute consensus** that something which is used for military purposes, any military purposes … that is a military objective … *[continued at 1.00.11]* **But absolutely, the whole group agreed on that.**" (1.00.14) "Ok, a lot of people are always asking questions about, 'what about civilians?' 'Cause you know, today, civilians are cyberwarriors. We did not struggle very much with that. I add this only because there appears to be in the press and so forth a lot of talk about this. In our view, and the view of the group I mean this was the uniform view of the group, the whole group agreed with this, there's **absolutely no prohibition** in humanitarian law, the law of war, on civilians participating in hostilities." (1.05.22) "But that is a fair criticism. So if someone says 'this is a Western view,' oh yes it is, I mean, this is, these are Germans	is that? That's because in this case where we started was by telling you that the essential interests are affected in a very grave and imminent way … And what did I tell you about necessity? If you're replying in necessity … and it affects another state, that's ok. So long as what? So long as his essential interests aren't affected." (35.26) "Alright. This scenario is different than all the others. The reason it's different it's **easier** in a sense … This is classic state-on-state. So let me go through this … Why do I say likely? Because remember there is a school of thought that requires some form of physical damage … my response is **as a matter of law it's not crystal clear** that data qualifies as physical in nature … So that's why I say it's not quite certain but you know my personal view is [x]." (37.10) "Although I'm in absolute, 112% agreement with Professor Hathaway, this is a **very fuzzy area** of the law. So that's why I'm not gonna tell you this is a prohibited intervention." (38.57) "But the legal community is divided here so we really can't **answer** that **question.**" (40.13) "**Is it ok? Answer: yeah. It's ok as a what? As a countermeasure. It's ok as a countermeasure**." (40.34) "It seems to me that	

classically defensive in the, in the, in the context of Article 51?' And I would say 'yes' and I would say 'this has been well-demonstrated by state practice in the immediate aftermath of 9/11, **clearly** the Security Council saw this as self-defense' … **There is a problem with that case though.**"
(23.26) "This isn't a big issue. The bigger issue is … .Well, *[in hypothetical A]* there it's **much much more complex …** However, if *[hypothetical B]* **here the law is unclear.** And you have to do a case-by-case analysis looking at status, the target, why the person's doing this, the extent of damage and so forth."
(24.17) "'The question now is, 'ok, now I understand what it is, I understand who can do it where I can do it when can I do it?'"
(24.32) "However the question is 'can you respond before or after the attack has been conducted?' The before-the-attack question, there are three schools of thought. There's the old school of thought … .**Today most**

distinguishing yourself the law has long been that ruses are permissible … "
(1.13.27) "**It is certainly perfidious, it is certainly not perfidy.** And the war crime is perfidy and requires perfidious conduct in, in connection with an intent to kill, wound, or, if you're a Protocol party, capture."
(1.14.07) *[response to other panelist]* "… I, I wanted to give an alternative viewpoint, **and it's a viewpoint that I think is more conventional** because I was concerned … with a little bit of your discussion of continuous combat function … "
[he proceeds]
(1.14.28) "I think you have to **very clearly distinguish** between characterization for the sake of targeting and characterization for the sake of detention or other activities. With regard to targeting there are two

and Americans and Canadians, Swedes, I mean, you know, this is a very Western oriented approach. **But we got it right if you're taking notes."** *[laughter from the audience]*
(1.09.47) "**[T]here's absolutely no question** you can do that, pursuant to the law of countermeasures."
(1.11.41) "The one place where we **struggled** a little bit … *[continued at 1.12.10]* We **disagreed** on this issue."
(1.14.40) "We, we operated from the general premise that there's not a new dimension, I know that's in all the books, but we said 'nonononono, what **we're talking about is cyber infrastructure, cyber infrastructure is located someplace, it may be located in the high seas, it may be located in air space, it may be located on territory, but it is located in some place that is governed by international law'.**"
(1.18.16) *[in response to a question]* "With regard to *in bello* …

it's **crystal clear** in this case that that is … that's **clearly, clearly** a breach of B's sovereignty. However, does it qualify as a countermeasure? My **answer** here is that probably it does, but it does raise the question of proportionality …. and be **very very very careful** here. **We're not talking** about the harm … **what we're talking about** is the wrong … "

(continued)

	CyCon 2012 (I)	CyCon 2012 (II)	CyCon 2012 (III)	ILD 2012	Brown 2013	LENS 2013	CyCon 2014	PILAC 2015
			people think this is something quaint and old and historical. The – there are two other schools of thought. One school of thought would apply … the Caroline-standard, which is temporal … However this standard doesn't work very well in the case of terrorism or in the case of cyber because you don't know it's, exactly when it's gonna come … And so therefore today **I think the emerging view** and I would **almost say the prevailing view** is this: that you have to look at three things."	categories of people, there are members of the armed forces and there are civilians. **Forget combatants, don't use that term. There are members of the armed forces, and there are civilians."** (1.15.32) **"I don't agree with this. We've all written on this, I don't agree. But that's, that's how it plays out."** (1.16.01) *[in response to another panelist's presentation, which he disagrees with]* "That's targeting, that's **very clear.**" (1.17.41) "So, I, I saw your, your pitch and but **I'm worried** because that exact pitch was made as we started the DPH process. **Because a number of us were here** *[pointing at the audience]*, **and this was *exactly* the argument that was made."**		we were **pretty certain** that any, any damage to civilian objects, or injury to civilians, sufficed." (1.18.36) "[C]ause I mean you know Wolff [Heintschel von Heinegg] and myself, we're really **classic international lawyers, we believe** the *in bello* has nothing to do with *ad bellum*, and vice versa. **Nothing. There's an absolute void, it may never be crossed.**"		

	CyCon 2012 (I)	CyCon 2012 (II)	CyCon 2012 (III)	ILD 2012	Brown 2013	LENS 2013	CyCon 2014	PILAC 2015
***Lex lata*, with regard to the *Tallinn Manual* specifically**	(3.11) "**It is a *restatement* of the law. It does *not* make law. There is no effort to progressively develop the law.** This was an attempt to say 'we now have cyber, how does the law of *bellum* and *in bello*, how does that body of law apply in the cyber context?'" (13.54) "I emphasize that it is … not *lex ferenda*, it is *lex lata*. If you ask me what armed attack *lex ferenda* is **you'll get a different answer** than what we put in the Manual. **Because we asked 'what is the law *now*?' …** August was the date we picked. In **August 2012, what's the law, not, where is the law going,** that's for scholars to write about."	(18.26) *[on the definition of 'attack']* "[I]f the consequences are really severe for the population, that is an attack. I, that may be, in my mind, **that may be *lex ferenda*, what the law *will* be, at this point, I don't believe it's the law today.**" (20.42) " … my **mission** is to find **what the law *is today* …** "	(12.28) "The classic example … is bringing down the New York Stock Exchange. Or doing something that undermines the economy of a state … Is this an armed attack? According to the conventional understanding the answer is 'no'. However, a group of scholars have argued that what you should do is dispense with the idea that … the attack has to be of a particular nature … And that the only question you should ask is 'how severe are the consequences?' … I will tell you that, I mean, this, this approach appeals to me, **but I'm in the business of finding what the law is today** not what the law will be seven years from now, and today, the **predominant opinion** among states and among scholars is **clearly**, death, damage, injury or death. This is **the agreed upon interpretation**."		(1.05.38) " … we did not try to be creative, in fact, every time someone did try to be creative, as director, I would slap them. Because we did not wanna be accused of being creative, we wanted to to be ***slave* to what's called *lex lata*, the law as it is today**. Not the law as it is a month from now, or a year, or ten years, but *today*. Because states make law, not law professors." (1.13.45) "[A]gain, **we were doing *lex lata***, we were doing the law as it is, we had a case on point, that was a famous ICJ case, so that's why we drew that line … I would expect that law to, the interpretation to change over time … "	(26.49) "What we decided was we wanted to do simply **a restatement of the existing law.** We did not want to go **out on the ledge**. We wanted to figure out, how would the **extant law, the law that we have today**, the *lex lata*, how would it apply in the cyber context." (1.06.23) "The other **criticism, and it's fair, is,** we were *very very very* **conscious about the fact that we don't have the right to say what law is, he does** *[pointing at someone in the audience]*. He does state practice, **I don't do state practice, ok? And *opinio juris*, and so forth. So we said, 'let's make sure we don't do *lex ferenda*, let's make sure** we are **in no way** trying to suggest **what the law should be'**. Our goal is to say, **'what is the law, *right* now,'** it was **June 2012**, that was the date. In **June 2012, 'what is the law today?'**."		(47.14) "**We swore on a stack of Bibles in front of ten bishops** *[laughter from the audience]* **that we would never never never delve into *lex ferenda*, that we would be strictly tied to *lex lata* …** " (48.28) *[in response to a question by an audience member]* " … but your point is … a very very good one, it's just we were *very* hesitant about getting out ahead of **where we thought states would** … your interpretation, consequentiality, is one of the minority positions that we said. Some people said consequentiality was *lex lata*. *Lex lata*, not *lex ferenda*." (52.10) "[T]he object of attack is in fact *an object* as understood in IHL …. (*cont.* 52:42) I will tell you that I anticipate that in five years, that will change. I'm writing, *urging* it to change. Because of the concerns you have. **But we we wanted to maintain fidelity to the law as we believe states would interpret it on *that* date.**" (54.49) "Although we pretty uniformly agreed that was the law, virtually anyone who's worked with a government thought that there were few ideas stupider than outsourcing the conduct of military operations to civilian entities, including intelligence agencies. It was, there was almost universal consensus, from the ICRC representatives, in their personal capacity I add, to Mike Schmitt at a war college that that was an incredibly stupid idea, for all sorts of reasons. But not for reasons of law. But not for reasons of law. **And as I said we were slave to *lex ferenda*.**" *[Schmitt says here, 'we were slave to* lex ferenda,' *but, given the foregoing and all the other references to the groups' adherence to* lex lata, *he obviously misspeaks here.]*

	CyCon 2012 (I)	CyCon 2012 (II)	CyCon 2012 (III)	ILD 2012	Brown 2013	LENS 2013	CyCon 2014	PILAC 2015
Future	(21.13) *[on armed attack]* "As I told you yesterday, I think that law will **be different in seven years,** but it's not today." (21.18) "Attack, we had brutal, bloody battles, thank god we are friends, over the issue of 'what does an attack … mean today?' However, I think in the last couple of, of literally weeks, the ICRC and those who are on the other side **are coming to an accommodation** that the international law community will find acceptable. **So I think that one's gonna be resolved by the Manual.**"	(16.13) "I think **we're starting to emerge the point** in the IHL community that if you do interfere with the functionality, it doesn't work … *[continued at 16.54]* I think **slowly but surely the international community is now accepting this premise.** There are some alternative views in terms of what qualifies as an attack … " (18.40) *[on a target-based view of attack]* "And then finally there's a group that has been saying for a long time that the issue is not the consequence, but instead the status of a target. **In other words** if you shoot cyber at civilians, or you shoot cyber at civilian objects, then that's a violation of international humanitarian law, irrespective of the consequences, unless the consequences are truly *de minimis*. I believe that it's fair to say that this viewpoint, **which was very strong, early on, ten**	(14.15) "What about data? … There's prevailing opinion today that merely attacking data is not enough … You have to destroy *things* … This again is the prevailing opinion. But if you look at the, the, the other view, **the view that *may* be emerging,** well, you don't have to look at that, because you don't look at nature. You look at consequences. So if the consequence-based, the severity view takes hold, again, **it's not the law today, but if it takes hold, then this might very well change.**" (28.25) "**Where's the future going?** I gave you ***lex lata***, the law as it is today. **Where do I anticipate the future's going?** There are two possibilities … *[continued at 29.06]* In my mind, the best guess is the bar will lower and the first thing we're going to see is any kind of massive disruption with economic infrastructure in a country. **But that's *not* today, that's seven, eight, nine years from now** when state practice begins to crystallize."	(10.06) "However, there's a process going on which you may have heard about called the *Tallinn Manual* … **and I think we're sort of coming to resolution** that we're both … *[referring to an ICRC lawyer in the audience]* **I think we're about to put this debate to rest.**" (11.27) "Do I anticipate that the standard will stay here? **Well, I'm a *lex lata* guy, not a *lex ferenda* guy, I told you what I think the standard is, I think it may evolve over time as we look at state practice, because I think states may treat massive economic attacks, or if someone takes control of your critical infrastructure** … as armed conflict. **Maybe. But, again, I'm a *lex lata* guy,** let's watch this space, see what happens with regard to states … " (23.17) *[text on the last slide]* "**Expect standards to evolve.**"	(45.03) " … I believe at least as June 2012, that was the law, I anticipate that international views on that particular aspect will change over time, I expect it to change relatively rapidly. And a number of the experts said, 'you don't have to wait for change, we believe that's the law now,' ok?" (1.13.45) "[A]gain, **we were doing *lex lata*,** we were doing the law as it is, we had a case on point, that was a famous ICJ case, so that's why we drew that line … I would expect that law to, the interpretation to change over time … International law, you must understand the nature of international law. **It, the the understanding of international law evolves over time to keep track with changing context** … " (1.29.41) "With regard to a treaty I'm not horribly optimistic, that's, I mean, that's beyond our ambition. Ok?"	(45.24) "My personal view is, I think the current law is damage, destruction, injury or death, and **I don't think that will be the current law ten years from now. I'm absolutely convinced the law will shift to the severity standard.** But we, but I'm sort of a classic international lawyer, I think you need some state practice before that happens, and so forth." (51.26) *[on forceful countermeasures]* " … **watch this space,** because this wasn't horribly important when *Oil Platforms* came out, it's **überimportant** today, because of cyber warfare." (1.06.54) "I will tell you, that **I am a firm believer that this body of law will evolve, it will evolve quickly through state practice,** because some of the Rules that we came up with that we say are the law, we believe they're the law, **states are not going to be willing to accept** …		(34.10) *[on data as an object – the slide is called "Schmitt View"]* "**Here's my view of what I think what will will happen.** I think the majority view is going to prevail because **states are not going to be willing** to give up their ability to for example conduct operations against data … **states simply will not accept** the notion that data is an object, period … " (35.28) "**I have suggested in, in a couple of articles that maybe what we will see happen,** is we will see the emergence of a new customary norm over time. And my, my idea is, is that we should not be able to conduct military operations against something that is related to what I call 'essential civilian functions'. This is a completely undeveloped idea, it's a very transparent **attempt by a scholar to try and get his gig out there, 'ah it's the Schmitt idea'.**" *[laughter]* (36.22) "**I think that we'll never be able to do this by treaty,** forget it. It's not gonna happen. It's too sensitive, it's too fluffy and so forth, but **we may see state practice.** You may very well see operations where you avoid striking data that would fall into this category, and if we can talk about it now, my idea is we can fold it into rules of engagement that will create the state practice necessary to form the

years ago this was a very strong viewpoint, is slowly fading away. Because these folks are struggling to answer questions like, 'well, but what's the difference with psyops?' … **So I think this view is fading away,** but there's still a few **dinosaurs** out there that hold it."

(20.22) "Let me tell you what Mike Schmitt thinks **the future is going to be.** I believe that the, the threshold for damage, necessary to qualify an operation as an attack, will drop somewhat. Because I believe that this argument about severity has legs. I mean it makes sense to me … My gut tells me, the human gut says we ought to be worried about how serious something is, not the nature of something. **So I think we will see this threshold drop over time through state practice.** That the, the prohibition will be a little bit lower."

(21.08) *[following his reference to 'let me tell you what Mike Schmitt thinks the future is going to be – severity rather than*

(23.48) "**NIAC, I think you're almost never gonna see … I think you'll almost never see this, you have the problem with regard to the enforcement of LOAC,** you have to decide whether or not that's customary or not, you have to decide it is customary before you even get there.

[he proceeds]

(24.06) I think the intensity level is going to be *very* hard to reach. Because it's not just the intensity of a single act, it's the intensity of a number of acts that are all related, **so I think that's unlikely. And I think that, I believe that these standards are likely to evolve over time, as we start to see what happens as states become concerned about operations, we'll see them begin to evolve.** But you know, we're not making new law here, this is **naturally the way international law evolves every day in in areas other than cyber.**"

Armed attack is a good example. I am **absolutely convinced** that if the United States were to suffer a massive cyberattack that caused no damage or injury but massively disrupted our way of life, we would consider that an armed attack. I'm *absolutely* convinced. The problem is, international law requires, you gotta have the state practice, not 'I think that's what they'll do'. You actually have to have, so, international law, customary law, will be made by the breach of extant norms, and **that's what I anticipate will be happening.**"

basis for a new norm, but, we'll see."

(38.28) "It'd be very hard to have a cyber organized armed group, an exclusively cyber organized armed group, that's – like Anonymous – that, because, the organized armed group, has to have some command structure, has to have a means of enforcing discipline … so we **won't see** a lot of that. **What we'll see** is individuals who will participate in hostilities, exactly like they did in the Georgia case … "

(42.40) *[in reference to a slide]* "Vectors, directions of the body of law."

(42.42) "You must remember that international humanitarian law is a balancing act between military necessity and humanitarian considerations. *Every single rule* is a reflection of this balance … **That balance is shifting, activities in cyberspace, *infinitely* more important than they were five years ago …** "

(43.07) "**Expect the law to shift** into a greater protection of your activities in cyberspace, because that will seen, be seen as a humanitarian consideration. How will that play out with regard to attacks? **The functionality test, particularly my approach, will be widely accepted,** *[laughter from the audience]* **the Schmitt, widely accepted, universally accepted!**"

(43.30) "With regard to data, **I anticipate seeing emergence**

(continued)

CyCon 2012 (I)	CyCon 2012 (II)	CyCon 2012 (III)	ILD 2012	Brown 2013	LENS 2013	CyCon 2014	PILAC 2015
	nature of the consequences] "**There is a danger, it could go the other way**. Because, listen, I teach in a War College, I know this. Capabilities always seek targets. When a capability is developed, war fighters, thinkers, operators, always say 'I can do this' … But I'm hoping the first bullet is more accurate." *[Schmitt refers here to a bullet on a PowerPoint slide]* (21.53) "I do believe that economies will be seen as a civilian object, **over, *over* time.**" (21.59) " … I'm absolutely pessimistic about the idea of new law in this area. These, this change will come not through the revolution of new law, but rather through the evolution of contemporary understandings of the, of the current international humanitarian law."						**of a new customary norm**, because it's just too hard. Both approaches are unsatisfactory, **expect to see a new norm emerge**. And with regard to participation, ***it can't be the case*** that you can drop a bomb on every seventeen-year old kid that's hacking into your systems, military systems. So I believe *that* requirement will become more demanding. But at the other, on the other hand, the notion that you have to strike while they're attacking you doesn't make sense in cyberspace, so the *timing* will be broader. So, you'll require a greater impact on enemy forces but your targetability, the window of opportunity to target will be broader." (49.15) "[G]enerally, severity of consequences is not an approach taken in IHL. So, although we were sensitive to that and we believe, **I believe that's where the law is going**, as I said … " (52.10) "[T]he object of attack is in fact *an object* as understood in IHL …. (*cont.* 52:42) I will tell you that I anticipate that **in five years**, that will change. I'm writing, *urging* it to change. Because of the concerns you have. **But we we wanted to maintain fidelity to the law as we believe states would interpret it on *that* date.**"

	Space							
	CyCon 2012 (I)	CyCon 2012 (II)	CyCon 2012 (III)	ILD 2012	Brown 2013	LENS 2013	CyCon 2014	PILAC 2015
Nonlawyers		(0.01) "Yesterday I started my presentation by telling you that as **lawyers we're** particularly upset about the use of the word 'attack'. Because attack, as used in the technical or operational sense, is not the same as the term 'attack,' **as used in the legal sense**. Now yesterday I told you that, **in the legal sense**, we have problems as well." (5.26) "It is **important to emphasize**, that in, that when we are talking about attacks, **as a matter of law, as a legal term of art**, we don't care if you're shooting at the person because you are conducting offensive operations, or you're shooting at the person because they're trying to kill you and you're defending yourself. An attack is simply transmitting violence from yourself to civilians, civilian objects, or military objectives, combatants." (5.56) **"For the techies** who often worry about defensive	(0.04) "Since I've come to this conference I think I've heard the term 'attack' about fifty times every single day. And it has caused me a panic. And so therefore I'm delighted that Katharina's asked me to give not one but two presentations on the term 'attack'. When **we're** using the term 'attack,' **lay folks** normally think of computer network attack … But that's not at all **the world according to the lawyers**. Because the term 'attack' in international law is a legal term of art. It has particular significance. And so what I'm going to do today and tomorrow morning is talk to you about that **legal significance.** Because it's creating an awful lot of confusion between **the nonlawyer and the lawyer community**." (1.07) "In international law the term 'attack' appears in two different places. The first is in the *jus ad bellum*, and the second is in the *jus in bello*. **Let me explain for those who don't deal with conflict studies what**	(7.02) "So let's do a **basic** legal analysis." (7.26) "[W]e get two factual criteria. The first is that there must be an armed conflict, that is a ***legal* term of art**. Ok? That's not a descriptive term, it's a ***legal* term of art**. You must have **what is legally known as** an armed conflict." (9.55) "There is a **well-known battle between mostly myself and Knut Dörmann** from the ICRC that has been going on for years, Knut would take it much further than that." (11.03) "[M]y friend Wolff von Heinegg and I think, disagree on this. **But in my view**, if you have to reload the operating system, that means you have to fix it, that means it's damaged that means it's an attack that means it's an armed conflict. **So I think we're about to put that to rest** – what about Stuxnet?"	(16.46) "The format of the book is … very important. There are black-letter rules that are absolutely unexceptionally quite boring. Because we had to get unanimity among the group. **So trying to get twenty international lawyers to agree on anything, that's quite a task. Even a single sentence was hard** … So what you get here, what you get here in the black-letter that unanimous decision is very very, or very very broad principles of law." (29.31) "We did have some hints. The first thing that would *make* sense was just to use **lay terminology** … but **we said it's not so easy in international law**, although that's what we understand we mean by use of force in law it means something slightly different." (36.46) "[T]his is **a technical-legal point,** what we said was that state involvement lies along a continuum." (39.04) " … **I can make that argument, I'm a good lawyer, I could also make the other argument.** But you can fashion what **we call** a colorable argument, an argument that doesn't make you laugh out loud, for self-defense in that case, but it's very complicated." (41.58) "This is the Rule we came up with, we basically say, whether or not something is an armed attack depends on its scale and effects, **that's lawyers' speak**, the reason we came up with that term, is because that's a term that's used in this famous opinion … I'll show you what it means in a second." (45.25) *[Question from the audience: " … do you include the imminent threat of an armed attack?"]* "Absolutely, this is – are you a lawyer?" –"Eh, I guess I let that slip." –"Yeah ok *[laughter from the audience]*. It's a very good lawyer question." (46.39) "[T]he classic law of anticipatory self-defense, that's **a legal term** … it generally was understood in, in, in terms of time … this doesn't make sense in the context of, of terrorism … you don't have warning … so **a number of us in the aftermath of 9/11 started**	(38.19) "How direct is it … for the lawyers in the audience, is there a direct causal connection between the act that you engaged in and the consequence that you're focused on … " (42.46) "If you have an operation that is mounted in self-defense against a cyber armed attack, then you must meet all other requirements of law of self-defense, we won't go into 'em, but **for the lawyers again**, necessity and proportionality and then of course you have the temporal factor, immediacy and imminency." (57.44) "[B]ecause **we're lawyers we** have to argue, it's our nature."	(0.42) "What I'd like to do is give you what I call a **dangerously brief** introduction to the legal framework we'll be applying today." (1.19) "So let me start **in the beginning**. States have obligations under international law, that's all we'll be talking about today, international law. I know the first day here in Tallinn we spend looking at a variety of norms, I'm not talking political norms, I'm not talking sociological norms, I'm not talking ethical norms, I'm talking **hard law** which is found in **only two places**. In treaties, and in customary international law." (3.40) *[on the Corfu Channel case]* "If you own the stuff, if you're in control of the stuff, that means you have an obligation to ensure that stuff, or those activities,	(22.00) *[on operations really being 'attacks' for the purposes of IHL]* "So then it begs the question, as **lawyers we** have to ask 'what? So what's *attacks* mean?' **Ok?** 'Now we know what operations mean, what's attacks mean?'" (26.57) "However, **because we were lawyers**, and there were some **law professors**, we had to argue. We came up with something elegant, but let's have an argument because **that's what we do in law**. Ok?"

(continued)

	Space							
	CyCon 2012 (I)	CyCon 2012 (II)	CyCon 2012 (III)	ILD 2012	Brown 2013	LENS 2013	CyCon 2014	PILAC 2015
		cyber stuff, don't worry about this distinction **as a matter of law**." (6.04) "The first point up here is violence, and this is very important, because we're wanting to know 'what does attacks really mean in practice?' And the concept of violence is again repeated over, and over, and over. And it kinda means, classic violence. What you think of **in lay terms** as a violent act."	**the difference is**." (3.20) "There's a ***lay* meaning to the word**, every time I see the Department of Defense Dictionary definition, **I break out in hives, there's the *lay* meaning to the word, and then there's a legal meaning**, and in fact there are *two* **legal meanings**, and you must not confuse the **two legal meanings**, because they're very very very distinct." (6.34) "So that begs the question, 'ok, then what is an armed attack?' Unfortunately, **or fortunately for lawyers and law professors** the term is not defined in international law anywhere, in any authoritative place in international law. But we have some clues." (8.17) "In fact in a very famous case, the … *Nicaragua* case, which has been cited over and over here, also known as the Paramilitary Activities case, **its formal name** … " (19.17) *[disagrees with previous speaker]* "**But the rest of the audience is bored, this is something two law professors argue about**."	(1.17.41) "So, I, I saw your, your pitch but **I'm worried** because that exact pitch was made as we started the DPH process. Because a number of **us** were here *[pointing at the audience]*, **and this was *exactly* the argument that was made.**"	**looking at this problem, and I will tell you what I came up with** … " (53.01) "The other thing is called the plea of necessity, it's again a, kind of a **technical legal thing** … " (53.30) " … but it's affecting your, and **this is the legal term**, essential interest … " (54.57) "Well the law here – there's we're not a party to this treaty but we recognize it as binding on us, for some **technical legal** reasons … " (57.18) "So a couple of us said 'well **we're purist lawyers** and the law doesn't apply' and we 'wowowowowow, stop, stop, that's crazy. So I can kill someone by for example poisoning a water system, I can kill people poisoning a water system using cyber but it's not prohibited by the law of war because I didn't, you know, release physical force?' **So we quickly got over that**, but we still had the issue of 'attack' to deal with, and the definition that we find in law, cause **you can't ignore the law**, you can't say 'ah that's not convenient here'. So what we said was 'what they really meant was in, in using the word violence was shorthand for violent consequences'." (1.20.58) "As a matter of law, a ceasefire does not end a conflict, *[referring to someone on the front row]* – I know it was called something else, but, the terminology's changed, *[addressing the audience again]* – **I'm I'm getting a lawyer look.**" (1.21.38) "[I]f we're at war, what **we lawyers** would call an armed conflict, that's **the legal term** … "		don't harm your neighbors … **in law it's known** as the principle of due diligence." (4.30) "[T]he United Kingdom had a right to pass through that strait in **what we would call** transit passage." (5.11) "[T]he question that **we lawyers** have not gotten our arms around is, 'yeah, but do I have to do something without knowing that harm's gonna occur just to make sure it doesn't occur?' And the international community is divided on this, I don't think there's such a duty." (6.33) "Whatever you do, even if it's not authorized, **that's called *ultra vires***, that's an act of Japan."	

	CyCon 2012 (I)	CyCon 2012 (II)	CyCon 2012 (III)	ILD 2012	Brown 2013	LENS 2013	CyCon 2014	PILAC 2015
Other(s) (lawyers) who don't really understand the law		(7.59) "So, over and over, particularly in the early days of cyber, the question was 'does this rule apply to cyber operations?' The answer today is **absolutely 'yes,'** it's, there's **absolutely no question** whatsoever, anyone who argues this point **doesn't know what they're talking about**. Because there's **almost unanimity** on this point. **You should not worry** about the fact that the *means* are not violent, **you have to** focus on the consequences of the operation. **It's not the nature, it's the consequences**." (19.03) *[on an instrument-based view of attack]* "I believe that it's fair to say that this viewpoint, **which was very strong, early on, ten years ago this was a very strong viewpoint, is slowly fading away**. Because these folks are struggling to answer questions like, 'well, but what's the difference	(6.51) "First of all, the big question that was asked … 'well … does an armed attack have to be kinetic? … Because of the word 'armed'. And therefore, does it exclude cyber stuff?' The answer is 'no'. The International Court of Justice has answered this question in the *Nuclear Weapons* Case … it matters what the consequences are. And in fact state practice supports this, **this should be no epiphany.** State, every state would believe that if you conduct a radiological attack or a chemical attack against another state and it's not kinetic in nature every state would agree that this is an armed attack. **This is a question asked by scholars that need not be asked, this question has been asked and answered, this is settled law**."	(1.17.41) "So, I, I saw your, your pitch and but **I'm worried** because that exact pitch was made as we started the DPH process *[ICRC, Direct Participation in Hostilities]*. **Because a number of us were here** *[pointing at the audience]*, **and this was *exactly* the argument that was made.** And you can say what you like about the DPH-study but **the one *major* advance has been to *solve* that** by the admission on the part of the ICRC, to their credit, of the notion that armed forces will extend to cover these people for the purposes of targeting. **So, the reason I spike this, I, I feel like *déjà vu*, I'm not in 1999 anymore, but I'm back with Nils Melzer at the start of the DPH-guidance**."	(1.19.30) "Here I would not say that any of those … operations were armed attacks. **I don't believe they were armed attacks, and I, and I believe most people who are knowledgeable about this area of law** would not say that they were armed attacks. That means that your remedy is not a use of force."	(28.43) *[pointing to a powerpoint slide]* "These were the experts, unusual mix of people. We wanted people who understood use of force issues, and we wanted people who understood warfare. **We were joking about a scholar, who will remain nameless, in the hallway, who has written an outrageous article and we were joking about it because the guy just simply doesn't understand** the context of warfare. So in this group what we did was we picked people who in some way, form or fashion kind of *got* conflict." (1.00.14) "Ok, a lot of people are always asking questions about, 'what about civilians?' 'Cause you know, today, civilians are cyberwarriors. We did not struggle very much with that. I add this only because there appears to be in the press and so forth a lot of talk about this. In our view, and the view of the group I mean this was the uniform view of the group, the		

(continued)

	CyCon 2012 (I)	CyCon 2012 (II)	CyCon 2012 (III)	ILD 2012	Brown 2013	LENS 2013	CyCon 2014	PILAC 2015
		with psyops?' … So I think this view is fading away, but there's still a few **dinosaurs** out there that hold it."				whole group agreed with this, there's absolutely no prohibition in humanitarian law, the law of war, on civilians participating in hostilities. **This is a myth invented by somebody, not a lawyer, that knows anything about humanitarian law. There's no prohibition on civilians participating in hostilities, whether it's cyber or kinetic, ok? … What happens though, is when that civilian participates in the hostilities, they, there are several consequences …**"		

	CvCon 2012 (I)	CvCon 2012 (II)	CvCon 2012 (III)	ILD 2012	Brown 2013	LENS 2013	CvCon 2014	PILAC 2015
Academics	(10.49) "We also wanted to pick people who had **practical experience, we did not want this to be a group of eggheads,** exploring the **mysteries** of the International Law Commission's Articles on State Responsibility … So we wanted to get people who had **been there, done that,** have thought through these problems in a **practical sense**." (13.54) "I emphasize that it is … not *lex ferenda*, it is *lex lata*. If you ask me what armed attack *lex ferenda* is you'll get a different answer than what we put in the Manual. Because we asked 'what is the law *now*?' … August was the date we picked. In August 2012, what's the law, not, where is the law going, **that's for scholars to write about.**"			(4.45) "Now, I always adopt the classic bifurcation. I don't buy this notion of transnational armed conflict or all that other creative stuff, **generated by professors that are desperate to have an original thought so they can get tenure**." *[laughter from the audience]*	(14.35) "So this was twenty independent scholars … This is twenty guys … **that's all it is. Twenty scholars, it's our view,** and nothing more than that." (1.09.57) " … we did not try to be creative, in fact, every time someone did try to be creative, as director, I would slap them. Because we did not wanna be accused of being creative, we wanted to to to be *slave* to what's called *lex lata*, the law as it is today. Not the law as it is a month from now, or a year, or ten years, but *today*. Because states make law, not **law professors**." (1.04.05) "So what we were trying to do was bring together people that had **three characteristics. They had to be really really good international lawyers to make the team. The second characteristic is, they also had to have some affiliation, with not the military, but with people who dealt with the battlefield** … but they had to be people	(25.10) "By this time, there are now lots of conferences. But all the conferences are the same. They are conferences where **academics come together and what they do is say 'wow this is really hard' … and that's all they did, ask questions.** So my response to these folks in Estonia was 'not really interested, these conferences really bore me, I'm busy, call me back when you're ready to start answering some questions.'" (28.12) "[E]veryone wanted us to emphasize that we were speaking only in our personal capacity. Because no one wanted **a bunch of academics** to steal their discretion. You know what I mean, if you're the Air Force General Counsel the last thing you want is some **academic** at the Naval War College determining what your cyber rules of the game were. **So this is a, a purely an academic exercise, twenty folks trying to figure out what *they* believe the law to be.**"		(15.18) " … the only requirement that was consistent across all twenty is the person that **made it** onto what we called the international group of experts had to have **experience** as a as a … **practicing legal adviser** … people who had *done* this. So if you were **just purely** an academic **you didn't make the cut**." (15.52) "If there are **purely academics**, I *do* respect you, ok?" *[smiles, small laughter from the audience]* (18.01) *[on the agreed deadline for Tallinn 2.0]* "And we hope to finish next year, we we've promised the, the manuscript to Cambridge University Press in early 2016, **but because we want to maintain our reputations as academics,** we will in fact *not* meet that deadline *[laughter from the audience]* … " (35.28) "I have suggested in, in a couple of articles that maybe what we will see happen, is we will see the emergence of a new customary norm over time. And my, my idea is, is that we should not be able to conduct military operations against something that is related to what I call 'essential civilian functions'. This is a completely undeveloped idea, it's a very transparent **attempt by a scholar to try and get his gig out there, 'ah it's the Schmitt idea'**." *[laughter]* (52.18) "Your your confused look is an appropriate look, because exactly as I said to the professor, we were very acutely sensitive, that we were trying to capture, **that's why you had to have been a state legal adviser,** acutely sensitive to … what we were trying to do is, to **capture for state legal advisers** what the international community is likely to say when there is an attack … But we we wanted to maintain fidelity to the law as we believe states would interpret it on *that* day." (52.59) "**Because our audience was not, academic, was not a law student or a professor,** our audience consisted, our intended audience were legal advisers and ministries of foreign affairs, ministries of defense, militaries, private companies that might engage in cyber operations, NGO's, practitioners, and **they need to know, not theoretically 'does this make sense?' but 'what, what's going to be the call?'**."

(continued)

	CyCon 2012 (I)	CyCon 2012 (II)	CyCon 2012 (III)	ILD 2012	Brown 2013	LENS 2013	CyCon 2014	PILAC 2015
					who had provided *actual* legal advice about conflict situations. We did not want **pure academics** who might not be able to contextualize as well as people who had **actually given legal advice,** because we knew who our audience was."	(1.02.59) "There are criticisms of the Manual, the first thing you do in **academia,** when **someone else does something good,** you immediately pronounce to the world how stupid it is, and they made lots of mistakes, so we're we're experiencing that now …" (1.04.40) "We decided that because this was the first shot, at this topic, that it was much more important to have the right people in the room to identify the law and how it applied in the cyber context, than it was to have widely representative participation in the project. It's our sense that *that international* participation should come in the form of treaty negotiations, or whatever, **but we were just twenty academics and practitioners that were trying to solve a problem, or trying to figure out what the law was in an area that no one seemed to know any answers**. But that is a fair criticism."		

	CyCon 2012 (I)	CyCon 2012 (II)	CyCon 2012 (III)	ILD 2012	Brown 2013	LENS 2013	CyCon 2014	PILAC 2015
The group of (legal, technical) experts involved in the Manual, and the process' observers	(0.56) "I got a phone call a couple weeks later and the phone call basically said … 'we're ready to start answering these questions, we'll give you as much money as you need in order to answer the questions and **you can design your own group**'." (1.48) "This is a product that represents the **personal views of the participants** that were involved in the process **and nothing more.** It's twenty or so **smart people** who got together that were tired of asking questions and said 'let's take a shot at answering some of these questions'." (4.20) "And then we spend a little time saying 'who are the **best people in the world** that we think would **form a cohesive group** to attack these problems?'" (7.45) "And then we had some technical experts that were part of the small drafting group because we knew we didn't understand cyber well enough to, to do it alone. They were instrumental, they were with us *every* step of the way." (8.43) *[on the technical experts]* "So at any rate, they were with us, and they kept us **honest** throughout, they explained when we were getting off track." (8.52) "We have send that out to peer reviewers, **select individuals who are experts** in a particular area of the law." (9.45) "Just wanted to show you who the groups of, group of experts were. This was *critical* because we needed to pick people – I, I've been through a number of these processes and listen, the most important … rule is, don't, **not to get the smartest people**				(19.07) " **… we also had a technical team with us at all, all the time, it was very, very important technical team,** since you're computer scientists, you'll probably understand this." (20.25) "We had a technical team. We also had three observers with us. They had the right to participate, and they participated and very very very actively, in fact they also drafted some of the Manual, however, they didn't have the right to vote … so they were from, United States Cyber Command, because, the legal adviser, **in fact *the* legal adviser from United States Cyber Command, because he was the one we felt that was most likely to know what the challenging legal issues were.** We had someone from NATO because they provided us the money, so we had to have someone from them. And then we invited someone from the International Committee of the Red Cross because **the ICRC is the entity … that kind of controls our body of law, humanitarian law, and they're very very good lawyers.** And so we had them there as well. Again they sat there, they were like one of us but when we got to the point where as director I said 'ok we're gonna vote' … they did not get a vote." (1.04.05) "So what we were trying to do was bring together people that had **three characteristics. They had to be really really good international lawyers to make the team. The second characteristic is, they also had to have some affiliation, with not the military, but with people who dealt with the battlefield** … but	(26.05) **"We, we decided to do a manual because it was a long lineage of doing manuals.** For the legal historians … the Oxford Manual, the **Brussels Manual, from the nineteenth century,** and so forth. There had been manuals recently, the '95 Manual on Naval Warfare … Professor von Heinegg was the rapporteur for that project, was integral to that; the San Remo Manual, **there's a San Remo Manual also on non-international armed conflict that I did with Charles Garraway from the UK and Yoram Dinstein from Israel, there was a Harvard Manual on Air and, Air and Missile Warfare … led by Yoram Dinstein, a number of us were involved** *[points at the audience]* … so we thought a manual might help." (28.43) *[pointing to a powerpoint slide]* "These were	[(0.48) "This morning you had, no kidding, a *masterclass* in international law. You had two scholars who are **truly at the world class level** and then you had a young scholar who is **clearly moving in that direction**."] *[The above quote does not quite fit this category: it has been included here, however, as it indicates a similar process, whereby Schmitt designates the level at which other lawyers/scholars are functioning – see the second half of Chapter 5.]* (4.40) *[on a previous speaker correcting the Manual]* "Something else she mentioned this morning, in fact she did it so well **I've actually changed this slide,** in the Manual, we say that there's a lack of consensus over whether there's a	(15.02) "How did we do it? We brought twenty experts from around the world, **a very politically incorrect group of experts,** because we knew we were doing this for **the first time,** so we **really didn't care if we had geographical distribution,** etcetera etcetera, we took the **twenty best people we could find,** the only requirement that was consistent across all twenty is the person **that made it** onto what we called the international group of experts had to have **experience as a as a … practicing legal adviser** … people who had *done* this. So if you were **just purely** an academic **you didn't make the cut.**" (16.10) *[on lack of technical knowledge]* "I've got this **ancient phone** that opens up like this *[gestures]*. So we were acutely aware of our limitations and so what we did was **we were accompanied at all times by a technical team that provided us advice.**" (16.22) "And then there were three advisers, **one from United States Cyber Command, the senior lawyer from**

(continued)

	CyCon 2012 (I)	CyCon 2012 (II)	CyCon 2012 (III)	ILD 2012	Brown 2013	LENS 2013	CyCon 2014	PILAC 2015
	in the room, but you wanna get people that can play well together because they're gonna be with each other for a *long, long, long* time … *[continued at 10.27]* So the number one criterion is to get people who were ***nice***. But fortunately there were **lots and lots and lots of *brilliant*,** nice people around. **And so then, we picked people who we knew were a specialist in the field, who really knew IHL or the *jus ad belllum* in a *very, very, very* deep sense**." (11.17) "In addition to the group of experts we had a group of observers … because we wanted, we wanted to have entities represented in the room that could, that could, could provide ***realism*** to how our customers would react. **And so the ICRC is a good example, no one knows humanitarian law better than the ICRC, Cyber Command, no one's doing this more than Cyber Command, ACT, sponsor of the CCDCOE.** These folks participated in the process throughout, fully as members of the group of experts, except, they did not get a vote … But they were **instrumental** throughout." (12.17) "Then we had a group of technical advisers … who kept saying **'listen Mister Potato Head, that's not the way the world works in cyber'.** And they, they've read the Manual, they provided examples to us, and so forth." (12.36) "[W]e had peer-reviewers, we went out to individuals who we thought had **particular expertise**, not in the overall subject, but in a particular area. I'll give the example of my friend Charles Garraway … **who's a *real* expert in detention**. So I				they had to be people who had provided *actual* legal advice about conflict situations. **We did not want pure academics who might not be able to contextualize as well as people who had actually given legal advice, because we knew who our audience was**. And the third is, is that we we needed to, we needed to pick people who liked each other and got along and played well together because we would go to Estonia when it was thirty-five degrees below zero and be locked in a room together … and I'd been involved in a major project at Harvard, five year project, in which that wasn't a criterion and it was really really brutal and awful and mean and everything like that and it ended in a disaster, and so I knew that we had to get people that worked together. **In the future though, without the slightest doubt, we need to have greater inclusivity**." (1.05.24) "This is nothing more, and you should interpret it as nothing more, than twenty people who got together to try and figure out what the law is, this is our best shot, it is not state practice, we'll see if it it stands up to criticism. And finally we did not try to be creative, in fact, every time someone did try to be creative, as director, I would slap them. Because we did not wanna be accused of being creative, we wanted to to to be ***slave* to what's called *lex lata*, the law as it is today**. Not the law as it is a month from now, or a year, or ten years, but *today*. Because states make law, not law professors … we wanted to try and capture that law and then allow states to determine what they wanted to do with this project." (1.25.32) *[audience question: "So is*	the experts, unusual mix of people. We wanted people who understood use of force issues, and we wanted people who understood warfare … So in this group what we did was we picked people who in some way, form or fashion kind of *got* conflict … **everyone had to have some kind of hook, some, they had to understand the context in which we were going to play."** (30.46) "It was a **pretty distinguished, very friendly group."** (30.49) "I'd been in these projects before, so when we picked them … **we picked people we liked and could get along with …** We'd be in previous projects where it became bloody and awful, so we picked *nice* people, **you had to be *nice* to get in this group."** (1.03.10) "There are some assertions that are fair … one of them is that we in virtually every Rule indicate our opinion as to whether or not	duty to prevent. But **as she corrected the twenty international world class experts**, it isn't really a, a, a controversy over whether there's a duty to prevent. It's a controversy over whether there's a duty to take preventive measures." (9.48) *[in reaction to the comment that the* Tallinn Manual *will make people think in terms of armed conflict or* jus ad bellum *in case of cyber operations]* "I wanna avoid that propensity in this conference, we're talking about active defense. But the mere fact that Professor Hathaway gives a **brilliant lecture** on countermeasures, or Professor Gill gives a **brilliant [lecture]** on self-defense … doesn't mean that's all you have, there are many many remedies in	**United States Cyber Command, to keep us honest, because we wanted to make sure we were dealing in the realm of of of the real,** and and that individual was the one that knew **what was really happening**." (16.38) "We had an International Committee of the Red Cross representative, because they basically **own humanitarian law**, and they're **always spectacular attorneys** …" (16.47) "And then we had **a representative from NATO**, primarily because NATO provided us the **cash** for the project, and **if you give us money you get a seat at the table** *[laughter from the audience]* **so NATO was there as well**." (21.20) *[on the notion of 'operations']* "Well, the group – **we spent three years thinking** about this so in the next four minutes I will summarize it." *[light laughter from the audience]* (22.44) *[on interpreting 'attacks']* "[A]nd then we looked at Commentaries both by the ICRC and by a a a group of **very famous legal scholars** led by Michael Bothe, a German, and they again are talking about violence

said 'Charles, can you look at the detention, tell us did we get it right, have we missed anything?' And so forth."

(14.31) "What we said, was that, 'it is customary law, or is applicable in NIAC or IAC, in, in accordance with *us*.' In other words, **we are the authority, we have twenty high-speed people here, through our years and decades of experience**, we are agreeing that this is customary, we are agreeing this is applicable in IAC or applicable in NIAC."

(16.25) "*[Other sources included]* the Air and Missile Warfare Manual and the NIAC Manual because those are both restatements of customary law as well, again we weren't *bound* by those, but it was persuasive evidence **because of the caliber of the people that were involved in those projects**."

(17.30) "[T]his is what distinguishes it from most other manuals. Most importantly, we knew we were embarking on, on, on a voyage into unknown territory. We understood that. People catch me in the hallway to tell me how stupid it is to write a manual before you've had an actual cyber war. But we think it was important to do that."

(21.44) "Blockade was the hardest. We have the **world's blockade expert** in the audience … literally **the number one guy in the world** there, of course, I don't wanna put words in his mouth but **he was asserting** there's *[no?]* such thing as blockade, **we had another guy who said** 'you're crazy' we never could resolve cyber blockade. So there's a long commentary on it and then say 'we're not sure'. Ok?"

the goal of the project to adopt some kind of framework in the United Nations some time in the future?"] "Absolutely not. We have no goal. Ok? … But I'm serious, here here's here's what we wanted to do, I'm very serious. We don't have any aspirations whatsoever. Here's the problem. We had a bunch of lawyers together, ok, we – most of us knew each other. I knew most of these people. We watched what happened in Estonia, and we watched what happened in Georgia, and we watched all the international legal community flail around trying to figure out what in the world is the law … then all these conferences started … and we said 'hey, maybe we can help those guys out' … *[continued at 1.26.52]* And what we said is 'we think we can contribute by stepping back … and we'll try to come up with either a solution or options for the legal adviser.' What the state does with it … is up to the state … We don't have any aspirations, we just wanted to help … *[continued at 1.28.20]* **My aspiration is that it's on the book shelf of someone that sits in the Ministry of Foreign Affairs in Romania.** And all of a sudden something bad happens they pull it out and they go 'wow I wonder' and then they see not our Rule … they see the Commentary. And they go 'ok. Ok, now I've got a huge jump start' … And what happens, I was the Dean of a center … we worked with government officials. And what will happen is, the Romanian MFA attorney will call the Bulgarian MFA attorney and say 'listen, are you watching what's happening here? This is what I'm thinking what do you think?' Or a Rule is customary in nature or it's simply treaty-based … some of the criticism is 'but you guys didn't review state practice'. We did look at state practice but not in a comprehensive way … **my reply is, 'yes, but we've looked at, we were twenty people that are fairly senior**, and we looked at all of the previous efforts to identify state practice, **so if there was a consensus view in the community that something was in fact customary** we simply were restating what the consensus view in the community [was]' … "

(1.04.11) "A big big big criticism that we get a lot, is that if you look at it, it's sort of a gathering of the usual suspects … This is a fair criticism. This is a fair criticism. We thought about including folks from China, and Russia, and we talked at great length about this. We decided that because this was international law … "

(13.33) "And finally, here, we heard, again a **brilliant** lecture of Terry Gill is the **top guy** in the world on self-defense, so you should feel, feel honored to have him here … "

(38.10) "Well again I wanna emphasize that there were three different views **in the international group of experts or there are three different views generally.**"

and physical force."

(24.52) *[on the cyber application of the notion of attack]* "Since you're at Harvard, you should be frustrated with this definition. And you should say to yourself 'golly, that can't be the rule. It can't be the rule.' And the reason it can't be the rule is because you can engage in all kinds of cyber operations during an armed conflict that can have *devastating* consequences for a civilian population but that don't *break* things. And don't *injure* people. That they for example collapse an economy would just be an example. And so we we had a *long*, long debate about this …"

(26.01) *[talking about the way the functionality test came about]* "There's a … non-attribution, but **a very brilliant person** working for a certain organization that's dedicated to humanitarian causes … "

(32.10) *[on data as an object]* "And, perhaps most importantly, remember I told you that **everyone had been a legal adviser, a lot of us said 'we do these operations all the time,** this is called a psyop. A psychological operation. Are you telling me that I

(continued)

	CyCon 2012 (I)	CyCon 2012 (II)	CyCon 2012 (III)	ILD 2012	Brown 2013	LENS 2013	CyCon 2014	PILAC 2015
	(22.13) "The last point … is this, ok? **We were only trying to set out to tell folks what *we*, just this group of twenty people thought was the law applicable in *ad bellum* and *in bello*** … *[continued at 22.55]* **Don't have a cyber operation, reach up there and grab the Manual and say 'the *Tallinn Manual* will answer the question'**. Because *in most cases* issues addressed in the *Tallinn Manual* are not relevant. Because you're not approaching either the armed conflict threshold or in the *ad bellum* sense the use of force or armed attack threshold. So I don't want to have the problem, you know, if you have a hammer, like the *Tallinn Manual*, every problem – cyber operation – is a nail."				they'll call their person in NATO and say 'what are you hearing? Did you guys think about the *Nicaragua* standard?' 'Oh yeah'. So that's what I'm hoping. That it jumpstarts the analysis in a sophisticated way. That we were able to have the debates that they would have … And then I hope that they adopt sensible rules of engagement … And with regard to a treaty I'm not horribly optimistic, that's, I mean, that's beyond our ambition. Ok? We have very modest goals."	the first shot, at this topic, that it was much more important to have the right people in the room to identify the law and how it applied in the cyber context, than it was to have widely representative participation in the project. It's our sense that *that international* participation should come in the form of treaty negotiations, or whatever, **but we were just twenty academics and practitioners that were trying to solve a problem, or trying to figure out what the law was in an area that no one seemed to know any answers**. But that is a fair criticism." (1.05.45) "The other thing is is that I have to be honest with you, for those of you who've been through these sorts of efforts, **if you have three years, we had three years, period, three years,** we had cash for three years, I was the project director, my name is Schmitt, it's		can't hack into the enemy's database and put a clown nose on their leader's face? Well that would require me, wouldn't it, to go in and manipulate data! Are you telling me that's illegal now? That's silly. That's silly.' And so the majority said, 'data, not an object'." (54.49) "Although we pretty uniformly agreed that was the law, **virtually anyone who's worked with a government** thought that there were few ideas stupider than outsourcing the conduct of military operations to civilian entities … "

not an Irish name, it's a German name, we were gonna finish in three years, and the problem is, **the broader, the more diverse the representation, the more impossible it becomes to move forward, at all, so we picked people that we knew could stay focused**, heavy sprinkling of Germans, people who had come from Germany a century ago, and so forth, in order to meet the three year window."

	CyCon 2012 (I)	CyCon 2012 (II)	CyCon 2012 (III)	ILD 2012	Brown 2013	LENS 2013	CyCon 2014	PILAC 2015
Himself in the third person	(20.16) *[on levée en masse applied to cyber]* "But the whole population, like **Mike Schmitt**, I'm not capable of spontaneously rising up against any invader. **Why?** 'Cause I wouldn't know how to fire a virus if, if, if it fell down in front of me."	(20.22) **"Let me tell you what Mike Schmitt thinks the future is going to be.** I believe that the, the threshold for damage, necessary 'to qualify an operation as an attack, will drop somewhat. Because I believe that this argument about severity has legs. I mean it makes sense to me … My gut tells me, the human gut says we ought to be worried about how serious something is, not the nature of something. **So I think we will see this threshold drop over time through state practice.** That the, the prohibition will be a little bit lower. **There is a danger, it could go the other way.** Because, listen, I teach in a War College, I know this. Capabilities always seek targets. When a capability is developed, war fighters, thinkers, operators, always say 'I can do this' … But I'm hoping the first bullet is more accurate." *[Schmitt refers here to a bullet on a PowerPoint slide]*		(1.17.20) *[talking about those who argue there is a distinction between civilians and combatants, and those who argue the existence of three categories, lawful and unlawful combatants, and civilians]* "Why does it make a difference? Because if you **take the Schmitt view,** which the ICRC will soon be calling it *[laughter from the audience]* there is no gap between GC3 protection and GC4 protection, you either get three or you get four. If you take the Dinsteinian approach *[Yoram Dinstein]* then there is an issue with regard to the treatment that an individual gets."		(40.26) "By the way, this is **the Schmitt-test,** I didn't come up with the term … But at any rate, this is kind of sort of the Schmitt-test, that, that I came up with in '99, changed."	(37.10) "Although I'm in absolute, 112% agreement with Professor Hathaway, this is a very fuzzy area of the law. So that's why I'm not gonna tell you this is a prohibited intervention. I will also tell you that there's some scholars, I happen to be one of them, that says 'intervention isn't just about doing bad stuff in another state … it has some element of coercion, there's a requirement that you're doing it because you're trying to *make* the other state do something'. So I'm not sure that is the case here [scenario 3] so this scenario, at least as the facts given to us … **would not meet the Mike Schmitt test of intervention,** it would meet the test of some other people."	(23.13) *[the powerpoint slide here is titled 'Result in Cyber Context?,' which is about how to interpret the notion of 'attack' in the cyber context; the last bullet on the slide says]* **"Schmitt view: Object doesn't work as intended"** (28.52) *[on the functionality test]* "[O]r **the Schmitt view,** which is it just doesn't work." *[this is the same sheet as five minutes earlier]* (34.10) *[on data as an object – the slide is called '**Schmitt View**']* **"Here's my view of what I think what will will happen.** I think the majority view is going to prevail because states are not going to be willing to give up their ability to for example conduct operations against data … " (35.28) **"I have suggested in, in a couple of articles that maybe what we will see happen,** is we will see the emergence of a new customary norm over time. And my, my idea is, is that we should not be able to conduct military operations against something that is related to what I call 'essential civilian functions'. This is a completely undeveloped idea, it's a very transparent **attempt by a scholar to try and get his gig out there, 'ah it's the Schmitt idea'."** *[laughter]* (43.07) **"Expect the law to shift** into a greater protection of your activities in cyberspace, because that will seen, be seen as a humanitarian consideration. How will that play out with regard to attacks? **The functionality test, particularly my approach, will be widely accepted,** *[laughter from the audience]* **the Schmitt, widely accepted, universally accepted!"** (54.49) "Although we pretty uniformly agreed that was the law, virtually anyone who's worked with a government thought that there were few ideas stupider than outsourcing the conduct of military operations to civilian entities, including intelligence agencies. It was, there was almost universal consensus, from the ICRC representatives, in their personal capacity I add, **to Mike Schmitt at a war college** that that was an incredibly stupid idea, for all sorts of reasons. But not for reasons of law."

Bibliography

Aalberts, Tanja and Thomas Gammeltoft-Hansen (eds.), *The Changing Practices of International Law*, Cambridge University Press 2018

Aalberts, Tanja and Ingo Venzke, 'Moving Beyond Interdisciplinary Turf Wars,' in: *International Law as a Profession*, André Nollkaemper, Jean d'Aspremont, Tarcisio Gazzini and Wouter Werner (eds.), Cambridge University Press 2017, 287–310

Aalberts, Tanja E. and Wouter G. Werner, 'International Law,' in: *Routledge Handbook of International Political Sociology*, Xavier Guillaume and Pınar Bilgin (eds.), Routledge 2017, 36–45

Adams, Michael J., A *Warning About Tallinn 2.0 . . . Whatever It Says*, on 'Lawfare,' January 4, 2017, www.lawfareblog.com/warning-about-tallinn-20-%E2%80%A6-whatever-it-says (July 15, 2020)

Adamson, Liisi and Zine Homburger, 'Let Them Roar: Small States as Cyber Norm Entrepreneurs' (2019) 24 *European Foreign Affairs Review* 217

Adler-Nissen, Rebecca, *Why International Relations Theory Needs Bourdieu*, on 'e-International Relations,' October 23, 2012, www.e-ir.info/2012/10/23/why-international-relations-theory-needs-bourdieu/ (July 15, 2020)

Aldrich, Richard W., 'How Do You Know You Are at War in the Information Age?' (2000) 22 *Houston Journal of International Law* 223

Alschner, Wolfgang and Damien Charlotin, 'The Growing Complexity of the International Court of Justice's Self-Citation Network' (2016) 29 *European Journal of International Law* 83

Andersen, Hanne and Brian Hepburn, 'Scientific Method,' *Stanford Encyclopedia of Philosophy*, November 13, 2015, Edward N. Zalta (ed.), http://plato.stanford.edu/archives/sum2016/entries/scientific-method/ (July 15, 2020)

Antolin-Jenkins, Vida M., 'Defining the Parameters of Cyberwar Operations: Looking for Law in All the Wrong Places' (2005) 51 *Naval Law Review* 132

Aronsson-Storrier, Marie, *Publicity in International Law-Making: Covert Operations and the Use of Force*, Cambridge University Press 2021

Arvidsson, Matilda, 'The Subject in International Law: The Administrator of the Coalition Provisional Authority of Occupied Iraq and Its Laws' (PhD, Lund University 2017)

Askehave, Inger and John M. Swales, 'Genre Identification and Communicative Purpose: A Problem and a Possible Solution' (2001) 22 *Applied Linguistics* 195

Austin, Arthur, 'Footnote Skulduggery and Other Bad Habits' (1990) 44 *University of Miami Law Review* 1009

Austin, John, *How to Do Things with Words: The William James Lectures Delivered at Harvard University in 1955*, Clarendon Press 1962

Banjo, Shelly, 'Home Depot Hackers Exposed 53 Million Email Addresses,' *The Wall Street Journal*, November 6, 2014, www.wsj.com/articles/home-depot-hackers-used-password-stolen-from-vendor-1415309282 (July 15, 2020)

Barkham, Jason, 'Information Warfare and International Law on the Use of Force' (2001) 34 *New York University Journal of International Law and Politics* 57

Barlow, John P., 'A Declaration of the Independence of Cyberspace,' *Electronic Frontier Foundation*, February 8, 1996, www.eff.org/cyberspace-independence (July 15, 2020)

Barnsby, Robert E. and Shane R. Reeves, 'Give Them an Inch, They'll Take a Terabyte: How States May Interpret Tallinn Manual 2.0's International Human Rights Law Chapter' (2017) 95 *Texas Law Review* 1515

Baron, Jane B. and Julia Epstein, 'Is Law Narrative?' (1997) 45 *Buffalo Law Review* 141

Bavelas, Janet B., 'The Social Psychology of Citations' (1978) 19 *Canadian Psychological Review/Psychologie canadienne* 158

BBC News, 'UK Launched Cyber-Attack on Islamic State,' April 12, 2018, www.bbc.com/news/technology-43738953 (July 15, 2020)

'Stuxnet "Hit" Iran Nuclear Plans,' November 22, 2010, www.bbc.com/news/technology-11809827 (July 15, 2020)

Benatar, Marco, 'Cyber Warfare,' *Oxford Bibliographies*, March 27, 2014, last reviewed November 2, 2017, http://oxfordbibliographiesonline.com/view/document/obo-9780199796953/obo-9780199796953–0087.xml (July 15, 2020)

'The Use of Cyber Force: Need for Legal Justification?' (2009) 1 *Goettingen Journal of International Law* 375

Benvenisti, Eyal, 'Margin of Appreciation, Consensus, and Universal Standards' (1999) 31 *New York University Journal of International Law and Politics* 843

Bigo, Didier, 'Pierre Bourdieu and International Relations: Power of Practices, Practices of Power' (2011) 5 *International Political Sociology* 225

Bikundo, Edwin, 'Review of *the Politics of Justifying Force: The Suez Crisis, the Iraq War, and International Law* by Charlotte Peevers (2013) Oxford University Press, pp. 288, ISBN 9780199686957' (2014) 36 *Sydney Law Review* 727

Blum, Yehuda Z., 'Economic Boycotts in International Law' (1977) 12 *Texas International Law Journal* 5

Boeke, Sergei and Dennis Broeders, 'The Demilitarisation of Cyber Conflict' (2018) 60 *Survival* 73

Boer, Lianne J. M., '"Article 51 Authorizes": Writing International Law,' in: *Constructing the Authority of International Law*, Gleider Hernández and Giedre Jokubauskaite (eds.), submitted (on file with the author)

'"Echoes of Times Past": On the Paradoxical Nature of Article 2(4)' (2015) 20 *Journal of Conflict and Security Law* 5

'*Lex Lata* Comes with a Date; or, What Follows from Referring to the "Tallinn Rules"' (2019) 113 *AJIL Unbound* 76

'Narratives of Force: The Presence of the Writer in International Legal Scholarship' (2019) 66 *Netherlands International Law Review* 1

'"Restating the Law 'As It Is'": On the Tallinn Manual and the Use of Force in Cyberspace' (2013) 5 *Amsterdam Law Forum* 4

'"The Greater Part of Jurisconsults": On Consensus Claims and Their Footnotes in Legal Scholarship' (2016) 29 *Leiden Journal of International Law* 1021

Boer, Lianne and Arno Lodder, 'Cyberwar,' in: *Cyber Safety: An Introduction*, Rutger Leukfeldt and Wouter Stol (eds.), eleven international publishing 2012, 157–166

Boer, Lianne J. M. and Sofia Stolk (eds.), *Backstage Practices of Transnational Law*, Routledge 2019

Bond, James N., 'Peacetime Foreign Data Manipulation as One Aspect of Offensive Information Warfare: Questions of Legality under the United Nations Charter Article 2(4)' (MA, Naval War College 1996)

Bourdieu, Pierre, 'Force of Law: Toward a Sociology of the Juridical Field' (1987) 38 *Hastings Law Journal* 814

Bowett, Derek W., 'Economic Coercion and Reprisals by States' (1972) 13 *Virginia Journal of International Law* 1

Self-Defence in International Law, Manchester University Press 1958

Brooks, Terrence A., 'Private Acts and Public Objects: An Investigation of Citer Motivations' (1985) 37 *Journal of the American Society for Information Science* 34

Brownlie, Ian, *International Law and the Use of Force by States*, Oxford University Press 1963

Buchan, Russell, 'Cyber Attacks: Unlawful Uses of Force or Prohibited Interventions?' (2012) 17 *Journal of Conflict and Security Law* 211

Budd, John M., 'Citations and Knowledge Claims: Sociology of Knowledge as a Case in Point' (1999) 25 *Journal of Information Science* 265

Bueger, Christian and Felix Bethke, 'Actor-Networking the "Failed State": An Enquiry into the Life of Concepts' (2014) 17 *Journal of International Relations and Development* 30

Bueger, Christian and Frank Gadinger, 'The Play of International Practice' (2015) 59 *International Studies Quarterly* 449

Bumiller, Elisabeth and Thom Shanker, 'Panetta Warns of Dire Threat of Cyberattack on U.S.,' *New York Times*, October 11, 2012, www.nytimes.com/2012/10/12/world/panetta-warns-of-dire-threat-of-cyberattack.html?_r=0 (July 15, 2020)

Burgess, Sally, 'Packed Houses and Intimate Gatherings: Audience and Rhetorical Structure,' in: *Academic Discourse*, John Flowerdew (ed.), Pearson Education Limited 2002, 196–215

Butler, Judith, *Bodies that Matter: On the Discursive Limits of 'Sex,'* Routledge 2011

Cameron, Clinton E., 'Developing a Standard for Politically Related State Economic Action' (1991) 13 *Michigan Journal of International Law* 218

Camic, Charles, Neil Gross and Michèle Lamont (eds.), *Social Knowledge in the Making*, The University of Chicago Press 2011

Carter-Thomas, Shirley and Elizabeth Rowley-Jolivet, 'Analysing the Scientific Conference Presentation (CP): A Methodological Overview of a Multimodal Genre' (2003) 39–40 *ASp* 59

Carty, Anthony, 'Sociological Theories of International Law,' Max Planck Encyclopedia of Public International Law 2008, Rüdiger Wolfrum (dir.), https://opil.ouplaw.com/view/10.1093/law:epil/9780199231690/law-9780199231690-e735 (July 15, 2020)

Casey, Debra L. and G. Steven McMillan, 'Identifying the "Invisible Colleges" of the Industrial & Labor Relations Review: A Bibliometric Approach' (2008) 62 *Industrial & Labor Relations Review* 126

CCDCOE, 'About Us,' https://ccdcoe.org/about-us/ (July 15, 2020)

Charter of the United Nations, 26 June 1945, 1 UNTS XVI

Chen, Lung-chu, 'Perspectives from the New Haven School' (1993) 87 *American Society of International Law Proceedings* 407

Cienki, Alan, 'Language as a Prototype Category: Cognitive Linguistics Meets Multimodal Communication,' Inaugural Lecture Vrije Universiteit Amsterdam, September 14, 2015, slides on file with the author

'Spoken Language Usage Events' (2015) 7 *Language and Cognition* 499

'The Dynamic Scope of Relevant Behaviors in Talk: A Perspective from Cognitive Linguistics' (extended abstract), *Proceedings of the 2nd European and the 5th Nordic Symposium on Multimodal Communication 2015*, www.ep.liu.se/ecp/110/002/ecp15110002.pdf (July 15, 2020)

Clarke, Richard A. and Robert K. Knake, *Cyberwar: The Next Threat to National Security and What to Do About It*, HarperCollins 2010

Cohen, Julie E., 'Cyberspace as/and Space' (2007) 107 *Columbia Law Review* 210

Constable, Marianne, *Our Word Is Our Bond: How Legal Speech Acts*, Stanford University Press 2014

Constable, Marianne, Leti Volpp and Bryan Wagner (eds.), *Looking for Law in All the Wrong Places: Justice Beyond and Between*, Fordham University Press 2019

Corten, Olivier, 'Formalization and Deformalization as Narratives of the Law of War,' in: *New Approaches to International Law: The European and the American Experiences*, José María Beneyto and David Kennedy (eds.), T.M.C. Asser Press 2013, 251–272

Council of Europe, *Convention on Cybercrime*, November 23, 2001, ETS No. 185

Cover, Robert M., 'The Supreme Court, 1982 Term – Foreword: Nomos and Narrative' (1983) 97 *Harvard Law Review* 4

Cox, Stephen J., 'Confronting Threats through Unconventional Means: Offensive Information Warfare as a Covert Alternative to Preemptive War' (2005) 42 *Houston Law Review* 881

Craven, Matthew, Susan Marks, Gerry Simpson and Ralph Wilde, 'We Are Teachers of International Law' (2004) 17 *Leiden Journal of International Law* 363

Crawford Camiciottoli, Belinda, 'Collective and Individual Identities in Business Studies Lectures,' in: *Commonality and Individuality in Academic Discourse*, Maurizio Gotti (ed.), Peter Lang 2009, 141–162

Crawford, Emily, 'From Inter-state and Symmetric to Intra-state and Asymmetric: Changing Methods of Warfare and the Law of Armed Conflict in the 100 Years Since World War One,' in: *Yearbook of International Humanitarian Law 2014*, Terry D. Gill, Robin Geiß, Heike Krieger, Tim McCormack, Christophe Paulussen and Jessica Dorsey (eds.), T.M.C. Asser Press 2016, 95–118

Crawford, Michael, 'Utility Hack Led to Security Overhaul,' *Computerworld*, February 16, 2006, www.computerworld.com/article/2561484/security0/utility-hack-led-to-security-overhaul.html (July 15, 2020)

Cristobal, Kasia Solon, 'From Law in Blackletter to Blackletter Law' (2016) 108 *Law Library Journal* 181

Cronin, Blaise, *The Citation Process: The Role and Significance of Citations in Scientific Communication*, Taylor Graham 1984

Cuenca, Maria Josep, 'Form-Use Mappings for Tag Questions,' in: *Discourse and Perspectives in Cognitive Linguistics*, Wolf-Andreas Liebert, Gisela Redeker and Linda Waugh (eds.), John Benjamins 1997, 3–20

Cyber Law International, 'Another successful int'l cyber law capacity-building seminar for gov't officials,' Twitter, May 21, 2019, https://twitter.com/CyberLawInt/status/1130767015176802305 (July 15, 2020)

d'Amato, Anthony, 'On Consensus' (1970) 8 *Canadian Yearbook of International Law* 104

d'Aspremont, Jean, 'Cyber Operations and International Law: An Interventionist Legal Thought' (2016) 21 *Journal of Conflict and Security Law* 575

d'Aspremont, Jean, Tarcisio Gazzini, André Nollkaemper and Wouter Werner (eds.), *International Law as a Profession*, Cambridge University Press 2017

Dapray Muir, J., 'The Boycott in International Law' (1974) 9 *Journal of International Law and Economics* 187

Davenport, Tara, 'Submarine Cables, Cybersecurity and International Law: An Intersectional Analysis' (2015) 24 *Catholic University Journal of Law and Technology* 57

De Tomas Colatin, Samuele, A *Surprising Turn of Events: UN Creates Two Working Groups on Cyberspace*, CCDCOE INCYDER Articles, March 11, 2019, www.ccdcoe.org/incyder-articles/a-surprising-turn-of-events-un-creates-two-working-groups-on-cyberspace/ (July 15, 2020)

Degano, Chiara, 'Dissociation and Presupposition in Discourse: A Corpus Study' (2007) 21 *Argumentation* 361

Del Mar, Maks, 'Metaphor in International Law: Language, Imagination and Normative Inquiry' (2017) 86 *Nordic Journal of International Law* 170

Delanis, James A., 'Force under Article 2(4) of the United Nations Charter: The Question of Economic and Political Coercion' (1979) 12 *Vanderbilt Journal of Transnational Law* 101

Delerue, François, 'International Cooperation on the International Law Applicable to Cyber Operations' (2019) 24 *European Foreign Affairs Review* 203

Delibasis, Dimitrios, 'The Right of States to Use Force in Cyberspace: Defining the Rules of Engagement' (2002) 11 *Information & Communications Technology Law* 255

Dezalay, Yves and Bryant G. Garth, *Dealing in Virtue: International Commercial Arbitration and the Construction of a Transnational Legal Order*, The University of Chicago Press 1996

Dinstein, Yoram, 'Computer Network Attacks and Self-Defense,' in: *Computer Network Attack and International Law*, Michael N. Schmitt and Brian T. O'Donnell (eds.), Naval War College 2002, 99–119

War, Aggression and Self-Defence, Cambridge University Press 2005 (4th ed.)

War, Aggression and Self-Defence, Cambridge University Press 2012 (5th ed.)

War, Aggression and Self-Defence, Cambridge University Press 2017 (6th ed.)

(gen. ed.), 'Commentary on the HPCR Manual on International Law Applicable to Air and Missile Warfare,' Program on Humanitarian Policy and Conflict

Research, Harvard University 2010, https://georgetown.instructure.com/files/900391/download?download_frd=1 (July 15, 2020)

Director of National Intelligence, 'Background to "Assessing Russian Activities and Intentions in Recent US Elections": The Analytic Process and Cyber Incident Attribution,' January 6, 2017, www.dni.gov/files/documents/ICA_2017_01.pdf (22 July 2020)

Dorsett, Shaunnagh and Shaun McVeigh, *Jurisdiction*, Routledge 2012

Douzinas, Costas, 'Speaking Law: On Bare Theological and Cosmopolitan Sovereignty,' in: *International Law and Its Others*, Anne Orford (ed.), Cambridge University Press 2006, 35–56

Ducheine, Paul, Joop Voetelink, Jan Stinissen and Terry Gill, 'Towards a Legal Framework for Military Cyber Operations,' in: *Cyber Warfare: Critical Perspectives*, Paul Ducheine, Frans Osinga and Joseph Soeters (eds.), T.M.C. Asser Press 2012, 101–128

Dunlap Jr., Charles J., 'Perspectives for Cyber Strategists on Law for Cyberwar' (2011) 5 *Strategic Studies Quarterly* 81

Dunn Cavelty, Myriam, *Cyber-Security and Threat Politics: US Efforts to Secure the Information Age*, Routledge 2008

'Unraveling the Stuxnet Effect: Of Much Persistence and Little Change in the Cyber Threats Debate' (2011) 3 *Military and Strategic Affairs* 11

Dunoff, Jeffrey L. and Mark A. Pollack, 'International Judicial Practices: Opening the Black Box of International Courts' (2018) 40 *Michigan Journal of International Law* 47

Duszak, Anna, 'Us and Others: An Introduction,' in: *Us and Others: Social Identities across Languages, Discourses and Cultures*, Anna Duszak (ed.), John Benjamins 2002, 1–28

Duyvesteyn, Isabelle, 'Between Doomsday and Dismissal: Collective Defence, Cyber War and the Parameters of War' (2014) 38 *Atlantisch Perspectief* 20

Dyson, Tim and Valeria Cetorelli, 'Changing Views on Child Mortality and Economic Sanctions in Iraq: A History of Lies, Damned Lies and Statistics' (2017) 2 *BMJ Global Health* 1

Dzehtsiarou, Kanstantsin, *European Consensus and the Legitimacy of the European Court of Human Rights*, Cambridge University Press 2015

Efrony, Dan and Yuval Shany, 'A Rule Book on the Shelf? Tallinn Manual 2.0 on Cyberoperations and Subsequent State Practice' (2019) 112 *American Journal of International Law* 583

Eichensehr, Kristen E., 'Review of *Tallinn Manual on the International Law Applicable to Cyber Warfare*. Edited by Michael N. Schmitt. Cambridge, New York: Cambridge University Press, 2013. pp. xix, 282. Index. $120, cloth; $58.99, paper' (2014) 108 *American Journal of International Law* 585

Eichhorn, Lisa, 'Writing in the Legal Academy: A Dangerous Supplement?' (1998) 40 *Arizona Law Review* 105

European Commission, Migration and Home Affairs, 'Cybercrime,' https://ec.europa.eu/home-affairs/what-we-do/policies/organized-crime-and-human-trafficking/cybercrime_en (July 15, 2020)

Fenrick, William J., 'ICRC Guidance on Direct Participation in Hostilities' (2009) 12 *Yearbook of International Humanitarian Law* 287

Finnemore, Martha and Duncan B. Hollis, 'Constructing Norms for Global Cybersecurity' (2016) 110 *American Journal of International Law* 425

Fleck, Dieter, 'Searching for International Rules Applicable to Cyber Warfare – A Critical First Assessment of the New *Tallinn Manual*' (2013) 18 *Journal of Conflict and Security Law* 331

Foltz, Andrew C., 'Stuxnet, Schmitt Analysis, and the Cyber "Use-of-Force" Debate' (2012) 67 *Joint Force Quarterly* 40

Fortanet, Inmaculada, 'The Use of "We" in University Lectures: Reference and Function' (2004) 23 *English for Specific Purposes* 45

Foucault, Michel, 'Authorship: What Is an Author?' (1979) 20 *Screen* 13

The Archeology of Knowledge, transl. A. M. Sheridan Smith, Pantheon Books 1972

'The Order of Discourse,' in: *Untying the Text: A Post-Structuralist Reader*, Robert Young (ed.), Routledge & Kegan Paul 1981, 48–78

Geertz, Clifford, 'On Paying Attention,' in: *Fine Description: Ethnographic and Linguistic Essays by Harold C. Conklin*, Joel Kuipers and Ray McDermott (eds.), Yale University Press 2007, 27–30

The Interpretation of Cultures, Basic Books 1973

Gervais, Michael, 'Cyber Attacks and the Laws of War' (2012) 30 *Berkeley Journal of International Law* 525

Gilbert, Nigel, 'Referencing as Persuasion' (1977) 7 *Social Studies of Science* 113

Godden, David M., 'On Common Knowledge and *Ad Populum*: Acceptance as Grounds for Acceptability' (2008) 41 *Philosophy & Rhetoric* 101

Goldsmith, Jack, 'Cybersecurity Treaties: A Skeptical View,' in: *Future Challenges in National Security and Law*, Peter Berkowitz (ed.), Hoover Institution 2011, 1–16, http://media.hoover.org/sites/default/files/documents/FutureChallenges_Goldsmith.pdf (July 15, 2020)

Don't Get Too Excited About a US-China Arms Control Agreement for Cyber, on 'Lawfare,' September 21, 2015, www.lawfareblog.com/dont-get-too-excited-about-us-china-arms-control-agreement-cyber (July 15, 2020)

'How Cyber Changes the Laws of War' (2013) 24 *European Journal of International Law* 129

Goldsmith, Jack and Tim Wu, *Who Controls the Internet? Illusions of a Borderless World*, Oxford University Press 2006

Goodman, Seymour E., 'War, Information Technologies, and International Asymmetries' (1996) 39 *Communications of the ACM* 11

Goodrich, Leland and Edvard Hambro, *Charter of the United Nations*, Stevens and Sons Limited 1949

Grafton, Anthony, *The Footnote: A Curious History*, Harvard University Press 1997

Grant, Thomas D., 'Doctrines (Monroe, Hallstein, Brezhnev, Stimson),' Max Planck Encyclopedia of Public International Law 2014, Rüdiger Wolfrum (dir.), https://opil.ouplaw.com/view/10.1093/law:epil/9780199231690/law-9780199231690-e697 (July 15, 2020)

Gray, Christine, *International Law and the Use of Force*, Oxford University Press 2008 (3rd ed.)

'The Use of Force and the International Legal Order,' in: *International Law*, Malcolm D. Evans (ed.), Oxford University Press 2010, 615–647

Greenberg, Lawrence T., Seymour E. Goodman and Kevin J. Soo Hoo, *Information Warfare and International Law*, National Defense University Press 1998

Grigsby, Alex, *The United Nations Doubles Its Workload on Cyber Norms, and Not Everyone Is Pleased*, Council on Foreign Relations Blog, November 15, 2018, www.cfr.org/blog/united-nations-doubles-its-workload-cyber-norms-and-not-everyone-pleased (July 15, 2020)

Gross, Neil and Crystal Fleming, 'Academic Conferences and the Making of Philosophical Knowledge,' in: *Social Knowledge in the Making*, Charles Camic, Neil Gross and Michèle Lamont (eds.), The University of Chicago Press 2011, 151–179

Haataja, Samuli, *Cyber Attacks and International Law on the Use of Force: The Turn to Information Ethics*, Routledge 2019

Hacking, Ian, '"Style" for Historians and Philosophers' (1992) 23 *Studies in History and Philosophy of Science* 1

Hallaq, Weal B., 'On the Authoritativeness of Sunni Consensus' (1986) 18 *International Journal of Middle East Studies* 427

Handler, Stephanie Gosnell, 'The New Cyber Face of Battle: Developing a Legal Approach to Accommodate Emerging Trends in Warfare' (2012) 48 *Stanford Journal of International Law* 209

Hargens, Lowell L., 'Using the Literature: Reference Networks, Reference Contexts, and the Social Structure of Scholarship' (2000) 65 *American Sociological Review* 846

Harold, Scott Warren, *The U.S.-China Cyber Agreement: A Good First Step*, on the RAND Blog, August 1, 2016, www.rand.org/blog/2016/08/the-us-china-cyber-agreement-a-good-first-step.html (July 15, 2020)

Harris, Matthew, 'Metafiction in New Zealand from the 1960s to the Present Day' (PhD, Massey University 2011)

Harrison Dinniss, Heather, *Cyber Warfare and the Laws of War*, Cambridge University Press 2014

Haslam, Emily, 'Information Warfare: Technological Changes and International Law' (2000) 5 *Journal of Conflict and Security Law* 157

Hathaway, Oona A., 'The Drawbacks and Dangers of Active Defense,' in: *Proceedings of the 6th International Conference on Cyber Conflict*, Pascal Brangetto, Markus Maybaum and Jan Stinissen (eds.), NATO CCD COE Publications 2014, 39–50

Hathaway, Oona A., Rebecca Crootof, Philip Levitz, Haley Nix, Aileen Nowlan, William Perdue and Julia Spiegel, 'The Law of Cyber-Attack' (2012) 100 *California Law Review* 817

Helfer, Laurence R., 'Consensus, Coherence and the European Convention on Human Rights' (1993) 26 *Cornell International Law Journal* 133

Helmbrecht, Johannes, 'Grammar and Function of We,' in: *Us and Others: Social Identities across Languages, Discourses and Cultures*, Anna Duszak (ed.), John Benjamins 2002, 31–49

Helmersen, Sondre Torp, 'Finding "The Most Highly Qualified Publicists": Lessons from the International Court of Justice' (2019) 30 *European Journal of International Law* 509

Henderson, Errol A. and J. David Singer, '"New Wars" and Rumors of "New Wars"' (2002) 28 *International Interactions* 165

Henrard, Kristin and Elaine Mak, 'The Use of Consensus Arguments in Transnational Judicial Decision-Making: Confirming or Jeopardising Universal Human Rights,' June 4, 2014, http://papers.ssrn.com/sol3/papers.cfm?abstract_id=2444682 (July 15, 2020)

Henriksen, Anders, 'Lawful State Responses to Low-Level Cyber-Attacks' (2015) 84 *Nordic Journal of International Law* 323

'The End of the Road for the UN GGE Process: The Future Regulation of Cyberspace' (2019) 5 *Journal of Cybersecurity* 1

Hernández, Gleider, 'The Responsibility of the International Legal Academic,' in: *International Law as a Profession*, Jean d'Aspremont, Tarcisio Gazzini, André Nollkaemper and Wouter Werner (eds.), Cambridge University Press 2017, 160–188

Hoisington, Matthew, 'Cyberwarfare and the Use of Force Giving Rise to the Right of Self-Defense' (2009) 32 *Boston College International and Comparative Law Review* 439

Hollis, Duncan B., 'An e-SOS for Cyberspace' (2011) 52 *Harvard International Law Journal* 373

The Fog of Technology and International Law, on 'Opinio Juris,' May 15, 2015, http://opiniojuris.org/2015/05/15/the-fog-of-technology-and-international-law/?utm_source=feedburner&utm_medium=email&utm_campaign=Feed%3A+opiniojuris feed+%28Opinio+Juris%29 (July 15, 2020)

'Why States Need an International Law for Information Operations' (2007) 11 *Lewis and Clark Law Review* 1023

Holtermann, Jakob V. H. and Mikael Rask Madsen, 'European New Legal Realism and International Law: How to Make International Law Intelligible' (2015) 28 *Leiden Journal of International Law* 211

Horst, Maja and Alan Irwin, 'Nations at Ease with Radical Knowledge: On Consensus, Consensusing and False Consensusness' (2010) 40 *Social Studies of Science* 105

Huntley, Todd C., 'Controlling the Use of Force in Cyber Space: The Application of the Law of Armed Conflict During a Time of Fundamental Change in the Nature of Warfare' (2010) 60 *Naval Law Review* 1

Hyland, Ken, 'Constraint vs Creativity: Identity and Disciplinarity in Academic Writing,' in: *Commonality and Individuality in Academic Discourse*, Maurizio Gotti (ed.), Peter Lang 2009, 25–52

'Directives: Argument and Engagement in Academic Writing' (2002) 23 *Applied Linguistics* 215

Disciplinary Discourses: Social Interactions in Academic Writing, The University of Michigan Press 2004

'Stance and Engagement: A Model of Interaction in Academic Discourse' (2005) 7 *Discourse studies* 173

'"Small Bits of Textual Material": A Discourse Analysis of Swales' Writing' (2008) 27 *English for Specific Purposes* 142

Iasiello, Emilio, 'Are Cyber Weapons Effective Military Tools?' (2015) 7 *Military and Strategic Affairs* 23

Ingber, Rebecca, 'Interpretation Catalysts in Cyberspace' (2016) 95 *Texas Law Review* 1531

International Committee of the Red Cross, 'Treaties, States Parties and Commentaries,' www.icrc.org/applic/ihl/ihl.nsf/vwTreatiesHistoricalByDate.xsp (July 15, 2020)

International Court of Justice, *Reparation for Injuries Suffered in the Service of the United Nations, Advisory Opinion, ICJ Reports* 1949, p. 174 (1949)

Military and Paramilitary Activities in and against Nicaragua (Nicaragua v. *United States of America), Merits, Judgment, ICJ Reports* 1986, p. 14 (1986)

Legality of the Threat or Use of Nuclear Weapons, Advisory Opinion, ICJ Reports 1996, p. 226 (1996)

Armed Activities on the Territory of the Congo (Democratic Republic of the Congo v. Uganda), Judgment, ICJ Reports 2005, p. 168 (2005)

Jensen, Eric Talbot, 'Computer Attacks on Critical National Infrastructure: A Use of Force Invoking the Right of Self-Defense' (2002) 38 *Stanford Journal of International Law* 207

Johns, Fleur, 'Author's Response – Fleur Johns, *Non-Legality in International Law: Unruly Law*, Cambridge, Cambridge University Press, 2013, pp. 259, ISBN 9781107014015' (2014) 27 *Leiden Journal of International Law* 966

'Data, Detection, and the Redistribution of the Sensible in International Law' (2017) 111 *American Journal of International Law* 57

'From Planning to Prototypes: New Ways of Seeing Like a State' (2019) 82 *The Modern Law Review* 833

Non-legality in International Law: Unruly Law, Cambridge University Press 2013

Johns, Fleur and Annelise Riles, 'Beyond Bunker and Vaccine: The DNC Hack as a Conflict of Laws Issue' (2017) 110 *AJIL Unbound* 347

Johns, Fleur, Thomas Skouteris and Wouter Werner, 'Editors' Introduction: Alejandro Álvarez and the Launch of the Periphery Series' (2006) 19 *Leiden Journal of International Law* 875

Johnson, David R. and David Post, 'Law and Borders: The Rise of Law in Cyberspace' (1995) 48 *Stanford Law Review* 1367

Joyner, Christopher C. and Catherine Lotrionte, 'Information Warfare as International Coercion: Elements of a Legal Framework' (2001) 12 *European Journal of International Law* 825

Jurich, Jon P., 'Cyberwar and Customary International Law: The Potential of a "Bottom-up" Approach to an International Law of Information Operations' (2008) 9 *Chicago Journal of International Law* 275

Kabinetsreactie op het AIV/CAVV-advies Digitale Oorlogvoering, DVB/VD-38/12, April 6, 2012, www.tweedekamer.nl/debat_en_vergadering/commissievergaderingen/details?id=2012A01586 (July 15, 2020)

Kammerhofer, Jörg, 'Lawmaking by Scholars,' in: *Research Handbook on the Theory and Practice of International Lawmaking*, Catherine Brölmann and Yannick Radi (eds.), Elgar 2016, 305–326

Kanuck, Sean P., 'Information Warfare: New Challenges for Public International Law' (1996) 37 *Harvard International Law Journal* 272

Kell, Douglas, 'The Matthew Effect in Science – Citing the Most Cited,' http://blogs.bbsrc.ac.uk/index.php/2009/03/the-matthew-effect-in-science/ (May 16, 2016)

Kelly, Spencer, 'Hackers Outwit Online Banking Identity Security Systems,' BBC News, March 8, 2012, www.bbc.com/news/technology-16812064 (July 15, 2020)

Kendall, Sara, 'On Academic Production and the Politics of Inclusion' (2016) 29 *Leiden Journal of International Law* 617

Kennedy, David, 'The Politics of the Invisible College: International Governance and the Politics of Expertise' (2001) 5 *European Human Rights Law Review* 463

'Theses about International Law Discourse,' in: *German Yearbook of International Law*, Jost Delbrück, Rainer Hofmann and Andreas Zimmermann (eds.), Duncker & Humblot 1980, 354–391

Kent, Avidan and Jamie Trinidad, 'International Law Scholars as *Amici Curiae*: An Emerging Dialogue (of the Deaf)?' (2016) 29 *Leiden Journal of International Law* 1081

Kerschischnig, Georg, *Cyberthreats and International Law*, Eleven International Publishing 2012

Kessler, Oliver and Wouter Werner, 'Expertise, Uncertainty, and International Law: A Study of the Tallinn Manual on Cyberwarfare' (2013) 26 *Leiden Journal of International Law* 793

Kilovaty, Ido, 'Rethinking the Prohibition on the Use of Force in the Light of Economic Cyber Warfare: Towards a Broader Scope of Article 2(4) of the United Nations Charter' (2015) 4 *Journal of Law and Cyber Warfare* 210

Kittichaisaree, Kriangsak, *Public International Law of Cyberspace*, Springer 2017

Klabbers, Jan, 'On Epistemic Universalism and the Melancholy of International Law' (2019) 29 *European Journal of International Law* 1057

Kodar, Erki, 'Computer Network Attacks in the Grey Areas of *Jus ad Bellum* and *Jus in Bello*' (2009) 9 *Baltic Yearbook of International Law Online* 133

Koenders, Bert, Minister of Foreign Affairs of the Kingdom of the Netherlands, 'Foreword,' in: *Tallinn Manual 2.0 on the International Law Applicable to Cyber Operations*, Michael N. Schmitt (ed.), Cambridge University Press 2017, xxv–xxvii

Koh, Harold Hongju, 'International Law in Cyberspace' (2012) 54 *Harvard International Law Journal Online* 1

Kondoch, Boris, 'Jus ad Bellum and Cyber Warfare in Northeast Asia' (2013) 6 *Journal of East Asia and International Law* 459

Konzett, Carmen, *Any Questions? Identity Construction in Academic Conference Discussions*, Walter de Gruyter 2012

Korzak, Elaine, *The 2015 GGE Report: What Next for Norms in Cyberspace?*, on 'Lawfare,' September 23, 2015, www.lawfareblog.com/2015-gge-report-what-next-norms-cyberspace (July 15, 2020)

Koskenniemi, Martti, 'Between Commitment and Cynicism: Outline for a Theory of International Law as Practice,' in: *Collection of Essays by Legal Advisers of States, Legal Advisers of International Organizations and Practitioners in the Field of International Law*, United Nations 1999, 495–523

From Apology to Utopia: The Structure of International Legal Argument, Cambridge University Press 2005

'International Legal Theory and Doctrine,' Max Planck Encyclopedia of Public International Law 2007, Rüdiger Wolfrum (dir.), https://opil.ouplaw.com/view/10.1093/law:epil/9780199231690/law-9780199231690-e1618 (July 15, 2020)

'Law, Teleology and International Relations: An Essay in Counterdisciplinarity' (2012) 26 *International Relations* 3

'Letter to the Editors of the Symposium' (1999) 93 *American Journal of International Law* 351

(ed.), *Sources of International Law*, Ashgate 2000

The Gentle Civilizer of Nations, Cambridge University Press 2001

'The Politics of International Law – 20 Years Later' (2009) 20 *European Journal of International Law* 7

Kostyuk, Nadiya and Yuri M. Zhukov, 'Invisible Digital Front: Can Cyber Attacks Shape Battlefield Events?' (2019) 63 *Journal of Conflict Resolution* 317

Koulen, Sarah-Jane, 'Blind Justice and the Portraits on the Wall,' in: *Backstage Practices of Transnational Law*, Lianne J. M. Boer and Sofia Stolk (eds.), Routledge 2019, 91–107

Kratochwil, Friedrich V., *Rules, Norms, and Decisions: On the Conditions of Practical and Legal Reasoning in International Relations and Domestic Affairs*, Cambridge University Press 1989

The Status of Law in World Society: Meditations on the Role and Rule of Law, Cambridge University Press 2014

Lam, Christina, 'A Slap on the Wrist: Combatting Russia's Cyber Attack on the 2016 U.S. Presidential Election' (2018) 59 *Boston College Law Review* 2167

Langner, Ralph, 'Cracking Stuxnet, a 21st-Century Cyber Weapon,' March 2011, www.ted.com/talks/ralph_langner_cracking_stuxnet_a_21st_century_cyberweapon?language=en#t-5628 (July 15, 2020)

LaRae-Perez, Cassandra, 'Note: Economic Sanctions as a Use of Force: Re-evaluating the Legality of Sanctions from an Effects-Based Perspective' (2002) 20 *Boston University International Law Journal* 161

Larson, Erik, Patricia Hurtado and Chris Strohm, 'Iranians Hacked from Wall Street to New York Dam, U.S. Says,' *Bloomberg.com*, March 24, 2016, www.bloomberg.com/news/articles/2016–03-24/u-s-charges-iranian-hackers-in-wall-street-cyberattacks-im6b43tt (July 15, 2020)

Latour, Bruno, *The Making of Law: An Ethnography of the Conseil d'État*, transl. Marina Brilman and Alain Pottage (revised by the author), Polity Press 2010

Latour, Bruno and Steve Woolgar, *Laboratory Life: The Construction of Scientific Facts*, Princeton University Press 1986

Lawson, Sean, 'Does 2016 Mark the End of Cyber Pearl Harbor Hysteria?,' *Forbes*, December 7, 2016, www.forbes.com/sites/seanlawson/2016/12/07/does-2016-mark-the-end-of-cyber-pearl-harbor-hysteria/#7d486d7722c2 (July 15, 2020)

Leão Soares Pereira, Luíza, '*International Lawyers as Lawmakers*' (PhD, Cambridge University 2021, forthcoming)

Lee, Youngjae, 'International Consensus as Persuasive Authority in the Eighth Amendment' (2007) 156 *University of Pennsylvania Law Review* 63

Levi, Ron and Mariana Valverde, 'Studying Law by Association: Bruno Latour Goes to the Conseil d'État' (2008) 33 *Law & Social Inquiry* 805

Li, Sheng, 'When Does Internet Denial Trigger the Right of Armed Self-Defense?' (2013) 38 *Yale Journal of International Law* 179

Lillich, Richard B., 'Economic Coercion and the International Legal Order' (1975) 51 *International Affairs* 358

Lin, Herbert S., 'Offensive Cyber Operations and the Use of Force' (2010) 4 *Journal of National Security Law & Policy* 63

Lincoln, Bruce, *Authority: Construction and Corrosion*, The University of Chicago Press 1994

Little, Laura E., 'Hiding with Words: Obfuscation, Avoidance, and Federal Jurisdiction Opinions' (1998) 46 *UCLA Law Review* 75

Lodder, Arno R. and Lianne J. M. Boer, 'Cyberwar? What War? Meer in het Bijzonder: Welk Recht?' (2012) 38 *Justitiële Verkenningen* 52

Lynch, Michael, 'Circumscribing Expertise: Membership Categories in Courtroom Testimony,' in: *States of Knowledge: The Co-production of Science and the Social Order*, Sheila Jasanoff (ed.), Routledge 2004, 161–180

Mačák, Kubo, 'From Cyber Norms to Cyber Rules: Re-engaging States as Law-Makers' (2017) 30 *Leiden Journal of International Law* 877

'From the Vanishing Point Back to the Core: The Impact of the Development of the Cyber Law of War on General International Law,' in: *Defending the Core*, Henry Rõigas, Raik Jakschis, Lauri Lindström and Tomaš Minárik (eds.), NATO CCD COE Publications 2017, 1–14

'Is the International Law of Cyber Security in Crisis?,' in: *Proceedings of the 8th International Conference on Cyber Conflict: Cyber Power*, Nikolaos Pissanidis, Henry Rõigas and Matthijs Veenendaal (eds.), NATO CCD COE Publications 2016, 127–139

'On the Shelf, but Close at Hand: The Contribution of Non-State Initiatives to International Cyber Law' (2019) 113 *AJIL Unbound* 81

Macfarlane, Robert, *Landmarks*, Penguin 2016

Mahbuba, Dilruba and Ronald Rousseau, 'The Matthew Effect and a Relation with Concept Symbols and Defaults' (2011) 58 *Annals of Library and Information Studies* 335

Maogoto, Jackson, *Technology and the Law on the Use of Force: New Security Challenges in the Twenty-First Century*, Routledge 2015

Marcus, Sharon, Heather Love and Stephen Best, 'Building a Better Description' (2016) 135 *Representations* 1

Markovits, Richard S., 'Learning from the Foreigners: A Response to Justice Scalia's and Professor Levinson's Professional Moral Parochialism' (2003) 39 *Texas International Law Journal* 367

Marks, Susan, 'False Contingency' (2009) 62 *Current Legal Problems* 1

Martin, James R. and Peter R. R. White, *The Language of Evaluation*, Palgrave 2005

Mauranen, Anna, *Cultural Differences in Academic Rhetoric: A Textlinguistic Study*, Peter Lang 1993

McInnis, Raymond G. and Dal Symes, 'David Riesman and the Concept of Bibliographic Citation' (1988) 49 *College & Research Libraries* 387

Mégret, Frédéric, 'Thinking about What International Humanitarian Lawyers "Do": An Examination of the Laws of War as a Field of Professional Practice,' in: *The Law of International Lawyers: Reading Martti Koskenniemi*, Wouter Werner, Marieke de Hoon and Alexis Galán (eds.), Cambridge University Press 2017, 265–296

Meierhenrich, Jens, 'The Practice of International Law: A Theoretical Analysis' (2014) 76 *Law and Contemporary Problems* 1

Merry, Sally Engle, 'New Legal Realism and the Ethnography of Transnational Law' (2006) 31 *Law & Social Inquiry* 975

Mertz, Elizabeth, *The Language of Law School: Learning to 'Think Like a Lawyer,'* Oxford University Press 2007

Michael, James B., Thomas C. Wingfield and Duminda Wijesekera, 'Measured Responses to Cyber Attacks Using Schmitt Analysis: A Case Study of Attack Scenarios for a Software-Intensive System' (2013) *2013 IEEE 37th Annual Computer Software and Applications Conference* 621

Modderkolk, Huib and Kim Zetter, 'AIVD Speelde Cruciale Rol bij Sabotage Kernprogramma Iran,' *De Volkskrant*, September 2, 2019, www.volkskrant.nl/nieuws-achtergrond/aivd-speelde-cruciale-rol-bij-sabotage-kernprogramma-iran~ba24df9f/?referer=https%3A%2F%2Fwww.google.com%2F (July 15, 2020)

Moore, Stephen, 'Cyber Attacks and the Beginnings of an International Cyber Treaty' (2013) 39 *North Carolina Journal of International Law & Commercial Regulation* 223

Morell, Teresa, 'International Conference Paper Presentations: A Multimodal Analysis to Determine Effectiveness' (2015) 37 *English for Specific Purposes* 137

Morth, Todd A., 'Considering Our Position: Viewing Information Warfare as a Use of Force Prohibited by Article 2(4) of the UN Charter' (1998) 30 *Case Western Reserve Journal of International Law* 567

Musil, Robert, *The Man without Qualities*, [Der Mann ohne Eigenschaften], transl. Sophie Wilkins and Burton Pike, Picador 2011

Nakashima, Ellen, 'U.S. Developing Sanctions against China over Cyberthefts,' *Washington Post*, August 30, 2015, www.washingtonpost.com/world/national-security/administration-developing-sanctions-against-china-over-cyberespionage/2015/08/30/9b2910aa-480b-11e5-8ab4-c73967a143d3_story.html (July 15, 2020)

Navarrete, Iñaki, 'L'Espionnage en Temps de Paix en Droit International Public' (2016) 53 *Canadian Yearbook of International Law/Annuaire canadien de droit international* 1

Neff, Stephen C., *War and the Law of Nations: A General History*, Cambridge University Press 2005

Nguyen, Reese, 'Navigating *Jus ad Bellum* in the Age of Cyber Warfare' (2013) 101 *California Law Review* 1079

Nimis, Steve, 'Fussnoten: Das Fundament der Wissenschaft' (1984) 17 *Arethusa* 105

Noll, Gregor, 'Analogy at War: Proportionality, Equality and the Law of Targeting,' in: *Netherlands Yearbook of International Law* 2012, Janne E. Nijman and Wouter G. Werner (eds.), T.M.C. Asser Press 2013, 205–230

'International Law as Discipline and Doctrine,' in: *Routledge Handbook of International Law and the Humanities*, Shane Chalmers and Sundhya Pahuja (eds.), Routledge 2021, 36–44

'Theorizing Jurisdiction,' in: *The Oxford Handbook of the Theory of International Law*, Anne Orford, Florian Hoffmann and Martin Clark (eds.), Oxford University Press 2017, 600–617

North Atlantic Council, 'Wales Summit Declaration,' September 5, 2014, www.nato.int/cps/en/natohq/official_texts_112964.htm (July 15, 2020)

North Atlantic Treaty, 4 April 1949, 34 UNTS 243

Nouwen, Sarah M. H., '"As You Set out for Ithaka": Practical, Epistemological, Ethical, and Existential Questions about Socio-Legal Empirical Research in Conflict' (2014) 27 *Leiden Journal of International Law* 227

Ohlin, Jens David, 'Did Russian Cyber Interference in the 2016 Election Violate International Law?' (2016) 95 *Texas Law Review* 1579

Orakhelashvili, Alexander, 'Natural Law and Justice,' Max Planck Encyclopedia of Public International Law 2007, Rüdiger Wolfrum (dir.), https://opil.ouplaw.com/view/10.1093/law:epil/9780199231690/law-9780199231690-e730?rskey=ijHlQr&result=19&prd=EPIL (July 15, 2020)

Orford, Anne, 'Critical Intimacy: Jacques Derrida and the Friendship of Politics' (2005) 6 *German Law Journal* 31

'Epilogue: Critical Intimacy and the Performance of International Law,' in: *Backstage Practices of Transnational Law*, Lianne J. M. Boer and Sofia Stolk (eds.), Routledge 2019, 174–178

'In Praise of Description' (2012) 25 *Leiden Journal of International Law* 609

'On International Legal Method' (2013) 1 *London Review of International Law* 166

Reading Humanitarian Intervention: Human Rights and the Use of Force in International Law, Cambridge University Press 2003

'Scientific Reason and the Discipline of International Law' (2014) 25 *European Journal of International Law* 369

Ottis, Rain, 'Analysis of the 2007 Cyber Attacks against Estonia from the Information Warfare Perspective,' in: *Proceedings of the 7th European Conference on Information Warfare and Security*, Dan Remenyi (ed.), Academic Publishing Limited 2008, 163–168

Oxford English Dictionary Online, "attend, v.," Oxford University Press, June 2020, www.oed.com/view/Entry/12780 (July 15, 2020)

"doctrine, n.," Oxford University Press, June 2020, www.oed.com/view/Entry/56322 (July 15, 2020)

Pareto, Vilfredo, *The Mind and Society, volume I*, Harcourt, Brace and Company 1935

Pascual, Esther, *Imaginary Trialogues: Conceptual Blending and Fictive Interaction in Criminal Courts*, LOT 2002

Paul, Danette, 'In Citing Chaos: A Study of the Rhetorical Use of Citations' (2000) 14 *Journal of Business and Technical Communication* 185

Paust, Jordan J. and Albert P. Blaustein, 'The Arab Oil Weapon – A Threat to International Peace' (1974) 68 *American Journal of International Law* 410

Peevers, Charlotte, *The Politics of Justifying Force: The Suez Crisis, the Iraq War, and International Law*, Oxford University Press 2013

Peil, Michael, 'Scholarly Writings as a Source of Law: A Survey of the Use of Doctrine by the International Court of Justice' (2012) 1 *Cambridge Journal of International and Comparative Law* 136

Pellet, Alain and Daniel Müller, 'Article 38,' in: *The Statute of the International Court of Justice: A Commentary*, Andreas Zimmermann, Christian J. Tams, Karin Oellers-Frahm and Christian Tomuschat (eds.), Oxford University Press 2019 (3rd ed.), 819–962

Perelman, Chaïm and Lucie Olbrechts-Tyteca, *The New Rhetoric: A Treatise on Argumentation*, University of Notre Dame Press 1969

Permanent Court of International Justice, 'Advisory Committee of Jurists, Procès-Verbaux of the Proceedings of the Committee, June 16th–July 24th 1920, The Hague,' www.icj-cij.org/pcij/serie_D/D_proceedings_of_committee_annexes_16june_24july_1920.pdf (May 15, 2016)

Peters, Anne, 'International Legal Scholarship Under Challenge,' in: *International Law as a Profession*, André Nollkaemper, Jean d'Aspremont, Tarcisio Gazzini and Wouter Werner (eds.), Cambridge University Press 2017, 117–159

Petrov, Anton O., *Expert Laws of War: Restating and Making Law in Expert Processes*, Edward Elgar 2020

Philadelphoff-Puren, Nina and Peter Rush, 'Fatal (F)laws: Law, Literature and Writing' (2003) 14 *Law and Critique* 191

Pirker, Benedikt and Jennifer Smolka, 'The Future of International Law Is Cognitive – International Law, Cognitive Sociology and Cognitive Pragmatics' (2019) 20 *German Law Journal* 430

PoKempner, Dinah, 'Squinting Through the Pinhole: A Dim View of Human Rights from Tallinn 2.0' (2017) 95 *Texas Law Review* 1599

Poulson, Kevin, '"Cyberwar" and Estonia's Panic Attack,' *wired.com*, August 22, 2007, www.wired.com/2007/08/cyber-war-and-e/ (July 15, 2020)

Preciado, Michael, 'If You Wish Cyber Peace, Prepare for Cyber War: The Need for the Federal Government to Protect Critical Infrastructure from Cyber Warfare' (2012) 1 *Journal of Law & Cyber Warfare* 99

Pronto, Arnold N., 'Some Thoughts on the Making of International Law – Review of Boyle, Alan and Chinkin, Christine. *The Making of International Law*. New York: Oxford University Press, 2007. pp. 288. $95. ISBN: 9780199248193' (2008) 19 *European Journal of International Law* 601

Raboin, Bradley, 'Corresponding Evolution: International Law and the Emergence of Cyber Warfare' (2011) 31 *Journal of the National Association of Administrative Law Judiciary* 602

Rajkovic, Nikolas M., Tanja E. Aalberts and Thomas Gammeltoft-Hansen (eds.), *The Power of Legality: Practices of International Law and Their Politics*, Cambridge University Press 2016

Randelzhofer, Albrecht, 'Article 2(4),' in: *The Charter of the United Nations: A Commentary*, Bruno Simma (ed.), Oxford University Press 2002, 112–136

Remus, Titiriga, 'Cyber-Attacks and International Law of Armed Conflicts: A "Jus Ad Bellum" Perspective' (2013) 8 *Journal of International Commercial Law and Technology* 179

Report of the Group of Governmental Experts on Developments in the Field of Information and Telecommunications in the Context of International Security, 22 July 2015, A/70/174

Report of the Group of Governmental Experts on Developments in the Field of Information and Telecommunications in the Context of International Security, 24 June 2013, A/68/98*

Rheindorf, Markus, *Revisiting the Toolbox of Discourse Studies: New Trajectories in Methodology, Open Data, and Visualization*, Palgrave Macmillan 2019

Rid, Thomas, 'Cyber War Will Not Take Place' (2011) 35 *Journal of Strategic Studies* 5

Riles, Annelise, 'A New Agenda for the Cultural Study of Law: Taking on the Technicalities' (2005) 53 *Buffalo Law Review* 973

Collateral Knowledge: Legal Reasoning in the Global Financial Markets, The University of Chicago Press 2011

'Infinity within the Brackets' (1998) 25 *American Ethnologist* 378

'Models and Documents: Artefacts of International Legal Knowledge' (1999) 48 *International and Comparative Law Quarterly* 805

The Network Inside Out, University of Michigan Press 2000

Roberts, Anthea, *Is International Law International? A Study in the Globalization of Legal Education and Scholarship*, Oxford University Press 2017

Rodgers, John, 'Whose Citations Are They?' (2010) 9 *Journal of Medical English Education* 94

Rõigas, Henry and Tomáš Minárik, *2015 UN GGE Report: Major Players Recommending Norms of Behaviour, Highlighting Aspects of International Law*, CCDCOE INCYDER Articles, June 26, 2016, https://ccdcoe.org/incyder-articles/2015-un-gge-report-major-players-recommending-norms-of-behaviour-highlighting-aspects-of-international-law/ (July 15, 2020)

Roscini, Marco, *Cyber Operations and the Use of Force in International Law*, Oxford University Press 2014

'World Wide Warfare: *Jus ad Bellum* and the Use of Cyber Force,' in: *Max Planck Yearbook of United Nations Law*, Armin von Bogdandy and Rüdiger Wolfrum (eds.), Koninklijke Brill N.V. 2010, 85–130

Mansfield Park (1999), Miramax Films, BBC Films and Intermedia Films in association with the Arts Council of England, written and directed by Patricia Rozema

Ruiz-Garrido, Miguel F., 'Intensifying Adverbs in Academic Spoken Discourse: A Contrastive Study between English and Spanish,' in: *Multimodal Analysis in Academic Settings: From Research to Teaching*, Belinda Crawford Camiciottoli and Inmaculada Fortanet-Gómez (eds.), Routledge 2015, 61–82

Ruiz-Madrid, M. Noelia and Inmaculada Fortanet-Gómez, 'A Multimodal Discourse Analysis Approach to Humour in Conference Presentations: The Case of Autobiographic References' (2015) 173 *Procedia – Social and Behavioral Sciences* 246

Rush, Peter, 'An Altered Jurisdiction – Corporeal Traces of Law' (1997) 6 *Griffith Law Review* 144

Ruys, Tom, *'Armed Attack' and Article 51 of the UN Charter: Evolutions in Customary Law and Practice*, Cambridge University Press 2010

Šadl, Urška, 'Case – Case-Law – Law: *Ruiz Zambrano* as an Illustration of How the Court of Justice of the European Union Constructs Its Legal Arguments' (2013) 9 *European Constitutional Law Review* 205

Sahlane, Ahmed, 'Argumentation and Fallacy in the Justification of the 2003 War on Iraq' (2012) 26 *Argumentation* 459

Sala, Michele, 'Interpersonal and Interactional Markers in Legal Research Articles,' in: *Interpersonality in Legal Genres*, Ruth Breeze, Maurizio Gotti and Carmen Sancho Guinda (eds.), Peter Lang 2014, 63–86

'Plain Language in Legal Studies: A Corpus-Based Study' (2014) 16 *European Journal of Law Reform* 651

Sander, Barrie, 'Cyber Insecurity and the Politics of International Law' (2017) 6 *ESIL Reflections* 1

'The Sound of Silence: International Law and the Governance of Peacetime Cyber Operations,' in: *Silent Battle*, Tomaš Minárik, Siim Alatalu, Stefano Biondi, Massimiliano Signoretti, Ihsan Burak Tolga and Gabor Visky (eds.), NATO CCD COE Publications 2019, 1–21

Sanger, David E., *Confront and Conceal: Obama's Secret Wars and Surprising Use of American Power*, Crown Publishers 2012

'U.S. and China Seek Arms Deal for Cyberspace,' *New York Times*, September 19, 2015, www.nytimes.com/2015/09/20/world/asia/us-and-china-seek-arms-deal-for-cyberspace.html?_r=1 (July 15, 2020)

Sanger, David E. and Nicole Perlroth, 'U.S. Escalates Online Attacks on Russia's Power Grid,' *New York Times*, June 15, 2019, www.nytimes.com/2019/06/15/us/politics/trump-cyber-russia-grid.html (July 15, 2020)

Schaller, Christian, 'Beyond Self-Defense and Countermeasures: A Critical Assessment of the *Tallinn Manual*'s Conception of Necessity' (2017) 95 *Texas Law Review* 1619

Schauer, Frederick, 'Authority and Authorities' (2008) 94 *Virginia Law Review* 1931

Schlag, Pierre, 'The Faculty Workshop,' *University of Colorado Law School Legal Studies Research Paper Series, Working Paper Number 11–12*, June 3, 2011 https://scholar.law.colorado.edu/cgi/viewcontent.cgi?article=1144&context=articles (July 15, 2020)

'The Problem of the Subject' (1991) 69 *Texas Law Review* 1627

Schmitt, Michael N., 'Computer Network Attack and the Use of Force in International Law: Thoughts on a Normative Framework' (1999) 37 *Columbia Journal of Transnational Law* 885

'Cyber Operations and the *Jus Ad Bellum* Revisited' (2011) 56 *Villanova Law Review* 569

CyCon 2012 | Michael Schmitt: Tallinn Manual Part I, www.youtube.com/watch?v=wY3uEo-Itso (July 15, 2020)

CyCon 2012 | Michael Schmitt: Tallinn Manual Part II, www.youtube.com/watch?v=f_TC3y7g4aA (July 15, 2020)

CyCon 2012 | Michael Schmitt: Tallinn Manual Part III, www.youtube.com/watch?v=iPdLtZEhofc (July 15, 2020)

Global Conference on CyberSpace 2015, www.youtube.com/watch?v=re_ei2D1G7Q (July 15, 2020)

ILD 2012 | Panel Discussion: Cyber Conflict and the Law of Armed Conflict, www.youtube.com/watch?v=sglT6o5YIu4 (July 15, 2020)

International Law and Cyber Warfare, www.c-span.org/video/?311806–1/panelists-explain-new-cyber-warfare-manual (July 15, 2020)

'International Law in Cyberspace: The Koh Speech and Tallinn Manual Juxtaposed' (2012) 54 *Harvard International Law Journal Online* 13

LENS Conference 2013 | Michael N. Schmitt, The Law of Cyberwar: The Tallinn Manual, www.youtube.com/watch?v=vQBiLBrmJJI (July 15, 2020)

Michael N. Schmitt: PILAC Lecture on Cyber Operations and IHL: Fault Lines and Vectors, www.youtube.com/watch?v=ZWwrVAMSOT4 (July 15, 2020)

'Preemptive Strategies in International Law' (2003) 24 *Michigan Journal of International Law* 513

Re-conceptualizing International Law Frameworks in Response to the Threat of Cyber Warfare, www.youtube.com/watch?v=jDvP-z-f4tc (July 15, 2020)

'The Interpretive Guidance on the Notion of Direct Participation in Hostilities: A Critical Analysis' (2010) 1 *Harvard National Security Journal* 5

Tallinn Manual 2.0 on the International Law of Cyber Operations: What It Is and Isn't, on 'Just Security,' February 9, 2017, www.justsecurity.org/37559/tallinn-manual-2–0-international-law-cyber-operations/ (July 15, 2020)

The Tallinn Manual on the International Law Applicable to Cyber Warfare, https://brown.hosted.panopto.com/Panopto/Pages/Viewer.aspx?id=1962891D-B51E-4B88-BB05-A99F011762B4 (July 15, 2020)

'The "Use of Force" in Cyberspace: A Reply to Dr Ziolkowski,' in: *4th International Conference on Cyber Conflict*, Christian Czosseck, Rain Ottis and Katharina Ziolkowski (eds.), NATO CCD COE Publications 2012, 311–317

(ed.), *Tallinn Manual on the International Law Applicable to Cyber Warfare*, Cambridge University Press 2013

(ed.), *Tallinn Manual 2.0 on the International Law Applicable to Cyber Operations*, Cambridge University Press 2017

Schmitt, Michael N. and Bernhard Blumbergs, *Active Cyber Defense Case Studies*, https://ccdcoe.org/cycon/2014/app.html (May 13, 2016)

Schmitt, Michael and Sean Fahey, *WannaCry and the International Law of Cyberspace*, on 'Just Security,' December 22, 2017, www.justsecurity.org/50038/wannacry-international-law-cyberspace/ (July 15, 2020)

Schmitt, Michael N., Charles H. B. Garraway and Yoram Dinstein, *The Manual on the Law of Non International Armed Conflict With Commentary*, International Institute of Humanitarian Law 2006

Schmitt, Michael and Tim Maurer, *Protecting Financial Data in Cyberspace: Precedent for Further Progress on Cyber Norms?*, on 'Just Security,' August 24, 2017, www.justsecurity.org/44411/protecting-financial-data-cyberspace-precedent-progress-cyber-norms/ (July 15, 2020)

Schmitt, Michael N. and Liis Vihul, *International Cyber Law Politicized: The UN GGE's Failure to Advance Cyber Norms*, on 'Just Security,' June 30, 2017, www.justsecurity.org/42768/international-cyber-law-politicized-gges-failure-advance-cyber-norms/ (July 15, 2020)

Schweiger, Elisabeth, 'Listening to Silence: "Targeted Killing" and the Politics of Silence in Customary International Law' (PhD, University of Groningen 2018)

Segal, Adam, *The Development of Cyber Norms at the United Nations Ends in Deadlock. Now What?*, Council on Foreign Relations Blog, June 29, 2017, www.cfr.org/blog/development-cyber-norms-united-nations-ends-deadlock-now-what (July 15, 2020)

Shackelford, Scott J. and Richard B. Andres, 'State Responsibility for Cyber Attacks: Competing Standards for a Growing Problem' (2011) 42 *Georgetown Journal of International Law* 971

Sharp Sr., Walter G., *CyberSpace and the Use of Force*, Aegis Research Corporation 1999

Shklar, Judith N., *Legalism: An Essay on Law, Morals and Politics*, Harvard University Press 1964

Legalism: Law, Morals, and Political Trials, Harvard University Press 1986

Siddiqui, Sabrina, 'What the Mueller Report Tells Us about Trump, Russia and Obstruction,' *The Guardian*, April 18, 2019, www.theguardian.com/us-news/ng-interactive/2019/apr/18/mueller-report-trump-russia-key-takeaways (July 15, 2020)

Silver, Daniel B., 'Computer Network Attack as a Use of Force under Article 2(4) of the United Nations Charter,' in: *Computer Network Attack and International Law*, Michael N. Schmitt and Brian T. O'Donnell (eds.), Naval War College 2002, 73–98

Singer, Peter W., 'Stuxnet and Its Hidden Lessons on the Ethics of Cyberweapons' (2015) 47 *Case Western Reserve Journal of International Law* 79

Sivakumaran, Sandesh, 'The Influence of Teachings of Publicists on the Development of International Law' (2017) 66 *International and Comparative Law Quarterly* 1

Sklerov, Matthew J., 'Solving the Dilemma of State Responses to Cyberattacks: A Justification for the Use of Active Defenses against States Who Neglect Their Duty to Prevent' (2009) 201 *Military Law Review* 1

Skouteris, Thomas, 'The New Tribunalism: Strategies of (De)Legitimation in the Era of International Adjudication' (2006) 17 *Finnish Yearbook of International Law* 307

Small, Henry G., 'Cited Documents as Concept Symbols' (1978) 8 *Social Studies of Science* 327

Smolka, Jennifer and Benedikt Pirker, 'International Law and Pragmatics: An Account of Interpretation in International Law' (2016) 5 *International Journal of Language & Law* 1

Sperduti, Giuseppe, 'Consensus in International Law' (1976) 2 *Italian Yearbook of International Law* 33

Spiermann, Ole, '"Who Attempts Too Much Does Nothing Well": The 1920 Advisory Committee of Jurists and the Statute of the Permanent Court of International Justice' (2003) 73 *British Yearbook of International Law* 187

Stappert, Nora, 'A New Influence of Legal Scholars? The Use of Academic Writings at International Criminal Courts and Tribunals' (2018) 31 *Leiden Journal of International Law* 963

'Practice Theory and Change in International Law: Theorizing the Development of Legal Meaning through the Interpretive Practices of International Criminal Courts' (2020) 12 *International Theory* 33

Statute of the International Court of Justice, 26 June 1945, 1 UNTS XVI

Stinissen, Jan, 'A Legal Framework for Cyber Operations in Ukraine,' in: *Cyber War in Perspective: Russian Aggression against Ukraine*, Kenneth Geers (ed.), NATO CCD COE Publications 2015, 123–134

Stolk, Sofia, '"The Record on Which History Will Judge Us Tomorrow": Auto-History in the Opening Statements of International Criminal Trials' (2015) 28 *Leiden Journal of International Law* 993

Stolk, Sofia and Renske Vos, 'International Legal Sightseeing' (2020) 33 *Leiden Journal of International Law* 1

Sullivan, Gavin, '"Taking on the Technicalities" of International Law – Practice, Description, Critique: A Response to Fleur Johns' (2017) 111 *AJIL Unbound* 181

Swales, John M., 'Evaluation in Academic Speech: First Forays,' in: *Academic Discourse: New Insights into Evaluation*, Gabriella Del Lungo Camiciotti and Elena Tognini Bonelli (eds.), Peter Lang 2004, 31–54

Swanson, Lesley, 'The Era of Cyber Warfare: Applying International Humanitarian Law to the 2008 Russian-Georgian Cyber Conflict' (2010) 32 *Loyola of Los Angeles International and Comparative Law Review* 303

Tanodomdej, Papawadee, 'The Tallinn Manuals and the Making of the International Law on Cyber Operations' (2019) 13 *Masaryk University Journal of Law and Technology* 67

Terry, Patrick C. R., '"Don't Do as I Do" – The US Response to Russian and Chinese Cyber Espionage and Public International Law' (2018) 19 *German Law Journal* 613

The Secretariat of the Advisory Committee of Jurists, 'Advisory Committee of Jurists, Documents presented to the Committee relating to existing plans for the establishment of a Permanent Court of International Justice,' www.icj-cij.org/files/permanent-court-of-international-justice/serie_D/D_documents_to_comm_existing_plans.pdf (July 15, 2020)

The White House, Office of the Press Secretary, 'Fact Sheet: President Xi Jinping's State Visit to the United States,' 25 September 2015, www.whitehouse.gov/the-press-office/2015/09/25/fact-sheet-president-xi-jinpings-state-visit-united-states (July 15, 2020)

Thomas, Sarah and Thomas P. Hawes, 'Reporting Verbs in Medical Journal Articles' (1994) 13 *English for Specific Purposes* 129

Thorne, Frederick C., 'The Citation Index: Another Case of Spurious Validity' (1977) 33 *Journal of Clinical Psychology* 1157

Tikk, Eneken, Kadri Kaska and Liis Vihul, *International Cyber Incidents: Legal Considerations*, Cooperative Cyber Defence Centre of Excellence (CCD COE) 2010

Tindale, Christopher W., *Fallacies and Argument Appraisal*, Cambridge University Press 2007

Tolppa, Maria, *Overview of the UN OEWG Developments: Continuation of Discussions on How International Law Applies in Cyberspace*, CCDCOE INCYDER Articles, March 23, 2020, https://ccdcoe.org/library/publications/overview-of-un-oewg-developments-continuation-of-discussions-on-how-international-law-applies-in-cyberspace/ (July 15, 2020)

Traynor, Ian, 'Russia Accused of Unleashing Cyberwar to Disable Estonia,' *The Guardian*, May 17, 2007, www.theguardian.com/world/2007/may/17/topstories3.russia (July 15, 2020)

Trubek, David M., 'Max Weber on Law and the Rise of Capitalism' (1972) 1972 *Wisconsin Law Review* 720

Tsagourias, Nicholas, 'Cyber Attacks, Self-Defence and the Problem of Attribution' (2012) 17 *Journal of Conflict and Security Law* 229

'The Legal Status of Cyberspace,' in: *Research Handbook on International Law and Cyberspace*, Nicholas Tsagourias and Russell Buchan (eds.), Edward Elgar Publishing 2015, 13–29

'The Tallinn Manual on the International Law Applicable to Cyber Warfare: A Commentary on Chapter II – The Use of Force,' in: *Yearbook of International Humanitarian Law 2012*, Terry D. Gill, Robin Geiß, Robert Heinsch, Tim McCormack, Christophe Paulussen and Jessica Dorsey (eds.), T.M.C. Asser Press 2014, 19–43

UNIDIR, 'Cyber Policy Portal,' https://cyberpolicyportal.org/en/ (July 15, 2020)

United Nations General Assembly, First Committee, Seventy-third session, 'Advancing Responsible State Behaviour in Cyberspace in the Context of International Security,' October 18, 2018, A/C.1/73/L.37

UNODA, 'Developments in the Field of Information and Telecommunications in the Context of International Security,' 2019, www.un.org/disarmament/ict-security/ (July 15, 2020)

'Fact Sheet,' July 2019, https://unoda-web.s3.amazonaws.com/wp-content/uploads/2019/07/Information-Security-Fact-Sheet-July-2019.pdf (July 15, 2020)

'Group of Governmental Experts,' www.un.org/disarmament/group-of-governmental-experts/ (July 15, 2020)

'Open-Ended Working Group,' www.un.org/disarmament/open-ended-working-group/ (July 15, 2020)

UNODC, Organized Crime, Emerging Crimes, 'Cybercrime,' 2016, www.unodc.org/unodc/en/cybercrime/index.html (July 15, 2020)

Valeiras Jurado, Julia, 'A Multimodal Approach to Persuasion in Conference Presentations,' in: *Multimodal Analysis in Academic Settings: From Research to Teaching*, Belinda Crawford Camiciottoli and Inmaculada Fortanet-Gómez (eds.), Routledge 2015, 108–132

Valverde, Mariana, '"Non-legality" and Society: Fleur Johns, *Non-legality in International Law: Unruly Law*, Cambridge, Cambridge University Press, 2013, pp. 259, ISBN 9781107014015' (2014) 27 *Leiden Journal of International Law* 961

van der Deijl, Emma, *Argumentum ad Populum: Classificatie, Beoordeling en Presentatie van de Populistische Variant* (MA, Leiden University 2017)

van Eemeren, Frans H., *Strategic Maneuvering in Argumentative Discourse: Extending the Pragma-Dialectical Theory of Argumentation*, John Benjamins 2010

van Hoof, Godefridus J. H., *Rethinking the Sources of International Law*, Kluwer Publishing 1983

van Keulen, Roos, *Introducing a Critical Stylistic Analysis: How Linguistic Features Contributed to the Tallinn Manual's Power Position* (LLM, Vrije Universiteit Amsterdam 2018)

van Steenberghe, Raphaël, 'Self-Defence in Response to Attacks by Non-State Actors in the Light of Recent State Practice: A Step Forward?' (2010) 23 *Leiden Journal of International Law* 183

Vass, Holly, 'Analysing Hedging in Legal Discourse Using Small-Scale and Large-Scale Corpora' (2015) 3 *Research in Corpus Linguistics* 27

Veilige Wereld – Veilig Nederland, 'The Hague Process: Courses on the International Law Applicable to Cyber Operations,' Facebook, May 16, 2017, www.facebook.com/VeiligeWereldVeiligNederland/posts/1373386999405061:0 (July 15, 2020)

Ventola, Eija, 'Interpersonal Choices in Academic Work,' in: *Linguistic Choice Across Genres: Variation in Spoken and Written English*, Antonia Sanchez-Macarro and Ronald Carter (eds.), John Benjamins 1998, 117–136

'Why and What Kind of Focus on Conference Presentations?,' in: *The Language of Conferencing*, Eija Ventola, Celia Shalom and Susan Thompson (eds.), Peter Lang 2002, 15–50

Ventola, Eija, Celia Shalom and Susan Thompson, 'Introduction,' in: *The Language of Conferencing*, Eija Ventola, Celia Shalom and Susan Thompson (eds.), Peter Lang 2002, 9–14

Venzke, Ingo, *How Interpretation Makes International Law: On Semantic Change and Normative Twists*, Oxford University Press 2012

'Semantic Authority,' in: *Concepts for International Law: Contributions to Disciplinary Thought*, Jean d'Aspremont and Sahib Singh (eds.), Elgar 2019, as downloaded from https://ssrn.com/abstract=2723851 (July 16, 2020)

'Understanding the Authority of International Courts and Tribunals' (2013) 14 *Theoretical Inquiries in Law* 381

Vernon, Thomas S. and Lowell A. Nissen, *Reflective Thinking: The Fundamentals of Logic*, Wadsworth Publishing Company 1968

Vienna Convention on the Law of Treaties, 23 May 1969, 1155 UNTS 331

Viswanathan, S., '"Illeism with a Difference" in Certain Middle Plays of Shakespeare' (1969) 20 *Shakespeare Quarterly* 407

von Bernstorff, Jochen, 'International Legal Scholarship as a Cooling Medium in International Law and Politics' (2014) 25 *European Journal of International Law* 977

Vos, Renske, 'Europe and the Sea of Stories: Operation Sophia in Four Absences' (PhD, Vrije Universiteit Amsterdam 2021)

Waldock, Claud H. M., 'The Regulation of the Use of Force by Individual States in International Law' (1952) 81 *RCADI* 455

Wallace, David and Mark Visger, 'Responding to the Call for a Digital Geneva Convention: An Open Letter to Brad Smith and the Technology Community' (2017) 6 *Journal of Law & Cyber Warfare* 3

Walton, Douglas, *Appeal to Popular Opinion*, Pennsylvania State University Press 1999

Walton, Douglas and Fabrizio Macagno, 'Common Knowledge in Legal Reasoning about Evidence' (2005) 3 *International Commentary on Evidence* 1

Wampole, Christy, 'The Conference Manifesto,' *New York Times Opinionator*, May 4, 2015, http://opinionator.blogs.nytimes.com/2015/05/04/the-conference-manifesto/?_r=0 (July 15, 2020)

Watkin, Kenneth, 'The Cyber Road Ahead: Merging Lanes and Legal Challenges' (2013) 89 *International Law Studies* 472

Watson, J. S., 'Legal Theory, Efficacy and Validity in the Development of Human Rights Norms in International Law' (1979) 1979 *University of Illinois Law Forum* 609

Waxman, Matthew C., 'Cyber-Attacks and the Use of Force: Back to the Future of Article 2(4)' (2011) 36 *Yale Journal of International Law* 421

Weber, Cynthia, 'Performative States' (1998) 27 *Millennium* 77

Weissbrodt, David, 'Cyber-Conflict, Cyber-Crime, and Cyber-Espionage' (2013) 22 *Minnesota Journal of International Law* 347

Weller, Marc, *An International Use of Force in Salisbury?*, on 'EJIL: *Talk!*,' March 14, 2018, www.ejiltalk.org/an-international-use-of-force-in-salisbury/ (July 15, 2020)

Werner, Wouter G., 'Absence, Restatement and Imagination: The Tallinn Manual on International Law Applicable to Cyber Operations,' in: *Repetition and International Law*, Cambridge University Press 2021, forthcoming (on file with the author)

'Godot Was Always There: Customary Law as Restatement Practice,' in: *Repetition and International Law*, Cambridge University Press 2021, forthcoming (on file with the author)

'International Law: Between Legalism and Securitization,' in: *Security: Dialogue Across Disciplines*, Philippe Bourbeau (ed.), Cambridge University Press 2015, 196–218

'The Use of Law in International Political Sociology' (2010) 4 *International Political Sociology* 304

Werner, Wouter G. and Lianne J. M. Boer, '"It Could Probably Just as Well Be Otherwise": Imageries of Cyberwar,' in: *Risk and the Regulation of Uncertainty in International Law*, Mónika Ambrus, Rosemary Rayfuse and Wouter Werner (eds.), Oxford University Press 2017, 39–55

West, Robin, 'Reconsidering Legalism' (2003) 88 *Minnesota Law Review* 119

Wetlaufer, Gerald B., 'Rhetoric and Its Denial in Legal Discourse' (1990) 76 *Virginia Law Review* 1545

White, Howard D., 'Citation Analysis and Discourse Analysis Revisited' (2004) 25 *Applied Linguistics* 89

Wikipedia, 'Schmitt Analysis,' https://en.wikipedia.org/wiki/Schmitt_Analysis (July 15, 2020)

Wingfield, Thomas C., *The Law of Information Conflict: National Security Law in Cyberspace*, Aegis Research Corporation 2000

Winter, Steven L., 'Transcendental Nonsense, Metaphoric Reasoning, and the Cognitive Stakes for Law' (1988) 137 *University of Pennsylvania Law Review* 1105

Woltag, Johann-Christoph, *Cyber Warfare: Military Cross-Border Computer Network Operations Under International Law*, Intersentia 2014

'Cyber Warfare,' Max Planck Encyclopedia of Public International Law 2015, Rüdiger Wolfrum (dir.), http://opil.ouplaw.com/view/10.1093/law:epil/9780199231690/law-9780199231690-e280?rskey=okuUsx&result=1&prd=EPIL (July 15, 2020)

Wolter, Detlev, *The UN Takes a Big Step Forward on Cybersecurity*, on 'Arms Control Association,' September 4, 2013, www.armscontrol.org/act/2013_09/The-UN-Takes-a-Big-Step-Forward-on-Cybersecurity (July 15, 2020)

Wood, Sir Michael, 'Teachings of the Most Highly Qualified Publicists (Art. 38 (1) ICJ Statute),' Max Planck Encyclopedia of Public International Law 2010, Rüdiger Wolfrum (dir.), http://opil.ouplaw.com.vu-nl.idm.oclc.org/view/10.1093/law:epil/9780199231690/law-9780199231690-e1480?rskey=DbiJzV&result=1&prd=OPIL (July 15, 2020)

Wortham, Anna, 'Should Cyber Exploitation Ever Constitute a Demonstration of Hostile Intent That May Violate UN Charter Provisions Prohibiting the Threat or Use of Force?' (2012) 64 *Federal Communications Law Journal* 643

Wright, Jeremy, Attorney General, QC, MP, 'Cyber and International Law in the 21st Century,' May 23, 2018, www.gov.uk/government/speeches/cyber-and-international-law-in-the-21st-century (July 15, 2020)

Yang, Wenhsien, 'Stance and Engagement: A Corpus-Based Analysis of Academic Spoken Discourse Across Science Domains' (2014) 5 *LSP Journal* 62

Young, Katharine G., 'The Minimum Core of Economic and Social Rights: A Concept in Search of Content' (2008) 33 *Yale Journal of International Law* 113

Ziolkowski, Katharina C., 'Computer Network Operations and the Law of Armed Conflict' (2010) 49 *Military Law and the Law of War Review* 47

'*Ius ad bellum* in Cyberspace – Some Thoughts on the "Schmitt-Criteria" for Use of Force,' in: *Proceedings of the 4th International Conference on Cyber Conflict*, Christian Czosseck, Rain Ottis and Katharina Ziolkowski (eds.), NATO CCD COE Publications 2012, 295–309

The text of the scene from *Twelfth Night* is taken from http://shakespeare.mit.edu/twelfth_night/full.html (July 16, 2020).

Index

For EU product safety concerns, contact us at Calle de José Abascal, 56–1°, 28003 Madrid, Spain or eugpsr@cambridge.org.

www.ingramcontent.com/pod-product-compliance
Lightning Source LLC
LaVergne TN
LVHW011812200926
848484LV00005B/1164
* 9 7 8 1 1 0 8 4 8 4 8 3 1 *